Fringe Nations in World Soccer

Soccer is the most popular mass spectator sport in the world, gaining huge media coverage and reaching all levels of society in countries all around the world. More than just entertainment, soccer has proved to be a reflection of national, cultural, community and ethnic identity as well as an indication of the development and international status of post-colonial nation states. For those nations still at the fringes of the modern global game, soccer represents a vision of potential commercialisation, capable of generating foreign reserves and bringing in considerable economic power.

This book explores aspects of the development of soccer in countries which have recently been marginalised in world soccer or have only erratic success on the international stage. These fringe nations include a greater part of Africa, the USA, Australia, Israel, India, Nepal, Bhutan, Burma, Indonesia, Thailand, Maldives and Sri Lanka, and while these countries are rarely noticed by the global football media, they nonetheless have great potential to excel, and many have a rich soccer heritage that still holds a place of central importance in the every day life of the people.

This book was previously published as a special issue of *Soccer and Society*.

Kausik Bandyopadhyay, an Academic Editor of Soccer and Society, teaches Modern Indian History and the History of Sport in the Department of History at the University of North Bengal, India.

Sabyasachi Mallick is a sports journalist with Kick Off, the official soccer magazine of the Indian Football Association, Kolkata, India.

Sport in the Global Society

General Editors: J. A. Mangan and Boria Majumdar

Fringe Nations in World Soccer

Sport in the global society
General Editors: J.A. Mangan and Boria Majumdar

The interest in sports studies around the world is growing and will continue to do so. This unique series combines aspects of the expanding study of *sport in the global society*, providing comprehensiveness and comparison under one editorial umbrella. It is particularly timely, with studies in the aesthetic elements of sport proliferating in institutions of higher education.

Eric Hobsbawm once called sport one of the most significant practices of the late nineteenth century. Its significance was even more marked in the late twentieth century and will continue to grow in importance into the new millennium as the world develops into a 'global village' sharing the English language, technology and sport.

Other Titles in the Series

America's Game(s)
A Critical Anthropology of Sport
Edited by Benjamin Eastman, Sean Brown and Michael Ralph

British Football & Social Exclusion
Stephen Wagg

From Fair Sex to Feminism
Sport and the Socialization of Women in the Industrial and Post-Industrial Eras
Edited by Roberta J Park and J A Mangan

The Future of Football
Challenges for the Twenty-first Century
Edited by Jon Garland, Dominic Malcolm and Mike Rowe

Football, Europe and the Press
Liz Crolley and David Hand

The Football Manager
A History
Neil Carter

This Great Symbol
Pierre de Coubertin and the Origins of the Modern Olympic Games
John J MacAloon

The Games Ethic and Imperialism
Aspects of the Diffusion of an Ideal
J A Mangan

Doping in Sport
Global Ethical Issues
Edited by Angela Schneider and Fan Hong

Africa, Football and FIFA
Politics, Colonialism and Resistance
Paul Darby

Scoring for Britain
International Football and International Politics, 1900–1939
Peter J Beck

Encyclopedia of British Football
Edited by Richard Cox, Wray Vamplew and Dave Russell

Football Culture
Local Conflicts, Global Visions
Edited by Gerry Finn and Richard Giulianotti

Football: The First Hundred Years
The Untold Story
Adrian Harvey

Olympism: The Global Vision
From Nationalism to Internationalism
Edited by Boria Majumdar and Sandra Collins

France and the 1998 World Cup
The National Impact of a World Sporting Event
Edited by Hugh Dauncey and Geoff Hare

A Social History of Indian Football
Striving to Score
Boria Majumdar and Kausik Bandyopadhyay

Sport, Civil Liberties and Human Rights
Edited by Richard Giulianotti and David McArdle

Modern Sport – The Global Obsession
Edited by Boria Majumdar and Fan Hong

Barbarians, Gentlemen and Players
A Sociological Study of the Development of Rugby Football
Kenneth Sheard and Eric Dunning

Athleticism in the Victorian and Edwardian Public School
The Emergence and Consolidation of an Educational Ideology
J A Mangan

Fringe Nations in World Soccer

Edited by Kausik Bandyopadhyay and
Sabyasachi Mallick

Routledge
Taylor & Francis Group

LONDON AND NEW YORK

First published 2008 by Routledge
2 Park Square, Milton Park, Abingdon, Oxon, OX14 4RN

Simultaneously published in the USA and Canada
by Routledge
270 Madison Avenue, New York, NY 10016

Routledge is an imprint of the Taylor & Francis Group, an informa business

Transferred to Digital Printing 2009

© 2008 Kausik Bandyopadhyay and Sabyasachi Mallick

Typeset in Minion by Genesis Typesetting Ltd, Rochester, Kent

British Library Cataloguing in Publication Data
A catalogue record for this book is available from the British Library

Library of Congress Cataloging in Publication Data

ISBN 10: 0-415-37822-2 (hbk)
ISBN 10: 0-415-49487-7 (pbk)

ISBN 13: 978-0-415-37822-2 (hbk)
ISBN 13: 978-0-415-49487-8 (pbk)

CONTENTS

SERIES EDITORS' FOREWORD

SPORT IN THE GLOBAL SOCIETY was launched in the late nineties. It now has over one hundred volumes. Until recently an odd myopia characterised academia with regard to sport. The global *groves of academe* remained essentially Cartesian in inclination. They favoured a mind/body dichotomy: thus the study of ideas was acceptable; the study of sport was not. All that has now changed. Sport is now incorporated, intelligently, within debate about *inter alia* ideologies, power, stratification, mobility and inequality. The reason is simple. In the modern world sport is everywhere: it is as ubiquitous as war. E.J. Hobsbawm , the Marxist historian, once called it the one of the most significant of the new manifestations of late nineteenth century Europe. Today it is one of the most significant manifestations of the twenty-first century world. Such is its power, politically, culturally, economically, spiritually and aesthetically, that sport beckons the academic more persuasively than ever- to borrow ,and refocus, an expression of the radical historian Peter Gay- 'to explore its familiar terrain and to wrest new interpretations from its inexhaustible materials'. As a subject for inquiry, It is replete, as he remarked of history, with profound 'questions unanswered and for that matter questions unasked'.

Sport seduces the teeming 'global village': it is the new opiate of the masses; it is one of the great modern experiences; its attraction astonishes only the recluse; its appeal spans the globe. Without exaggeration, sport is a mirror in which nations, communities, men and women now see themselves. That reflection is sometimes bright, sometimes dark, sometimes distorted, sometimes magnified. This metaphorical mirror is a source of mass exhilaration and depression, security and insecurity, pride and humiliation, bonding and alienation. Sport, for many, has replaced religion as a source of emotional catharsis and spiritual passion, and for many, since it is among the earliest of memorable childhood experiences, it infiltrates memory, shapes enthusiasms, serves fantasies. To co-opt Gay again: it blends memory and desire.
Sport, in addition, can be a lens through which to scrutinise major themes in the political and social sciences: democracy and despotism and the great associated movements of socialism, fascism, communism and capitalism as well as political cohesion and confrontation, social reform and social stability.

The story of modern sport is the story of the modern world-in microcosm; a modern global tapestry permanently being woven. Furthermore, nationalist and imperialist, philosopher and politician, radical and conservative have all sought in sport a manifestation of national identity, status and superiority.

Finally, for countless millions sport is the personal pursuit of ambition, assertion, well-being and enjoyment.

For all the above reasons, sport demands the attention of the academic. *Sport in the Global Society* is a response.

J. A. Mangan
Boria Majumdar

Series Editors
Sport in the Global Society

Prologue: The Real Peoples' Game

Kausik Bandyopadhyay

Soccer, the most popular mass spectator sport in the world, is a game where humanity comes alive with one goal. The game has always remained a marker of identities of various sorts. Behind the façade of its obvious entertainment aspect, it has proved to be a perpetuating reflector of cultural nationalism, distinctive ethnicity, community or communal identity, cultural specificity as well as representative of models of development and international status for post-colonial nation states. For those nations, which still remain at the periphery of world soccer, the game signifies a vision of potential commercialization of sport capable of generating foreign reserves and of flexing economic muscle. The imaging and prioritization of the game as a 'national' or 'international' event in public opinion and the media also play a critical role in transforming the soccer culture of a nation.

The present volume seeks to explore some aspects of the variety of dispensations of 'development' in the field of soccer in countries which, even with their potential to excel at the highest level or with a heritage of soccer glory and culture, in recent times have either become a marginal presence in world soccer or have been experiencing a somewhat choked state of growth despite occasional flurries at the international circuit in the past. It is, however, important to note at the outset that 'Fringe Nations' does not offer any rigid conceptualization of marginalized or underdeveloped soccer states in the world. It may make more sense when we apply the term 'fringe' to those nations or even peoples or groups of peoples (women, for example), which/who approach the game in a meaningful socio-economic perspective or with a sound developmental vision. In these 'fringe' nations, which include the Australian continent, a greater part of Asia and Africa, the USA, and some parts of Europe and Latin America (as will be evident in the volume), soccer culture still holds a place of central importance in the everyday life of the masses.

Socio-Historical studies on soccer can afford a domain where scholars can honestly blend the *intellectual* with the *popular* without really disturbing their respective sanctities. The way the contributors of this volume have approached soccer's varied significance in a range of states intends to make the point that intellectualizing the popular and popularizing the intellectual can go hand in hand and generate a synthetic genre of scholarship.

Globally, soccer has long been a site which articulates the complexities and diversities of the everyday life of nations. In view of such complexities, it is easy to comprehend that a single volume, even when paying attention only to the fringe nations, can only scratch the surface. *Making It Happen* attempts to reveal at least part, if not the whole, of the process of how significant soccer was/has become for these fringe nations – politically, economically, culturally and emotionally.

Soccer in most countries acts as a marker of social identity/difference and progresses as an emblem of nationalism, which constitutes the focus of some of the chapters of the book. These chapters have attempted to establish soccer's credibility as a viable theme in the study of national/regional/local dichotomies in social history and cultural studies. Use of lively personal anecdotes and experiences in some essays is a deliberate act to highlight this point. Drawing upon J.A. Mangan's suggestion, *Making It Happen* brings forth the pertinent question of 'the autonomy of sport as a manifestation of indigenous popular culture, and local, regional and national negotiation and resistance in the face of global movements'.[1]

The essays on men's soccer in the volume are arranged in a geographical sequence starting with Australia and ending with the USA. Nations are chosen according to availability of scholarly intervention and literature, and studies offer as far as possible the most recent state of scholarship on issues and dimensions hitherto either ignored or seen in a different light. The volume begins with Roy Hay's stimulating discussion of 'Our wicked foreign game', that is, soccer and why 'soccer has not become the main code of football in Australia'. He examines the role of soccer in Australian public life emphasizing the game's position of secondary importance to rugby or Australian Rules in different regions. His essay draws on international comparisons with the USA or white British colonies to argue that in a uniquely multicultural country like Australia and one with established sporting traditions, *different* domestic experience of the game could shape the past, present and future of soccer in the country. Given the cultural diversity of the state, Hay concludes, it should work towards a strategic competitive advantage for the popularization of soccer in contemporary Australia when the nation has qualified after a while for the World Cup finals in Germany. As a follow up to the Australian case, Nick Guoth also explores a somewhat similar condition soccer enjoys (suffers from) in New Zealand. While rugby union, with its tremendous masculine appeal, has become an emblem of the country's national identity, soccer, the other oldest football code, remains marginalized to the former code. Guoth investigates the reasons why soccer was unable to acquire a central place in New Zealand's national identity. Surveying a wide array of literature on nineteenth-century New Zealand football, he tries to develop theories that should provide the reader with a better understanding of how, in that period, the game of soccer developed in New Zealand and how it succumbed to rugby as the country's national sport.

India may rank 130th in current FIFA ratings, yet the rich heritage of local football culture in India is fascinating enough to invite comparison with that of Brazil, Argentina, Italy or England. However, whenever soccer-loving Indians try to take pride in their legitimate achievement in the game, they look back either to the first worthy indigenous club Mohun Bagan's victory in the IFA Shield in 1911 or to India's Asian Games win of 1951 or 1962. Dwaipayan Sen's essay reconsiders the first momentous event in Indian soccer history, examining the varied responses to, and larger meaning of, the historic event. The essay intends to destabilize rigidly imperialist or nationalist historical interpretations of this event. By focussing his analysis on the varied responses to the phenomenon of Indians having defeated the British, he argues that in each case the writer of the report brought his (in all cases) ideological commitments to bear on his interpretation of the victory. Sen's analysis of an entire range of newspaper reports documents how the larger meaning of Mohun Bagan's victory came into being only through the very particular connotations football had acquired in the cultural and political schema of early-twentieth-century Bengali society. His analysis also tries to reveal how received notions of modernity, tradition, race, governance and masculinity acquired significantly different and, at times, conflicting meanings in the minds of the football and Mohun Bagan-crazed newspaper correspondents, and presumably, the newspaper-reading public. Sen accounts for the larger significance of this event in terms of the differences and similarities both between, and within, nationalist (Indian) and imperialist (British) interpretations.

The national sport of Iran is wrestling; many of its sports halls as well as football stadiums are named after its greatest wrestling legend, Gholamreza Takhti. Yet Iran's first place in the 1998 world wrestling championships, held in Teheran, caused far less excitement in Iran than the country's mere participation in the 1998 soccer World Cup, while Iran's qualification for the 2006 World Cup finals has created a greater stir in recent times. In Iran nationalism peaks around football probably because many consider collective action a truer test of a country's spirit than individual talent. Given the Islamic Republic's persistent attempts to keep global culture at bay, the widespread popularity of football in Iran calls for some explanation. The transition from wrestling to football as Iran's most popular sport, as H.E. Chehabi's essay argues, therefore reflects the social and political changes that have occurred in the country. Chehabi finds it striking as to how this shift in tastes is congruent with the Durkheimian notion of transition from mechanic to organic solidarity. His article attempts to show that the history of football in Iran has been intimately intertwined with politics, both domestic and international. Successive Iranian regimes have tried to use sports for internal and external legitimation. The author's aim is to analyze the interplay between the popularization of football, social change, state policies and politics *tout court*. The game's persistent popularity in Iran shows that Iranians' insertion in global culture has continued unabated.

One of the striking paradoxes in contemporary world soccer has been the enduring tension between loyalties towards national and club teams. This trend has affected not only the elite soccer nations, but has sent its ripples to developing, as well as underdeveloped, soccer powers. Amir Ben-Porat considers this nation-club dichotomy in the context of Israeli football. His essay analyzes a shift in the loyalty of Israeli football supporters, from the uncontested primacy afforded to the national team, to split loyalties expressed through a concrete conflict between loyalty to the local club and loyalty to the national side. This shift, according to him, is related directly to the transformation of Israeli society, which increasingly has undergone change, moving towards a more capitalist-oriented society. Under the impact of globalization *inter alia* commercialization of soccer, the game in Israel has been commodified, which in turn has transformed the game for the clubs, the players and the fans. Consequently, in the 1990s, fans faced a situation in which their loyalty to the national side was threatened by a clash with their loyalty to their club, a paradox that remains unresolved. People still come in their thousands to support the national team. Many, who have no special local club, give the national side backing because it is a symbol of the nation-state. But it appears that for the fanatic, argues Ben-Porat, the national selection has lost its prerogative over his local club. When the interests of the local club clash with that of the national selection, the fan finds him/herself in an awkward situation. Some hesitate, but many others have made a decision, 'my football club is "my castle" and everything else comes second.'

Africa, for quite some time now, has become an important source of overseas recruits for Asian, European and Latin American clubs. Raffaele Poli attempts to assess the status of African players in European football players' labour market. Taking the implementation of the Bosman Law in 1995 as the entry point, Poli argues that the resultant salary hike of star footballers playing in well-off clubs of major leagues leads to the emergence of an ever-increasing economic gulf separating clubs of the G-14 organization from the rest of the European clubs. The essay subsequently examines the viability of Jean-François Bourg's theory of the existence of a 'segmented' labour market in European professional football. The latter part of the essay concentrates on African players' status through a statistical analysis of their presence in 78 professional and semi-professional leagues of UEFA member countries, which reveals that, in comparison with migrants of other origins, Africans are more concentrated in the lower levels of competition. Indeed, as Poli argues, in the context of an economic polarization and of a 'segmented' labour market which needs a constant renewal and circulation of players, African footballers are particularly sought after, not only because of their value as footballers, but also because they allow the clubs' recruiters to make substantial financial savings through a form of wage dumping.

Chris Bolsmann offers a review of Peter Alegi's *Laduma! Soccer, Politics and Society in South Africa*. Bolsmann rightly notes that Alegi's contribution is part of an increasing body of academic work concerned with football in South Africa. Moreover, it contributes to the social history of sport in the country. The interplay of soccer, politics and society in the first 75 years of the last century has been explored by Alegi in a historical perspective. The discussion by Bolsmann on this worthy work assumes special significance in the context of South Africa's success in international soccer in the last ten years and its victory in the bid to hold the 2010 World Cup.

As part of security measures taken for George W. Bush's 2003 visit to Gorée Island in Senegal, residents were, according to those interviewed, taken to a soccer stadium and locked inside. In their words, 'Da fa mélni Diaam mo gna watt': 'It was like slavery had returned'. How is one to understand this discourse of slavery emerging more than 150 years since it was outlawed in French territories? And why is this narrative aimed at the United States, when President Abdoulaye Wade has done so much to cultivate amiable relations with this superpower nation? In the aftermath of 9/11, George W. Bush praised Senegal for being among the most democratic of the world's Islamic nations. Why, then, this coercive treatment – or at least the impression of it – from the standpoint of Goréeans? More importantly, why was a soccer field chosen to be the stage for this political spectacle? Michael Ralph tries to address these questions in the context of Senegal's recent soccer history and economic imperatives. Ralph shows how Senegal's effort to promote itself as an anti-terrorist Islamic nation while aggressively pursuing privatization is linked to the way soccer is promoted internally, for the purposes of national cohesion, and externally, as evidence of Senegalese potential. Both developments spring, the author argues, from the most dominant feature of the nation's post-Independence 'crise economique': a labour shortage that has encouraged the state to pursue foreign direct investment as the most feasible way to bolster revenue while the youth engage in sport as the best way to escape career unemployment. Beyond this link, according to Ralph, these two pursuits – foreign finance and sport – are two salient features of President Wade's political programme. Even more to the point, they are strategies that presuppose and entail a particular kind of neoliberal subject – both at the level of the individual athlete and the nation writ large – in the way these domains are intertwined in the political imagination. He draws upon the implications of Senegal's success in the 2002 World Cup and argues that the 'sporting faith' manifest in such success was shaped and, in turn, reinforced the nation's political strategies, economic development and cultural resources.

The programme of national development for an economically-backward nation is commonly perceived in economic terms. But it encompasses more than just improved living conditions. For example, it includes improvement of the production capabilities of the populace through the education and improved health of its youth. Sam Mchombo, in his effort to explore alternative strategies to development, considers Malawi youths' love of soccer as a viable means to achieve a greater end, such as to combat the increasing advent of AIDS. Sport, and particularly soccer, has been perceived as a useful ploy to save the youth, restore their health and, given the scarcity of financial resources, determine ways in which the youth could be encouraged to channel their energy and vigour to the development of the country, admittedly, a modified notion of development. Mchombo's point is interesting as it raises soccer's role in human life beyond mere entertainment or leisure pursuit. While soccer sometimes serves the agenda of election in Malawi politics, the redirection of the sport to serve as means to ends that are nebulous and removed from the immediate concerns of game results requires some explanation. Mchombo offers a number of potential roles soccer could perform in Malawi in particular, and in African nations in general: soccer helps people come out of poverty; it heightens one's chances of success as a political leader; it is exploited by interested groups/peoples to attain socio-political ends; and yet it fosters, like the Malawi Youth Soccer Project in which the author himself is involved, youth alia national development. However, as Mchombo argues, such exploitation of soccer for non-sports purposes becomes compatible with the goals of national development only when the concept of development is clearly articulated. In Malawi, as he emphasizes, the exploitation of soccer for community service, to combat HIV/AIDS through increased awareness and education, to contribute to gender equity, etc., originated independently. Malawi Youth Soccer Project has therefore become able to inspire people from, or working in, other African countries.

David Hassan's article on Northern Ireland examines the long-standing silence of northern nationalists, Irish nationalists living in Northern Ireland, in attending home international matches. Hassan draws attention to a range of political, social and ideological reasons for which he believes large numbers of this community have stayed away from games for more than three decades. His second focus of attention is the recent decision by the British government to build a new national sports stadium on the outskirts of the capital city, Belfast. Viewed together, these developments give rise to a broader argument, as the essay posits, that notwithstanding the well-founded opposition northern nationalists have had towards symbols of unionist hegemony in Northern Ireland, including the Irish Football Association (IFA), it is now time to move on. In so doing it offers an ideal opportunity for all concerned to contribute to the birth of a new political and social context in this most divided of western societies.

While the success of the US national soccer team has startled many around the world in the last decade, the failure of the game to develop into a major US sport has continued to puzzle most of the international sporting world. Sandra Collins's article reviews the recent history of soccer in the US and analyzes several cultural and economic factors, including the US television sports broadcasting market, in order to argue that for the foreseeable future, soccer in the US remains problematic. Despite the growth of the US soccer market since the 1994 World Cup, the US Major League Soccer (MLS) teams continue to struggle despite their anticipated market potential. The economics of professional sports, according to Collins, has much to do with this failure. With the global flows in professional sport, argues Collins, talented US players opt for overseas clubs in order to earn higher salaries. The equation is simple enough for the author. High salaries cannot be paid by the MLS teams without major television or cable network contracts, and there are no contracts due to the lack of a large fan base to support such contracts. This being the case, how will a large and loyal fan base for US soccer emerge? Collins addresses this question through her essay. She argues that the recent draft choice of 14-year-old Freddy Adu as the youngest player in soccer history may prove to be a shrewd one in helping to create a star system within the US soccer world. One cannot overlook, however, the powerful draw of cultural nationalism that sport evokes. For Collins, the popularity of baseball, basketball or football in the US has much to do with how these sports have come to be identified with being American.

The last two essays deal with the sociology and history of women's soccer in the Republic of Ireland and the USA respectively in a comparative perspective. Whether the future of global soccer is *feminine*[2] or not, these essays intend to make the point that women's football has its own autonomous domain capable of generating radical changes in gender and social relations. Katie Liston expects her article to be considered as an attempt to develop a more adequate sociological model for the females' increasing involvement in a traditionally associated male sport like soccer in Ireland. Her work assumes special significance in view of her elite-level involvement as a player in women's soccer since 1995, and the use of the data and in-depth interviews she gathered in that capacity. Favouring a more fruitful application of the figurational sociological approach, Liston examines Bourke's arguments to understand the consequences of increasing interdependence between the sexes in Ireland, one aspect of which includes the increasing female participation in traditionally male-dominated sports such as soccer since the 1970s. In contrast to other researches in the field, she argues that changes in the self-images and social make-up of male and female athletes are inextricably bound up with changes in the social structure of gender relations in the wider society. Thus, according to her, the development of women's soccer in Ireland can be meaningfully understood, in sociological terms, by looking at the position of soccer in the overall status hierarchy of sports, female and male athletes' positions within soccer, and the consequences of social relations for the self-conceptions of males' and females' habituses.

The stellar success of the 1999 Women's World Cup final and the US women's team's worthy performance in it envisaged a bright future for women's soccer in the USA. Fanfare and attendance for the tournament was unprecedented, while the final between the USA and China saw a phenomenal television rating. The Women's United Soccer Association (WUSA) was launched to cash in on this excitement and interest around women's soccer and a women's professional league was formed to cater to that trend. Unfortunately, interest, attendance and television ratings all came to a halt within three years resulting in the disbanding of the league. Sean F. Brown addresses this perplexing question of failure of the WUSA in face of the wild success of the 1999 World Cup. Brown explains this failure in terms of definite strategic, socio-economic and cultural factors. Strategically, argues Brown, the league suffered from saturation of the market (locations in major sports markets with a plethora of other sporting options) and a marketing strategy that seemed to outreach the demand for women's professional soccer (reliance on corporate sponsorship rather than grassroots approaches). According to him, the reconciliation of the enormously popular 1999 World Cup Final and the unlikely failure of the WUSA need to be understood in the context of relational complexities between critical events and sport. The failure of the Cup Final to spur long-term interest in women's professional soccer, argues Brown, resulted from critical mistakes in the establishment and marketing of women's professional soccer made by the WUSA. The essay also attempts to answer questions about the nature of sport spectatorship in the United States, and whether the ideas of American Exceptionalism vis-à-vis soccer continue to be viable given this event analysis. Culturally, he points out, the success of the 1999 World Cup final had more to do with expressions of nationalism by American viewers and less to do with soccer itself. The essay in fact details an instance of positive nationalism (the viewing of a particular sporting event because of the nationalistic implications of the event).

Although we put forward a hypothetically valid notion of 'Fringe Nations' in world soccer, as mentioned at the outset, this is no rigid conceptualizing. Rather, as the essays in the present volume show, the historical roots and growth, cultural adoption and appropriation, and developmental patterns and potentials of the game in the countries discussed defy any simplistic homogenization and offer more variability than affinity.

Sports history, it can be justly claimed, is peoples' history. Starting from this premise, the essays in this volume not only examine the potentials and complexities of on-field development of soccer but also study the role of soccer in shaping peoples' lives in colonial and post-colonial histories. More importantly, the essays concentrate on exploring the relationships between the national, regional and local in the history and development of soccer in the countries studied. This is expected to generate future forays into more specialized regional and local studies. As James Walvin has suggested, 'more emphasis needs to be placed on local studies without losing sight of the broader context'.[3] *Making It Happen* also shares Walvin's notion that 'general structures do indeed have a place, but they will inevitably be subjected to the qualifications of specific and local peculiarities'.[4] Walvin has further remarked:

> Like many other forms of social behaviour, sporting activity is largely socially and historically determined. Thus the sports historian and sociologist need to reach beneath the surface, behind the obvious facts of sporting history, if their studies are to be any more than yet another quasi-antiquarianism masquerading as serious social history.[5]

This volume, in the same vein, adopts a more didactic approach, which considers soccer as a mirror of society and culture. However, at the same time, it puts equal emphasis on, and gives valid weight to, results and scores, lists and tables, data and statistics, as and when required.

It is the staggering mass following at all levels transcending age, space or time that makes soccer different from any other sport in the world. Yet as in other sports, performance and non-performance are equally revealing in soccer as well. The craze and status of the game, as well as the future of soccer, is revealed from this graph of performance or non-performance. In the developing and underdeveloped nations with potential for development, soccer is now confronted with the changing realities of the global game and the accompanying challenges of globalization: commercialization, professionalization and mediatization. In the face of these, when growing competition among elite football clubs in developed soccer bastions have become obvious and when FIFA, world's apex body of soccer, has recently put so much emphasis on the exercise on standardization, access to capital, competitive mass media and sponsorship – new priorities under globalization have altered the balance of power in international, national and local rivalry affecting the game in the fringe nations. *Making It Happen* is thus an attempt to address the antecedent, present and future of soccer in the 'Fringe Nations'.

Notes

[1]   Mangan, 'Series Editor's Foreword', viii.
[2]   FIFA president Sepp Blatter remarked a few years back that 'the future of football is feminine'.
[3]   Walvin, 'Sport, Social History and the Historian', 10.
[4]   Ibid.
[5]   Ibid., 8.

References

Mangan, J.A. 'Series Editor's Foreword.' In *Football Culture: Local Contests, Global Visions,* edited by Gerry P.T. Finn and Richard Giulianotti. London & Portland, OR: Frank Cass, 2000.
Walvin, James. 'Sport, Social History and the Historian.' *The British Journal of Sports History 1,* no.1 (1984): 1–15.

'Our Wicked Foreign Game': Why has Association Football (Soccer) not become the Main Code of Football in Australia?

Roy Hay

Introduction

Soccer, 'our wicked foreign game', is not the main code of football in any state in Australia, but is probably the second in most states if measured by spectator attendance or participation.[1] In Victoria, Australian rules is number one, while in New South Wales, rugby league is the dominant code. The phenomenon is not unique to Australia. None of the white dominions of the old British Empire or the former British colony, the United States, has soccer as its main code, with the exception of South Africa where the non-white population has taken up Association Football.[2] In most of these countries soccer is characterized as a migrants' game, even though many of the migrants playing or watching the game are of second or later generations. Explanations for the secondary position of soccer in Australia ought therefore to be compared with those for these other countries, and if we seek a comprehensive explanation of this phenomenon then the Australian story ought not to vary too much from those applied to the others, unless it can be clearly shown that Australian experience and conditions were indeed different.[3] This essay concentrates on the domestic experience in Australia, with a view to introducing and outlining some of the issues which might be drawn into an effective international comparison.

Before doing that, though, it is worthwhile to look more closely at the true position of soccer in Australia today. If the men's code is secondary, that is not necessarily true of the women's game in Australia. Women's soccer is also the top code in the United States where the team is the current Olympic champion and runner-up to Germany in the FIFA Women's World Cup. In Australia, the women's game is at least as popular as any of the other codes of football. The national team has qualified for the Women's World Cup and the Olympic Games. Women's soccer is claimed to be the fastest growing sport in the country. Separate organizations for women's soccer (and indoor soccer, futsal) have now been brought together under the Football Federation of Australia. Women's matches were played alongside men's games at the Olympic Games in Australia in 2000 and when the men took part in a friendly international against Iraq in 2005. It is arguable that an opportunity exists to turn soccer into a more appealing game to families by involving women as players, administrators and spectators, as well as mothers of the next generation.

It is also easy to underestimate the significance of soccer in Australia by simply relying on the mainstream media. Even though they are very rubbery, participation rates in the football codes, particularly among boys and girls up to the age of 15, show soccer leaving the other football codes in its wake. 'The sports that attracted most boys were outdoor soccer (with a participation rate for boys of 20 per cent), swimming (13 per cent), Australian rules (13 per cent) and outdoor cricket (10 per cent). For girls, the most popular sports were netball (18 per cent), swimming (16 per cent), tennis (8 per cent) and basketball (6 per cent).'[4] Female registrations in soccer in New South Wales rose by 28.5 per cent between 2002 and 2003, reaching 23,305 in the latter year. Junior female registrations (6–17 years) were up by over 30 per cent.[5] In 2005 an 18 per cent increase in total registrations to 14,000 in Sydney's north shore district of Ku-ring-gai put extreme pressure on facilities for soccer in the area.[6]

Crowds for competitive international soccer matches in Australia, especially World Cup qualifiers, have been excellent. Fédération Internationale de Football Association (FIFA) World Cup qualifiers against Iran in 1997 and Uruguay in 2001 drew capacity attendances to the Melbourne Cricket Ground (MCG) and over 100,000 saw the Olympic Games final in Melbourne in 1956. An average of 47,000 spectators attended double headers at the MCG during preliminary rounds of the Sydney Olympics of 2000, even though this tournament was limited to male players under the age of 23 and the programme each night had one male and one female game. When Australia played 93,000 were present.[7] National Soccer League (NSL) crowds between 1977 and 2003 were often regarded as woeful by comparison with those of the Australian Football League (AFL), but, particularly in Perth and Adelaide, they were not wildly out of line with rugby union or rugby league crowds. Also, Australian attendances are comparable to those in the top leagues in many countries around the world, for example Scotland with the major exception of Celtic

Table 1   Attendance[a] at selected sporting events – 1999 and 2002[8]

	1999		2002	
	Persons	Attendance rate[b]	Persons	Attendance rate[b]
	'000	%	'000	%
Australian rules	2509.2	16.8	2486.2	17.1
Horse racing	1756.4	11.8	1865.2	12.9
Motor sports	1574.3	10.6	1473.4	10.2
Rugby league	1501.1	10.1	1464.6	10.1
Cricket (outdoor)	942.5	6.3	866.2	6.0
Soccer	621.2	4.2	801.9	5.5
Rugby union	446.2	3.0	673.6	4.6
Harness racing	534.8	3.6	508.3	3.5
Basketball	526.0	3.5	434.4	3.0
Tennis	444.0	3.0	393.5	2.7
Dog racing	276.4	1.9	232.3	1.6
Netball	248.7	1.7	219.7	1.5

(a) Attendance at a sporting event, match or competition as a spectator by persons aged 15 years and over in the 12 months prior to interview in April 1999. The 2002 survey referred to people aged 18 years and over.

(b) The number of people who attended, expressed as a percentage of the civilian population aged 18 years and over.

There were changes in the survey methodology between these two surveys, so the figures should not be used for comparison without reference to the Explanatory Notes in the 2002 document. The 2002 document records different figures for 1999.

and Rangers, the Old Firm.[9] Nevertheless, despite its occasional triumphs on the field and its precocious establishment of the first national league of any of the football codes, soccer in Australia has never come close to establishing itself as the primary form of football in a country which is often said to be obsessed by sport.[10] Why is this?

There is no single reason. Some explanations lie outside the code, others inside. Many reach back into the history of the game since its inception in the nineteenth century. They set a pattern which became established very early and influenced perceptions of the game thereafter, being reinforced again and again by developments within the code and in the wider society.[11]

Formative Stages

In the early part of the nineteenth century games of football were not as rigidly defined and codified as they later became. Bill Murray argues that timing is critical and that once a sport becomes established in a society it is difficult to dislodge. He also attributes the lack of impression made by soccer in the United States and the white dominions in part to social snobbery. As a predominantly working-class game, soccer did not receive support from British elites seeking to influence their colonial brethren. Nor did it appeal to colonial elites. He also suggests that the greater availability of open space and grass militated against the development of soccer compared with cricket and Australian rules, which were more suitable to societies with more land, though football and soccer both developed in the inner cities and the near suburbs where land was at a premium.[12]

There is obviously a class dimension to the status of football in Australia. Football has been a working-class, professional game, while cricket and rugby union, though often transcending classes in certain localities, have tended to be associated with middle-class and upper-class groups whose social leadership resisted challenge effectively until at least the turn of the twentieth century.[13] As a general rule British officials and teachers did not promote soccer and the process was left to seamen, engineers, artisans and the like.[14] As Richard Holt puts it, 'Football also failed to become officially established as an institution of Empire'.[15] Australia's elites, with certain exceptions which will be addressed later, have not warmed to soccer and indeed have kept clear of all the football codes until relatively recently. Lower-class migrants, on the other hand, have taken to the game. This invites comparison with the United States where, according to Foer, the two social groups which have supported the game are elites and Latin-American immigrants.[16]

The sources of early British migrants to Australia may have been significant. If they were predominantly drawn from the lower orders of urban London, rural Southern England, Ireland and Highland Scotland, they would have been less likely to have brought a species of soccer with them than if they had come from the North of England or the central belt of Scotland, where the game had a much greater hold by the 1880s. This hypothesis is put forward as speculation rather than established fact at this stage, but it is worth exploring.[17] According to James Jupp, 'Despite a widespread belief in Australia that a high proportion of English free settlers came from the industrial North, there is little evidence from available figures that this was true until the 1880's'.[18] The North was also under-represented in assisted migration figures between the 1860s and the 1880s.[19] J.C. Docherty mentions the political and social concerns of immigrants to Newcastle in New South Wales and their strong collectivist approach, but does not explain how this became a pioneering area in the development of soccer in Australia, just as it was in Newcastle-upon-Tyne in England. Scottish migrants were also over-represented in the Newcastle area.[20] Jupp, on the other hand, asserts that 'Soccer established a mass following in the Hunter Valley region, where there was a concentration of immigrants from Scottish and North East mining areas, but otherwise was unable to displace rugby and Australian rules'.[21] If the migration boom of the 1880s had a higher proportion of northern English and Scottish migrants then it is probably significant that this was the decade in which soccer became prominent for the first time as a separate code in Australia, with the foundation of a number of clubs in the major eastern cities and industrial centres and the first interstate matches taking place.[22]

The English-speaking migrants to these new colonial societies did not absolutely need their sports to assist them to come to terms with the places in which they found themselves. Some subsequent generations of migrants did. We will be returning to this point later. Nevertheless, the Scottish and English migrants who set up clubs in Australia began a tradition of naming them after their homelands or geographic areas, or used terms which were current in the names of existing clubs overseas, so we have Caledonians, Northumberland and Durhams, Rangers, Celtics, Fifers and others to mark the newcomers.[23] These clubs became enclaves where new migrants could find like-minded people at a time when there were few domestic organizations in Australia catering for them.[24] Some British migrants were brought to Australia by soccer clubs, or joined them within days of arrival, including the father of the former Australian cricket captain, Bobby Simpson, who was offered £50 a season to play for Granville in Sydney around 1926. Jock Simpson was probably a rarity, since semi-professional soccer was uncommon in Australia in the 1920s.[25] More typical would be the experience of William MacGowan, who was signed up to play with Ford's soccer club in Geelong as soon as his feet touched Australian soil in Melbourne in 1926.[26] Ford had set up its assembly plant in Victoria in that year, and its workers very quickly entered a team in the local league. By the 1950s semi-professionalism was more common and overseas players were actively sought out by Australian clubs.[27]

Andrew Dettre has attempted to trace the colonial pattern to the very origins of European Australia. He argues that the early involuntary migrants left their stamp on the culture and the sports in Australia and elsewhere: 'Those people [early British settlers in Australia, America, Canada and South Africa] included convicts and others similarly disillusioned and determined to forget what they had left behind. Theirs was a rough, tough life-style and when it came to diversion they preferred a form of blood sport. Hence we saw the development of rugby, Australian football, gridiron and ice hockey.'[28] It is an interesting thesis, but it is hard to accommodate the attraction of cricket in this interpretation. It was cricket which became Australia's national sport in the nineteenth century, precisely because it was a sport in which Australia could compete with the colonial metropolis.[29]

Australians proved they could organize themselves on a private enterprise basis to compete effectively against the English at cricket by the 1880s, whereas a similar group of Australian soccer players would have been completely out of their depth against British professional footballers, as proved to be the case as late as the 1960s. The same would have been true of the other English-speaking dominions. Low-standard soccer did not appeal to British migrants used to top-class professional games in England and Scotland.[30] Indeed, the earliest 'international' matches played by representative Australian teams were relatively light-hearted affairs between Western Australian selections and the English cricket tourists led by A.C. McLaren in 1902 and 'Plum' Warner in 1904, both of which ended in large wins for the cricketers.[31] It was not until the 'bodyline' tour of 1932–33 that the Hakoah club in Melbourne beat the English cricketers in a match which was the last activity of the tourists before they set sail for Sydney and home in March 1933.[32]

Domestic Influences

There was little or no indigenous culture of ball games to be drawn on in Australia. Despite recent anachronistic attempts to link Australian rules to Aboriginal prototypes, there is no sign of an indigenous activity which could embrace or be translated easily into soccer.[33] John Sugden and Bill Murray, among others, have tried to explain the spread of soccer around the world and, like Murray, I remain unconvinced by those accounts which concentrate solely on the role of the European proselytizers and fail to examine what was already there in the popular consciousness which could relate to this peculiar sport.[34] We need to go back to the local sources and the travellers' tales with a view to finding out what 'sports' or cultural activities existed prior to the appearance of soccer in a whole range of countries if we are to explain why it took off in some parts of the world and not elsewhere. We have to undertake the kind of archaeological work which Neil Tranter has done for parts of the central belt of Scotland, which has undermined the notion that popular forms of football had been eliminated by Calvinism, Puritanism and the industrial revolution.[35] We also need to be aware of the problems inherent in transforming indigenous cultural practices into modern sports. There is no simple conversion mechanism.[36]

The precocious establishment of domestic codes of football in Australia, New Zealand, the United States and Canada inhibited the spread of migrant games. What later became known as Australian rules, rugby union and American football were all functioning sports with substantial followings by the mid- to late-nineteenth century. Hence it was relatively harder for another code to overturn their position in the consciousness of the natives. For a period the various codes co-existed, but soon in each society one code became dominant in popular estimation. In Australia, one significant feature is that the main codes, Australian rules and rugby league, were regionalized, divided by 'the Barassi line', that demarcated the areas that played these sports.[37] That line did not follow the border between Victoria, where Australian rules developed, and New South Wales, which plumped for rugby league, but took in the Riverina bounded by the Murrumbidgee (since that part of New South Wales had been orientated towards Melbourne rather than Sydney), the national capital Canberra and the whole of South and Western Australia and the Northern Territory. Since Australian rules expanded nationally in the 1990s and rugby league established a toehold in Melbourne with the Melbourne Storm, the line has become blurred, but for most of last century it marked a real division.[38]

The popularity of the early established codes of football was reinforced by some explicit antagonism exhibited by these codes as they fought for their patches. In this they were regularly backed by the domestic media and local authorities. Examples abound from Australian experience as soccer clubs were pilloried in the press and refused permission to use football and cricket ovals or banished to remote areas within municipalities at the behest of established sporting bodies. A Mr Thomas of Western Australia remarked in 1909, 'The opposition to the game everywhere is stupendous and only continued self sacrifice on the part of its votaries can keep the flag flying'.[39] During periods of rapid expansion soccer clubs sought extra fields on which to play and this brought them into direct competition with the existing domestic football clubs. Even in the 1930s, when economic depression affected all the football codes, soccer found it hard to get a share of or take over underused football ovals.[40]

All codes of football had a boost at the end of the Second World War, but Australian rules was struggling for a period thereafter. Its attendances were not keeping pace with the growth of the Melbourne or Victorian population.[41] Yet soccer could not make as much headway as it wished, thanks in part to the effective opposition of Australian rules and rugby league. John Kallinikios charts the difficulties faced by migrant soccer bodies in the years after the Second World War in obtaining adequate pitches in the Melbourne suburb of Footscray, with the powerful Yugoslav club JUST banished to what became Schintler Reserve amidst warehouses and transport facilities.[42]

Another factor inhibiting the growth of soccer was the failure to get teachers or police in states other than NSW heavily involved in the game.[43] These local community leaders have had a major influence on the development of sport around the country and relatively few of them have been strong promoters of soccer.[44] Similarly, the game made little impact on Australia's private school system until the last two decades when some elite schools began to take up the game, often driven by students who were devotees of the game and descendants of migrants. By comparison, in the United States, soccer struggled to make headway in the college system, which provides the bulk of recruits to the National Football League.[45]

The Organization of Soccer in Australia

The internal politics and maladministration of the sport have not helped improve the image and acceptance of the game. There has been a species of self-inflicted ghettoization.[46] Though clubs and ethnic groups will deny it, some migrant clubs have become bastions of particular communities in Australia.[47] These are not always national groups with a particular ethnic composition, as the media tend to portray them. Often they are sub-national or regional, or have a specific religious affiliation, but they retain an attachment to an 'imagined community' overseas which often seems parochial or offensive to outsiders.[48] They seem to be, or can be portrayed as being, 'un-Australian', though this term is as contentious and undefined as its United States' equivalent has been in that country's chequered past.[49]

The code was also wracked for much of its early post-war history by a conflict between amateur and professional groups within the administration of the sport and its clubs. Since only amateurs could take part in the Olympic Games which were to be held in Melbourne in 1956, there was a considerable incentive to ensure that the game was kept free of any taint of professionalism, just at the point when its popularity was taking off as a spectator sport which allowed the emergence of semi-professionalism on a significant scale for the first time. By 1957 the professionals were in the ascendancy, but momentum had been lost and the code was subject to a major split and suspension by FIFA for the poaching of players from European clubs without paying transfer fees. The resulting battles within the code were not ended until at least 1962. The structure which was set up at that time, with the Australian Soccer Federation as the creature of the state federations, which were the main stakeholders, proved in the end to be a contributor to the persistence of divisions within the code. Arguably, this held back later development when the promotion and costs of maintaining the Australian national team became relatively more onerous, though others would point to qualification for the World Cup in 1974 and the setting up of the National Soccer League in 1977 as successes for the ASF.

In another sense there has been a failure to make the sport Australian. This is a very controversial claim. What we mean by 'Australian' is not static but highly malleable. Soccer was the first code of football to establish a national league in 1977.[50] The code had a very torrid time trying to do so, but then so did the Victorian Football League, later the Australian Football League (VFL/AFL) in the 1980s and 1990s. The soccer league was not truly national, in that all the teams taking part came from New South Wales, Victoria, Queensland, South Australia and the Australian Capital Territory, though Western Australia and New Zealand were to join many years later.[51] But soccer was probably ahead of its time and the country was not quite ready for a national league, as it was still bound up in local, state and parochial concerns. By 2004 the concept of national leagues was well established and it was at that point that a major crisis occurred in Australian soccer, which led to the demise of the existing national league and its planned replacement by a smaller A-League. Unfortunately, this resulted in a hiatus of two years, which had an appalling effect on the careers of many young Australians.

Throughout soccer's history in Australia there have been incidents of financial mismanagement, corruption and the burning of sponsors. Whether soccer has been worse than other codes in these areas is a moot point, but the code has a poor record of financial probity over the years. High-profile cases involving the president of the Australian Soccer Association and the national coach in the 1990s led to parliamentary inquiries and police investigations.[52] While during the currency of their sponsorship business and government organizations profess to be delighted with the results they obtain from soccer, it often becomes clear in retrospect that they did not feel that they obtained the promised benefits. There have been successful long-term sponsorships, however, such as those by the Ampol Petroleum Company in the 1950s and 1960s, by Phillips in the 1970s and by Diabetes Australia in the 1990s.

It is often argued that soccer has shown a persistent failure to obtain and hold media coverage, particularly free-to-air commercial television. Crude conspiracy theories abound to explain these results, but often the code has not been able to provide an attractive product for hard-headed commercial realists in the media industries. David Hill's almost obsessive desire for mainstreaming the game led him to sell the rights to televising soccer to Channel Seven in a long-term deal, only for the television company to broadcast matches solely on its pay-TV operation, which had a very poor take-up at the time. It is a chicken-and-egg problem, however: if soccer can produce the continuing audience then it will attract free-to-air commercial television, but television exposure is seen as necessary to achieve a broader audience for the game. The initiative has to come from the sport itself.[53] Meantime, soccer has had to rely largely on the tireless work of Dominic Galati, Les Murray, the late Johnny Warren and their colleagues at SBS.[54]

According to Bill Murray, in the United States the people who organized the game were not interested in it as a game in its own right. Many were baseball park owners looking for extra use of their capital investment.[55] In Australia there have been examples of outsiders becoming involved in the game for largely extrinsic reasons, but the majority of those who developed and financed the game started with, and retained, a commitment to soccer.[56]

Bill Murray also argues that in the United States works teams were used by socially-conscious employers to help damp down labour troubles in the textile towns of New England.[57] There is not much evidence of this in Australia, where works teams were usually the initiative of the workers themselves who then sometimes managed to get a little sponsorship from their employer.[58] A few companies did embark on more ambitious schemes of social control through sport and welfare in the 1920s, but on the whole these were in decline within a decade. As Philip Mosely remarks, 'Soccer in New South Wales has traditionally been a working class recreation, with little bourgeois involvement to speak of'.[59] As far as can be ascertained, the few employer-sponsored initiatives had little influence on the growth of the game in Australia.[60]

Soccer and Migration

Repeatedly, soccer would have its status as a migrant game reinforced in the White Dominions and the United States. Major waves of inward migration saw a boom in the number of people playing and watching soccer in all these countries. Bill Murray talks about a golden period of soccer in the United States in the 1920s, when it seemed that the game might force itself into a wider consciousness.[61]

In Australia the great waves of migration in the 1880s, the decade before the First World War, the 1920s and the period after the Second World War saw the growth in the popularity of soccer as a participant sport among migrants, but only in the last of these periods did it become a consistent mass spectator sport and by that time the migrants who flocked to soccer were from non-traditional sources; first northern then southern Europe. So the implications of post-war migration and the success of soccer kept up the image of a migrants' game. Its organization remained ethnic rather than district. The massive post-war migration gave a huge boost to soccer in Australia, turning it from a largely participant sport into a semi-professional spectator sport attracting crowds in excess of 10,000 to matches at state league level in New South Wales and Victoria and proportionately high numbers in South Australia, Queensland and Western Australia. Though British migrants produced many of the players, the bulk of spectators were drawn from the ranks of non-British immigrants.

These migrants, arriving in a strange society which welcomed their labour but expected them to become assimilated Australians and to eschew links with their homelands, found very few institutions catering for them. Soccer clubs became one of the places where migrant groups could gather for more than just the sport. Aside from providing them with recreation and entertainment in a sport with which many were familiar, unlike Australian rules or cricket, the soccer clubs assisted migrants in a variety of ways. They helped migrants to establish an identity that was both Australian and related to their homeland. Many migrants were and are fiercely proud of both societies. Soccer gave them a chance to compete at something in which they could succeed through their own efforts and with skills that were often superior to those of Australians of longer standing.

The sport introduced them to many Australian concepts and ideological beliefs, such as fair play, mateship, fierce competition followed by convivial celebration or commiseration. Frank Lowy, now the President of the Football Federation of Australia and the second richest man in Australia, learned about the customs and practices of his new home at the Hakoah club in Sydney.[62] Lowy's involvement in soccer preceded his rise into the Australian moneyed elite, but a few influential business people helped promote the game, including Sir William Walkley of the Ampol Petroleum Company and more recently Nick Tana in Perth, Western Australia.[63] A significant number of business leaders among the ethnic communities used soccer on their climb to the top; Harry Mrksa of Melbourne Croatia and Metro Travel, one of the largest travel agencies in Australia in the 1980s, and Branko Filipi, a leading house builder in South Australia and later in Victoria, are two examples.

Yet, by emphasizing migrant groups and their particular characteristics and by conducting business and social activities in languages other than English, the soccer clubs were creating barriers for Australians of long standing, who were not prepared to work at overcoming their initial feelings of strangeness when they came into contact with these new clubs and their members. There was a fear of the 'foreigner', exacerbated by war and not entirely offset by the fact that large numbers of Australian service men and women now had some first-hand experience of countries other than their own.

Local Support for Soccer

As I have already noted, access to facilities was sometimes blocked by other codes or local authorities. On the other hand, there are examples of local, state and national institutions contributing to the development of the game. For example, the Western Australian Football League donated half the proceeds of a pre-season friendly between East Freemantle and South Fremantle in 1909 to assist a soccer tour of the eastern states.[64] The Attorney-General, Septimus Burt, is said to have offered a contribution to the cost of buying Perth Oval around 1905, but the British Football Association of Western Australia did not have enough money to pay its share. Much later the state authorities in South Australia helped develop the Hindmarsh Stadium in Adelaide, while the Western Australian government assisted in providing a ground for Perth Glory in the 1990s.

Local authorities could be persuaded to cooperate and assist soccer on occasion. The Prahran ground was floodlit for night soccer in 1954. Bill Thomas of the Victorian Amateur Soccer Football Association mentioned the high esteem in which his colleague John Oliphant was held by Prahran Council for the manner in which he had conducted negotiations on behalf of soccer.[65]

In the past 20 years soccer has benefited from significant funding through the Australian Institute of Sport and state institutes via the Australian Sports Commission (ASC) and from state programmes designed to improve the health of the population. Diabetes Australia (Victoria) has been a major sponsor of the Victorian Soccer Federation. Also, the Federal Government provided financial backing for the Crawford Inquiry and Report into Australian soccer in 2002–03.[66] When the report was accepted by the government and the soccer authorities, a AUS $15 million Federal Government grant was made via the ASC so that the debts of Soccer Australia could be paid off and the group presided over by Frank Lowy could make a fresh start.[67] Lowy insisted that the government money come without strings, relying on his own profile and commitment to achieve what he promised.[68]

Geographical Factors

What Geoffrey Blainey referred to as the tyranny of distance affects all codes in Australia, but it is particularly influential on the game that is played by the majority of countries in the world. Australia is virtually an automatic participant in the finals of rugby league and rugby union world competitions, with their very restricted lists of participants, while Australian rules has its ersatz and unhistorical competition with the Gaelic Athletic Association's version of football. But the national soccer team has to climb an almost impossible ladder to reach the final stages of the FIFA World Cup, which consists of an easy run against all the countries of Oceania, with the occasional exception of New Zealand, followed by a two-game play-off against a battle-hardened team from South America, Europe or Asia.

One bad game at this stage and the World Cup dream is over for another four years, with consequent loss of media exposure, not to mention the financial boost, which comes from World Cup qualification. In 1997 David Hill, then President of the Australian Soccer Federation, adopted a typical crash through or crash approach, hiring the high-profile former England manager Terry Venables to coach the national team through the qualifiers. All went well until the final match in Melbourne when the Socceroos threw away a two-goal lead to allow Iran to qualify on the away goals rule. The subsequent let down, and the financial problems which were an inevitable consequence, set back the code significantly. Hill had also conducted a campaign against the ethnic clubs in the National Soccer League, which had the effect of polarizing the forces within the game while undermining the viability of the clubs, which had helped to develop the code.

A recent development has also had some deleterious effects on the code. For many years Australia imported players from overseas, many of whom took Australian citizenship and went on to play for the national team. Thanks in part to the training facilities at the Australian Institute of Sport and the various state institutes, Australia is now producing junior players who can compete successfully in FIFA's restricted age competitions at under-17, under-20 and under-23 Olympic level. To complete their soccer education, however, the best of these players have to go overseas to test themselves against the stars of Europe and South America. The result is that elite Australian players are now based largely in Europe, where high-level competition and training is available.[69] The perennial conflict between club and country is exacerbated because of the distance Australian players have to travel to take part in matches for their national team. The Australian authorities have responded by playing some friendly matches in London to reduce the travel burden and ensure the greater accessibility of star players.

So Australia has only reached the World Cup final stages twice, in 1974 and 2006, though it has come very close on at least four other occasions.[70] In 2005, under the new Football Federation of Australia chaired by Frank Lowy, Australia has become a member of the Asian Football Confederation, which will give it a more competitive but less daunting, less sudden-death, route to the major international competitions.[71] In turn, this will increase the travel burdens on Australia's overseas-based players, because they will be required to be available for many more competitive matches, not all of which fall in the weeks in the international calendar which FIFA is beginning to develop.

We have noted the impact of the outward migration of elite players to test themselves at the highest level in Europe and the implication for the Socceroos, the national team. But the absence of the best players overseas weakens the appeal of the domestic competitions, which are now staffed by players seen to be of a lower calibre. One of the expressed aims of the Football Federation of Australia is to attract players back to this country in their prime to raise the standards and promote the game. To do so they need to offer the players a full-time professional contract at a level which is competitive, when lifestyle and family issues are taken into account, with that offered in Europe by second-tier clubs. There is no reasonable prospect of Australian soccer being able to offer the equivalent of the remuneration packages of a top Premier League club in England or Italy.

Violence and Soccer

There is no doubt that soccer in Australia has been influenced by perceptions that it is a uniquely violent game as far as its fans and spectators are concerned.[72] There are serious questions about the perceived level of violence and the reality.[73] The level of on-field violence is no worse than in Australian rules or rugby league. Indeed, some of the violence in rugby league internationals between England and Australia was so vicious that Tony Collins was led to wonder why the 'Battle of Brisbane' in 1932 did not cause a ripple in Anglo-Australian relations, unlike the 'bodyline' cricket test series, which followed soon after.[74]

Spectator violence is often attributed to European ethnic politics even when very little of the latter is involved. For example, in the 1950s and 1960s Maltese clubs like George Cross had a reputation for having very rowdy fans. George Cross was suspended from Victorian competition, as was Geelong (when it was taken over by an Italian group and played as IAMA – Italian-Australian Migrant Association), though neither had political problems with other groups in the league.

On the other hand, clashes among migrants from Yugoslavia, between Serbs and Croatians (less frequently between Greeks and Macedonians), often had a political edge.[75] Episodes in 2005 revived all the old fears and hatreds. At the match between Sydney United (Croatian) and Bonnyrigg White Eagles (Serbian) on Sunday 13 March at Edensor Park in Sydney there was a confrontation between rival supporters prior to the game.[76] Representatives of both clubs denied any ethnic link and said that they were cooperating to avoid hooliganism. Sydney United said that the people involved were not known to the club, though White Eagles named various people to the authorities.[77] Another match, in the Illawarra region of New South Wales, was postponed for fear of a repetition of the events in Sydney.[78] The same charges and replies can be found in the cases of incidents going back at least to the 1950s in Australia.[79] They were repeated when South Melbourne (Greek) and Preston Lions (Macedonian) supporters clashed at Bob Jane Stadium in Melbourne in the Victorian Premier League on Sunday 17 April 2005.[80]

The FA and FIFA and the World Game

Bill Murray argues that the lack of interest of the Football Association (FA) and the Scottish Football Association in the game in Australia and the other dominions inhibited its growth. The logistics of proselytizing tours ruled out a visit by full-strength English representative teams in the early days. When a side was sent it was largely second-tier players and yet it was still far too strong for the locals. One-sided matches were less attractive to spectators. Even in the USA, where tours by top-class British clubs were regular events from the 1920s onwards, the game did not dent the hold of American football.[81] However, the FA is said to have made a large cash grant for the development of soccer in New South Wales and Queensland in 1931.[82] The timing was not good, being in the midst of the Great Depression, but apart from this donation Australian soccer was not the recipient of a large amount of FA support. A few trophies were offered for local competition. On the other hand, the pools companies provided a regular financial subvention to Australian soccer in return for the use of Australian fixtures and results in the northern hemisphere summer.

The development of soccer in Australia was never smooth. There were divisions in the code over the distribution of resources between elite teams and those at a lower level, something which is almost endemic in soccer around the world. Should the money the game generated be retained at the elite level to advance standards, exposure and further commercial gain, or should some of it be redistributed to assist junior development and competition outside the elite to increase the future pool of talent and participation in the code? In Australia these common dilemmas were compounded by divisions over the organization of the code. Should it be organized on a district or local basis, or should teams draw on particular ethnic or other interest groups? Should migrants join existing clubs and leaven the game as skilled individuals, helping in the process with their assimilation into mainstream Australian society, or should they be allowed to form 'national groups' to play with and be supported by people of similar migrant background? These tensions boiled over at intervals in the history of the game in Australia.

Splits, divisions and breakaways are not unique to soccer in Australia and have been part of the game in most parts of the world. In the United Kingdom, the Football League was set up in 1888 to give the leading professional clubs a regular competition and to channel the resources of the new mass audience to them. It remained under the umbrella of the Football Association, but the relationship was an uneasy one. In 1992 an internal coup within the FA enabled the leading clubs to form a Premier League separate from the Football League, once again driven by commercial concerns. In both cases the innovating group prospered, though the results for the rest of the code in England remained problematic. So it is not inevitable that a split or a breakaway will have a deleterious effect on the game in the longer run.[83] Nevertheless, the splits which occurred in Australia in 1927 and between 1957 and 1962, whatever their commercial impact, reinforced negative stereotypes about the game, the influence of ethnicity, politics and impressions of difference from the other codes of football. The role of migrants in the changes in the game was not interpreted positively by those observing the game from the outside.

Soccer in Australia was also disrupted by the suspension of the Australian Soccer Football Association by FIFA when member clubs recruited players from European clubs, primarily from Austria, Holland and Malta, in the1950s without paying a transfer fee in compensation. Though the suspension allowed some of these clubs to prosper by hiring talented overseas stars and hence generating revenue from spectators, participation in FIFA tournaments and tours by high-profile overseas teams were prevented. Subsequently, FIFA, particularly under the presidencies of Joao Havelange and Joseph Blatter, has become more involved with the game in Australia, but largely through the anomalous Oceania Confederation. It is arguable that being a large fish in this particular pond had not benefited the game in Australia. Oceania has had direct qualification for the various under-age tournaments but not for the critical World Cup, the only confederation with no guaranteed place.[84]

Other Possibilities

The soccer scoring system is often cited as a cause of the failure of Australians to embrace the game. Australians are said to prefer high-scoring games like Australian rules or basketball. Baseball is another low-scoring minority sport in Australia. But experimental rule changes overseas to increase scoring rates did not find widespread acceptance, for example 'beer matches' in Scotland, sponsored by a brewery, with rule changes and consequently higher scoring. So there is no guarantee that higher scoring in soccer would produce a greater response in Australia.

Women were not integrated into the game until very recently in Australia. Whereas Australian rules has always drawn a significant number of female spectators, soccer has tended until recently to draw on a predominantly male audience.[85]

Though women have played the game recreationally and competitively since the nineteenth century, and indeed attracted an audience of over 50,000 to a match between two of the leading teams in England in 1920, its regrowth in the last 20 or 30 years has been remarkable.[86] In England the number of adult women's teams has gone from 80 to over 1,000 in a decade. Women's soccer attracted some of the largest attendances at the Olympic Games in Atlanta in 1996 and it is claimed that the 1999 World Cup in the United States was the largest sporting event involving women ever held. The crowd at the final in Los Angeles exceeded that for the men's World Cup held at the same venue in 1994, television coverage in the United States was on a par, sponsorship of the game and its leading players increased dramatically in that country, and even the ball used in the competition was specially designed.[87]

Australia has participated in that growth, if on a smaller scale.[88] In Victoria alone, 62 teams took part in official league competitions under the auspices of the Victorian

Soccer Federation in 1999.[89] Every girl in Victorian primary schools receives some chance to play the game as part of the curriculum. The game has been historically much stronger, in both indoor and outdoor varieties, in New South Wales, South Australia, Queensland and the ACT. It is said that a match in Brisbane in 1925 attracted nearly 10,000 spectators and women's soccer was played during the Depression in Lithgow, New South Wales.[90] By 1978 an estimated 60,000 women played soccer, and Australian representative player Julie Murray gained a professional contract with Fortuna in Denmark in 1990.[91] The Australian women's team qualified for the World Cup in 1999 and 2003. Australia hosted the Olympic women's tournament in Sydney in 2000 and mounted an ultimately unsuccessful bid to stage the women's World Cup in 2003. Success in this would have had implications for any bid for the men's World Cup in the new millennium.

Women's participation rates remain lower than for males.[92] There are still a number of barriers to equal treatment in the sport, including shortage of facilities, lack of qualified coaches, very limited media coverage and promotion of female role models, continuing prejudice against women playing soccer and the expectations of women regarding sporting activity.[93] Yet women's soccer in Australia is continuing to expand rapidly.

The Future

The future may not be like the past, despite the false dawns which have occurred at regular intervals in Australia. Four days after Johnny Warren's death, Ray Chesterton wrote in the *Sydney Daily Telegraph*: 'Soccer's failure is cultural. It wants to impose world thinking on Australia without acknowledging this is a unique country with established sporting traditions. Soccer in Australia should be called abandon all hope.'[94] The current Chief Executive Officer of the Football Federation of Australia, John O'Neill, disagrees: 'The history of the game has a tradition of immigrants to Australia at various stages of our history, bringing a passion for football with them, e.g. Anglo-Celts, Italians, Greeks, Eastern European and more recently Asians. Thus, the opportunity exists to unify the game as Australian, reflecting the fact that Australia is a multicultural country. In fact, I believe this is a source of strategic competitive advantage, that the cultural diversity will indeed assist football to become a more popular sport.'[95] He may be optimistic and the test will come with the new A-League and the Asian connections, which his organization is fostering, along with Australia's qualification for the 2006 World Cup finals.

Acknowledgements

I am deeply grateful for the critical comments, references and support of Bill Murray, John Kallinikios, Brian Stoddart, J. Neville Turner, Andrew Howe, Greg Stock, Nick Guoth, Peter Smith, Richard Kreider, John Harms and colleagues in the Melbourne chapter of the Australian Society for Sports History.

Notes

[1]   'Our wicked foreign game' was quoted by V.J.M. Dixon, editor of *Soccer News*, in his editorial of 24 July 1954, 2. He was writing about the forthcoming tour of a New Zealand team to Victoria: 'The usual panic is on in the home of another code [Australian Rules Football] and all clubs are combining to make sure "Our Wicked Foreign Game" shall not use any of their hallowed ovals.' He went on to say that the difficulty had been overcome and a suitable venue arranged. Brunswick Oval, home of the Fitzroy Cricket Club and the Fitzroy Football Club ground, was to be used on 11 and 14 August 1954 for games against Victoria and Australia respectively (*Soccer News*, 31 July 1954, 7 and 10).

[2]   Though rugby union has a much higher media profile at international level. That may change when South Africa hosts the FIFA World Cup in 2010. It is interesting that in the last two or three years a few youngsters in some of the black townships have taken up Australian rules, claiming that the game has less imperial baggage than either rugby union or soccer. Expatriate Australians and the Australian Football League (AFL) have been partially responsible for this small beginning, including former Melbourne player Brian Dixon (Peter Blucher, 'Lions Recruit Australia's Expert on Irish Footballers', *Age*, Sport, 22 April 2005, 5). See also Australian Football League, *Australian Football in South Africa*. David Matthews, General Manager, Game Development, Australian Football League, also supplied information.

[3]   Markovits and Hellerman's *Offside* is a stimulating account of United States' experience, but its comparisons are largely with Europe and not at all with the British dominions, with the limited exception of Canada and the role of ice hockey.

[4]   Children's Participation in Cultural and Leisure Activities, Australia, Australian Bureau of Statistics, 2000 (4901.0).

[5]   'Soccer NSW posts record registration numbers', Soccer New South Wales website, Sunday 24 Aug. 2003, <www.soccernsw.com.au/mr240803rego.html>.

[6]   'Soccer boom worsens grounds crisis on Sydney's North Shore', Relay of Ku-ring-gai & District Soccer Association media release, Soccer New South Wales website, 11 April 2005, <media@soccernsw.com.au>.

[7]   Hay, 'Sports Mad Nations'.

[8]   Sports Attendance, Australia, Australian Bureau of Statistics, April 1999 and Dec. 2003 (4174.0).

[9]   Hay, 'Soccer and Social Control in Scotland, 1873–1973'.

[10] In 2005 the Australian Soccer Association changed its name to the Football Federation of Australia and was followed by some of the state federations as they embraced football as the name by which the code would officially be known. Since the 1880s the game has been known successively as British football, soccer football, soccer and, more derisively, 'wogball' during the period of post-Second World War migration (Talia Cerritelli, 'Football: A code divided', Victorian Soccer Federation website, March 2005, <www.soccervictoria.org.au>, accessed 23 March 2005, by which time the VSF had become the Football Federation of Victoria, following Western Australia and the Northern Territory).

[11] Murray, *Football*, 79.

[12] Murray, *The World's Game*, 20.

[13] For an introduction of great breadth and sophistication see Chapter Four, 'Empire and Nation', in Holt, *Sport and the British*, 203–79. Holt makes the point that football was of British origin but not really 'English' in the sense of being a game embraced by the social and political leadership of the imperial power (237).

[14] Mangan, *The Games Ethic and Imperialism*.

[15] Holt, *Sport and the British*, 237.

[16] Foer, *How Soccer Explains the World*.

[17] Richard Holt uses a similar argument to explain the failure of football to become the dominant sport in South Wales (Holt, *Sport and the British*, 247).

[18]   Jupp, *The Australian People*, 300.

[19]   Ibid., 301.

[20]   Docherty, 'English Settlement in Newcastle and the Hunter Valley'.

[21]   Jupp, *The Australian People*, 343; see also Mosely and Murray, 'Soccer'.

[22]   Hay, 'British Football, Wogball or the World Game?'; Mosely, 'The Game'.

[23]   Mosely, 'A Social History of Soccer in New South Wales, 1880–1956'.

[24]   Hay, 'Oral History, Migration and Soccer in Australia, 1880–2000'.

[25]   Doug Aiton, 'Settling the Score', Conversations, *Sunday Age*, Agenda, 8 December 1996, 5.

[26]   Oral information from MacGowan's daughter, Lilias Burke, Geelong Historical Record Centre, Geelong, 6 April 1994.

[27]   'Most [migrant soccer star players] have their fares paid by their supporters here, and are found jobs with a future', *Soccer News*, 19 Aug. 1961, 3.

[28]   Quoted by Laurie Schwab, 'Will we Embrace Soccer at Last?', *Sunday Age*, 28 Feb. 1993, 12.

[29]   Hay, 'The Last Night of the Poms'.

[30]   The unwary might be misled by references to matches between England and Scotland played in Australia from the 1880s onwards. These were games of association football played between migrants from these countries or their descendants. Similarly, the New World Cups played for in the 1950s onwards extended the catchment for tournaments to the post-war migrants, from Europe in particular.

[31]   'English Cricketers as Footballers', *Referee*, 2 April 1902, 8; Kreider, *A Soccer Century*, 23–5. A South Australian selection was also trounced by the cricketers in 1904.

[32]   Hay, 'Sidelight on Bodyline'.

[33]   Hay, 'How Footy Kicked Off: Origins of our Great Game Unclear', *Geelong Advertiser*, 6 Nov. 2004, 37.

[34]   Murray, *Football*; Murray, *The World's Game*; Sugden, 'USA and the World Cup'; Sugden and Tomlinson, *FIFA and the Contest for World Football*.

[35]   Tranter, 'The Chronology of Organised Sport in Nineteenth Century Scotland: A Regional Study I – Patterns'; Tranter 'The Chronology of Organised Sport in Nineteenth Century Scotland: A Regional Study II – Causes'; see also Holt, 'Working Class Football and the City'.

[36]   See Bale and Cronin, *Sport and Post-colonialism*, especially the Introduction.

[37]   'Australia is divided by a deep cultural rift known as the Barassi Line. It runs between Canberra, Broken Hill, Birdsville and Maningrida (Arnhem Land) and it divides Australia between rugby and rules' (Turner, 'The Ron Barassi Memorial Lecture 1978', 290). The line (as well as the lecture) was named after Ron Barassi, senior, the father of Ronald Dale Barassi, one of the most impressive and innovative players and coaches of Australian rules. My thanks to David Nadel for confirming the origins of the phrase.

[38]   Rugby league has also expanded, setting up or incorporating teams in Melbourne and New Zealand.

[39]   Kreider, *The Soccerites*, 221. I am indebted to Richard Kreider for allowing me to read his book prior to publication.

[40]   'J.J. Liston (who is better known as President of the Victorian Football Association, was also President of the Victorian Soccer Football Association until his death during the Second World War) desired to convert some of the VFA grounds to soccer and in 1937 he sought financial aid from the English Football Association but nothing more was heard of the idea' (J.O. Wilshaw, 'Soccer Aid to VFA', *Sporting Globe*, 6 June 1953, 7).

[41]   Sandercock and Turner, *Up Where, Cazaly?*, 226. The authors attribute the relative decline of Australian rules in Melbourne at that time to the conditions at suburban grounds, the decline of inner-urban populations, the higher share of recent, non-English speaking migrants in these suburbs, and a changing attitude to competitive sport in schools (227–30). Most codes of football experienced a decline in attendances from the immediate post-war peaks, so the rapid growth of soccer in Australia seemed particularly threatening in the 1950s and 1960s.

[42]   Kallinikios, 'Sporting Realities and Social Meanings'.

[43]   Schoolmaster, 'The Future in the School', *Soccer News*, 31 July 1954, 1 and 4.

[44]   Incidents of on-field violence in Australian rules and rugby league have encouraged some parents to try soccer for their children, though off-field violence by soccer fans may have had the opposite effect.

[45]   Murray, *Football*, 259.

[46]   Mosely, *Ethnic Involvement in Australian Soccer, 1950–1990*; Bradley, *Report to Australian Soccer Federation on Structure and Organisation of Australian Soccer*; Hay, 'Marmaras's Oyster or Seamonds' Baby?'; Hay, 'Croatia'.

[47]   Hay, '"Those bloody Croatians"'.

[48]   Hughson, 'The Bad Blue Boys and "the magical recovery" of John Clarke'. For a fuller analysis see Hughson, 'A Feel For the Game'.

[49]   Simon Hill, 'Can you smell the fear?' Parts 1 and 2, SBS website, accessed 6 June 2005, <http://wwiii.sbs.com.au/opinions/index.php3?id=58677>.

[50]   Hay, 'The Origins of the Australian National Soccer League'.

[51]   Western Australia applied for the original National Soccer League in 1975, but the application was not accepted, almost certainly because of transport costs (Memo to Members of the Executive Committee of the Australian Soccer Federation by the President, Sir Arthur George, 1 Dec. 1975, 3). The memo refers to resolutions of the Executive Committee of the ASF on 12 July 1975. I am indebted to Nick Guoth for supplying me with copies of documents relating to the formation of the NSL in 1975–77.

[52]   Stewart, *Report to Australian Soccer Federation on the Transfer of Australian Soccer Players.*

[53]   As Nick Tana puts it, 'As a marketer, I understand the networks' attitude is "Get your runs on the board and show us your credentials and away we go". It's not up to them to make our product, it's up to us to make our product. We here in Perth are a good example of what one can do by virtue of forcing the networks into coming and knocking on our doors, because once you put, pardon my French, bums on seats, and there's excitement and things are happening around football, then all of a sudden the networks are wanting to get involved because they're being forced by public pressure. So what comes first? We have to get our game in order, and that is happening now' ('Sports Factor', ABC Radio National, 11 March 2005).

[54]   Though Galati was owed over AUS $2 million by Soccer Australia and eventually settled for AUS $300,000 under persuasion from Frank Lowy (Solly, *Shootout*, 300; see also Harper, *Mr and Mrs Soccer.*

[55]   Murray, *Football*, 258.

[56]   Following the transfer of the young Australian-Croatian Mark Viduka from his Melbourne club to Dinamo Zagreb in 1995, expectations were raised that investors could make money by identifying Australian talent and exporting it to major overseas clubs, but these were not realized.

[57]   Murray, *Football*, 258.

[58]   Mosely, 'Factory Football'.

[59]   Ibid., 33.

[60]   Branko Filipi's sponsoring and employment of Croatian migrants in Adelaide and Melbourne was significant in the early period of post-war migration (Hay, 'Croatia', 61).

[61]   Murray, *Football*, 261–4.

[62]   Margo, *Frank Lowy*, 108. Lowy was a prime mover in Westfield shopping complexes.

[63]   Walkley was instrumental in the settlement with FIFA in 1962–63, which brought an end to Australia's suspension from the world body for poaching players from overseas. He became President of the Australian Soccer Federation after the tragic death of Dr Henry Seamonds in 1963, and later Chairman of the Oceania Confederation of FIFA in 1968, a year after he was knighted. Perth businessman Tana said, 'I do a lot of business in Asia, and football is a door-opener. It's a political door-opener and it's a business door-opener and it's just a general conversation door-opener. It is an incredible tool, and if we use it correctly, we will definitely have very, very strong links with Asia, bearing in mind that that is their first sport' ('Sports Factor', ABC Radio National, 18 March 2005).

[64] *West Australian*, Saturday 24 April 1909, quoted in Kreider, *The Soccerites*, 62.

[65] *Soccer News*, 31 July 1954, 10.

[66] Independent Soccer Inquiry, Australian Sports Commission, Canberra, 2003 (Crawford Report).

[67] Michael Lynch, 'The Round-ball Revolution', *Age*, 31 Oct. 2004.

[68] Solly, *Shootout*, 8.

[69] The FFA has about 150 overseas players on its database, of whom about 40 are playing in the first division in their respective countries and about a dozen of those in the English Premier League, the Italian Serie A, La Liga in Spain and the Bundesliga in Germany, the top four competitions in Europe (Information from Peter Smith, Communications Department, FFA, by email, 14 April 2005).

[70] As this essay goes to press, Australia has just earned a place in the 2006 World Cup finals by beating Uruguay in the qualifiers.

[71] Michael Cockerill, 'Hopes High Switch to Asia will help us Soccer it to 'em', *Sydney Morning Herald*, 11 March 2005.

[72] Vamplew, *Sports Violence in Australia*; Adair and Vamplew, 'Not so far from the Madding Crowd'.

[73] O'Hara, *Crowd Violence at Australian Sport*.

[74] Tony Collins, '"Ahr Waggy" – Harold Wagstaff and the making of Anglo-Australian Rugby League Culture', 5th Annual Tom Brock lecture, North Sydney, 4 July 2003, 12.

[75] Hay, 'A New Look at Soccer Violence'.

[76] There was another small-scale but ugly incident at the end of another match between these clubs at Parramatta Stadium on 1 May 2005 (Stephen Gibbs and AAP, 'Soccer thugs out of control', *Sydney Morning Herald*, 2 May 2005). A committee of inquiry's report into the first incident was tabled in the NSW State Parliament on 5 May ('Report of the independent panel of inquiry into the crowd disturbances at the Sydney United sports centre on Sunday 13 March 2005', Soccer New South Wales website, <http://www.soccernsw.com.au/home/AA/2005/IPR_April_2005.pdf>).

[77] *Australian and British Soccer Weekly*, Tuesday 15 March 2005, had a full-page report on the match on p.13, and on p.9 Greg Stock mentions the crowd trouble in his opening paragraph. The television, radio and mainstream print media carried extensive reports on the incidents, which provoked Soccer New South Wales to appoint an independent board of inquiry into the matter (Ben Sharkey, 'Riot police called out to match', news.com.au, 14 March 2005; Michael Cockerill and Les Kennedy, 'Clubs face fan lockout after brawl', *Sydney Morning Herald*, 15 March 2005; Sheree Went and Paul Carter, 'Lockouts, bans possible for ethnic clubs', <news.com.au>, 15 March 2005; 'Hooligans read riot act', SBS, <theworldgame.com.au>, 15 March 2005).

[78] *Geelong Advertiser*, 19 March 2005, 22.

[79] Hay, 'A New Look at Soccer Violence'; Mosely, 'European Immigrants and Soccer Violence in New South Wales, 1949–1959'; Vamplew, 'Sports Crowd Disorder'; Danforth, 'Is the World Game an Ethnic Game or an Aussie Game?'; Hughson, 'Football, Folk Dancing and Fascism'; Warren, *Football Crowds and Cultures*.

[80] Michael Lynch and Andrea Petrie, 'Clubs face Expulsion after Fans Clash at Soccer Match', *Age*, News, 19 April 2005, 5. For previous incidents involving South Melbourne and Preston and the political context see Hay, 'A New Look at Soccer Violence', 55–7. A correspondent to the Melbourne *Herald-Sun* argued that Australia's multicultural policies were to blame for the ethnic tensions involved (Jud Field, 'Soccer Trouble from Old Ideas', *Herald-Sun*, 20 April 2005, p.19). I owe this reference to John Kallinikios.

[81] Murray, *Football*, 261.

[82] Cameron, *The Second Australian Almanac*.

[83] It could be argued that cricket and rugby league prospered in the long run from the interventions of Kerry Packer in cricket in the 1970s and Rupert Murdoch in rugby league in the 1990s, even though the short term consequences were adverse.

[84]   Following promises made during his election campaign by Blatter, Oceania was briefly awarded a place, but this was withdrawn in part because of political opposition from South America and partly because of internal chaos within the Australian and Oceania soccer authorities.

[85]   Hess, '"Ladies are specially invited"'; Wedgwood, 'We have Contact!'. However, Sir Arthur George(opoulos), former President of the Australian Soccer Federation, remembers: 'When I used to go to Sydney Olympic matches I'd feel like a foreigner. The emotion, the abuse and the carrying on. Women used to go in their hundreds, but then a small minority [of men] took over, with the bad language, etc.' (Quoted in Solly, *Shootout,* 27.)

[86]   Williamson, *Belles of the Ball,* 31; for a summary of the state of play see Pfister *et al.,* 'Women and Football – A Contradiction?'.

[87]   *Women in Sport,* 10.

[88]   The trials and early growth of women's soccer in Australia are outlined in Watson, *Australian Women's Soccer.*

[89]   Calculated from Victorian Soccer Federation, Women's League Tables, 25 July 1999.

[90]   Kreider, *A Soccer Century,* 151.

[91]   Stell, *Half the Race,* 255. Since then several players, including Dianne Alagich and Alison Forman, have won contracts overseas.

[92]   Australian Bureau of Statistics, 'Participation in Sport and Physical Activities', *Year Book Australia,* 1998 (1301.0).

[93]   Scraton *et al.,* 'It's Still a Man's Game?'.

[94]   The World Game, SBS website, <http://wwiii.sbs.com.au/opinions/index.php3?id=51794>, accessed 16 Nov. 2004.

[95]   Devlin, 'John O'Neill and his Dreams and Targets'. This article originally appeared in *Football Business International,* at <www.soccerinvestor.com>.

References

Adair, Daryl and Wray Vamplew. 'Not so far from the Madding Crowd: Spectator Violence in Britain and Australia: A Review Article.' *Sporting Traditions 1* (Nov. 1990): 95–103.

Australian Football League. *Australian Football in South Africa: A Unique Opportunity for the AFL.* Melbourne: AFL, Oct. 2004.

Bale, John and Mike Cronin, eds. *Sport and Post-colonialism.* Oxford: Berg, 2003.

Bradley, Graham. *Report to Australian Soccer Federation on Structure and Organisation of Australian Soccer.* Sydney: Australian Soccer Federation, 18 May 1990 (Bradley Report).

Cameron, Angus, ed. *The Second Australian Almanac.* Sydney: Angus & Robertson, 1986.

Danforth, Loring M. 'Is the World Game an Ethnic Game or an Aussie Game? Narrating the Nation in Australian Soccer.' *American Ethnologist 28,* no.2 (2001): 363–87.

Devlin, Barry. 'John O'Neill and his Dreams and Targets.' *FIFA Magazine 4* (April 2005): 51–3.

Docherty, J.C. 'English Settlement in Newcastle and the Hunter Valley.' In *The Australian People: An Encyclopedia of the Nation, Its People and Their Origins,* edited by James Jupp. Cambridge: Cambridge University Press, 2001.

Foer, Franklin. *How Soccer Explains the World: An Unlikely Theory of Globalization.* New York: Harper Collins, 2004.

Harper, Andy. *Mr and Mrs Soccer.* Sydney: Random House Australia, 2004.

Hay, Roy. 'Soccer and Social Control in Scotland, 1873–1973.' In *Sport: Money, Morality and the Media,* edited by Richard Cashman and Michael McKernan. Kensington: New South Wales University Press, 1981.

———. 'British Football, Wogball or the World Game? Towards a Social History of Victorian Soccer.' In *Ethnicity and Soccer in Australia. Studies in Sports History, no.10,* edited by John O'Hara. Campbelltown: Australian Society for Sports History, 1994.

———. 'Marmaras's Oyster or Seamonds' Baby? The Formation of the Victorian Soccer Federation, 1956–1964.' *Sporting Traditions 10,* no.2 (1994): 3–24.

————. 'Croatia: Community, Conflict and Culture: The Role of Soccer Clubs in Migrant Identity.' In *Sporting Nationalisms: Identity, Ethnicity and Assimilation,* edited by Michael Cronin and David Mayall. London: Frank Cass, 1998.

————. 'A New Look at Soccer Violence.' In *All Part of the Game: Violence and Australian Sport,* edited by Denis Hemphill. Sydney: Walla Walla Press, 1998.

————. 'Sidelight on Bodyline.' *Baggy Green: Journal of Australian Cricket 4,* no.1 (2001): 19–21.

————. 'Sports Mad Nations: Some Research Already Done.' *Australian Society for Sports History Bulletin 33* (Feb. 2001): 18–24.

————. '"Those bloody Croatians": Croatian Soccer Teams, Ethnicity and Violence in Australia, 1950–1999.' In *Fear and Loathing in World Football,* edited by Gary Armstrong and Richard Giulianotti. Oxford: Berg, 2001.

————. 'Oral History, Migration and Soccer in Australia, 1880–2000.' In *Speaking to Immigrants: Oral Testimony and the History of Australian Migration: Visible Immigrants Six,* edited by A. James Hammerton and Eric Richards. Canberra: History Program and Centre for Immigration and Multicultural Studies, Research School of Social Sciences, Australian National University, 2002.

————. 'The Last Night of the Poms: Australia as a Post-colonial Sporting Society.' In *Sport and Post-colonialism,* edited by John Bale and Mike Cronin. Oxford: Berg, 2003.

————. 'The Origins of the Australian National Soccer League.' Paper delivered to the Sporting Traditions XV Conference, Melbourne, 14 July 2005.

Hess, Rob. '"Ladies are specially invited": Women and the Culture of Australian Rules Football.' *International Journal of the History of Sport 17,* nos 2/3 (June/Sept. 2000): 111–41.

Holt, Richard. 'Working Class Football and the City: The Problem of Continuity.' *British Journal of Sports History 4* (May 1986): 5–17.

————. *Sport and the British: A Modern History.* Oxford: Clarendon Press, 1989.

Hughson, John. 'A Feel for the Game: An Ethnographic Study of Soccer Support and Identity.' Ph.D. diss., University of New South Wales, Sydney, 1996.

————. 'The Bad Blue Boys and "the magical recovery" of John Clarke.' In *Entering the Field: Studies in World Football,* edited by Gary Armstrong and Richard Giulianotti. Oxford: Berg, 1997.

————. 'Football, Folk Dancing and Fascism: Diversity and Difference in Multicultural Australia.' *Australia and New Zealand Journal of Sociology 33,* no. 2 (1997): 167–86.

Jupp, James. *The Australian People: An Encyclopedia of the Nation, Its People and Their Origins.* Cambridge: Cambridge University Press, 2001.

Kallinikios, John. 'Sporting Realities and Social Meanings: The Transformation and Representation of Soccer in Victoria, 1945–1963.' Ph.D. diss., University of Melbourne, 2004.

Kreider, Richard. *A Soccer Century: A Chronicle of Western Australian Soccer from 1896 to 1996.* Perth: Sports West Media, 1966.

————. *The Soccerites.* Cloverdale, Western Australia: SportsWest Media, 2005.

Mangan, J.A. *The Games Ethic and Imperialism: Aspects of the Diffusion of an Ideal.* Harmondsworth, Middlesex: Viking, 1986.

Margo, Jill. *Frank Lowy: Pushing the Limits.* Sydney: Harper Collins, 2001.

Markovits, Andrei S. and Stephen L. Hellerman. *Offside: Soccer and American Exceptionalism.* Princeton: Princeton University Press, 2001.

Mosely, Philip. 'Factory Football: Paternalism and Profits.' *Sporting Traditions 1* (Nov. 1985): 25–36.

————. 'A Social History of Soccer in New South Wales, 1880–1956.' Ph.D. diss., University of Sydney, 1987.

————. 'The Game: Early Soccer Scenery in New South Wales.' *Sporting Traditions 2* (May 1992): 135–51.

————. 'European Immigrants and Soccer Violence in New South Wales, 1949–1959.' *Journal of Australian Studies 40* (March 1994): 14–26.

————. *Ethnic Involvement in Australian Soccer, 1950–1990.* Canberra: Australian Sports Commission, 1995.

Mosely, Philip and Bill Murray. 'Soccer.' In *Sport in Australia: A Social History,* edited by Wray Vamplew and Brian Stoddart. Cambridge: Cambridge University Press, 1994.

Murray, Bill. *Football: A History of the World Game.* Aldershot: Scolar Press, 1994.

——. *The World's Game: A History of Soccer.* Champaign, IL: University of Illinois Press, 1996.

O'Hara, John, ed. *Crowd Violence at Australian Sport. Studies in Sports History, no.7.* Campbelltown: Australian Society for Sports History, 1992.

Pfister, Gertrude, Kari Fasting, Sheila Scraton and Ana Bunuel Heras. 'Women and Football – A Contradiction? The Beginnings of Women's Football in Four European Countries.' *European Sports History Review 1* (1999): 1–26.

Sandercock, Leonie and Ian Turner. *Up Where, Cazaly? The Great Australian Game.* St Albans, Herts: Granada Publishing, 1981.

Scraton, Sheila, Kari Fasting, Gertrude Pfister and Ana Bunuel Heras. 'It's Still a Man's Game? The Experience of Top Level European Women Footballers.' *International Review for the Sociology of Sport 34,* no.2 (1999): 99–111.

Solly, Ross. *Shootout: The Passion and the Politics of Soccer's Fight for Survival in Australia.* Milton, Queensland: John Wiley Australia, 2004.

Stell, Marion K. *Half the Race: A History of Australian Women in Sport.* Sydney: Angus & Robertson, 1991.

Stewart, Hon D. G. *Report to Australian Soccer Federation on the transfer of Australian Soccer Players,* Australian Soccer Federation, December 1994.

Sugden, John. 'USA and the World Cup: American Nativism and the Rejection of the People's Game.' In *Hosts and Champions: Soccer Cultures, National Identities and the USA World Cup,* edited by John Sugden and Alan Tomlinson. Aldershot: Arena, 1994.

Sugden, John and Alan Tomlinson. *FIFA and the Contest for World Football: Who Rules the People's Game?* London: Polity Press, 1998.

Tranter, Neil. 'The Chronology of Organised Sport in Nineteenth Century Scotland: A Regional Study I – Patterns.' *International Journal of the History of Sport 7,* no.2 (1990): 188–203.

——. 'The Chronology of Organised Sport in Nineteenth Century Scotland: A Regional Study II – Causes.' *International Journal of the History of Sport 7,* no.3 (1990): 365–87.

Turner, Ian. 'The Ron Barassi Memorial Lecture 1978.' In *The Great Australian Book of Football Stories,* edited by Garrie Hutchinson. Melbourne: Viking O'Neil, 1983.

Vamplew, Wray. *Sports Violence in Australia: Its Extent and Control.* ACT: Australian Sports Commission, 1991.

——. 'Sports Crowd Disorder: An Australian Survey'. In *Crowd Violence at Australian Sport. Studies in Sports History, no. 7,* edited by John O'Hara. Campbelltown: Australian Society for Sports History, 1992.

Warren, Ian. *Football Crowds and Cultures: Comparing English and Australian Law and Enforcement Trends. Studies in Sports History, no.13.* Campbelltown: Australian Society for Sports History, 2004.

Watson, Elaine. *Australian Women's Soccer: The First 20 Years.* Canberra: Australian Women's Soccer Association, 1994.

Wedgwood, Nikki. 'We have Contact! Women, Girls and Boys Playing Australian Rules Football.' Ph.D. diss., University of Sydney, 2000.

Williamson, David J. *Belles of the Ball: The Early History of Women's Soccer.* Devon: R & D Associates, 1991.

Women in Sport 4, no.1 (1998): 10.

Loss of Identity: New Zealand Soccer, its Foundations and its Legacies

Nick Guoth

The historiographical cupboard of New Zealand soccer is bare. Sports historian Charles Little registered his disbelief in 2002[1] and since then very little has changed. Yet the variance in literature discussing rugby, in this small window of time, has continued to provide evidence of the fact that rugby, and not soccer, is, and has always been, portrayed as the national sport of New Zealand.[2] While this essay cannot change the ever-strong current of feeling between the two sports and their different histories, it is hoped that, like Little's paper, it may provide a basis for more work to be done on this subject.

Only recently historians have suggested answers to the question of why rugby was chosen, and here these reasons will be explored, and expanded, to reveal a solid theory for the separation of the football codes. For New Zealand, timing was the key, and this combined with the legacy of soccer's failings generated rugby's emergence. More importantly, masculinity was not significant when the separation occurred, but provincial identity through rivalries, developed and assisted in the choice of rugby.

Public schools have played an important role in the development of the football codes, first in England, and then in New Zealand. The relationship between these public schools, England and football, integrated within New Zealand history will be the opening topic of this paper, and through this, a general discussion is provided on the origins of football in New Zealand. It will also investigate and present the arguments relating to the way soccer was viewed in comparison to rugby, embodying subject areas of media coverage and missionary activities, amongst others, to define the failings of soccer, whether intentionally or without reason. A brief discussion on comparative studies of the United States is diagnosed for further exploration.

English Origins, Public Schools and Early Football

The introduction of rugby to New Zealand has been credited to Charles John Monro,[3] when he returned from Christ's College, Finchley in England and offered the game as an alternative to the football of the day in Nelson. Two years prior, on Saturday 31 May 1868, a group had met to form the Nelson Football Club[4] which Arthur Swan, in his extensive history of rugby football, states played both Association and Victorian rules football.[5] Monro explains, in an article for the *New Zealand Free Lance* in 1925, that he remembers the game being played in Nelson as early as 1861 at a venue known as 'The Green'. Monro describes the game in that 'there was no club then, and it only amounted to rough and tumble and a punt about'.[6] Historians have then attributed to the schoolboy network the spread of rugby through the country, with Monro himself performing some of the missionary duties. This included a trip to Wellington later in 1870, which led to a game being played between Nelson and Wellington at Petone on 12 September. Monro's effort was not the only insurgence by an ex-English public school boy into the New Zealand system. Influences existed throughout the country, both before and after Monro, with some tending towards the rugger style and others, the dribblers' version. Arguments were to continue throughout the provinces during this period, with both versions of football putting forward their case. The origins of this controversy are found in the English sporting history of earlier decades.

Delving back to the roots of rugby and its separation from soccer in mid-nineteenth century England provides some remarkable points of discussion. The near removal of folk foot-ball[7] at the end of the eighteenth century 'owing to industrialisation and the changes in social patterns' saw the game become more of a public school sport.[8] Yet the anarchy of the sport, familiar with the pre-industrial lower-class game of the country towns and villages,[9] was still an integral part in the first half of the nineteenth century. Eventually, the elitist public schools were to codify their games and remove the worst of the violence. Public schools, also seen as sporting schools, believed athleticism to be vital for the boys' health and moral well-being.[10] In each school's case, the type of game was based on a number of constraints, including the size of the field and quality of surface. James Walvin provides an interesting assessment of this point, asserting that by the 1850s and 1860s other schools adopted football as the winter physical recreation and the form of the game depended on which school the master had attended as a boy or young teacher.[11] Walvin uses the schools of Charterhouse, Eton, Harrow, Rugby and others to provide his examples. Most of these used the dribbling style of the game,[12] which in some cases allowed catching the ball but not carrying, while the latter, Rugby, by 1841, promoted the carrying of the ball.[13] Adrian Harvey, in his discussion on the rules of football, divides these, in relation to public school football of the day, into two categories – those used by Rugby, and the rest. Rugby, Harvey states, was distinguished from others by the level of permissible violence, the extent to which the ball could legitimately be handled and the large numbers of players involved in the game. The others were the ancestors of Association football. The Cambridge codification meetings of 1848 and 1863, as Walvin states, were brought about by members of the public schools while in the formative years of association football, the ex-public school pupils performed missionary activities to spread the game. From the 1850s onwards, new forms of gentlemanly recreation began to appear throughout the country.[14] Steven Tischler also provides a pair of defining examples from the period where conflicting rules caused concern for those wishing to participate in a game of football.[15]

Walvin's commentary generates some justification for the apparent lack of rugby in New Zealand until Charles Monro set the game in motion from Nelson in 1870. It follows that the proportion of dribbler public-school immigrants was far larger than that of the rugbyites, and thus lends credence to the theory that the exportation of sport from England was made up of soccer and cricket. Greg Ryan, while viewing the relationship between cricket and class in nineteenth-century New Zealand, adds evidence to this theory stating that there was a disproportionate number of public school and Oxbridge graduates reaching parts of New Zealand between 1850 and 1880.[16] Further to this, it can be asked whether public school tradition rather than linkage was more important in the spread of football in New Zealand. The following section probes this theory.

Historians, however, have for the most part, ignored this fact when examining the origins of rugby and its establishment in New Zealand. The Monro effect awoke the sleeping giant of the rugbyite public school New Zealander. Certainly the veritable army of Tom Browns spread themselves throughout the British Empire, yet they were in New Zealand well before 1870. Len Richardson, for example, attributes the emergence of rugby to those with Oxbridge degrees in one hand and rugby ball or cricket bat in the other, calling most of these 'the colonial founding fathers'.[17]

Early New Zealand Football

There is evidence of numerous forms of football, though more in the line of folk-football, throughout the colony centres before 1870. The style of football varied from town to town, as had been the case in the public schools back in England and Scotland. Montague Shearman, in his late-nineteenth-century discussion on football, informs us that for the 25 years following the 1863 codification of Association rules, the game had altered little, especially for the style of play.[18] Shearman defines Association football in the early days as a dribblers' game. 'Skill in dribbling is something more than go-ahead, fearless, headlong onslaught on the enemy's citadel; it requires an eye quick at discovering a weak point and "nous" to calculate and decide the chances of successful passage.'[19] Viewing a report from the Melbourne *Age* of a game between Victoria and NSW in 1883, Philip Mosely notes that both heading and dribbling were keenly mentioned; yet there was no 'explicit description of passing the ball'. He attributes the usage of dribbling to the possibility that, of those who represented NSW on that day, most were of English origin. This was based on their names and that 'the passing game had been slower to take on in England than north of the border'.[20]

New Zealand, more so than Australia, was settled by the English. Wellington and Nelson were founded by the New Zealand Company. Most of the original settlers came from London or nearby counties. The colonization of Taranaki was initially with folk from Devon and Cornwall. The denominational colonies of Christchurch (founded 1850) and Otago (1848) were established by the Church of England and the Free Church of Scotland respectively.[21] Auckland was slightly different by the 1850s with a large population of Australians, some driven by imperialism.[22] The style of game in New Zealand would thus have followed that in England, especially with the influx of public school English. A small number of individuals were influential in the development of football in New Zealand.

In Christchurch, the first recorded game of football was in 1854 as part of a festival to celebrate the anniversary of settlement.[23] From at least 1860, Christ's College started playing a variant of football, and by 1862 the game was based upon rules that were established at the Radley College in England.[24] Chairing the committee to draw up the rules was George Harper, youngest son of the first Anglican bishop of Christchurch, Henry Harper. Prior to attending Christ's College, George had played football at Radley College and Eton. The first game was fought out on Thursday 29 April 1862 with the venue being Raven's Paddock in Rolleston Avenue.[25] Radley, founded in 1847, did not take up soccer until 1881 and was exposed to the Winchester rules in 1864, when they played their first school football match against Bradfield.[26] While there is little evidence of the rules of football at Radley, Ryan and Small provide a copy of those formulated at Christ's College in 1862, which refer to the handling of the ball and throwing between the posts as a method of scoring a goal. The rules were more a mixture of the two football codes with more emphasis towards Association variants than those devised at Rugby.[27] Significantly, though, Harper is the first possible instance of a student from an English public school exporting his version of football to a New Zealand school.

Members of Radley College may have conveyed their game to Christ's College in Christchurch, yet it was through the impetus of R.J.S. Harman that led to the Christchurch Football Club (CFC) being formed on 3 September 1863. The Club is regarded as the oldest football club in New Zealand.[28] The CFC adopted the rules of Christ's College, and this facilitated regular competition between the two. Geoff Vincent, in his work on early Canterbury football, describes the game as one of scrimmages, rushes and dribbles with holding the ball kept to a minimum. It had thus evolved to resemble Association football 'as it was played in England before 1870'.[29]

Over the next decade, changes occurred in many ways. A number of rugbyites from Britain infiltrated the CFC in the early 1870s and attempted to transform the way the game was being played. Yet the CFC, without any believed threat to their manliness, rejected this version of football. Vincent uses an example from the *Lyttleton Times* dated 25 May 1875 which said 'any player who picked up the ball was "collared", after which "a general scrimmage" ensued. "Pleasure and science are postponed to fatiguing strain of body and weight of flesh", wrote one observer, "Time is lost making up the numerous quarrels that of necessity ensue, when the rules are so varied and complex … and above all, it is exceedingly dangerous and brutal". Rugby football was pronounced demonstrably inferior to the "prettiest, most scientific, easiest, and least hazardous … dribbling game" devised and played by the CFC.'

The style of the code appeared solidly founded and had abandoned any divergence. Yet within only a year of the above quote, the idea of Association football had been all but put aside. Vincent supports the overwhelming reason as being the effect of the Auckland rugby tour of 1875. Rugby was fully adopted by the Canterbury Football Club in March 1876 and three years later the Canterbury Rugby Football Union was founded. It took another 13 years for a corresponding Association of soccer to form in the province.[30]

Even so, it was not all rugby in Canterbury as Christ's College refused to give up its own rules.[31] Football expanded in Christchurch and moved from the public schools to the working-class suburbs. Richardson, while not providing dates, outlines that even after the formation of local rugby clubs, self-regulated games of football were played, sometimes by 'pub-teams' where informality, custom and spontaneity flourished. Some of these were eventually swept up by the more formal rugby clubs, as were the Sydenham boys by the Sydenham Rugby Football Club in 1882.[32]

Accounts about the history of football in Auckland vary between both rugby and soccer historians, suffice to say that the earlier versions were related to that played at Westminster College in England. Literature demonstrates that three people initially were crucial in the development of the game in the northern province – F. Whitaker, Charles Dacre and William Robinson. While the former two were from dribbling schools, and transplanted their version of the game to the locals, they were to join with Robinson eventually in playing rugby both in Auckland and for the province. The earliest recollection of football in the city was a game at the Auckland Domain in 1868, yet most agree that the game would have been played in some way prior. Considering the number of Australians present in the city, the style of game probably was a mix of Victorian and Association rules.[33]

In his book on the first 100 years of Association football in New Zealand, Tony Hilton lays a large amount of the claim for the founding of football in Auckland to Charles Craven Dacre.[34] Born in Sydney, Australia, in 1848, he emigrated to Auckland 11 years later before being sent to England for schooling. Dacre went to Clapham Grammar and in 1864 was playing football under the rules for his school, and for London Athletic and Clapham Rovers, the version of the game shifting between each of the three. Dacre also participated in the first game under 'modern day' Association rules representing Surrey against Middlesex. Before departing the English shores he had made a name in cricket as well as Association football, a one-time secretary of the Football Association. Of the assortment of rules he had played under, Westminster was the version that Dacre brought with him to New Zealand.[35]

Dacre's return to New Zealand saw him take up farming, yet he was still very interested in the game of football. Before 1870 there was little football played in most of the North Island, essentially owing to the Maori wars that plagued the island. Cricket also was in abeyance until 1865 when hostilities receded.[36] Although the mainstay of the British regiments had sailed away, it was left to the colonists, a portion of whom would have come from Auckland, to sustain the fighting with the Hau hau over the following five to seven years.[37] The men of Auckland were presumably engaged in these encounters. For Dacre, like Monro, his arrival was timely. Yet, as with the Radley College members who set Christ's College on its way in Christchurch nearly a decade prior, Dacre passed on his knowledge of the sport from Clapham in June 1871 to assist in the forming of the Auckland Football Club.

On Saturday 11 June 1870, with the HMS Rosario lying in Auckland Harbour, a game was arranged. Whitaker, an old Westminster boy, was one of the main organizers. The sailors brought the goalposts and the ball from the ship. There were numerous reports on the match, although none provided a score. The *New Zealand Herald* stated that the 'Jack Tars' of the Rosario proved victorious after a hard struggle.[38] Robinson, in his discussion on the history of rugby in Auckland to the English, describes the rules played that day –

> The rules under which this match was played were of non-descript sort, no offside, no picking up, no holding, but shoving over anywhere, anyone, and anyhow.[39]

At this stage of history, the literature and the facts presented in the Auckland newspapers of the time vary. Not discrediting Robinson, but the three documents all appear to replicate the same text. Each reproduces the recollections of Robinson, which in a number of cases bear little resemblance to what can be garnished from the *New Zealand Herald* and the *Daily Southern Cross*. The two crucial items of disagreement relate to the formation of the Auckland Football Club and discussions surrounding games between Auckland and the Thames Club. The most fitting scenario appears that while Robinson was correct with the date of the first game in 1870, he was one year out with everything else.

The second recorded match against the Rosario appears to have been contested on 3 June 1871 with another local game two weeks later. It was consequent to this game that the Auckland F.C. was established.

> A meeting was held last night, at half-past seven o'clock, in Robertson's Buildings, of a number of gentlemen desirous of forming a football club in this city … A draft copy of rules was read, and, after various amendments and additions had been made, the rules were adopted in their amended form. It was resolved that the club should date its existence from the 22nd June, 1871, and should be called the 'Auckland Football Club'.[40]

Robinson states that a ball was obtained from Melbourne. Two more games were played against the Rosario with the Aucklanders being the more successful. The rules chosen for these games were Westminster, but somewhat modified, with an influence of Victorian rules. Whitaker was said to be an able exponent of the dribbling game. Affirmation of further games is provided in the first annual meeting of the Club on

2 May 1872 where it was stated that several matches had been contested, chiefly with the crews of man-of-war ships in the harbour. At this meeting a sub-committee was formed to revise the code, consisting of F. Whitaker, T. Henderson and A. Boardman, and further a challenge would be made to the Thames Club. Robinson described the rules of the day as without offside, but which allowed players to run with the ball, bouncing it every five yards, and kicking it between the posts under a tape. The Victorian rules element soon discarded meant games were played under something like Association rules, yet problems still existed and eventually the rules were to change again.[41]

With the arrival of C.B. Mercer and Gore, new guidance appeared to help settle the problems of code choice. Both from Wellington College (England), and in conjunction with Whitaker and others, a set of rules based on those played at that school were drafted at the 1873 Annual Meeting. These were supplemented by an old Lillywhite Guide and were made only 33 in number. In the preview to a game to be played on 26 April 1873, the *New Zealand Herald* provided some reasoning behind the change in rules.[42]

> The club has lately adopted a new code of playing rules based on the Wellington Club. The rules previously played were introduced by the officers of the Rosario, when the first football match was played in Auckland; but, being totally different from those of any other club in existence, have been discarded for the rules now approved of.[43]

Further descriptions asserted the rules to be vastly superior to those formerly played under, and generated what may be termed a 'prettier game'. Following a number of games in Auckland, on 13 September 1873 the first match under these rules was played against the Thames Club, with a drawn score line. Rugby became the dominant sport, and it was not long before the first major inter-provincial tour took place in 1875.[44]

New Zealand's early soccer heroes, Charles Dacre and his brother Life, were exponents of both versions of football, Charles having participated in the first inter-provincial rugby match for Auckland against Canterbury and scoring the first try and points for his province. When Dacre met an unfortunate accident on the rugby field, the sport of soccer petered out with his absence from the game.[45] Games were rarely played, and those mostly against visiting ships. It took ten years before, at a meeting held on 31 May 1887, the Auckland FA was formed.[46]

The history of Wellington football is a little less complicated than Auckland. Yet, unlike the other provincial centres, there appears no specific individual who helped transform his version of the English game to the locals. Instead, the game was occurred as a result of locals getting together at special events like fetes. An article in the *Wellington Independent* in early 1866 stated that at an upcoming fete the 'amusements will consist of cricket, football and other rural English sports'.[47] The same paper, four days later, gave an extensive description of the fete, including that of a 'friendly game of cricket', yet there was no mention of any football being played.[48] This is the earliest documentation of football in the central province. Anders Wiren, in his book on the silver jubilee of Wellington rugby, quotes this reference; although he also alludes to the possibility of the game being played much earlier. In citing William Garrard's work on early rugby history of Canterbury, Wiren states that the people who brought football to Christ's College in the early 1850s were three members of well-known Wellington families.[49] A game was played in September 1868, not long after the establishment of the Nelson FC, between two companies of the 18th Royal Irish. The game was to involve a team of civilians, but an insufficient number put in an appearance. There was eagerness in the writer's words to continue football in Wellington. 'We should like to see these manly, healthy, open air exercises more resorted to by those whom sedentary pursuits render occasional out-door exercise essential to their health and happiness.'[50] However, it took another two years before the game of football was played with interest. The arrival of the Rosario in mid-1870 helped promote the need to provide a Wellington team. In late August of that year, the two met with the 'men of war' winning one goal to nil. The report in the local paper showed the game to be of the dribbling version, played with pluck and spirit, where each member took at least one tumble. The article described the game as a rough one, 'but nothing occurred to destroy the good temper even for an instant'.[51]

The arrival of Monro and his Nelson team, via sponsored passage by Sir Julius Vogel on the Government steamer 'Luna', was the big event of the year and a match arranged between Nelson and Wellington on 12 September 1870 became the first inter-provincial contest.[52] The more organized Nelson won two goals to one. The *Wellington Independent*'s report on the engagement stated: 'as so often happens in this game, different codes of law prevailed in the minds of the players, but without for an instant promoting ill-feeling, or bringing about a feeling of dissatisfaction, so that, the Nelson men carried the day'.[53] The game showed the need for organization and in May the following year, the Wellington Club was established at a meeting of some 30 enthusiasts at the Branch Hotel. The Wellington Club adopted Victorian rules initially, but following a meeting on 24 June 1871, the version of the game to be played was changed to rugby.[54] The new club's first game was played on 22 July and later that year it won a game against a combined Nelson Club and Nelson College Club team by a solitary goal.

The period from early 1874 until June the following year saw the game in disarray. The Wellington Club nearly folded, mainly owing to the disinterest of the players. The *Evening Post* described the situation as one that 'unfortunately, on account of the apathy displayed by the youths of this city, who prefer the part of "lookers on" to that of joining in the game, we can seldom raise fullsides, which obliges us to curtail those rules to suit members'.[55] A number of attempts were made to establish matches including a game with the HMS Blanche, but none eventuated. Even the annual pilgrimage to Nelson was abandoned with football in Wellington appearing to have died a natural death.[56] While 1874 saw the near cessation of football in Wellington, the next year was one of both confusion and solidarity. The indifference of the past year had carried forward and a growing movement for the implementation of Victorian rules existed. So much so that along with the Wellington Club, two new clubs both under Victorian rules were formed. Eventually a set of unique, hybrid rules was developed and the games began to be contested under these rules. A problem came to head when the annual Nelson contest meant that rugby rules had to be used. Eventually, the decision was to return to that game, and following the Auckland tour later that year, it was solidly set as the version of football in Wellington.[57]

The Wanganui Club was established in 1872 following a game instigated by the Nelson Club captain, A. Drew. Although the match itself turned into a 'rough-and-tumble' game, it was sufficient to generate interest in the small seaside town. The club played a number of 'Town' v 'Country' matches as well as a series against the Armed Constabulary in each of the following years. On 24 January 1874, the Taranaki Club was formed, bringing the game to New Plymouth. The *Taranaki Herald* of the day stated that football existed for some time prior and was happy to see that finally a club had been formed. That year the game was introduced into the Waikato region, and in late September two Waikato teams contested a match played along rugby lines, with one of the teams containing a number of Auckland players, including the Whitaker brothers.[58] Other areas to commence playing rugby over the following years were Hawkes Bay and Marlborough.

In Dunedin, it was George Samuel Sale of Rugby school who provided the influence on local football. Rex Thompson, in his paper on early Otago rugby, notes that the games played prior to 1870 were a blend of rugby, Association and/or Victorian rules. He provides an example of what is believed to be the earliest report of a football game in the province on 31 May 1869.[59] This appears rather hard to believe, considering that Dunedin was settled by Scotsmen who would have brought their variant of the game and later in the 1860s by Australians, who sought their fortunes on the Otago goldfields and conveyed their own version of the game.[60] By 1871, Sale was to impose his influence. He had returned to New Zealand from England to take up a chair at the newly established University of Otago, not only with his experiences from Cambridge and Rugby, but also having been Commissioner of the South Island's West Coast goldfields and, more importantly, the first editor of the *Christchurch Press*. Thompson lays significant importance on Sale and his part in the development of rugby football. 'Tall and strongly built, and now in his early forties, Sale was to become not only "the moving spirit of university sport", but also the moving force behind the establishment of rugby football in his adopted province.'[61] It took only two months for the first rugby game to be organized, involving players from both the Otago Boys' High School and the University. In March 1872, the Dunedin Football Club was established. Thompson states that a major dilemma befell the members as to the version of the rules, and that the experience of Sale provided the solution. By June 1872, it was unanimously resolved that carrying the ball, which was banned previously, would now be allowed.

The Dunedin FC was now a rugby club, but this did not mean that they were to play rugby all the time. On a trip to Oamaru, some 75 miles north, the Dunedin club had to vary their game, and at a request from the Oamaru Football Club there was some play without handling. Dunedin was superior and won in all instances.[62] Over the next few years, the problems of other clubs not choosing rugby saw a rebellion in the Dunedin FC to such an extent that in May 1875 a vote was taken and Association rules adopted.[63] Yet the Australian influence from the gold-digging migrants still kept their version alive and games were played either under Victorian or

Association rules and on one occasion with one half under rugby and the other under Association rules.[64] Thompson summarized the predicament facing rugby in 1875 by stating it was struggling for acceptance, and its future as the dominant code of football in Dunedin was by no means certain at this time.[65] The game lacked impetus and firm direction. Yet, in only two years, rugby became the ascendant code of football in Otago. The main reason, the arrival of Auckland in late 1875, will be extrapolated later in this paper, although in the intervening time the Dunedin FC became the last home of Association rules in the province with all other clubs finally moving to rugby.[66]

The history of Association rules over the period from the mid-1870s to the early 1890s is vague and assumptions can be made that only rare social games were played during this time. For the five years following the formation of the Auckland Football Association, Otago and Wellington founded their associations and in 1891 the first meeting of the newly established New Zealand Football Council was held in Wellington.[67] John Small, in his book on Canterbury soccer, explains that the New Zealand Football Association moved to Christchurch, owing to the need for a major ground, Lancaster Park being that property. In 1893, the headquarters moved back to Wellington.[68]

The men of the Auckland Association Football Club, created prior to the formation of the Auckland Football Association in 1887, 'preferred it to rugby on account of its more scientific nature, open play, and total absence of packed scrums'.[69] The number of players increased so rapidly that an Association was formed with eight teams playing for the Cup in 1887. In April 1882, one year after Christ's College formally decided upon rugby rules, the Canterbury Association Football Club was formed. It lasted only a few years and in 1890 the Christchurch Association Football Club was established, but it too only survived for a short time and it was not until 1903 that the Canterbury Football Association was founded.[70]

Turning Point

Football in New Zealand prior to the mid-1870s was a mish-mash of various codes, none of which stood out. Only in one or two centres had one variant of the game shown itself as more dominant than the others. One of these was Auckland. The decision to play rugby in Auckland in 1873 was the most significant choice made in New Zealand sporting history. The reasoning appears to be somewhat against common present beliefs. While Nauright expounds rugby and its relationship with masculine identity (and certainly there was a link in times after the sport's beginnings), there is evidence that Association football, and not rugby, was the more masculine, in relation to violence, of the games, when played in Auckland.

The early games of football between Auckland and the Thames Goldfields were 'rough and tumble' adventures. Injuries were not uncommon and casualties numerous. An extract from the Auckland RFU history, describing the 1871 match, states:

> The play was apparently very rough, as the report says that W. Cussen was knocked insensible by a charge from Donovan, Bull got two ribs broken, Jennings had two

teeth knocked out, and Dunlevy was kicked in the groin, and had to be taken to hospital.

Shortly after this it was thought advisable to alter the rules to Rugby Union.[71]

Robinson declares that this was the trigger to change the rules to those played at Wellington College, yet evidence shows a gradual refinement of the rules by a select committee for each season. Certainly the arrival of Gore and Mercer provided an impetus, yet the change was made and the 1873 match between the Goldfields and Auckland was under rugby rules.

In 1873, Auckland sent a cricket team to districts in both the North and South Islands. Having been highly successful on this tour, the northern province of Auckland came 'into notice very much'. Robinson was the captain of this team, and together with leading rugby enthusiasts, a decision was made 'to follow in the footsteps of lovers of kindred sport'. Thus, in 1875, it was proposed to 'invade' the southern provinces.[72] At the same time, there was another conflict in the making, this one of a political nature. Julius Vogel, the Treasurer in the ministry of William Fox, propounded a 'go-ahead' policy. This involved expanding and improving the infrastructure within New Zealand, especially in the field of transport. He proposed to borrow £10m and as security for this overseas loan intended to set aside a public estate of six million acres along the new railway lines and roads. The provincial governments weren't of the same opinion as Vogel and attempted to hinder the progress of the new. In turn, Vogel took the only action he could, and in 1876, he abolished the provincial governments, thus centralizing all control in Wellington.[73]

The loss of, or at least a significant dent in, provincial identity by the centralization of government, generated a void. The rugby tours of 1875 till 1877 by Auckland, Canterbury and Otago respectively, became the fillers. Vincent supports this theory stating 'the demise of the provinces, and the relocation of power to the central government in Wellington, prompted the middle classes in many parts of New Zealand to search for a new means of maintaining provincial identity and expressing civic pride. Contests between representative sports teams were widely considered to be the ideal solution.'[74] Improvements in transport, initiated by Vogel, had in turn facilitated in the development of inter-provincial rugby rivalry and thus provincial identity. Just as Monro some five years earlier had provided impetus for the expansion of rugby across the Cook Strait to Wellington and regions nearby, the Auckland tour turned around the thoughts of footballing entities throughout the Colony and set in motion the dominance of rugby over the other codes.

Role of the Media

The use of the media is one area that has rarely been addressed when examining the topic of identity. Newspapers have always played an important role in transporting sport to the masses, and raising public consciousness. It provides, as Scott Crawford states, not just the results and outcomes, but the more subtle nuances of the various sports.[75] The descriptions provided in nineteenth-century newspapers would attempt to give the reader a feeling of participating in the event. Accounts could include descriptions of the garments worn by the spectators. In New Zealand, too, the printed media played a crucial part in the growth and consolidation of rugby as the major football code in New Zealand in the mid-1870s.

In New Zealand, many newspapers in the 1860s were established with an expectation of making a profit. The 1870s saw a marked expansion in the number of papers, especially with the opening of the trans-Tasman cable in 1876 and the telegraph in the 1880s, and the establishment of the United Press Association resulted in a uniform press service allowing newspapers the position of establishing a national identity.[76] The uniformity came about through provision by one source and by regulating what news was to be published. In this the local editor became a 'gatekeeper' in determining what readers saw.[77]

Crawford postulates that from the mid 1860s onwards, there was increasing evidence that sporting activity held a certain fascination for newspaper readers. This was based on the fact that the 'mass of the population in colonial New Zealand read for entertainment, not for instruction'. He rightly asserts that the ideal source of entertainment were the sports pages. He extends this point further to argue that the newspapers were a method of local propaganda, displaying 'regional pride' by comparing what was happening in the local town with others. Finally, he concludes that the newspapers had always been an important tool in bringing about a uniform national consciousness around sport. Certainly, they had the ability to galvanize a province or country around a sport if they wished, something that is still being done today. Through this, one possible theory relating to soccer postulates the use of newspapers as a propaganda tool and that the owners/editors of the major regional papers were all rugby devotees. While probably somewhat far-fetched, the idea is not to be discarded. George Sale, who helped to set up rugby in Otago, was the first editor of the *Christchurch Press* in the 1860s. Julius Vogel, who sponsored the Nelson team on its trip to Wellington in 1870 through his position in government, was the founder of the *Otago Daily Times*. A newspaper or periodical thrives on circulation and thus there is a designated need to provide what the reader wants. By giving the public more information on rugby than soccer, the print media generates a 'rolling-stone' effect where exposure garnishes interest and this leads to more coverage. Propaganda, while possibly not on the agenda of the editors and writers, is created through continuous and heavy exposure.

The fact that the media controlled what the people wanted to see could be influenced by the slightest change in circumstances. A clear example occurred in 1875 when the *Lyttleton Times* provided a glowing report on why the current version of football was better than the 'dangerous and brutal' rugby. Yet, when it came to the tour by Auckland of a rugby team just three months later, the paper exalted the quality of the game, while trying to promote provincial identity. The use of the media further assisted in entrenching attitudes of masculinity in rugby. They were seen to provide both positive and negative effects on the readers. An example of such a contrasting report may be reproduced here: 'There were no broken limbs – though the Doctor was on the Ground; but several singlets were seen flying about, some few ounces of blood were sprinkled on the ground, and some of the players were limping about testifying to the strength of their opponents.'[78]

Bill Keane, in one of the extremely rare papers looking at New Zealand soccer, states that 'success brings flexibility' and that 'winning teams generally attract more favourable attention and support'.[79] For developing sport in the nineteenth century, the role of media in portraying a team was thus evidently significant while the quantity of media coverage rarely equates to the success of a team in present times.

Spreading the Game and Not

Missionary ventures also provided impetus to the growth of rugby in New Zealand. From the Auckland FC venture south in 1875 to the major tours a little over a decade later, enthusiasm was aroused and club organization formalized. Similarly, the annual pilgrimage into the countryside by city-based teams was seen as a vital cog in the development of the sport.[80] Dunedin's goldfield's tour is a prime example.

The first major tour took place in the second half of 1875, with an Auckland select travelling the South to challenge regional teams from Canterbury, Otago, Nelson, Wellington and Taranaki. The tour not only helped to provide a catalyst for rugby, but also created a feeling of regional identity. This tour, more so than the game itself, became the reason why rugby acquired the support it did from both the media and the general public. Examples exist of the local newspapers furnishing glowing reports on the game, in the name of provincial identity. In Dunedin, the tour match was eventually to provide great public interest in the sport, even before it had taken place, such was the importance of winning. A half-holiday was held to allow for workers to attend the mid-week match at Southern Oval.[81]

For Otago, and the Dunedin FC, the decision of choosing rugby over their own, more dribbling style of rules, did not take place for another two years. In 1876, with the Dunedin FC playing Association rules and the Union club, rugby, a compromise had to be reached for the annual game between the two clubs. With Dunedin refusing to play under rugby rules, the game consisted of half with Victorian rules and the other half using Association. Yet, it is noted by Thompson that the game with Oamaru was played under rugby rules.[82] In 1877 Dunedin toured the country, and this Thompson attributes as the final straw that saw the Dunedin FC accept rugby as its sport. He quotes from Sean O'Hagan:

> Rugby was already entrenched as the New Zealand game in most parts of the country and was the only game to play if Dunedin was to make a name for itself on the tour. The coming tour dominated the activities of the Dunedin Club members during the first half of the year ... and a couple of rugby games were played against Union.[83]

Regional identity became the focus of moulding the style of football for New Zealanders and this was attained through inter-provincial rivalry. It is questionable whether there was any linkage between old public school friends in organizing these tours. A review of the current literature does not appear to show any concrete evidence. Yet, the fact that teams toured and the quality and quantity of support altered from negative to positive does show that these were highly significant. It was not going to be too long before regional identity was to develop into one held by a nation.

E. Stoddart's English tour of 1888 was essential in developing a link between the Home country and their far-distant cousins. The linkage with the mother country promoted enthusiasm amongst the spectators, especially those teetering on the decision of which sport to follow. More importantly, it provided the masses with a quality of competition unseen in any other winter code, a quality where the game was played at the highest level.

The inability of a soccer team from England to visit either Australia or New Zealand had the opposite effect, and one so damaging it could never recover. The first overseas team to tour New Zealand was a New South Wales selection in 1904, and the first time a New Zealand team played against another country in a full international was not until June 1922, some 34 years after Stoddart's men had arrived.

Comparative Studies: USA

A brief look at the existing comparative studies that analyze the situation faced by soccer in the United States of America may be of relevance here. The Americans were able to develop their own game of football, grid, based on elements from rugby. Discussion some two decades ago suggested the concept of 'sport space'. This theory expounds that there is a finite domain available for all sports to exist within and, if one sport was to take up a significant amount of that domain, no other sport could co-exist to its fullest extent. Tony Mason projects the theory to argue that this 'space' or 'gap', once plugged, leaves no 'room' for new sports to be introduced.[84] Andrei Markovits transposes this theory to the context of several other countries, stating, for example, that rugby in New Zealand and Australian rules football in Australia filled the available space left by cricket, which had occupied the major portion.[85]

Further work by Markovits expands this theory. Not only is the space limited, but it can be crowded out from both above and below. For American soccer, the argument reveals that baseball, the American pastime, 'got in first' and attacked from below while Walter Camp's new brand of football, which we know as gridiron, came from above.[86] His work mirrors that of John Sugden, who not only argues about soccer being crowded out, but adds that basketball emerged as the third, home grown, national pastime.[87] The concepts appear feasible, yet Waddington and Roderick contend that when one begins to examine the assumption, its inadequacies become immediately apparent.[88] Their comments are quite valid, and although the works of Mason, Markovits and Sugden are discredited, some of their theories also have merit. In New Zealand, there appeared a vacuum in the sport space prior to the mid-1870s and although Association rules, rugby and Victorian rules coexisted, none could gain such prominence to over-rule the other and be the major sport. If we look specifically at the situation surrounding the 1875 Auckland rugby tour and its ability to fulfil regional identity, then we may have a classic example of 'sport space'. In this case, the space works through identity, and as we have already shown, timing was everything. When Julius Vogel centralized a number of government functions, a space for provincial identity became available, although some portion of it may have been there previously. Yet, when the rugby tours eventuated, it allowed the public to embrace a sport that represented their *region* of New Zealand, and in doing so, filled the void. While unconvinced that Victorian rules could have done this, there is sufficient evidence, based on the games in the provinces previous to the tour, that had it been an Auckland soccer tour in 1875, the identity space would also have been closed.

Other Theories of Soccer's Demise

The demise of the Association version of football in New Zealand has roots in areas other than those shown in the above discussions. Returning to comments of Shearman and Mosely, evidence shows that the game in New Zealand would have followed more in line with dribbling. Scott Crawford, in his paper interpreting rugby and the New Zealand society, makes the point that rugby demonstrates a 'feeling of shared purpose', which he defines as an essential ingredient for survival. This Crawford backs up with an extract from Hughes' book *Tom Brown's Schooldays*, which adds to the theme of a 'team' game.[89] Thus, how important was it for the New Zealand sportsman to play a team game versus one in which individualism was integral? Crawford provides further statements on this topic where he asserts that in the pre-1870s period 'there was a stable sporting base for team sport regional loyalty and regional identity'.[90] The significance of team versus individual would have extended into the period of the initial growth of football. This is an area, which requires some more detailed study.

   The existence of Association football in New Zealand during the two decades following Monro's return was tenuous. The drive to push rugby into the fore meant that soccer would need to re-invent itself, or, at the very least, expand on what bare support it did have. The relevant socio-economic climate hindered this possibility. Miles Fairburn investigates this using Wellington as a clear example, believing that most of the population were limited in pursuing leisure activities. 'With such a small pool of potential supporters to draw upon, collective leisure had a lower capacity to arise, specialise, take permanent institutional shape, and provide services and amenities.'[91] Fairburn shows the flimsy nature of the social fabric on account of institutions that tended to be short-lived. This he illustrates through the cases of cricket and rugby in Wellington.[92] The impact on Association football was certainly felt. The lack of any constructive game in Auckland, bar the odd adventure with a passing ship, would have been the norm throughout the country.

   Len Richardson develops another theory for the promotion of rugby in centres similar to Otago. He postulates that regional identity extended to the need for a sport that was not attached to Australia, that being 'aerial ping-pong'. He argues, by quoting Geoffrey Blainey, that most football at the time was of the Victorian or English rules. This identity need, according to him, was fuelled by the fear of colonial bastardization and thus Richardson concludes that it led to George Sale promoting rugby in Dunedin.[93] Richardson maintained that the colonial founding fathers guarded their 'grand old game' zealously.

Conclusions

The arrival of football to New Zealand was in part a public school phenomenon and, separately, a result of the need to provide an identity first to the provinces and then to the country. The earliest forms of the game were of the same folk-football variants that co-existed throughout England in the previous years. Unfortunately, there has been only superficial research done on these origins and further investigation is warranted. As in England, Association rules and rugby fought each other for the rite of passage as the main sport, yet unlike in England it was to be rugby that won through in New Zealand. Association rules, which were also to wage war with Victorian rules, suffered from its poor establishment and timing, and the eventual veracity of the rugby enthusiasts to push their game.

Rob Hess summarizes the problem as follows:

> given that the rules of virtually all types of football were still in a state of flux, games of any code had a very tenuous foothold during these formative years, and the direct influence of charismatic and forceful personalities had a significant impact in terms of the development of all organised sports, including what type of football would be played in any particular circumstance.[94]

English public schools provided the key players for the development of football in New Zealand. Individuals stood out in most of the centres and pushed their own agenda, some successfully and others not so. Eventually rugby was to become dominant throughout and although soccer was not to die out, it was placed into the backwater of winter sports.

When the Auckland rugby team ventured south, it fulfilled the basic need for provincial identity. This, coupled with the governmental centralization of the mid-1870s and the significant improvements in transport infrastructure, saw rugby, and not any other variant of football, become the dominant sport in New Zealand. Continuing inter-provincial matches helped promote a rivalry, and thus it was simple to extend to a national identity when the English toured in 1888. This essay has tried to analyze the reasoning why the Aucklanders decided on rugby, but not the reasoning behind those in the other provinces of New Zealand. A more detailed analysis of the decisions made in these centres is also required and should include areas of study such as the origins of those involved, their schooling and the environment around them.

Soccer has had to suffer a number of legacies from the nineteenth century. The lack of organizational aptitude on the part of the early clubs playing Association rules to formulate regional teams prior to that of the Auckland rugby tour meant they were unable to fill a void in provincial identity, one that as soon as rugby stepped in, was plugged. Whether soccer could have succeeded had the tour been of the dribbling game is uncertain, and considering what appears to be poor management in the soccer of the day compared with rugby, it looks inevitable that rugby would eventually have taken over.

It is, however, important to note that religion, social and class interference and other aspects of New Zealand culture that shaped the development of the colony from the middle to the late nineteenth century, had in their various ways influenced football and its participants. The scope of the present discussion has not allowed these items to be discussed in any depth and further research is required. This essay has hopefully provided a number of avenues of thought in the description of soccer's inability to lead the country in sport and further to be able to 'catch up' owing in some part to the effects of media and missionary activities of rugbyites. It also hopes to induce others to venture into the topic of New Zealand soccer history, and not let it become 'the forgotten game'.

Acknowledgements

The author would like to thank those numerous people who have assisted in the development of this paper, especially Greg Ryan whose help and encouragement has been immeasurable.

Notes

[1]   Little, *The Forgotten Game.*
[2]   Greg Ryan in the introduction to his book *Tackling Rugby Myths*, disagrees with the concept of the 'national game' tracing back to the 1870s, believing more that it wasn't until the twentieth century that the game became truly national, owing to factors like coverage, etc.
[3]   Swan, *History of New Zealand Rugby Football*, 1.
[4]   *Nelson Evening Mail*, 1 June 1868, 2.
[5]   Swan, *History of New Zealand Rugby Football*, 1.
[6]   *New Zealand Free Lance*, 1 April 1925, 40–1. The article is a letter to 'Touchline' by Charles Monro and describes the earliest history of rugby in Nelson and Wellington, including how the Wellington team was formed for the first Nelson game and the problems of finding a ground.
[7]   Many early texts gave the term as 'foot-ball'. There appears to be no history to this, nor any date when the two words were merged. I will use the more common 'football' in the remainder of this paper.
[8]   Walvin, *The People's Game.* Joseph Strutt, in his book *Pastimes of the People of England* wrote 'it was formerly much in vogue among the common people of England, though of late years it seems to have fallen into disrepute, and is but little practised' (79). His verdict is probably not to be taken too seriously. Magoun counters his arguments showing prime examples of continuity as well as proof of the game being played disregarding the Sabbath laws. See also Magoun, *History of Football.*
[9]   Tischler, 'A Social History of Football', ii.
[10]   Whyte, 'Building a Public School Community'.
[11]   Walvin, *The People's Game*, 37.
[12]   Heading was not introduced until much later (c. 1870) and thus when the ball was in the air, a player would catch it, step a few paces back and then kick it back into play.
[13]   Harvey, 'An Epoch in the Annals of National Sport' discusses the rules of different football games in the nineteenth century and provides an example of Rugby's 1846 rules to show that picking the ball up off the ground was not legal and he cites Hughes to suggest that there was little handling prior to 1841.
[14]   Walvin, *The People's Game*, 44.
[15]   Tischler, 'A Social History of Football', 66–8.
[16]   Ryan, 'Cultural Baggage'.
[17]   Richardson, 'The Invention of a National Game', 1.
[18]   Shearman, *Athletics and Football*, 359.

[19] Ibid., 362.

[20] Mosely, *The Game*, 138.

[21] Sinclair, *A History of New Zealand*, 76.

[22] Ibid., 85.

[23] In England prior to industrialization and the removal of free time, games were held on Shrove Tuesday and other holidays like Christmas. It was generally common to use holidays to get people together with a game of football.

[24] Vincent, '"To Uphold the Honour of the Province": Football in Canterbury c.1854–c.1890.', 15.

[25] Ryan, 'Sport in Christchurch', 333, and Small, *Canterbury Soccer*, 3.

[26] Money, *Manly & Muscular Diversions*, 67–8.

[27] Ryan, 'Sport in Christchurch', 334. These rules saw a ground of 150 yds by 76 yds with goals 12 yds apart and sticks 6 feet out of the ground. A player who caught a kick from an opponent could run with it and throw it into the goal, and a goal would be won when the ball is fairly kicked or thrown between the goal-sticks. See Small, *Canterbury Soccer*, 3 for the complete set of 14 rules. These rules were amended in 1865, 1872, 1876 and in 1877.

[28] Ryan, 'Sport in Christchurch', 333.

[29] Vincent, '"To Uphold the Honour of the Province": Football in Canterbury c.1854–c.1890.', 13.

[30] Ibid., 16–18.

[31] Ibid., 23.

[32] Richardson, 'The Invention of a National Game'.

[33] Auckland Rugby Football Union, *Rugby in Auckland*, 5.

[34] In July 1922 Ces Dacre represented Auckland against the first Australian team and then played for New Zealand in the third test match, also in Auckland. Ces was a brother of another Life Dacre, both of whom were probably grandsons of either Charles or Life.

[35] Hilton, *An Association with Soccer*, 18.

[36] Ryan, 'Cultural Baggage'.

[37] Sinclair, *A History of New Zealand*, 129.

[38] *New Zealand Herald*, 11 June 1870, 3 and 13 June 1870, 4.

[39] Robinson, *Rugby Football in New Zealand*, 5–6.

[40] *Daily Southern Cross*, 22 June 1871, 3.

[41] *New Zealand Herald*, 3 May 1873, 5, *Daily Southern Cross*, 3 May 1872, 2. Two more games were played against the Rosario in 1872 with the Auckland FC winning 1-0 and 4-0. A letter sent to the *New Zealand Herald* on 5 June 1872 was of interest in that it showed that the size of the crowd was quite significant, yet most of these were located in the middle of the field and hindered the progress of the game.

[42] *New Zealand Herald*, 9 April 1873, 2, Robinson, *Rugby football in New Zealand*, 8–9, and Auckland RFU, *Rugby in Auckland*, 7–8. Robinson lays some claim to being important in the rule changes, although there is no evidence to prove or disprove this.

[43] *New Zealand Herald*, 26 April 1873, 2.

[44] *New Zealand Herald*, 5 May 1873, 2 and 15 Sept. 1873, 3, *Daily Southern Cross*, 15 Sept. 1873, 3.

[45] Hilton, *An Association with Soccer*, 19.

[46] Houston, *Association Football in New Zealand*, 23, and Auckland RFU, *The Football Annual for Season 1888*, 70.

[47] *Wellington Independent*, 9 Jan. 1866, 5.

[48] Ibid., 13 Jan. 1866, 5.

[49] Wiren, *The Jubilee of Rugby Football in Wellington*, 4.

[50] *Wellington Independent*, 29 Sept. 1868, 2.

[51] Ibid., 23 Aug. 1870, 2.

[52] Charles Monro, in an article in the *New Zealand Free Lance*, 1 April 1925, explains that while he was in Wellington with his father, who was a member of Parliament at the time, he 'blushingly' asked Vogel, the Colonial Treasurer and Minister for Marine, to give the Nelson team a

passage on the Luna. Monro explains this as 'to my surprise and joy, he not only consented, but he immediately telegraphed to Capt. Fairchild to bring them over'.

[53] *Wellington Independent*, 13 Sept. 1870, 2.

[54] Swan, *History of New Zealand Rugby Football*, 5–6. Swan uses extracts from the *Wellington Independent*, *Daily Advertiser* and the *Evening Post* of the day. These provide a fairly detailed description of the way the Club trialled the new game.

[55] *The Evening Post*, 5 Aug. 1874.

[56] Swan, *History of New Zealand Rugby Football*, 45–7, *The Evening Post*, 5 Aug. 1874 and *The New Zealand Times* (Wellington), 14 Sept. 1874.

[57] Swan, *History of New Zealand Rugby Football*, 46–50. Swan presents some of the rules of the new hybrid code, a mixture of rugby and Victorian rules, with an emphasis on the latter.

[58] Swan, *History of New Zealand Rugby Football*, 15–17 and 19–23.

[59] Thompson, 'Provincial Rugby in New Zealand'.

[60] Richardson, 'The Invention of a National Game'.

[61] Ibid., and Griffiths, *Otago University at Cricket*, 6.

[62] *Evening Star*, 29 May 1873.

[63] Ibid., 5 May 1875.

[64] *Otago Daily Times*, 12 July 1875.

[65] Thompson, 'Provincial Rugby in New Zealand'.

[66] *Otago Daily Times*, 3 June 1876.

[67] Houston, *Association Football in New Zealand*, 23–31. Also inaugurated, constituted or founded were Canterbury and Otago in 1889, Wellington in 1891, Southland in 1903, Hawkes Bay and Taranaki in 1905, Wanganui in 1908, Buller in 1910, Westland in 1918 and Nelson and Southland in 1921. Others were established in the later years, although Houston is unsure when the Waikato FA came into being. In 1922, it was called the South Auckland FA when the Australians toured. Houston's book states that Taranaki was founded approximately in 1928, yet evidence from recent work done by Taranaki soccer historians shows 1905 as the correct date.

[68] Small, *Canterbury Soccer*, 6–7.

[69] Auckland RFU, *The Football Annual for Season 1888*, 70.

[70] Small, *Canterbury Soccer*, 4–8.

[71] Auckland RFU, *Rugby in Auckland*, 6–7. Note that this match was more likely played in 1872, based on evidence presented earlier in this essay.

[72] Robinson, *Rugby Football in New Zealand*, 9–10. See also *New Zealand Herald*, 16 June 1873, 2, for an item about a meeting of the cricketers to discuss a possible provincial team and the formation of a cricket association.

[73] Sinclair, *A History of New Zealand*, 136–8.

[74] Vincent, '"To Uphold the Honour of the Province": Football in Canterbury c.1854–c.1890.', 18.

[75] Crawford, 'A Sporting Image'.

[76] Harvey, 'Bringing the News to New Zealand'.

[77] Kielbowicz, *News in the Mail*, 4. He states that this role continued in the telegraph era as well.

[78] *Otago Daily Times*, 28 Aug. 1873.

[79] Keane, '"Ex-pats" and "Poofters"', 56.

[80] Richardson, 'The Invention of a National Game'.

[81] Thompson, 'Provincial Rugby in New Zealand' quoting from *Evening Star*, 22 Sept. 1875. Half-day holidays to attend sporting events were not uncommon, and continued well into the twentieth century. See the 1922 Australian soccer tour.

[82] Thompson, 'Provincial Rugby in New Zealand' quoting from *Otago Daily Times*, 3 June 1876 and 10 June 1876.

[83] O'Hagan, *The Pride of the Southern Rebels*, 17.

[84] Mason, *Association Football and English Society*, 78–9.

[85] Markovits, 'The Other American Exceptionalism'.

[86]   Markovits and Hellerman, *Offside*.
[87]   Sugden, *USA and the World Cup*, 231 and 235.
[88]   Waddington and Roderick, 'American Exceptionalism', 28–49.
[89]   Crawford, 'A Sporting Image', 60.
[90]   Ibid., 56.
[91]   Fairburn, 'Local Community or Atomized Society', 156.
[92]   Fairburn cites the following examples: of the ten Wellington Cricket Clubs engaged in senior
       competition between 1883 and 1900, six had folded by 1900; and that it had been estimated 65
       rugby clubs were formed in Wellington between 1871 and 1899 of which some 54 collapsed.
       However, Fairburn does not take into account the possible effects of the 1890s depression.
[93]   Richardson, 'The Invention of a National Game'.
[94]   Hess, 'Case Studies in the Development of Australian Rules Football', 150.

References

Auckland Rugby Football Union. *The Football Annual for Season 1888.* Auckland: H. Brett, 1888.
————. *Rugby in Auckland, 1883–1967; Official history of the Auckland Rugby Football Union Inc.*
       Auckland: Auckland RFU, 1968.
Crawford, Scott. 'A Sporting Image: The Emergence of a National Identity in a Colonial Setting,
       1862–1906.' *Victorian Periodicals Review 21,* no.2 (Summer 1998): 56–63.
Fairburn, Miles. 'Local Community or Atomized Society: The Social Structure of Nineteenth
       Century New Zealand.' *New Zealand Journal of History 16* (1982): 146–65.
Griffiths, George J. *Otago University at Cricket.* Dunedin: Otago Heritage Books, 1978.
Harvey, Adrian. '"An Epoch in the Annals of National Sport": Football in Sheffield and the Creation
       of Modern Soccer and Rugby.' *International Journal of the History of Sport 18,* no.4 (Dec
       2001): 53–87.
Harvey, R. 'Bringing the News to New Zealand: The Supply and Control of Overseas News in the
       Nineteenth Century.' *Media History 8,* no.1 (2002): 21–34.
Hess, Robert. 'Case Studies in the Development of Australian Rules Football, 1896–1908.' Ph.D.
       diss., Victoria University, 2000.
Hilton, Tony. *An Association with Soccer: NZFA Centenary 1891–1991.* Auckland: The Sporting Press
       Ltd, 1991.
Houston, John. *Association Football in New Zealand.* Wellington: A.H. & A.W. Reed, 1952.
Keane, William F. '"Ex-pats" and "Poofters": The New Zealand All Whites.' *Culture, Sport, Society 4,*
       no.3 (Autumn 2001): 49–64.
Kielbowicz, Richard B. *News in the Mail: The Press, Post Office, and Public Information, 1700–1860s.*
       New York: Greenwood Press, 1989.
Little, Charles. 'The Forgotten Game: A Reassessment of the Place of Soccer within New Zealand
       Society, Sport and Historiography.' *Soccer and Society 3,* no.2 (Summer 2002): 38–50.
Magoun, Francis P. Jnr. *History of Football: From Beginnings to 1871.* Bochum-Langendreer: Verlag
       Heinrich Pöppinghaus O.H.-G., 1938.
Markovits, Andrei. 'The Other American Exceptionalism: Why is there no Soccer in the United
       States?' *International Journal of the History of Sport 7,* no.2 (1990): 230–64.
Markovits, A. and S.L. Hellerman. *Offside: Soccer and American Exceptionalism.* Princeton: Princeton
       University Press, 2001.
Mason, Tony. *Association Football and English Society, 1863–1915.* Brighton: Harvester Press Ltd,
       1980.
Money, Tony. *Manly & Muscular Diversions: Public Schools and the Nineteenth-Century Sporting
       Revival.* London: Duckworth & Co., 1997.
Mosely, Philip. 'The Game: Early Soccer Scenery in New South Wales.' *Sporting Traditions no.2* (May
       1990): 135–51.

O'Hagan, Sean. *The Pride of the Southern Rebels.* Dunedin: Pilgrim South Press, 1981.

Richardson, Len. 'The Invention of a National Game: The Struggle for Control.' *History Now 1,* no.1 (1995): 1–8.

Robinson, William W. *Rugby Football in New Zealand: Its Development from Small Beginnings.* London: Pall Mall Press, 1905.

Ryan, Greg. 'Cultural Baggage, Cricket and Class in Nineteenth Century New Zealand.' *History Now 1,* no.1 (1995): 9–13.

———. 'Sport in Christchurch.' In *Southern Capital: Christchurch: Towards a City Biography 1850–2000,* edited by J. Cookson and G. Dunstall. Christchurch: Canterbury University Press, 2000.

———. ed. *Tackling Rugby Myths: Rugby and New Zealand Society 1854–2004.* Dunedin: University of Otago Press, 2005.

Shearman, Montague. *Athletics and Football.* Badminton Library, 4th ed., London: Longmans, Green & Co., 1894.

Sinclair, Keith. *A History of New Zealand.* London: A Lane, 1980.

Small, John. *Canterbury Soccer.* Christchurch: Mainland Soccer, 2003.

Strutt, Joseph. *Pastimes of the People of England.* London: 1801.

Sugden, John P. 'USA and the World Cup: American Nativism and the Rejection of the People's Game.' In *Hosts and Champions: Soccer Cultures, National Identities and the USA World Cup,* edited by J.P. Sugden and A. Tomlinson. Aldershot: Arena, 1994.

Swan, Arthur C. *History of New Zealand Rugby Football.* Christchurch: New Zealand Rugby Football Union, 1948.

Thompson, Rex W. 'Provincial Rugby in New Zealand: Otago's Academic Pioneers'. *Journal of Sports History 23,* no.3 (Fall 1996): 221–7.

Tischler, Steven. 'A Social History of Football in England to 1914.' Ph.D. diss., Columbia University, 1978.

Vincent, Geoffrey. '"To Uphold the Honour of the Province": Football in Canterbury c.1854–c.1890.' In *Tackling Rugby Myths: Rugby and New Zealand Society 1854–2004,* edited by Greg Ryan. Dunedin: University of Otago Press, 2005.

Waddington, I. and M. Roderick. 'American Exceptionalism: Soccer and American Football.' *The Sports Historian, 16* (May 1996): 28–49.

Walvin, James. *The People's Game: A Social History of British Football.* London: Allen Lane, 1975.

Whyte, William. 'Building a Public School Community 1860–1910.' *History of Education 32,* no.6 (Nov 2003): 601–26.

Wiren, Anders F. *The Jubilee of Rugby Football in Wellington, October 1879–1929.* Wellington: Wellington Rugby Football Union, 1930.

Wiping the Stain Off the Field of Plassey: Mohun Bagan in 1911

Dwaipayan Sen

Introduction

> If the Bengalees ever win this trophy – defeating all European teams – they may well claim to have wiped off the stain of the field of Plassey.
>
> President Watson of the Calcutta Football Club at the annual football dinner in 1892, *Amrita Bazaar Patrika*, 4 Aug. 1911.

On 29 July 1911, Mohun Bagan became the first Indian football team to win the Indian Football Association (IFA) Shield defeating several British civilian and military teams on Calcutta's football grounds. The scenes of explosive jubilation and rejoicing that followed defied people's imagination. Nobody left the maidan (football field) for several hours. Ganen Mallik, news correspondent for *Amrita Bazaar Patrika* wrote:

The scene that followed was beyond description. Hats, handkerchiefs, umbrellas and sticks were waved and the tremendous cheering shook heaven and earth. It was as if the whole population had gone mad and to compare it with anything would be to minimise the effect.[1]

The Bengalee's correspondent added:

There were great rejoicings in the students' messes in all parts of the city. In some places where the inmates returned rather early there was illumination. Everywhere the streets were thronged with crowds all mad with excitement. Shouts of 'hurrahs' echoed and re-echoed from all parts of the town. The enthusiasm was universal. Young children became all joy to see the beaming appearance of their elders without realising what the matter was.[2]

Mohun Bagan's adoring fans escorted the triumphant football team through the city via the Kali temple to the club secretary Sailendranath Basu's home amidst women blowing conches, and traffic jams that lasted well into the evening. During the post-victory celebrations on the maidan, an elderly *sanyasi* (monk) approached one of the winning team's members and said, 'We are thrilled that you have overcome the military team, but when will you pull that down?' He was pointing to the Union Jack flying over Fort William. The footballer responded, 'The next time we beat the English on the football pitch'.[3] Coincidentally, (or perhaps unwittingly decreed by this footballer), Mohun Bagan would not win the IFA Shield again due to various unfavourable circumstances until 1947, the year India won independence.

The question that faced members of Bengali society at this juncture was the larger meaning of Mohun Bagan's victory. What impact did the victory have on the Indians and the British? The varied responses to this question are the central objects of my analysis. Studying the responses to such a sensational event allows one to gauge how Mohun Bagan's victory affected, and was interpreted by, various notions of the Bengali, and/or Indian (taken here as Hindu, male and upper caste/class, a minority in Bengal) national self.[4] An analysis that attends to the fluidity and shifting contexts and interests of national identity with regard to Mohun Bagan's victory allows for an understanding of the past that does not privilege any one meaning of an event.

Historians have interpreted the significance of this event in two ways. Tony Mason and Paul Dimeo argue that the larger meaning of Mohun Bagan's win signified the success of imperial 'hegemony' over colonial subjects, or native submission to British 'cultural imperialism'.[5] Boria Majumdar, Kausik Bandyopadhyay and Soumen Mitra, on the other hand, interpret Mohun Bagan's victory as a clear expression of anti-imperial nationalist sentiments. The second argument is intended as a counter to the first. As Majumdar claims, 'While the English press saw it [Mohun Bagan's win] as a success of the imperial strategy of the "civilising mission", vernacular reports clearly looked upon it as a triumph of Bengali/Indian nationalism'.[6]

This essay intends to destabilize rigidly imperialist or nationalist historical interpretations of this event. By focussing analysis on the varied responses to the phenomenon of Indians having defeated the British, it argues that in each case the writer of the report brought his ideological commitments to bear on his interpretation of the victory. Therefore, my analysis of an entire range of newspaper reports documents how the larger meaning of Mohun Bagan's victory came into being only through the very particular connotations football had acquired in the cultural and political schema of early twentieth-century Bengali society. This analysis tries to reveal how received notions of modernity, tradition, race, governance and masculinity acquired significantly different and, at times, conflicting meanings in the minds of the football and Mohun Bagan crazed newspaper correspondents, and presumably, the newspaper-reading public. I account for the larger significance of this event in terms of the differences and similarities *both between and within* nationalist (Indian) and imperialist (British) interpretations. Therefore, I offer an understanding of Mohun Bagan's victory not in terms of normative imperialist and nationalist interpretations, but by taking into account the racist, non-racist, modernist and traditionalist dimensions of these intersecting, conflicting and inter-penetrated perspectives.

For a moment, all societal divisions seemed to have dissipated due to the overwhelming enthusiasm in the wake of Mohun Bagan's victory. Given that we know that this period in Indian history was marked by exacerbated racial and growing socio-cultural tensions, what seems most significant about the discourse on Mohun Bagan's victory is the extent to which newspaper reporters sought to reject, disprove and negate the experience of imperial racism. Contrary to preceding scholarly arguments, I argue that Mohun Bagan's victory was interpreted as simultaneously a critique and appraisal of both imperialist and nationalist policies launched from the grounds of universalism.

Contemporary Meanings of the Victory

Only when the reality of Mohun Bagan's win had started to sink in, did news correspondents begin to debate the larger meaning of this event that had publicly undone the myth of British superiority and its co-dependent, Indian inferiority. Indeed, the articles that were published after the win differed markedly from the ones charting the development of the IFA tournament in that the former were overtly concerned with providing lessons or morals to the story of Mohun Bagan's triumph, while the latter merely provided a journalistic account of each match. The main frameworks with which scholars have generally perceived Mohun Bagan's win have either been an imperial or nationalist one. This analytical section seeks to break with what Manu Goswami, following Rogers Brubaker, has called 'methodological nationalism', or, as the case may be 'methodological imperialism' in the above surveyed scholarly literature.[7]

Furthermore, I examine how cultural and religious issues of the day were literally read into the text of Mohun Bagan's win, as well as the varying nodes of significance it held for different people. It is the 'co-production' of colonial and nationalist forms that concerns us here. An analysis that is attentive to the pitfalls of methodological nationalism or imperialism charts the dynamics of the discourse generated by Mohun Bagan's win *between and within* Indian and British news correspondents, rather than simply asserting its (hermetically sealed) nationalist or imperialist significance. Mohun Bagan's win, while no doubt accorded the seat of nationalist importance, also represented a society caught up in a surge of universalism. Indeed, one of the hotly debated topics regarding this victory was the presence or absence of racial antagonism. The ability of football to eliminate racial barriers was necessarily a contradictory affair in colonial Calcutta – but what seems most significant in this light was the public concern over perceiving Mohun Bagan's win as a means towards friendship and establishing equality between colonizer and colonized. What is most notable about this win given the stark divisions in the imperial society of early twentieth-century Calcutta is the momentary, near fantastic sense of joyous unity that was experienced as a result of this victory. Furthermore, the different and, at times, conflicting perspectives news correspondents brought to bear on the significance of Mohun Bagan's win are precisely what mark this momentary unity.

The Bengalee

In a lengthy editorial piece titled 'The Mohan Bagan Victory and its Lessons', the correspondent for *The Bengalee* sketched out in some detail what he thought were the larger lessons to be learnt from the conditions of Mohun Bagan's success. Speaking of the enthusiastic public response, he wrote,

> More than a hundred thousand people witnessed the game, and the news of the Mohun Bagan victory spread like wildfire from one part of the town to the other. Indeed even our people in the Muffusil had been deeply stirred ... Especially have our young men, the most susceptible of the community, who naturally take to sports, been carried away by the prevailing feeling. All this is healthy excitement and will give a fresh impetus to manly sports; and outdoor sports have a beneficial effect on the body and the mind. When our young men are convinced that the possession of a good and strong physique is one of the essential conditions of success in manly games, and in a still larger sense, in the higher game of life, they will turn their attention to the abolition of those customs which interfere with the physical development of the race.[8]

The understated assumption here is the contingency of our young men being convinced 'that the possession of a good, strong physique' is one of the essential conditions in the higher game of life. Once this has happened, according to the correspondent, our young men will turn to abolish those customs interfering with the physical development of the race. Which customs? Which race?

> We have in mind the pernicious custom of child-marriage which saps the manhood of our people and seriously handicaps us in the great competition of nations. This unhappy usage peculiarly affects the youthful generation, and their resolution in the matter will sound its death-knell.[9]

How does one explain the distance covered between Mohun Bagan's victory and earnest cries for abolishing child marriage? Within the logic of moderate nationalist thought, 'pernicious customs', and there were many, were precisely the very reason 'our people' lagged behind in the 'great competition of nations'. Mohun Bagan's victory was thus couched within the larger debate between orthodox Hindu traditionalists and liberal Hindu modernists, but within the same register, anticipated the to-be of sovereign nationhood once manliness in the higher game of life had been attained. For us to succeed in the great competition of nations, all pernicious customs needed to be weeded out before 'manhood' could be assumed. The correspondent, however, had bigger fish to fry. He continued,

> An Anglo-Indian contemporary who, on the whole has given a fair report of the match, reminds us that we must not crow too loudly, for a single swallow does not make a summer. That is perfectly true, and it is wise and morally healthful to practice self-restraint amid the exuberance of our rejoicings. That indeed is the dictum of our sacred books, and the immemorial habit of our people. But the memorable success of Saturday would be lost upon us, if it failed to enhance the self-respect of our people or to disclose their immense potentialities for adaptation and progress. The Bengali is no longer the timid and weak-kneed representative of the race whom Macaulay so foully libelled.[10]

Self-restraint, sacredly ordained and of immemorial habit tempered by enhancement of self-respect. Or, a disclosure of the 'immense potentialities for adaptation and progress'. These are the range of meanings that Mohun Bagan's victory signified for this correspondent. What exactly is meant by adaptation and progress we are not yet told, but the strong note of enthusiasm for modernization is unmistakable. It is important also to note that this call for modernization, as much as it despised pernicious custom, nevertheless drew upon the 'dictum of our sacred books' and the 'immemorial habit of our people'. To be a liberal, moderate nationalist did not mean eschewing what tradition had bequeathed to 'our people'. Indeed, Mohun Bagan's victory could be celebrated, but just not too much. Instead, Bengalis could take quiet satisfaction in the fact that Mohun Bagan's victory,

> and other similar instances are but the outward manifestations of the great transformation in the character and the stamina of our people which has taken place within less than the life-time of a generation. The Bengalees possess a great and inherent capacity for adaptation. Among the Indian races, they were the first to appreciate the benefits of English education and they have enormously profited by it. In manly sports introduced from the West, they are well in the front. When Mr. Spencer, the balloonist, came over here and made his descents with the parachute, the Bengalees were the first to follow in his wake in such aerial exploits. All this is exceedingly hopeful and encouraging. But a great deal yet remains to be done. We have excellent materials but they need to be improved. *With all our affectionate reverence for the past, we must not be blind to the forces of modern progress. We must bow to them. We must assimilate them into our social system and into the usages of our everyday life. We must accept the truths of modern science and practice them for the betterment of the race, for the improvement of the body and the mind.* (Emphasis added.)[11]

Bengali propensity for adaptation is proved by their primacy in English education, manly sports introduced by the West, and although a stretch, their aerial exploits. But this is clearly not enough. Blindness to the forces of modern progress is indeed what the correspondent believes is partially responsible for 'our peoples' pernicious customs'. Adaptation thereby means assimilating the forces of modern progress 'into our social system and into the usages of everyday life'.[12]

Mohun Bagan's victory is clearly grist for the argument that Bengalis must modernize 'with all our affectionate reverence for the past'. Following this, in a flourish of functionalism, the correspondent hammered his point home ending with an ominous warning:

> The individual units must be rendered efficient to ensure the efficiency of the community. What severe physical and mental training must each member of the Mohan Bagan team gone through to ensure the efficiency of the team! We have to apply this lesson to the larger life of the community, make every unit of it physically and mentally strong by purging our social system of usages which interfere with the development of the race, and then but not till then, all will be well with us.[13]

In the teleology of this correspondents' thought, manhood, both individual and collective would simply not be attained until adaptation to modernity had purged the social system of those ills, such as child marriage in this case, that interfered with the development of the race. As of right now, our people, the race, the bodily incarnation of the community was afflicted due to pernicious social customs. Modernity was the force that would eradicate these vices and set us on the right path towards progress, development and manhood.

Consider now, what another news correspondent writing for *Amrita Bazaar Patrika*, edited by Kali Prasanna Chatterji, had to say of this analysis in another extended editorial entitled 'The Manliness of the Bengalis'. I discuss this particular article in some detail in due course, but for the moment I excerpt the relevant passage to emphasize the contrast in prevalent perceptions of manliness:

> Here we shall digress a little. There are people who attribute the physical deterioration of our race mainly to early marriage. But be it noted here that the fine race of whom Lord Minto spoke in such rapturous terms, were the fruits of that system of marriage. The eleven of the Mohun Bagan football team are, we believe, also the products of early marriage. The latter, remind us that not only do they come from the ancient stock but they have in them all the elements of manliness which characterised their ancestors a century ago.[14]

For this particular news correspondent, manliness was hardly something recently acquired by our race. Mohun Bagan's manly legacy does not begin with a football club. The source of its players' manliness is found in the ancient stock of which they are descendants. Indeed, their manliness is characterized by the customs of their ancestors, not by their adaptation to the forces of modern progress. Here is the kernel of one of the central tensions regarding the significance of Mohun Bagan's victory.

To stay with *The Bengalee* newspaper however, there was another article next to the one I have previously discussed at length called 'Mohun Bagan's Success'. The writer claimed that he was bringing to light 'an equally important aspect which deserves attention' that other writers had not as yet reflected upon. He wrote,

> We have in our leading article today as well as in our leaderette on the subject in Sunday's issues dealt with one aspect of the success of the Mohanbagan team. There is yet another and equally important aspect which deserves attention. Manly games, like commerce and industrialism, are symbolical of a great and growing change in human affairs. The keynote of this change is the substitution for the racial hatred and jealousy of a bygone age, of a spirit of friendly rivalry.[15]

Was this really the case? Was racial hatred and jealousy truly of a bygone era, and the spirit of friendly rivalry the dawn of a new age? Arguably this was blind idealism, but there is a sincere conviction to the correspondents' narrative that hints at the universalistic and humanist potential of Mohun Bagan's victory. Here we have an instance of Boria Majumdar's argument regarding the crucial distinction between English language and vernacular sources being called into question. For *The Bengalee* was widely acknowledged as one of the major nationalist organs – indeed, none other than Surendranath Banerjea, President of the Congress, was its editor. Simply because one wrote in English, and one denied the current existence of racial hatred – did this preclude the possibility of simultaneously being truly nationalist? Apparently, not. The correspondent continued,

> From this point of view, the invention of a new game which finds acceptance among the nations of the world like a new discovery in the domain of science which can be applied to the bettering of human life is one more link which binds together the different branches of the human family. It is also, and for the same reason, an imperial asset of great value. It seems to us that it would be a very good thing if means could be found to take the Mohan Bagan team over to England. They are sure to meet with a reception there which cannot fail to bring the two countries even closer together than they are today. It will also create a profound impression upon the English public regarding the capabilities of the race. Prince Ranjit Singh, the Indian cricketer, is one of the most popular figures in England and the British public hang upon his words as eagerly as if he were an Englishman and a cabinet minister.[16]

One could simultaneously be a nationalist, and a humanist, even if one were at the receiving end of the colonizers' gaze. Manly games, industrialism and commerce are devoid of their specifically imperial content and origins and can be 'applied to the bettering of human life', and 'is one more link which binds together the different branches of the human family'.

To be sure, however, football was also an instrumental 'imperial asset' insofar as it was a means by which the English public's impression of our race could be improved. Mohun Bagan, were they to go to England, like Ranjit Singh would gain the popularity of the British, another step closer towards 'bringing the two countries closer together'. The insistence on denying the racial difference between the 'two countries' was part of the moderate nationalist response to imperial racism, and the very universal, humanist grounds from which nationalists critiqued the imperial government for their unjust, illiberal policies. The foregoing evidence suggests that Mohun Bagan's victory was instrumental in this process.

Nationalist Newspaper Sources in the English Press

The *Modern Review,* a journal edited by a prominent member of the Brahmo Samaj (a reform Hindu sect), had a brief but presumably more mature lesson to offer in 'The Success of Mohun Bagan' than those who were 'losing their heads over a successful football match' – the writer proclaimed,

> The winning of the challenge shield at the football tournament by the Mohun Bagan football club has given us sincere pleasure. It is undoubtedly an achievement to be

proud of. We are only sorry that there has been some foolish writing on this topic in some of our papers. We are, however, glad that the members of the winning team themselves have kept their heads remarkably cool, as all good sportsmen ought to. Why should we lose our heads over a successful football game, when we know that we are capable of much higher things requiring both manliness and the qualities of leadership and combination?[17]

Of the news sources that covered and commented on these events, there were a series of Bengali-owned English newspapers as well as Bengali-owned Bengali, or vernacular, journals which noted the absence of racial tensions, praised the British expressing their gratitude, and acknowledged that the mutual pride Bengalis and Britishers must feel upon Mohun Bagan's victory. Mohun Bagan's football triumph thus signified a universalistic premise within its nationalist enthusiasm. It is on these grounds that Boria Majumdar finds 'the English press' not quite 'nationalist', and Paul Dimeo and Tony Mason find the essence of imperial 'hegemony' or native submission to British cultural imperialism. Arguing against both these positions, I extend another line of argument. Imperial praise was not praise of the lived phenomenon of a racist and oppressive government in Bengalis' lives, but a patriotic assertion of 'their nation's', their 'race's', 'their peoples'' instrumental role in the dynamics of that Empire. Furthermore, perceiving racial absence in Mohun Bagan's win did not make one less nationalist – for to return a racist gaze would be no better than the British themselves. The argument for an absence of racial divisions was in some ways the bedrock of the moderate nationalist ideology – by 'reasserting precisely the claims to universality of the modern regime of power', to borrow Partha Chatterjee's words, Indian 'nationalism fought relentlessly to erase the marks of colonial difference'.[18] Let us turn to a consideration of these Bengali sources.

The Telegraph, edited by Surendra Nath Bose, *Indian Empire*, by Kesab Chandra Banerji, and the *Indian Mirror*, by Rai Norendranath Sen Bahadur, head of the Maha Bodhi Society, commanded the third, fourth and fifth largest circulations of 'Native-owned English Newspapers' as categorized by the Bengal Special Department. This department's publication, *Report on the Native Newspapers of Bengal* is a standard archival source for contemporary scholars.[19]

The writer for *The Telegraph* had the following to say with regard to Mohun Bagan's victorious match:

> The Telegraph is pleased to see that the victory of the former was well taken by the English population of Calcutta and says that this is as it should have been for it was a fair contest, fairly and gallantly fought on both sides in a friendly spirit, without anything like race hatred and rancour finding any place in the heart of the combatants. Those who had been looking forward to a bombardment of Fort William by Bengali athletes as also those who had been long aiming for a military revolt against peace and order were equally disappointed. The game throughout was most exhilarating and square, and there was nothing like ill motive on either side.[20]

The *Indian Mirror* in describing the momentous events of 29 July, claimed that, 'the Jap's victory over the Russians did not stir the East half as much as did the match between the two said teams'. The journal concluded by adding the caveat that 'the large-mindedness of the European community in admitting a Bengali team to take part with them in sport, ought to arouse a deep sense of gratitude'.[21]

One must be careful here to distinguish these narratives that praise and admire the British from what Tony Mason has called the 'essence of hegemony'. Additionally, one cannot assume that all newspapers in the English press concluded that, 'sports had been successfully used to civilise the natives'[22] because they lauded the absence of racial feeling. Instead, we could understand this 'absence of racial hatred' and 'praise for the European community' as a crucial part of the moderate nationalist strategy of putting themselves on equal footing with their masters, or of beating their masters at their own game not on 'their' terms, but 'ours'. These narratives should be understood within the contextual dynamics of not just colonial oppression, but also the dynamics of nationalist assertion upon the imperial project. To observe the dynamics of difference *within* this nationalist assertion however, let us turn to Muslim perceptions of this victory.

The Bengalee had reported that,

> The venue of the Mahomedan Sporting club was another scene of unusual excitement. Some of the members of the Mahomedan sporting who assembled there were simply mad with excitement on the victory of their Hindu brethren. They were dancing, jumping and even rolling on the ground. It was the same feeling of pride that was uppermost in the Mahomedan mind as in the Hindu mind.[23]

Bear in mind that while the collectivities that are usually consistently evoked by *The Bengalee's* correspondent are 'the nation', 'our people', 'the race', in this case we have two separate, already distinguished identities – Hindus and Muslims – united by 'the same feeling of pride'. This report, however, is from the perspective of a Hindu. *The Comrade*, a journal founded and at that time edited by Maulana Mohamed Ali, 'heartily joined the chorus of praise and jubilation over the splendid victory of Mohun Bagan'.[24] *The Mussalman*, (circulation 800) edited by A. Rasul and M Rahman, wrote that,

> It is worthy of note in this connection that although the Mohun Bagan was a team composed of Bengalee Hindus, the jubilation in consequence of its success was not confined to any particular race or creed. It was a sense of universal joy, which pervaded the feelings of the Hindus, the Mahomedans and the Christians alike. The members of the Moslem Sporting Club were almost mad and rolling on the ground with joyous excitement on the victory of their Hindu brethren.[25]

While the correspondent of *The Mussalman* concurs with *The Bengalee* correspondent's rendition of the events, the universal joy of the victory is experienced via carefully specified categories of religious community – Hindu, Muslim and Christian, rather than, race, nation, people. He does not evoke 'the nation' or 'our people'. This difference reveals discrepancies in how Mohun Bagan, as corporeal representative of 'the nation' as a category of thought and practice, was prefigured in the minds of our newspaper correspondents. Indeed, Bengali Hindus seem to have experienced the universal joy of the victory through racial and national categories of interpretation – Bengali Muslims, on the other hand, experienced the same universal joy through the lens of religious community categories.

Nationalist Newspaper Sources in the Bengali Press

Basumati, Nayak and *Hitavadi* were all Bengali newspapers, the latter two edited by Priya Nath Guha and Panchcowri Banerji. They had circulations of 3,000 and 30,000 respectively. Remember again Majumdar's argument that only vernacular sources revealed the truly nationalist connotation of this victory by foregrounding the charged racial atmosphere of the matches. Instead, I demonstrate that these Bengali sources shared much in common with their Bengali-owned English counterparts. The *Nayak* boasted,

> Indians can hold their own against Englishmen in every walk of art and science, in every learned profession, and in the higher grades of the public service. Among sports, in cricket, Prince Ranjit Singh and the Bombay team have beaten Englishmen on their own ground. It only remained for Indians to beat Englishmen in that peculiarly English sport, the football. It thrills every Indian with joy and pride to know that rice-eating, malaria-ridden, barefooted Bengalis have got the better of beef-eating, Herculean, booted John Bull in that peculiarly English sport. Never before was there witnessed such universal demonstration of joy, men and women alike sharing it and demonstrating it by showering of flowers, embraces, shouts, whoops, screams and even dances.[26]

Again, in this instance, Mohun Bagan stands in for rice-eating, malaria-ridden and barefooted Bengalis, or Indians holding their own against Englishmen. One must not miss the sentiment of nationalist assertion this correspondent felt upon witnessing Mohun Bagan's victory, nor forget that this era was the start of a long nationalist struggle to wrench influential seats in public service from the colonial government. Feats like Mohun Bagan's victory in football and Ranjit Singh's success in cricket are all evidence of Indians being able to 'hold their own' against their British counterparts. Likewise, this correspondent may have hoped for more opportunities for Indians to 'hold their own' in the field of government. Thus, he had two lessons to offer. He declared that,

> The first of these lessons is that the rice-eating Bengali is capable of learning everything to perfection and beating even his teachers. Teach him warfare and he will prove as clever and indomitable as the Japanese. The second lesson is the magnanimous equanimity of the Englishman. Amid the taunts and jeers of exultant Bengali youths, Englishmen, even at the bitter hour of defeat, never lost for a moment their equanimity, nay, had the generosity to express their admiration for their conquerors, to take them up on their shoulders and dance in glee, so that everyone could see why the English are the rulers of India. May the English be victorious! Would that they showed the same equanimity in the work of administration that they have shown in sport![27]

'The magnanimous equanimity of the Englishman.' 'May the English be victorious!' Surely this is not what Majumdar had in mind when he wrote that only vernacular sources reveal the true extent of the nationalist connotation accorded to this event. The first lesson we have already heard once before via *The Bengalee's* correspondent. The second lesson, however, is new to us. This equanimity that Bengalis allegedly publicly experienced on the football field is one that is also desired in the political boardrooms of the day. This correspondent is discretely criticizing the imperial government. One must not therefore interpret such sources as succumbing to cultural imperialism on account of their admiration of their ruler's equanimity on the sports field. Indeed, what is at play in the English response to Mohun Bagan's victory is their being held to their own standards by Bengalis. Thus, English 'generosity to express their admiration for their conquerors' becomes valuable within the moderate nationalist mindset in the context of the former's position as colonizers. The grounds of loyalism, as Seth reminds us, were precisely where the most powerful critique of imperialism was launched.

The most provocative statement however, is 'so that everyone could see why the English are the rulers of India'. What is the logic behind a statement such as this? What does it tell us about the power dynamics between the colonial rulers and their colonized subjects? Contrary to most depictions of colonial rule, this statement gives us access to a certain level of affinity across the colonial divide, of accepting the game as emblematic of civil competition. It might be argued that the English are the rulers of India because they too had learnt how to admit defeat. The symbolism of the powerful accepting defeat in a colonial arena hinted at much larger prospects in the nationalist mind. The gradual levelling of the playing field, so to speak, would eventually and inevitably give way to the formation of the Indian nation-state. Thus, our correspondent is quick to add, 'Would that they showed the same equanimity in the work of administration that they have shown in sport'.

In a following issue of *Nayak* another article was published regarding the reasons for Bengalis' 'uncommon powers for success' with reference to Mohun Bagan's victory. The writer stated, and then asked,

> The Bengalis have proved themselves to be possessed of uncommon power for success in every department of life. What is it that has made the Bengali mind so full of sterling qualities? What is it that has preserved these qualities in them during more than a thousand years of foreign subjection? It is not surely their fish-eating, for then all peoples living on sea-coasts would have been as intelligent and as efficient as they are. It is, as a matter of fact, their religion, which has stocked their mind with such a perennial store of high and noble qualities. It may be asked, if it is their religion which makes them great, then why does India bear foreign yoke?[28]

This writer offered the first avowedly religious, in this case, Hindu interpretation of the foregone event. Even though he had not even specified which religion, one can easily guess by the familiar tropes of 'a thousand years of foreign subjection' and the question, 'then why does India bear foreign yoke?' The writer has already established that it is in fact their religion and not their fish-eating 'which has stocked their mind with such a perennial store of high and noble qualities', 'preserved through a thousand years of foreign subjection' and is now proving 'themselves to be possessed of uncommon power for success in every department of life'. The question then remains, why is India still under 'foreign yoke?' The correspondent returned, in a typically primordialist register,

> The reply to this question is that Hindus fell from their religion and were conse-quently punished by foreign subjection. The germ of Hinduism, however, still lurks in them, and so they still excel in many things. The soil and the atmosphere of India are particularly fit for the preservation of the Hindu spirit. The great fertility of the

Indian soil and the equability of the Indian climate, reduce the struggle for existence and make men in India less selfish and egotistic than people living in other parts of the world, and better fitted for preserving and developing the higher and nobler qualities of man.[29]

Working backwards from this point, the 'higher and nobler qualities of man' are equated with Hinduism. These qualities consist of 'less selfishness and egotism than people living in other parts of the world'. Having been sustained by the soil and atmosphere of India, the Hindu spirit has lived on in dormancy having been toppled as the result of foreign domination. Foreign domination is the punishment for Hindus 'falling from their religion'.

To return to the primary question however, 'what is it that has made the Bengali mind so full of sterling qualities?' one sees that the link formed to Mohun Bagan's victory is their comparatively less selfishness and egotism in wake of the overwhelming enthusiasm over their victory. Indeed, the club secretary Sailendranath Bose had published the following letter in *The Statesman* in response to the exuberant outpouring of adulation and calls for 'something to be done' to honour Mohun Bagan from both English and Bengali quarters:

> To The Editor of the Statesman,
>
> Sir, As it is impossible to reply to the numerous letters I have received, I beg leave to offer through the medium of your paper my hearty and grateful thanks to the large number of our friends and admirers who have so kindly thought fit to encourage the players of the club by their congratulations and offer of entertainments, etc. At the same time it is the decision of the management of the Club that it is not desirable to make a fuss over last Saturday's success, as the Club in general and the players in particular look upon it as the result of practice and study of the Science of the game under the guidance and with the help of their numerous friends, both European and Indian.
>
> It is hoped therefore that it would not be misconstrued if the players have to decline with great regret (which they do through your paper) any offer of entertainment in any other shape, though they very gratefully appreciate the same.[30]

For the writer in *Nayak*, like those in *The Bengalee* and *Amrita Bazaar Patrika* self-restraint was understood as a specifically Hindu, and in some cases ancient, feature of Bengalis. For Sailen Bose, however, this self-restraint stemmed from the fact that the players in particular looked upon their victory as 'the result of practice and study of the Science [capital S] of the game under the guidance of both European and Indian friends'. Even Sailen Bose, at the centre of everybody's adoration, not only denied the overtly nationalist (read, Bengali) cause of his victory, but instead attributed it to both European and Indian friends – and explicitly stated the players' perception that it was the result of studying and practicing a 'Science'. It is also important to note however, that the Mohun Bagan players had visited the Kali temple to offer their prayers and thanks for good fortune both before and after the match. This duality is instrumental in understanding the psyche inhabited by the bhadrolok conscience – both the religiosity of paying obeisance to Ma Kali and the scienticity of football, existed simultaneously.

Returning to analysis of Bengali newspapers however, the *Basumati* offered some of the most meaningful lessons, both then and now. The correspondent's text began by bestowing lavish praise upon Mohun Bagan:

> May Mohun Bagan ever triumph! Bengal and the Bengali are honoured by your victory. The whole of Bengal rings with your triumph. We have seen Bengalis assembled on various occasions of danger, distress, and sorrow, such as that of Partition, the Consent Bill, and the death of a great man. But never before did we witness such a vast concourse, such a vast demonstration of joy.

> Mohun Bagan has infused a new life into the lifeless and cheerless Bengali. The Bengali seems to feel anew the pulsation of life. Delighted at your striving, God has poured the electric fluid of enthusiasm into the veins of Bengalis. The Bengalis will never be able to repay the debt they owe you for infusing the revivifying nectar into their lifeless body.[31]

The correspondent introduces the figure of the 'lifeless and cheerless Bengali's body'. This collective historical figure jars with earlier evocations of the both modern and ancient manliness of the Bengalis. There are thus three distinct sexualities of the imagined Bengali man – the masculine modern, the masculine ancient and the lifeless present. (There was yet another, whose imagined form had not yet materialized – the Indian [Bengali] soldier in the British army.) Nevertheless, 'God has poured the electric fluid of enthusiasm into the veins of Bengalis'. What is unique however is that no previous event, the Partition, the Consent Bill, nor the death of a great man, ever brought together so many people. And in this case, people are brought together not in danger, distress or sorrow, but in joy. The journalist then drove though a crucial point in my own analysis of this event:

> They are greatly mistaken who seem to find race-antagonism in this national victory. Race-antagonism has nothing to do with it. There is nothing of meanness in the tide of patriotism that has rushed into the silted up life stream of the Bengali. By your victory sports has been turned into a unifying force, an occasion of common rejoicing.[32]

Mohun Bagan's 'national' victory in this interpretation had nothing to do with racial antagonism. Sport itself had been turned into a unifying force such was the joy of the event. How does a historian confront instances such as these that fly in face of both elite and popular memory of a violent colonial past characterized amongst other relations by explicit racial tensions? Is it the silted-up life-stream our reporter refers to that induced Bengalis to look upon this event as a source of pride? Or perhaps, the phantasmic joy from Mohun Bagan's win witnessed a collective forgetting, however so momentary, of the racially charged atmosphere of those days. Indeed, the insight I glean from this source is that nationalism as experienced in lieu of Mohun Bagan's victory did not necessarily (pre)suppose a racial bias towards the British.

A line from a poem published in the journal *Manasi* testifies to the extent the similar uplifting sentiment of racial barriers having been surpassed existed even within the 'Bengali', that is vernacular, imagination. The poem was a tribute to Mohun Bagan by one Karunanidhan Bandyopadhyay. One of the couplets in the poem ran as follows: 'Deshe bideshe rotlo aaji, bango-jubaar maan; tootay gechhey shaday kaloye, mithha babodhann.' (The fame of Bengali youth has spread at home and in the world, False divides in white and black have been at long last hurled/[broken]).[33]

In another article in *Manasi*, Charuchandra Mitra set himself the task of explaining the reason for Bengalis' complete joy in light of Mohun Bagan's win. Although we have encountered the majority of his argument via other sources, he made a direct reference to the noteworthiness of Mohun Bagan's victory for the country's nationalist politicians. Saluting Sailendranath Bose for his commendable deeds as club secretary he wrote,

> Tomar anushthheyo karmer shaphhollo dekhiya shokolay shikhoon, thyagay shaktir shanchay hoay na – ekikoron ball pauya jaye, kahakeo thyag korilay cholibay na, grohon korithay hobay. Tumi jayroop ethogooli jubokkay premer mohun-doray ekshathhey bandhiaychho amadiger samajnetharao jodi khudro sharththo upekkha koriya premalingan dvara shokolkay aaponar korithay cheshthha koren, thaha hoilay samajer unnoti shigrihi amader korayotto hoibay. (May all learn from having seen the results of your worthy efforts, there is no accumulation and development of strength in abandonment – this is how one attains might; it simply won't work if we neglect anybody, we have to accept and realize this. The way you have bound so many youths in unity with the thread of love, if our society's leaders would but curb their self-interest just a little and by means of affectionate embrace made everyone their own, if that were to happen, society's good fortunes would improve rather quickly.)[34]

Mohun Bagan's victory was thus seen as accomplishing what nationalist politicians had hitherto been unable to do – uniting Indians under one banner. But what was of consequence to this reporter was that the lesson of exemplary teamwork of Mohun Bagan that presumably did not leave behind or 'abandon' any one player could be applied to the sphere of national politics. Indeed, if the leaders of the country set aside their own narrow interests, and did not abandon certain sections of society, the general welfare would improve. Mitra reveals the prevailing sense of disillusionment amongst Bengalis with the political direction (or lack, thereof) of the nationalist movement. One might certainly read Mitra's reference to nationalist leaders' self-interest as a direct criticism of their policies.

The last Bengali source I consider cast doubts on the true extent of the English population's positive reception of Mohun Bagan's victory. In fact, this particular source was emblematic of a much more disillusioned section of Bengali public opinion – one that did not necessarily care to recognize the allegedly benign intentions of British rule, or see in Mohun Bagan's victory the intimations of the 'harmonious workings of two great races'. Writing in *Hitavadi* under the *nom-de-plume* of 'an old man', the correspondent argued that, 'How far the praise lavished by the Anglo-Indian papers of the Mohun Bagan team comes from the heart will be proved by the two following facts:'

> In praising this Bengali team, the *Englishman* [the newspaper] could not resist the temptation of having, without any regard to relevancy, a fling at the Bengali agitators of whom it spoke as follows – 'Political agitators gnashed their teeth in impotent rage to think that with all their fine fury they had never been able to collect such audiences as these.' Again, on the semi-final day when an Englishman and a Native Christian were travelling together in the same railway compartment, the latter, in all innocence,

enquired of his companion the result of the day's contest, to which the only reply he received was a slap on the cheek.[35]

The *Hitavadi's* correspondent then proceeded to draw out the implications of his observations, claiming that,

> Even the laudation, however, is not without a spice of tartness. And this is natural, for, the day this note of resentment is absent from the Englishman's report of a defeat sustained by him you may be sure that he is become quite as spiritless as ourselves.[36]

Again, we encounter the 'spiritless' Bengali, albeit within a critique of clandestine English resentment about their loss at Mohun Bagan's hands. Certainly, our correspondent has touched upon a sensitive issue – the English quarters of Calcutta had supposedly worn a mournful look in the first few days of August 1911.

One might however, look for clues as to what has made the Bengali quite so spiritless. According to this journalist, the Englishman would be as spiritless as the Bengalis on the 'day this note of resentment is absent from the Englishman's report of a defeat sustained by him'. If I insert the Bengali into this logic, by implication, what has made him so spiritless is his lack of resentment about the multiple defeats he has sustained. A feeling of impotency marks this Bengali's narrative, one that Mrinalini Sinha amongst many other notable scholars has insightfully commented upon at great length.[37] The unspoken suggestion, if I may be allowed the historical stretch, is that now is the time to resent. It is most certain that Mohun Bagan's victory in this light also gathered purchase as a public expression of resentment. Kausik Bandyopadhyay's, Boria Majumdar's and Soumen Mitra's essays, all foreground this perspective.

To attend to the journalist's central point however, English praise upon Bengali exploits was certainly mitigated by their own failure to live up to English moral standards. 'To accept defeat like a man', was perhaps the public guise under which the English laboured, as much as Bengalis sought to couch their pride and enthusiasm within self-restraint. Neither, it would seem, fully lived up to their own expectations of themselves.

Amrita Bazaar Patrika and English (i.e. Imperialist) Newspaper Sources

The Statesman, Englishman and *Empire* constitute this survey of English public opinion. I have distinguished between English newspapers run by Englishmen, and English newspapers run by Bengalis. The mere agreement over the lack of racial antagonism within the English press belies the crucially different positions and perspectives English- and Bengali-owned newspapers occupied within the colonial power structure. This examination of English positions is therefore interspersed with relevant excerpts from editorials in *Amrita Bazaar Patrika* (allegedly the 'most nationalist' of Bengali-owned English newspapers) to emphasize the extent of cross-referencing, dialogue, as well as argument across the colonial divide.

The English, as has already been suggested, were certainly as surprised at Mohun Bagan's victory as Bengalis were unable to control their enthusiasm. They were however, quick to assert that 'We see nothing in this evening's contest that need arouse any but the most friendly feelings, and whatever be the result, we trust that the losing side and their sympathisers will show a truly sportsmanlike temper'.[38] The *Amrita Bazaar Patrika* quoted a lengthier portion of the same excerpt from *Empire* in the now memorialized article, 'The Immortal Eleven'. Having described and temporarily excused the 'wild enthusiasm' of Saturday evening, the journalist, Ganen Mallik, qualified his own exuberance by writing,

> But if we are to be true to Hindu instinct and culture such triumphs should not at all be exploited for other ends than establishing the best of relations between the two races. These are divine events meant for facilitating the harmonious working of two great peoples by curbing to a certain extent the pride of the one and contributing to the growing self-consciousness of the other. The Indian, with his head raised erect by these incidents, will take his rightful place by the side of his ruler and give his best for the fulfilment of the work for which Providence has brought the two peoples together.[39]

Then, upon quoting a longer version of the above-mentioned portion of the *Empire*, he asserted, 'That is also the spirit of Hindu teaching'.[40] One should not lose the essential distinction between the *Empire's* 'true sportsman-like temper' and the *Amrita Bazaar Patrika's* repeated reference to 'Hindu' teaching, instinct and culture. Although both positions sought to efface the racially charged atmosphere of the era, they did so from completely different subject-positions.[41] One might certainly ask however, 'what is this "work" for which Providence has brought the two peoples together?' but I put this question on hold for the time being. The writer from *Amrita Bazaar Patrika* continued,

> We are also glad to say that the East Yorks throughout maintained a dignified attitude and did not resort to any questionable means for keeping up prestige. In fact, they allowed the Bengalees the fairest and fullest opportunity to rise to the height of their being in a new line of activity and thus deserve well of the latter. What we want to see most on this occasion is the absence of any exaggerated sense of superiority or pride. These occasions demand from us the Hindu spirit of working, without being either unduly elated or depressed at the result. We do not, of course, mean to say that we are not proud of our young men who have acquitted themselves so splendidly and won the admiration of all parties for their skill and agility. It is no joke to beat uniformly the three best military teams in the field and that with a clean hand. But we must not miss the true moral of the victory and make a sorry exhibition of ourselves in mere swaggering. Let us use these incidents to cultivate confidence in ourselves, to feed the legitimate ambition and aspiration of fulfilling ourselves; *but let also love and gratitude for those who are taking us by the hand and teaching us to win spurs in fresh fields and pastures new, fill our hearts.* (Emphasis added.)[42]

One has here, in a nutshell, the mainstream nationalist position towards the English in light of Mohun Bagan's success – 'use these incidents to cultivate confidence in ourselves, feed our legitimate ambition and aspiration of fulfilment', but simultaneously, 'love and gratitude for those who are talking us by the hand and teaching us to win spurs in fresh fields and pastures new'. The fine line that is occupied to balance loyalties between the imagined national self, seeking self-determination, and the hand-holding paternal ruler exemplifies the exigencies of the public face of Congress-style moderate nationalism. Finally, in a direct address to the Government of British India, Mallik conjured the desired imaginary Bengali military man whom I had previously mentioned:

> We also ask the attention of the Government to the moral of this incident. Is it not high time that they did some thing to give full play to the developing physical powers of our countrymen? Should these materials be allowed to rust unused?'

> … When all classes of Indians have thus given conclusive proof of their physical fitness, is it just and proper that they should still be denied an opportunity to be of some use to the Empire with their physical strength and other concomitant virtues? We hope that the incident which we have noticed today at such great length will lead the government to revise their estimate of Indian capacity. From games and foot-balling matches to actual field-service may appear to be a long leap. But the skill, physical fitness, discipline, courage and organization required in these sports are also held to be the essentials of active military service and it is illogical in the extreme to hold that those who shine in the one line will hopelessly fail in the other.[43]

The significance of Mohun Bagan's match had now departed from the grounds of racial amity to the Empire's frontline. According to Mallik, Mohun Bagan's 'skill, phys-ical fitness and strength, discipline, courage and organization' were all virtues required in active military service. Although there is an extensive history behind the reasons why Bengalis were not encouraged in military service as compared to other 'races' in British India, what is of concern here is that the moral of Mohun Bagan's victory was funda-mentally related to the imperial government's obligation to respond to Bengalis earnestly anticipated participation in the imperial army. Mohun Bagan came to stand for 'all classes of Indians' having 'thus given conclusive proof of their physical fitness'. It was considered sheer injustice to 'let rust unused these physical powers' in place of the potential opportunity to be 'of some use to the Empire'.

Turning to what *The Statesman* thought of these matters, having repeated the motions of establishing the absence of racial tensions, the newspaper's correspondent went further to state that the English community was as elated as the Indian commu-nity upon learning of 'their' defeat. To suggest otherwise would be, in his words, 'absurd'. Upon explaining the reasons and lessons for English devotion to sports and good temper, he indulged, 'the English people must have been bad pupils in the national school of good temper and chivalry if they did not welcome the triumph of the Mohun Bagan team, and cherish a strong desire to defeat them at the earlier opportu-nity'.[44] Apparently, some of them were. Next, in a passage that reveals the imperial intentions of football's origins and spread in British India,

> It is a cardinal belief with the Englishman that the great games are among the most valuable features of his civilization. He takes them with him to every clime and teaches them to every race. Nothing pleases him more than that in some part of the world he should discover pupils who beat their master.[45]

The writer then proceeded to make the point that Mohun Bagan should indeed go to England, like the Parsees before them in cricket, if only to encounter stiffer 'English' competition on the football field.

They will then discover that, while the military teams in India can give a very creditable exhibition of football, they are far from being the best exponents of that game which England can produce.

Somewhat more diplomatically, the correspondent concluded,

If the Mohun Bagan success were made the means of promoting the spread of healthy sports not only would a great benefit be conferred on the rising generation but an honour in keeping with the unselfish spirit of true sports would be rendered to the victorious team.[46]

He then took it upon himself to address the appeal raised in the previously mentioned *Amrita Bazaar Patrika* article that called upon the government's attention to the 'moral of this incident':

An Indian journal draws from the great event the inference that the Government ought to recognise the possession by Bengalis of the qualities which make good soldiers. It is much more desirable that the Bengalis themselves should perceive that, when physical energy has been developed by healthy sports, the effect ought to be to divert the attention of the most promising young men of the country from sedentary pursuits to out door occupations which are at present not agreeable to them, but which would be far more profitable to themselves than office employments and far more beneficial to the community. Agriculture calls for the assistance of trained minds in healthy bodies, and it will be strange if young men who have undergone the stimulating discipline of football and cricket do not feel the attraction of the career offered by farming and other industries which demand physical strength and endurance.[47]

Presumably standing in for the government, *The Statesman* spurned the plea for military service and responded instead with the promise of agriculture and industry. Mohun Bagan's players, rather than ideally becoming soldiers, would do better for themselves and their community on fields and in factories. Ganen Mallik of *Amrita Bazaar Patrika* did not wait long to respond. The same day, he published the previously alluded to article, 'Manliness of the Bengalis' to counter the 'side-issue' that *The Statesman* correspondent had raised.

Why does our contemporary evade the point and raise a side issue? What we contended for was that when the Indians could display such excellence in English manly games, which require not only physical endurance but such qualities as strong will, intrepid courage and powers of organization, they might as well be utilised in the battlefield.[48]

After describing the feats of Indian hunters, and asserting the century-old origins of the masculinity of the Bengali race via Lord Minto's rapturous letter written in 1807, Mallik proceeded to construct a mini-history of early eighteenth-century India in the following terms. Note the primordialist 'ideal self-subsisting village' civilizational undertone that informs Mallik's narrative of India before domination under the British crown:

In those days the people had their national games which were by no means less manly than the football and the cricket. Every village at that time had its gymnasium and it was a religious duty with its male inhabitants, young and old, to spend their evenings, and sometimes mornings, in physical culture. They had not to attend courts as litigants and lawyers and create discord among themselves: or to drive quills in Government or mercantile offices to earn a pittance to keep their bodies and souls together: or to resort to the press and the platform to bring about unrest in the land. They had enough of food: the prices of all necessary articles were cheap: fish, milk and vegetables were more than abundant: they had good drinking water and malaria and cholera were unknown: and the villagers, who then constituted the pick of the nation, were in this way able to grow physically and strike Lord Minto the way they did.[49]

An all too romanticized memory of the past, Mallik's nostalgic narrative encapsulates the history of British rule in India from the position of the normative Indian, Bengali man: In 'those' days male inhabitants had time for physical culture, food and drink was plenty, illness was 'unknown'. Now, he has to attend courts, create discord where there was presumably unity, drive quills in government or mercantile offices – or resort to the press and platform to bring about unrest. Yet again, two versions of the Indian man emerge – one who attends the colonial government or mercantile office, or one who resorts to the press and platform to bring about unrest in the land. Mohun Bagan's players were all undoubtedly of the former mould. Almost all of them worked in colonial government or mercantile offices, or attended universities. Alternately, it is also true that political extremism and/or terrorism were more a feature of Bengali youth than the more seasoned older Congress-style politicians and their partisans. Rupak Saha's novella, *Ekadashe Suryodoy*, literally 'Sunrise on the Eleventh', brings to light the intricacies of the relationship between moderates and extremists within the context of Mohun Bagan's IFA bid in 1911.

Ganen Mallik extended his own analysis of the situation of Bengali youth referred to by *The Statesman*'s correspondent. Initially agreeing with the latter's suggestion that 'our young men should devote a portion of their time to healthy sports', Mallik proceeded to refute the suggestion that they [Bengali youth] prefer 'sedentary pursuits' to 'outdoor occupations'. He argued that as Bengalis were beholden to pass University exams in a foreign tongue they had no time for leisure, articulating the acute dilemma between the pressures of formal education and salaried work/*chakri* or the pursuit of physical health (that is, in many ways, still with us in our present day).

> Our college and school students cannot spare even one hour for the training of their bodies if they have to pass their examinations successfully. It is also sheer necessity – the question of bread – that keeps a large section of our youths pinned to office employments.
>
> We cannot help repressing a smile at the proposal of 'the Statesman' that, Indians, including, we believe, the Mohan Bagan team, 'who have undergone the stimulating discipline of football and cricket', should take to agriculture. Do English youths who distinguish themselves on the playground ultimately turn to agriculturalists? And then, where will the millions of Indian peasants go to earn their bread if they are ousted from their occupation by superior men like trained and educated Indian youths? No, Mr. 'Statesman', they deserve a better career than that of hewers of wood and drawers of water.[50]

In Mallik's mind, the agricultural profession and the millions of Indian peasants in its practice were clearly inferior to the superiority of 'trained and educated Indian youths'.

The 'better career' that he desires for Bengali men is military service. There is of course however, the dilemma of *chakri* referred to above, that keeps Bengali men from cultivating physical fitness. Mohun Bagan's victory thus emerges within the constraints experienced by Bengali youth of this era. 'The question of bread' thereby informs this understanding of the conditions of Mohun Bagan's win.

I close this analytical section with an anecdote from a retired member of the Mohun Bagan club who had later taken up correspondence with *Amrita Bazaar Patrika* from his residence in Bhagalpur. The news of Mohun Bagan's triumph had, as has already been noted, spread all over the province of Bengal. This passage perhaps best captures the sense of consolation and re-affirmation of historically bruised Bengali, and Indian, pride:

> The wave of enthusiastic admiration which is agitating the metropolis just now over the well-deserved victory of the Mohun Bagan team has reached our distant town as well. It is the talk in every circle. A congratulating telegram has already been despatched by the Bengalee football players of this town and a special fixture is announced today in honour of the occasion. Your humble correspondent is an old footballer who remembers with pride that he was once a member of this immortal club. In this connection I remember some memorable words uttered by Mr. Watson of the [exclusively English] Calcutta Football Club when presiding over the annual Football Dinner in 1892 or 1893 – they were to this effect – 'If the Bengalees ever win this trophy – defeating all European teams – they may well claim to have wiped off the stain of the field of Plassey.' Herein old footballers there may bear me out. And, should we not congratulate Mr. Watson (I hope he is alive to-day) on the fulfilment of his prophecy?[51]

The Battle of Plassey on the 23 June 1757, was the conventional cut-off point in standard nationalist historical time when British colonialism in India 'began'. Robert Clive and Mir Jafar's machinations gave rise to a strengthening of the bureaucratic and economic ties that the East India Company had established by then. Mohun Bagan's victory had punctured the realm of the political, to use President Watson's words, 'wiped off the stain of the field of Plassey', setting back the historical clock by a century and a half to when 'India' was unconquered by the British. In 1911, the meaning gleaned from Mohun Bagan's victory put Indians back on par with their British rulers. The cruel irony of this liberal enthusiasm however, was that it would take more that three decades for the nationalist leadership to allegedly 'prove' their ability to conduct responsible government to their imperial rulers.

Conclusion

A central facet of the (contradictory) equalizing process between Bengalis and the British, or metonymically, 'wiping the stain off the field of Plassey', was the necessity to agree upon the absence of racial antagonism and to discard the underlying premise of racial inequality. In this manner, Mohun Bagan's victory was interpreted within the nationalist and imperialist psyche as simultaneously extending a nationalist, as well as universalist, counter-imperial appeal. But as I have argued throughout this paper, the universal joy that held Calcutta in sway for the first few days of August 1911 was experienced by newspaper journalists and presumably other spectators of Mohun Bagan's victory through the lens of their own ideological commitments. Therefore, even if all journalists agreed on the universal significance of this event, precisely how this event was universalized in the mind of each writer differed from case to case.

Thus, if for the *Bengalee's* correspondent, Mohun Bagan's victory signified the growing adaptation of the Bengali race to Western modernity, for *Amrita Bazaar Patrika's* Ganen Mallik, the victory was testament to the masculinity that characterized Mohun Bagan's Bengali ancestors. If for some nationalist journalists Mohun Bagan's victory stood as a critique of imperial policies, for others, the event was a clandestine critique of the failure of nationalist leaders to unite Bengali society due to their pursuit of narrow self-interests. If for some Bengali journalists this event signified the absence of racial antagonism, for others, it merely underscored the failure of the British to live up to their 'imperial games ethic'. If for Mallik it meant that the government ought to enlist Bengalis into the imperial army, for *The Statesman* it meant that the youth of Bengal should take to industry and agriculture. Emphasizing the dualities and inconsistencies in the meaning of Mohun Bagan's victory allows for a history of this event that does not restrict its significance to either an imperialist or nationalist register. Instead, one observes how the meaning of Mohun Bagan's victory emerged and was interpreted from each writer's specific vantage and perspectives of the cultural and political schema of the day.

As I have suggested, this cultural-political schema was not neatly separated into imperialist and nationalist categories of practice. On the contrary, it was precisely due to the inter-penetration of imperialist and nationalist interpretive practices – Hindu traditionalism/Western modernism, imperial racism/universalism, British imperialism/Indian nationalism, 'imperial games ethic'/Hindu spirit of 'working' – that Mohun Bagan's victory acquired such a range of allegedly contradictory, mutually reinforcing, as well as conflicting meanings. Consequently, as I have demonstrated, there were differences and similarities both between and within imperialist and nationalist interpretations of this event. Nevertheless, the universalist purchase of Mohun Bagan's victory is a feature common to almost all newspaper sources I have reviewed in this study: the sense of there having been a historical concession, or reparation, a reason for universal joy. President Watson's prophecy attests to that sentiment.

Acknowledgements

This is an abridged version of a thesis submitted to the Master of Arts Program in the Social Sciences at the University of Chicago, May 2005. I thank Dipesh Chakrabarty and Matthew Millikan for their helpful comments and criticisms. Also, my thanks to Boria Majumdar, for sending me sources from Kolkata that were unavailable in Chicago.

Notes

[1]   *Amrita Bazaar Patrika,* 31 July 1911.
[2]   *The Bengalee,* 30 July 1911.

[3]   Interview with Umapati Kumar, President, Mohun Bagan Club, in Mitra, 'Babu at Play'.

[4]   My use of the term 'event' is consistent with the following understanding offered by Marshall Sahlins: 'an event is not simply a phenomenal happening, even though as a phenomenon it has reasons and forces of its own, apart from any given symbolic scheme. *An event becomes such as it is interpreted.* Only as it is appropriated in and through the cultural scheme does it acquire an historical *significance.*' [My emphasis.] Sahlins, *Islands of History*, xiv.

[5]   Mason, 'Football on the Maidan', 150–1. Paul Dimeo, 'Football and Politics in Bengal', in Dimeo and Mills, *Soccer in South Asia*, 69.

[6]   Majumdar, 'The Vernacular in Sports History', 3076.

[7]   Goswami writes, 'Methodological nationalism is part of a broader national-state centric bias. Nation-state centric frameworks – the conflation of society and nation-state, the exaggerated privilege accorded to the national scale as unit of analysis – are an entrenched legacy, as various works have argued, of late nineteenth-century sociological and philosophical paradigms.' Goswami, *Producing India*, 19. Although Goswami utilizes the notion of methodological nationalism to explore the production of the spatio-temporal matrix of the nation form, this notion pertains to this discussion insofar as football matches were part of national cultural fields in colonial Calcutta. The point being, one must be attendant to the ways in which nationalist categories of practice are conflated with, or treated as, categories of analysis.

[8]   *The Bengalee*, 1 Aug. 1911.

[9]   Ibid.

[10]   Ibid.

[11]   Ibid.

[12]   What our correspondent does not mention however, and this is where his narrative seems to hover above the reality of his day, is that the majority of the population of Bengal did not have access to English education, or football or ballooning. Thus, when he invokes the 'nation', or the 'race', or 'our people', he is speaking about a very specific class of members who actively participated in constituting these categories. The 'masses' do not necessarily appear, or have a stake in the adaptation or progress of the nation. Indeed, they hardly exist in the grand vision of modernity our news correspondent imagines.

[13]   *The Bengalee*, 1 Aug. 1911.

[14]   *Amrita Bazaar Patrika*, 3 Aug. 1911.

[15]   *The Bengalee*, 1 Aug. 1911.

[16]   Ibid.

[17]   *Modern Review*, Sept. 1911, 307.

[18]   Chatterjee, *The Nation and Its Fragments*, 26.

[19]   A curious feature of this archive is that each newspaper's editor's caste is listed next to each name. Needless to say, every single editor was either Brahmin, Kayastha or Baidya – Bhadrolok. In July/August 1911, accounting for 2,000, 1,500 and 1,000 in distribution respectively, the *Telegraph*, *Indian Mirror* and *Indian Empire* were surpassed only by *The Bengalee* and *Amrita Bazaar Patrika*, both dominating the Bengali-owned English newspaper circulations at 6,500 and 3,000 respectively.

[20]   *The Telegraph*, 5 Aug. 1911, in *Report on Native-owned English Newspapers in Bengal*, week concluding 12 Aug. 1911, 992–3.

[21]   *Indian Mirror*, 30 July 1911, in *Report on Native-owned English Newspapers in Bengal*, week concluding 12 Aug. 1911, 992–3.

[22]   Majumdar, 'The Vernacular in Sports History'.

[23]   *The Bengalee*, 30 July 1911.

[24]   *The Comrade*, in 'Mohun Bagan Golden Jubilee Souvenir', 1939, 15.

[25]   *The Mussalman*, in ibid., 16.

[26]   *Nayak*, 30 July 1911, in *Report on the Native-owned Papers in Bengal*, week ending 5 Aug. 1911.

[27]   *Nayak*, 30 July 1911.

[28]   *Nayak*, 5 Aug. 1911.

[29] Ibid.
[30] *The Statesman,* 2 Aug. 1911.
[31] *Basumati,* 5 Aug. 1911, in *Report on the Native-owned Papers in Bengal,* week ending 12 Aug. 1911.
[32] *Basumati,* 5 Aug. 1911.
[33] *Manasi,* Ashvin (Bengali month), 1911. Kumar, *Mohun Bagan Omnibus,* 2.
[34] *Manasi,* Bhadro (Bengali month), 1911. Kumar, *Mohun Bagan Omnibus.*
[35] *Hitavadi,* 4 Aug. 1911, in *Report on the Native-owned Papers in Bengal,* week ending 12 Aug. 1911.
[36] Ibid.
[37] Consider, for instance, this depiction of Bengali, male self-perception published in *Nayak* on the 14 June 1911: 'We English-educated *Babus* are like dolls dancing on the palms of Englishman. The education which makes *Babus* of us, and gives us our food whether we are in service or in some profession, is established by the English. Our … political efforts and aspirations are all kinds of gifts of the English people … English education and the superficial imitation of English habits and manners have made us perfectly worthless, a miserable mixture of Anglicism and *swadeshism.*'
[38] *Empire,* 30 July 1911, in *The Bengalee,* 31 July 1911.
[39] *Amrita Bazaar Patrika,* 31 July 1911.
[40] Ibid.
[41] This relationship hardly constitutes what Tony Mason has called the 'essence of the mystery of hegemony'. Surely, pleas for the 'curbing to a certain extent the pride of one and contributing to the self-consciousness of the other' do not testify to any hegemonical hold over the Bengali consciousness. Neither should one accept Boria Majumdar's suggestion that English reports on account of their lauding of the absence of racial feeling were any less nationalist.
[42] *Amrita Bazaar Patrika,* 31 July 1911.
[43] Ibid.
[44] *The Statesman,* 3 Aug. 1911.
[45] Ibid.
[46] Ibid.
[47] Ibid.
[48] *Amrita Bazaar Patrika,* 3 Aug. 1911.
[49] Ibid.
[50] Ibid.
[51] *Amrita Bazaar Patrika,* 4 Aug. 1911.

References

Bandyopadhyay, Kausik. 'Das Bidroho.' *Ananda Bazar Patrika,* Robabisariyo, 25 Aug. 2002.
———. 'Race, Nation and Sport: Footballing Nationalism in Colonial Calcutta.' *Soccer and Society 4,* no.1 (2003): 1–19.
———. '1911 in Retrospect: A Revisionist Perspective on a Famous Indian Sporting Victory.' *The International Journal of the History of Sport 21,* no.3/4 (2004): 363–83.
Bandyopadhyay, Shantipriya. *Khelar Raja Phutbol.* Calcutta: Jnanthirthho, 1983.
Banerjea, Surendranath. *A Nation in Making: Being the Reminiscences of Fifty Years in Public Life.* London: Oxford University Press, 1925.
Basu, Jaydeep. *Stories from Indian Football.* New Delhi: UBS Publishers' Distributors Pvt. Ltd, 2003.
Bhattacharyya, Buddhadeva, ed. *Freedom Struggle and Anushilan Samiti.* Calcutta: Anushilan Samiti, 1979.
Chakrabarty, Dipesh. *Provincializing Europe: Postcolonial Thought and Historical Difference.* Princeton: Princeton University Press, 2000.

————. *Habitations of Modernity: Essays in the Wake of Subaltern Studies.* New Delhi: Permanent Black, 2002.

Chandra, Bipan, *et al. India's Struggle for Independence.* New Delhi: Viking, 1988.

Chatterjee, Partha. *The Nation and Its Fragments: Colonial and Postcolonial Histories.* Calcutta: Oxford University Press, 1995.

Das, Suranjan. *Communal Riots in Bengal: 1905–1947.* New Delhi: Oxford University Press, 1991.

Datta, Pradip Kumar. *Carving Blocs: Communal Ideology in Early Twentieth Century Bengal.* New Delhi: Oxford University Press, 1999.

Dimeo, Paul and James Mills, eds. *Soccer in South Asia: Empire, Nation, Diaspora.* London: Frank Cass, 2001.

Goswami, Manu. *Producing India: From Colonial Economy to National Space.* Chicago: University of Chicago Press, 2004.

Kumar, Sibram, ed. *Mohun Bagan Omnibus.* Calcutta: Prabhabati Prokashani, 1983.

Mason, Tony. 'Football on the Maidan: Cultural Imperialism in Calcutta.' In *The Cultural Bond: Sport, Empire, Society,* edited by J.A. Mangan. London: Frank Cass, 1992.

Majumdar, Boria. 'Sport in South Asia: Soccer in South Asia – Review Essay.' *The International Journal of the History of Sport 19,* no.4 (2002): 202–10.

————. 'The Politics of Soccer in Colonial India, 1930–37: The Years of Turmoil.' *Soccer and Society 3,* no.1 (2002): 22–36.

————. 'The Vernacular in Sports History.' *Economic and Political Weekly 37,* no.29 (2002): 3069–75.

Mitra, Soumen. 'Babu at Play: Sporting Nationalism in Bengal, 1880–1911.' In *Bengal: Yesterday and Today,* edited by Nisith Ray and Ranjit Roy. Calcutta: Papyrus, 1991.

Mukherjee, Haridas and Uma Mukherjee. *The Growth of Nationalism in India (1857–1905).* Calcutta: A.C. Ghosh, 1957.

————. *'Bande Mataram' and Indian Nationalism (1906–1908).* Calcutta: Firma K.L.M., 1957.

————. *India's Fight for Freedom or The Swadeshi Movement (1905–1906).* Calcutta: Firma K.L.M., 1958.

Mukherjee, Hirendranath. *India's Struggle for Freedom.* Calcutta: National Book Agency Pvt. Ltd., 1962.

Mukherjee, Kumar. *The Story of Football.* New Delhi: Publications Division, Ministry of Information and Broadcasting, Government of India, 2002.

Nanda, B.R. *The Moderate Era in Indian Politics: Dadabhai Naoroji Memorial Prize Fund Lecture.* Delhi: Oxford University Press, 1983.

Nandy, Moti. Translated by Banerjee Shampa. 'Football and Nationalism.' In *The Calcutta Psyche,* edited by Geeti Sen. New Delhi: India International Centre, 1990.

Pal, Bipinchandra. *Swadeshi and Swaraj (The Rise of New Patriotism).* Calcutta: Yugayatri Prakashak Limited, 1954.

Ray, Rajat Kanta. *Social Conflict and Political Unrest in Bengal, 1875–1927.* Delhi: Oxford University Press, 1984.

Rosselli, John. 'The Self-Image of Effeteness: Physical Education and Nationalism in Nineteenth-Century Bengal.' *Past and Present 86* (1980): 121–48.

Saha, Rupak. *Ekadashe Surjodoy.* Kolkata: Karuna Prokashoni, 1990.

Sahlins, Marshall. *Islands of History.* Chicago: University of Chicago Press, 1987.

Sarkar, Sumit. *Swadeshi Movement in Bengal, 1903–1908.* New Delhi: People's Publishing House, 1973.

————. *Modern India: 1885–1947.* Madras: Macmillan India Ltd, 1983.

————. 'The Conditions and Nature of Subaltern Militancy: Bengal from Swadeshi to Non-Co-operation, c. 1905–22.' In *Subaltern Studies III: Writings on South Asian History and Society,* edited by Ranajit Guha. New Delhi: Oxford University Press, 1984.

————. *Writing Social History.* New Delhi: Oxford University Press, 1997.

————. *Beyond Nationalist Frames.* New Delhi: Permanent Black, 2002.

Sengupta, Achintyakumar. *Kallol Yug.* Calcutta: M.C. Sarkar and Sons Pvt. Ltd., 1966.

Seth, Sanjay. 'Rewriting Histories of Nationalism: The Politics of "Moderate Nationalism" in India, 1870–1905.' *The American Historical Review 104,* no.1 (1999): 95–116.

Stoddart, Brian. 'Sport, Cultural Imperialism, and Colonial Response in the British Empire.' *Comparative Studies in Society and History 30,* no.4 (1988): 649–73.

The Politics of Football in Iran

Houchang E. Chehabi

In late 1997 Iranian football made international headlines. In an article on the Islamic summit held in Iran, the *Economist* wrote that almost 'anything can become a political football in Iran, including football'.[1] This attention was precipitated by the political ramifications inside Iran of the national team's tie against Australia in Melbourne on 29 November, which secured it a place in the 1998 World Cup. Since then, major international soccer games have often given rise to massive street demonstrations by young people. That football should cause so much excitement in Iran is not astonishing if one looks at it from a global perspective. Football is a game in which each team works together to try and occupy as much of the 'territory' of the other as it can, culminating in attempts symbolically to 'conquer' the other side's stronghold by kicking the ball into the goal.[2] The playing field thus becomes a metaphor for the competition between communities, cities and nations: football focuses group identities. The excitement that the game generates in Latin America is well known; Honduras and El Salvador even waged a brief 'soccer war' in 1969.[3]

But ask any Iranian what Iran's national sport is, and the answer will be 'wrestling', a discipline whose history in Iran goes back more than a thousand years, compared to the century that football has been known in the country. Until the introduction of Western sports and physical education, Iranian sports consisted on the one hand of the various folk games specific to different provinces,[4] and on the other of the exercises, including wrestling, practiced in the *zurkhanehs*, urban gymnasia found almost everywhere in Iran.[5] The only native team game of any importance was polo, which had thrived under the Safavids but disappeared during the troubles that followed their demise in the eighteenth century, only to be revived as a British import in the late Qajar period.[6] Physical exercises in Iran were therefore mostly individual in nature, which struck Iranian modernists as conducive to the individualism and lack of cooperative spirit that is commonly ascribed to the 'national character' of Iranians,[7] leading them to make the popularization of team sports part of their agenda for change. Nonetheless, until the mid-1960s freestyle wrestling, which resembles traditional Iranian wrestling and was therefore readily adopted by Iranians, remained Iran's most popular sport.[8] Iran's greatest sports legend, Gholamreza Takhti, was a champion in that discipline, and today in Iran not only sports halls but also many football stadiums are named after him.[9] Freestyle wrestling is the discipline in which Iranians have gained the highest number of medals since they started competing internationally at the 1948 London Olympics. Yet Iran's first place in the 1998 world championships, held in Teheran, caused far less excitement in Iran than the country's mere participation in the 1998 soccer World Cup: 'nationalism peaks because many consider collective action a truer test of a country's spirit than individual talent'.[10] Given the Islamic Republic's persistent attempts to keep global culture at bay, the widespread popularity of football in Iran calls for some explanation.

Football is by far the most popular sport in the world, and scholarly attempts to make sense of this popularity go back almost a century.[11] In a very basic sense, football embodies modernity:

> Nineteenth century individualism found in the spirit of the club a certain compensation for its solitude; democracy has visibly diminished the borders between [socio-economical] milieux, [new modes of] transportation have lifted the limitations imposed by vital spaces. The popularity of a local, national, and international athletic game that allows for restrained masculine aggressivity and technical skill to manifest themselves in inoffensive enterprises, that offers sensible and moderate satisfactions, and that allows the development of 'nationalist' and 'regionalist' cults without grave consequences is especially well adapted to this new world. Football is a game of this sort … A technical culture value of team work.[12]

While this may be an overly optimistic assessment of the 'inoffensiveness' of football fever, written before hooligan violence became an everyday occurrence, the social transformations that favoured the popularity of football in Europe also took place in Iran (and the rest of the Middle East), only later; the transition from wrestling to football as Iran's most popular sport therefore reflects the social and political changes that have occurred in the country. It is striking how this shift in tastes is congruent with the Durkheimian notion of transition from mechanic to organic solidarity: wrestling, in which all athletes do the same, has an elective affinity with mechanic solidarity, which is the solidarity brought about by the resemblance of the members of a group, while football (and other team sports) typifies what organic solidarity is all about, namely solidarity on the basis of a complementarity deriving from the division of labour.[13] Christian Bromberger, the French anthropologist who has written extensively about both Iran and football, observed that 'football values team work, solidarity, division of labour and collective planning – very much in the image of the industrial world which originally produced it',[14] but cautioned that football 'also underlines the role of chance, of cheating, of a judgement that can be argued about, i.e., the umpire's'.[15]

My aim in this article is not to give a history of Iranian football,[16] nor to present an anthropological study of Iranian football, but to analyze the interplay between the popularization of football, social change, state policies and politics *tout court*.

The Introduction of Western Sport to Iran

The introduction of Western sports in Iran is not well documented. At the Dar al-funun, the first modern school established in Teheran in 1851, the European officers on the teaching staff made their Iranian students exercise regularly. For this purpose, the school's theatre, which had never been used for dramatic performances, was transformed into a gymnasium. Like so many other cultural innovations, modern physical exercise also reached Iran through the military. Various methods were used: A German-educated officer by the name of Geranmayeh taught Friedrich Ludwig Jahn's gymnastics at the old Military Academy (*Madraseh-ye Nezam*),[17] in the Gendarmerie Swedish officers taught Per Henrik Ling's Swedish method,[18] and in the school of the Cossack Brigade Russian gymnastics was taught.[19]

The utility of physical exercise for national progress became a matter of public discussion after the constitutional revolution of 1906. Persian publications, both inside and outside Iran, stressed the importance of sport and physical exercise for creating a healthy nation that could revive the glories of ancient Iran.[20] In 1916 a man who can be called the father of modern sports in Iran, Mir Mehdi Varzandeh, returned to Iran from a lengthy stay in Belgium and Turkey, and began teaching physical education in Iranian schools. He met with resistance at first, but in 1919 the minister of education, Nasir al-Molk, made physical education part of the official curriculum of Iranian schools.[21] In June 1921, *Kaveh*, the influential journal published in Berlin, wrote:

> In the opinion of those who have immersed themselves in the secrets of nations' progress, [sport] is one of the main causes of national power, progress, independence, civilization, national survival, and especially chastity and seriousness of purpose, and is the origin of both individual and social virtues. Playing balls with the hands, *but especially with the feet*, horse riding, rowing, hunting, fencing, polo, and sledging ... have a huge importance in the lives of Europeans, and a direct connection with their progress. It is not for nothing that many learned people have said that *the secret of the grandeur, power, and progress of the British is football, i.e., playing ball with the feet*.[22]

In spite of the special place that football occupied in the modernist imagination, when in 1927 the Iranian parliament passed a law authorizing the ministry of education to introduce compulsory daily physical education in public schools,[23] the system used was the callisthenics developed in Sweden by Per Henrik Ling, which became known in Iran as *varzesh-e su'edi*, 'Swedish exercises'. Shortly thereafter, a physical education teacher training college was established under the directorship of Varzandeh, and it operated until 1934.[24] It seems that the clergy and religious opinion opposed the measure, as the exercises struck some traditional people as frivolous because they resembled dancing.[25]

Competitive Western athletic games were introduced to Iran by Iranians returning from Europe and by Europeans living in Iran. Like elsewhere in the world, British expatriates played a major role in the introduction of football to Iran.[26] In the Ottoman Empire the first football games had been played by British residents and non-Muslims,[27] and in Iran, too, the first record of any game that I have found involved British expatriates in Isfahan playing a team of Armenians in 1898. The sons of the prince-governor of the province, Zell al-Soltan, watched and then took to the game, which they found more enjoyable than cricket.[28] But as far as the general public was concerned, football was introduced to Iranians through three conduits of modernization: missionary schools, the oil industry and the military.

In British missionary schools games, including football, were part of the curriculum.[29] The same was true for the St Louis School, run by French Lazarists, which had one of the earliest varsity soccer teams.[30] And although nowadays one does not associate football with the United States, American missionaries preferred it to American football.[31] Physical education was an important part of the curriculum of the American School (later Alborz College), which had been founded by Presbyterian missionaries.[32] In a conscious effort to inculcate the value of cooperative effort, insufficiently fostered by traditional Iranian exercises, the director of the school, Dr Samuel M. Jordan (1871–1952), concentrated on ball games and made students take up pick and shovel to help build the school's football field.[33] In 1935 Jordan wrote:

> Iranian statesmen for years have mourned, 'We Iranians do not know how to cooperate'. But how do you teach people to cooperate, how do you teach them to 'play the game'? Obviously by playing games, and so we introduced football, baseball, volleyball, basket-ball – all those group games that we are using here in America, and naturally the boys took to them just as boys do everywhere in the world. The result is that physical education with all these group games is a regular part of the school program for all the schools of Iran and a year ago the Minister of Education took out from Columbia University a Ph.D. in physical education to head their department of Physical Education. Throughout the whole Empire, Young Iran is learning to 'play the game' of life.[34]

While missionary schools introduced football to the sons of the elite, working-class Iranians were acquainted with the game by the British employees of the Anglo-Persian Oil Company. These played football (as well as cricket, hockey, tennis, squash and golf) in the oil fields of Abadan and Masjed Soleyman; the latter area even boasting a football league and an annual international match between England and Scotland.[35] The local Iranian employees of the company first looked on, and then began replacing individual players on the teams, until they formed their own teams. These young Iranian football players met some hostility from their social environment for partaking in the games of the 'infidels', and were at times beaten up and pelted with stones. One reason for this hostility was that the players' shorts violated traditional dress codes, for the *shar'ia* advises men to cover their legs from the navel to the knee.[36] Elsewhere in the south of Iran, football was introduced by the British officers of the South Persia Rifles (1916–21) to the Iranian troops they commanded, who then spread the game among the population.

In Teheran, British residents connected with the legation, the consulate, the Imperial Bank and the Indo-European Telegraph Department held matches, mostly on the Meydan-e Mashq, which later came to be known as Tupkhaneh. Their games attracted the attention of young men who came to watch, and around 1908 Iranians started replacing individual players on the British teams. Soon Iranian football players formed their own teams, but faced a major problem in that balls were difficult to find. Some made do with inflated cow udders,[37] while others endeavoured to abstract out-of-bounds balls at British games. The onset of the First World War in 1914 put an end to the organized games among the British teams in Teheran, but by 1918 they started once more, again with some Iranian players. In 1920 a number of Iranians formed the first all-Iranian football club, which they called 'Iran Club'. Soon the alumni of the American college and the students of the School of Political Science also formed teams.[38] In 1919 or 1920 a number of Iranian and British football enthusiasts founded the football association (*Majma'-e futbal-e Iran*) to encourage Iranian players and popularize the game. The director of the Imperial Bank of Persia, James McMurray, became its president, and he was assisted by the legation doctor, A.R. Neligan; they each donated a cup to be awarded to winning teams. A year later the Iranian members of the association decided to take it over. They renamed it *Majma'-e tarvij va taraqqi-ye futbal* (Association for the Promotion and Progress of Football), and Reza Khan agreed to be its honorary president.[39] It became the first association to be registered at the State Registry, the newly founded *Daftar-e asnad-e rasmi*, and the first modern Iranian sports organization. It and published the rules of association football translated into Persian, and beginning in 1923 it organized soccer tournaments in Teheran.

To sum up, the British presence in Iran was instrumental in popularizing football in Iran, but other Westerners, like the Americans and the French, also helped through the schools they established. In places that had not much of a foreign presence such as Ardabil, it seems that the game was introduced in the 1920s by young men who had spent some time in the Caucasus.[40] Football matches were occasions on which Iranians, both Muslim and non-Muslim, and Europeans met. Perhaps it was precisely this that aroused the suspicion of some traditional circles. In March 1925, for instance, police had to step in when a group of youngsters, all bearing names that indicate their background in the milieu of artisans and small shop keepers, created disturbances at a game between a Teheran club and an Armenian team and insulted the Armenian woman spectators. The hooligans *avant la lettre* were arrested and condemned to fifty whip lashes.[41]

Football under Reza Shah

By the mid-1920s football had become a symbol of modernization, and soon the game was promoted at the highest levels of the state. In the summer of 1924, Reza Khan ordered regular athletic competitions to be held by the armed forces, and these included football games. Some of these took place in the provinces, such as one between members of the *tip-e mokhtalet-e Kordestan*, at which players still wore traditional *givehs*.[42] But the development of the game was hampered by the shortage of playing fields, most of which belonged to British or American institutions.[43] In the winter of 1925 at a session attended by the then speaker of parliament, Seyyed Mohammad Tadayyon in his capacity of head of the Association for the Promotion and Progress of Football, one of the players pointed out that it was a shame that the British had facilities but the Iranians did not. Tadayyon used his influence in the Majlis, and in the spring of 1926 the legislature approved a bill whereby a piece of land near the Darvazeh Dowlat, on which young men had played informally for a number of years, was purchased by the government to establish a permanent soccer field.[44]

After ascending the throne in late 1925, Reza Shah continued showing an interest in football. Thus in early 1926 he attended a match between an Iranian team and a team of British expatriates in Teheran, which the Iranians won.[45] Iranians had beaten Britons at their own game for the first time, and having thus gained in self-confidence, in the autumn of 1926, to show that relations between Iran and the Soviet Union had improved, the Iranian cabinet decided to send a team of 15 Iranian football players led by the director of the School of Physical Education, Mir Mehdi Varzandeh, to an international tournament in Baku.[46] The team played four matches against different teams from Baku, losing three and drawing one. Upon their return to Teheran, a satirical magazine, *Nahid*, made fun of their defeat on its front-page cartoon. Having expected a warmer welcome, a number of players took it upon themselves to ransack *Nahid*'s editorial offices, for which they were arrested and gaoled for a night.[47] However, one of the players who had played in Baku, Hoseyn Meftah, drew a more constructive lesson from the losses. Later he wrote:

> That trip had the advantage that we learned that dribbling and individualism (*takravi*) are of no use: each of us was good at individual moves ... this was what the people liked. But when we saw the foreign games and the Baku team[s] we learned that the purpose of football is something different from what we had pursued until then.[48]

In 1929 it was time for a return visit, and so a team from Baku was invited to play in Teheran in late November.[49] To impress the visitors, grass had been planted on the state-owned football field. The last of the three games, all of which were won by the visitors, was attended by Abdolhoseyn Teymurtash, the powerful minister of court. The humiliating defeats (11-0, 3-1, 4-0!), suffered on home grounds to boot, caused a lot of consternation, so much so that some young men gave up football altogether. In subsequent years the interest in football subsided, and newspapers hardly reported on those matches that did take place.[50] The activities of the Association of the Promotion and Progress of Football fizzled out, and beginning in the early 1930s a number of new organizations were formed to replace it.[51] These turned out to be ephemeral, but a new impetus was given to sport and physical education in 1934.[52] In January of that year, to remedy the inefficiency of previous *ad hoc* associations, the ministry of education set up a special Office of Physical Education. Its main function was to make schools establish football teams and then organize interschool competitions.[53] Competitions began a few weeks later, but teams again faced a severe shortage of playing fields.[54] This office was only in charge of school sport, however, and so a number of Iranian statesmen and educators founded the National Association for Physical Education (*Anjoman-e melli-ye tarbiyat-e badani*) in the spring of 1934.[55] From the outset, the association placed itself under the patronage of the Crown Prince, who had become the president of the Association for the Promotion and Progress of Football in 1929, but was by now studying in Switzerland.[56] To reorganize Iranian sports and scouting, an American and recent graduate of Columbia University by the name of Thomas R. Gibson was invited to come to Iran. For Gibson, who stayed until 1938, sport meant team sports: when a Japanese Judo master offered to introduce this discipline to the Iranian public, Gibson refused the offer, arguing that what Iran needed was team sports.[57] Gibson instituted competitions between school teams, mostly in soccer. Within a few months after his taking charge, 24 teams had been formed, all of them connected with educational establishments. The tournaments were attended by the highest dignitaries of the state.[58] Isa Sadiq, a prominent education official in those years, relates that in the beginning the public was so indifferent to spectator sports that the Physical Education Association had to resort to serving free tea and sweets to lure people to the football games.[59] Gibson also systematically sent coaches to the provinces to propagate modern sports, mainly football.[60] All over the country, football clubs were formed and playing fields were established, sometimes on abandoned cemeteries.[61]

In May 1936 the Crown Prince returned to Iran from abroad. As a boy growing up in Iran Mohammad Reza Pahlavi had enjoyed playing football, and at the Rosey School in Switzerland, where he spent five years, his athletic prowess had outshone his scholarly achievements and he had captained both the school's football and tennis teams.[62] Upon returning home, he took a personal interest in sports. An article published in 1936 by the official organ of the ministry of education reports that after he joined the football team of the Officers School which he now attended, that team never again lost a match and became the champion of the league of university faculties and high schools. Noting that matches in which he played attracted the enthusiastic attention of a public that thereby showed its deep attachment to the monarchy, the article added:

> His Highness the Crown Prince plays center forward, which is the most difficult and most technical position. Those who are familiar with this game, who are aware of the degree of difficulty of the center forward's duties, and who have had the honor of watching [the crown prince], will happily confirm that His Highness is a master and true champion in the way he defeats the opposing team by adroitly changing the attack line and distributing the ball to his teammates so as to put all of them to work and form a five-player attack line. The other point that all members of teams that

have played against the Officer's School and spectators have noted is his sense of justice, nobility, and fair play.[63]

In 1939, for the first time in Iranian history, national championships were held in a number of disciplines, including football. This was followed in 1940 by first attempts to create separate federations for each discipline, including football, attempts that bore fruit only after the war.[64]

To sum of the history of soccer in pre-First World War Iran, until the mid-1930s Western sports appealed to a small minority of Iranians and officially sponsored football remained largely an elite activity. This is apparent, for instance, from the names of referees in the early period, where we find the scions of major land-owning families like Sardar Akram Qarahghozlu, Arsalan and Abdollah Khal'atbari, and Ezam al-Saltaneh Zolfaqari.[65]

The age of Reza Shah was the golden age of varsity sports in Iran. The state's sponsorship of football in the rapidly expanding armed forces and in the equally rapidly expanding public educational system turned soccer into a popular pastime for young people. The result of these efforts was that, in spite of traditionalist resistance, football caught on. In 1935 an English observer wrote: '[Football] has conquered Persia too and is played all over the country … in towns and tiny hamlets, by most of the schoolboys and a few men. And it was a smart game, fast, clean, intelligent.' And he added the usual refrain about team-work:

> Many Persian schools play football several times a week, not only for its physical value but because it is believed to be a fine education in learning to play 'fair', a quality which Persians know the boys lack but which they wish to create, as they have seen, in the contact with Europeans, both in Persia and in Europe, how much it means in creating better human relationships.[66]

Football under Mohammad Reza Shah

Reza Shah left Iran in 1941, and only a few weeks after his departure, Ayatollah Kashani complained in a letter to the prime minister that the state had shamelessly turned a mosque into a football field and organized sports classes on its grounds.[67] But power was still largely in the hands of modernists, and so the state's promotion of football continued, although with less intensity than under Reza Shah.

During the Second World War, the presence of many Allied soldiers in occupied Iran allowed young Iranian men to measure their skills against foreigners. As a result of this experience, Iranian officialdom sensed a need to reorganize Iranian sports according to international criteria.[68] In anticipation of the 1948 Olympic Games in London, a national Olympic committee was founded in 1947, and it published guidelines for separate federations to be set up for each discipline. The national football federation was finally established in 1947, and soon thereafter joined the Fédération Internationale de Football Association, FIFA, the world governing body of soccer.

In the 1950s and early 1960s the national team lost most of its international games, including a highly politically-charged one against Iraq in 1962, which angered the Shah and caused Prime Minister Ali Amini to declare that if one had the 'honor of the homeland and the health of the young people' at heart, money earmarked for sending the Iranian soccer team to the Fourth Asian Games in Jakarta should better be spent at home.[69]

The fortunes of the national team began improving in 1964, as the Iranian side beat the national teams of Pakistan, Iraq and India to qualify for the Olympic Games in Tokyo. When the team returned to Teheran after a victorious game in Calcutta against India,[70] the government arranged a major welcome for them at the airport. Each player was driven to the city in an open jeep with a garland of flowers around his neck and an Iranian tricolour on each side.[71]

However, Iran's successes on the world's soccer fields paled in comparison with its triumphs on the world's wrestling mats. In the 1950s and 1960s Iranian freestyle wrestlers won many medals, culminating in national team winning the world championship of 1965 in Yokohama. These international successes combined with the sport's long tradition in Iran to make freestyle wrestling the most popular sport in Iran throughout the 1940s, 1950s and early 1960s.

It was only in the late 1960s that football became a major spectator sport. Iranian society was changing, as millions moved to the big cities, especially Teheran. A mass society resulting from urbanization favours a sport like football, which can be followed by tens of thousands of spectators in a stadium, spectators for whom the teams provide foci of loyalty and collective identification at the time when traditional community ties and rituals weakened.[72] Moreover, beginning in the mid-1960s television, which had come to Iran at the start of the decade, began broadcasting football games and thus brought it into people's homes.

The year 1968 stands out as a watershed in the history of Iranian football. For one thing, the death of Takhti in that year deprived wrestling of its most admired figure. But more importantly, in 1968 Iran and Israel were the finalists in the Asian Nations Cup, a quadrennial event taking place in between the world championships that is older than the European Nations Cup, and the game was to be held in Teheran. Only the previous year, Israel had defeated its Arab neighbours in the Six Day War, and the event had swung most Iranians' sympathies firmly behind the Arabs. Now, at a time when Arab sports teams were boycotting Israel, Iran, ever eager to espouse an independent line on the Arab-Israeli issue,[73] hosted a championship game.[74]

On the day of the game, 19 May, Teheran was rife with tension. Rumour had it that Habib Elqanian, a rich Jewish industrialist (who was executed in 1979), had bought 16,000 tickets to distribute to Jewish Iranians so that they could cheer for the visitors. As it happened, before the game the gates of Amjadiyeh Stadium were opened and the public were let in free of charge, generating new rumours that the Shah wanted to prove his pro-Islamic and pro-Iranian sentiment by making sure that Muslim Iranians cheered for the Iranian team.[75] During the game spectators were delirious, and anti-Semitic chants were heard, confirming the link between modern anti-Semitism in the Middle East and the creation of the state of Israel.[76] In the end the hosts beat the guests 2 to 1, and as Iran became Asian football champion, the joy was great in the stadium. *Noql*, sugar-covered almonds traditionally served on happy occasions, was thrown onto the field, and spectators remained on the grounds of the stadium for two hours chanting patriotic slogans, as police cavalry nervously guarded the nearby US embassy. The victory led to rumours that the government had bribed the Indian referee to let Iran win, or alternatively that the Israelis had lost on purpose, so that their ally, the Shah, might bask in the glory of having accomplished what the Arabs had failed to do: beat Israel.[77] From the point of view of many Iranian spectators, however, the match had not been a contest between nations but a contest between religious groups.[78]

The 1968 victory, witnessed by millions of people on television, made soccer a true mass phenomenon in Iran. Two popular singers, Vigen and Delkash, recorded songs to the glory of Iran's team. Players became frequent guests on radio shows and their photos were traded on street corners. More and more youngsters began playing informal games with cheap plastic balls on improvised fields with portable goals, a game that came to be known as *gol kuchak* (little goal).

In 1974, the year after the October War, Iran and Israel again faced each other in Teheran, this time as finalists in the Asian Games. Only one year after the quadrupling of oil prices had made it rich, the Iranian regime wanted to use the hosting of the Asian Games to enhance the country's international profile. If successful, the event might presage Olympic Games, the hosting of which in 1964 had consecrated Japan's membership in the rich countries' club. The Shah's aim was to be placed second in the overall medal count, after Japan, and he and his minister of court, Amir Asadollah Alam, followed the game on the radio.[79] This made the People's Republic of China, which ironically had been admitted to the Asian Games thanks to Iranian brokerage, the country to beat. To enhance its chances, Iranian officials persuaded the organizers (allegedly by dispensing liberal amounts of caviar and rugs) to give a medal to each one of a team's players in team sports: thus a victory against Israel would net Iran 17 medals, enough to place second. In the game only Israel scored, but it was an own goal, and so Iran won 1 to 0. Of course rumours immediately circulated that the Israelis had lost intentionally.

Domestically, too, football had a political charge. General Khosravani, a military man with close connections to the regime, was proprietor of a club named Taj (crown) which had a major soccer team. In the football league of Teheran Taj was the perennial rival of another team, Shahin. Taj and its offshoots Afsar and Deyhim (both synonyms of 'crown') were, because of their owner's affiliation with the army, associated with the regime, while Shahin had a more intellectual membership: its owner insisted that players not neglect their studies and many went on to become, to use a Persian expression, 'doctors and engineers'. The rivalry between Taj and Shahin thus had a political dimension, as oppositionists tended to cheer for Shahin. The latter team fell victim to intrigue and was dissolved in 1967, but its players formed a new team, Perspolis.

The rivalry between Perspolis and Taj, the reds and the blues, dominated Iran's pre-revolutionary football scene, especially after a national soccer league was started in 1974 (Takht-e Jamshid Cup); even today, video cassettes of their legendary matches can be purchased in Los Angeles.[80] The two teams had very different playing styles: Perspolis had an English coach and played a more spontaneous game, while Taj's coach was Yugoslav and gave the team a more Central European playing style.

In the 1970s Khosravani built up a chain of about 300 Taj clubs around the country, and the members of these clubs would perform in the annual rallies organized in Iran's stadiums on such occasions as the Shah's or the Crown Prince's birthday. Crown Prince Reza Pahlavi was a Taj fan, and his support for the team was shown during television broadcasts of matches, further identifying Taj with the regime. Also, in the mid-1970s Taj began publishing a sports periodical, which tried to gain readers by printing photos of players in the company of female film stars and singers. These two initiatives gave yet another pretext to religious oppositionists to identify official football as one aspect of the moral corruption propagated by the Pahlavi regime. However, Perspolis, although having a number of religious players on the team, could by no means be identified with the opposition: Princess Fatemeh Pahlavi was one of its major shareholders.[81]

In the last years of the Shah's regime, oppositionists sometimes alleged that the regime actually promoted football to keep the population apolitical, and for some of the Islamists who were beginning to appear on the scene the football craze of the 1970s was a sinister plot by the Shah to divert public attention from 'serious' matters. Upon occasion Islamist militants would even disrupt games.[82] Revolutionaries often have an ascetic streak,[83] and so the idea that pastimes detract from 'serious' pursuits and should therefore be rejected runs through many of them, religious or not.[84] Let us remember the three F's which Portuguese leftists claimed the Salazar regime used to keep people in line: Fátima, Futebol and Fado.[85]

But by the mid-1970s football had taken root in Iran. At the apex of society, the imperial family continued being directly involved in football. The national team's captain in 1947 was Mohammad Khatami, who later became a four-star general, commander of the air force, and a brother-in-law of the Shah,[86] and in the 1970s another close relative of the Shah's, Kambiz Atabay (his uncle was the husband of the Shah's oldest sister, Hamdam al-Saltaneh), came to head the Football Federation, and used his influence to promote the game more efficiently.[87] The Crown Prince, born in 1961, was a keen player and spectator, and often made the minister of court, Amir Asadollah Alam, play with him.[88] But Iranians of *all* social classes were passionately interested in soccer, either as players or as spectators, including seminarians: in Qom, Seyyed Ahmad Khomeini, the Ayatollah's younger son, played in the local Shahin team.

Under the first Pahlavi ruler, the state had promoted football for the educational value ascribed to it, but under the second ruler the game became above all a spectator sport, occasionally used to promote nationalism. This shift in emphasis is congruent with developments elsewhere in the world:

> Educators know that young people can discover in an exemplary fashion the value of joint social membership, obligingness, camaraderie, and fair play, as well as the value of fitness, initiative, vigor, and physical agility thanks to [practicing] football in a pleasant club atmosphere, but that is not 'real' football … 'real' football is the spectator sport.[89]

In the revolutionary upheavals of 1978 athletes played a minor role. Parviz Qelichkhani, arguably the country's best football player at the time, held a press conference in

California, where he played for the San Jose Earthquakes in the now defunct North American Soccer League, to announce that he would not join Iran's national team for the World Cup in Argentina (the first time Iran participated in that championship), to protest against repression in Iran. With the triumph of the revolutionaries in early 1979, soccer fell on hard times.

Football in the Islamic Republic of Iran

At a meeting with sportsmen soon after his return, Ayatollah Khomeini said: 'I am not an athlete but I like athletes', a phrase that became a mantra for sports functionaries of the new regime. But on the whole it is safe to say that sports did not feature very highly on the agenda of the revolutionaries.

Athletic contests are not expressly mentioned in the Koran. One game, *maysir*, is expressly forbidden (2:219 and 5:90-1),[90] and in compendia of jurisprudence the only sports that are mentioned are horse racing and archery, *sabaq* and *ramayah* in Arabic. The reason is that it is permissible for the competitors to bet on the outcome, and for third parties to set a prize.[91] According to the hadith, the Prophet practiced many sports in public, and encouraged his followers to do likewise.[92] Among Shi'ites, the first Imam, Ali b. Abi Taleb, has a formidable reputation as an athlete. But the founders of the Islamic republic were not traditionalists intent on turning the wheel of history back, but puritans reacting against what they saw as the hedonistic excesses of Iran's westernized elites. For instance, equestrian sports were at first frowned upon because of their elitist image, even though horse races are doctrinally approved. Iranians' football fever met with a lot of suspicion on the part of the revolutionaries, a suspicion that had an antecedent in England's experience two centuries earlier. A comparison with the English experience is instructive.

When James I and Charles I of England legalized on Sunday a certain number of popular amusements, contained in the *Book of Sports*, puritans were furious. They accepted sport 'if it served a rational purpose, that of recreation necessary for physical efficiency. But as a means of the spontaneous expression of undisciplined impulses, it was under suspicion; and in so far as it became purely a means of enjoyment, or awakened pride, raw instincts or the irrational gambling instinct, it was of course strictly condemned.'[93] When the Puritans came to power in England they had an opportunity to put theory into practice. 'Between the over-throw of the king and the restoration was much the most thorough-going governmental attempt to amend the sporting habits of the people that [England] has experienced.' But in the end even Oliver Cromwell had to come to terms with what Adam Smith might have called people's natural propensity to play and compete, and sport and games never completely disappeared, except on Sundays.[94]

Religiously inspired puritanism combined with revolutionary asceticism to affect the Islamic Republic's sports policies in the early years after the revolution. Elite sports such as horse racing, fencing and bowling were (temporarily) eliminated. Given the affiliation of many owners of sports clubs with the previous regime, all private clubs were nationalized. Chess, boxing and Kung fu were forbidden, the first because most

Muslim jurists associate it with gambling, the latter two because they inflict physical injury, which is contrary to the shari'a. At the same time martial arts like Karate and Taekwondo were positively encouraged, to the point that training facilities were provided in mosques. Women's sports competitions were discontinued until further notice, the reason being the athletes' insufficient covering during the competitions.[95] In Teheran, as if to avenge Reza Shah's seizing of mosque land to build sports facilities, the football field of Teheran University was appropriated to hold the ritual weekly Friday prayers at which the high theocratic dignitaries of the state address the nation on social and political matters.[96]

As for the major football teams, they were nationalized and renamed after the revolution. Taj became Esteqlal (Independence), and Perspolis became Piruzi (Victory);[97] players were not allowed to wear shirts with Latin letters on them. The rivalry between the 'blues' and the 'reds' continued, and for a while it had a new political dimension: Esteqlal had a few Mojahedin among its members (the club endorsed Mas'ud Rajavi, the leader of the Mojahedin, for the presidential elections in 1980), while Piruzi, which most people never stopped calling Perspolis, was more diverse. With the elimination of political pluralism in the early 1980s, the political dimension of the rivalry disappeared, but the rivalry itself remained and games between the two teams continued attracting huge and intensely partisan crowds.

In early 1980, while the national team was in Bushehr preparing for the Asian Games, it became the target of attacks. Demonstrators chanted the slogan 'The National Team's Training Camp is a Treason to the People', and a local Islamic propaganda organization published a pamphlet that asked:

> Would it not have been better if instead of spending a lot of money on this sort of entertainment, it were spent on sending some of our nation's young people abroad to acquire skills that our country needs? Would it not have been better if instead of spending this innocent and oppressed nation's blood on such useless pursuits, clinics were built and villages electrified? Would it not have been better if instead of clowning around like the British and the Americans in order to 'shine' in international arenas, [the players] shone in the company of the brothers of the Construction Jihad in our villages, where the simplest amenities are lacking? Have all our political, economic, and cultural problems been solved that we have turned to sport?[98]

Not only were they not solved, but soon a new problem was added to them: war.

On 22 September 1980, while the national team was in Kuwait playing in the Asian Nations' Cup, Iraq invaded Iran. Iran lost the game 2-1, inaugurating a long series of losses of the national team in the 1980s.[99] The new head of the national physical education organization said in the autumn that under conditions of war, there was no reason to hold football games.[100] But young men wanted to play, and so the official indifference to soccer led to the growth of improvised neighbourhood games (*gol kuchak*). The popularity of these games in neighbourhoods inhabited by people who formed the social bases of the new regime worried the new men in power, who would have preferred to see youngsters in the mosques rather than on the playing fields. When mosques were not full enough during the Ramadan months of the early 1980s, critical articles began appearing in the press that accused the counterrevolution of organizing these games. As one eye-witness explained it, the popularity of 'little goal' football had no political overtones, but signified merely that playing football was more fun than listening to preachers.[101]

The revolution had put an end to the Takht-e Jamshid Cup, but in 1981 a series of provincial leagues were formed, whose champions would then play each other for the national championship. Reflecting the ideology of the new regime, the cup was called Qods (Jerusalem) Cup. The continued popularity of football riled the fundamentalists, and in the autumn of 1983 an article in the organ of the ruling Islamic Republican Party complained bitterly that during the mourning month of Muharram 110,000 spectators had cheered and clapped for Esteqlal and Perspolis, and that spectator sports were a legacy of the Shah's regime which the revolution should have replaced with participatory sports.[102] A few months later the prime minister echoed this view when he called the cult of champions a legacy of imperialism.[103]

Major football games presented difficulties for the regime. They often led to troubles, and were sometimes cancelled.[104] In a country from which most public entertainment had been banished, attending football matches was one of the few remaining leisure activities for young men. From 1981 on, women were banned from stadiums, and the presence of tens of thousands of frenzied young males occasionally led to riots, one of the worst of which occurred on 9 October 1984. A game that had been scheduled for the Azadi Stadium, where the Asian Games had taken place a decade earlier, had been transferred to the Shahid Shirudi (formerly Amjadiyeh) Stadium in central Teheran because the city did not have enough buses to transport fans to the Azadi sports complex. The Shirudi Stadium has a much smaller capacity, however, and so many ticket holders were denied access to the premises. The game had to be stopped midway, spectators went on a rampage, and 19 were injured in clashes with security forces.[105] The underground or exiled opposition readily ascribed a political significance to the riots which they probably lacked, but like seventeenth-century English Puritans, who reported in 1647 that 'under pretence of football matches [there] have been lately suspicious meetings and assemblies at several places made up of disaffected persons',[106] the Islamic republicans feared large gatherings of excitable young men.[107] Sport per se was a healthy and therefore good thing, but the excitement it generated was not. Following the October riot, the official newspaper of the Islamic Republican Party published an article arguing that the event resulted from pandering to football fever and paying too much attention to European football.[108] A few months later, more research having been done on the incident, another article analyzed the destructive role of football in the Third World, argued that football fever was a colonialist plot, and concluded that the microbes that had befallen Iranian football in the Shah's time were still present. The article claimed that football games between two important clubs begot black markets in tickets and drugs, that the supporters were well organized and had come with prepared chants, and that, worst of all, when members of the Islamic Propaganda Unit tried to get spectators to chant Islamic slogans at the beginning of the match, spectators had made fun of them![109]

However, if the regime tried to stop football, it would antagonize precisely the popular classes on whose support it depended most.[110] The result was constant attempts in the press to contrast traditional Iranian values of chivalry with the commercialization, exploitation and hooliganism that characterize sports in the corrupt West.[111] Football remained the most popular sport among the young, and was a vehicle for carrying Western cultural influence into the country. Maradona's earring, Chris Waddle's haircut, and the German national team's uniforms were all imitated, much to the chagrin of regime hardliners. For the young men increasingly impatient with the officially enforced puritanism, football matches provided a means to vent their frustrations. Football is in many ways a ritual, and shares certain characteristics with a religious ceremony,[112] and it is perhaps precisely because of this that it was perceived as a threat by the hardliners in the regime.

In the late 1980s some of Iran's leaders began to realize that the post-revolutionary policy of frowning on all forms of entertainment was self-defeating, as it gave rise to illicit practices far more objectionable than the ones outlawed. One of the results of this was a greater emphasis on sports, presumably because a *mens sana* resides in a *corpus sanum*. Iranian television was hard pressed to produce programmes that people actually liked, and sporting events seemed innocuous enough, except that neither football players nor wrestlers cover their legs between the navel and the knee, and so conservatives were constantly criticizing the head of the radio and television organization, Mohammad Hashemi, younger brother of Ali-Akbar Rafsanjani. In the end, the matter of sports broadcasts was referred to Imam Khomeini himself, who in late 1987 issued a fatwa authorizing television not only to broadcast films featuring not totally covered women, but also sports events, provided viewers watched without lust.[113] After this ruling sports coverage expanded to the point where in 1993 a third channel was set up which broadcasts mainly sports. This policy still occasionally ran into opposition from revolutionary purists, for instance in 1994, when the coverage of the football World Cup in the United States prompted the newspaper *Jomhuri-ye eslami* to write that by broadcasting the games, television provided propaganda for America, Iran's enemy.[114]

A few months after the war with Iraq ended in 1988, it was in Kuwait that the national teams of Iran and Iraq played to a draw, in a show of peace replete with white pigeons. Politicians were finally becoming alert to the use of football.[115] In 1989 a new national soccer league was formed, and it was named Lig-e Azadegan, after the POWs who had come home. But the league does not function regularly: teams that play in international championships are excused from playing as often as others, leading to highly unconventional decisions that are regularly criticized by other teams and the press.[116] Football teams having been nationalized, the Armenian club Ararat was for a long time the only privately owned club, but in 1994 a new club, Bahman, was founded in Karaj and became quite successful for a while. The remaining top clubs are attached to companies, many of them state-owned, ministries, or other state organs. Perspolis is now attached to the ministry of industry, while its perennial rival Esteqlal is attached to the organization of physical education.[117] Other teams' names reflect their affiliations: Traktorsazi-ye Tabriz (Tabriz tractor works), San'at-e Naft-e Abadan (Abadan oil industry), Fulad-e Khuzestan (Khuzistan steel), and, reflecting Isfahan's role as cradle of Iran's textile industry, Poliakril-e Esfahan (Isfahan polyacrylic).[118]

In the early 1990s women's sports were revived through the initiative of Fa'ezeh Rafsanjani, the daughter of the then president, who scored very well in the 1996 parliamentary elections. After the existence of women's sports became an established fact,[119] the dossier of women's presence at male games was reopened. In July 1994, on the occasion of preliminary matches in the Asian Youth Cup, it was announced that women could attend football matches. The conservative newspaper *Resalat* objected to this, on the grounds that the disputes, fights and foul language prevalent at football matches made them inappropriate venues for families, an allusion to the bawdy chants of sports fans that usually elaborate metonymically on the fact that in a team sport the object of each team is to penetrate the other side.[120] *Jomhuri-ye eslami*, objected to women watching men in shorts. Nonetheless, on 18 July about 500 women, placed in a special section of the stadium separate from the men, attended a game between India and Bahrain. Only three days later the football federation rescinded its decision, stating that unfortunately some football fans had not been able to adapt themselves to the Islamic and humane norms that governed Iranian society: apparently a few women had encircled players and asked for their autographs.[121] The controversy would not go away, however, and on 22 February 1995, the head of the Physical Education Organization announced that he was personally in favour of allowing women to attend football matches but not wrestling and swimming events, in which men are not 'appropriately dressed'. Conservatives disagreed. The weekly sports paper *Pahlavan* pointed out that according to the shari'a obligatory coverage for a man extended from the knee to the navel, whereas the shorts of football players left players' thighs uncovered. To settle the question, the paper asked Iran's Supreme Leader, Ayatollah Ali Khameneh'i, for a fatwa on whether it was permissible (for men) to play team sports dressed in T-shirts and shorts in the presence of unrelated women, and whether women could watch them if they did not feel lust. On both issues Khameneh'i ruled that 'an unrelated women may not look at the naked body of an unrelated man, even if the intent is not deriving lust'.[122] Even this restriction did not satisfy one particularly sensitive cleric, Hojjat al-Islam Qara'ati, who called on Iranian athletes to foreswear shorts and tight-fitting uniforms.[123]

Gradually, then, Iran's rulers came to accept that football was undoubtedly Iran's most popular sport. By the early 1990s a number of companies were specializing in selling football videos, posters and magazines. International football lore was eagerly adopted by young Iranians in spite of all the government's exhortations to resist the West's 'cultural aggression'. Even newspapers published by regime figures report extensively on international football, so much so that in 1993 the head of the Wrestling Federation, who doubled as Iranian Defense Minister, said in an interview that although the only sport in which Iran was successful internationally was wrestling, the press emphasized football, adding: 'if we're not careful, football will destroy wrestling'.[124] It is only natural that the two disciplines became entangled in the factional struggles of the 1990s. The newspaper *Salam*, spokespiece of the more liberal wing of the regime until it was closed down, emphasized football in its sports coverage, while *Resalat*, the organ of the conservatives, stressed wrestling.[125] In the presidential election of May 1997, many football players endorsed Mohammad Khatami, while

Ali-Akbar Nateq Nuri, the official candidate after whose martyred brother a major annual wrestling tournament is named, was endorsed by some of the country's top wrestlers. Khatami won with a landslide.

The greater support of the state for sport in general and soccer in particular after the end of the Iran/Iraq War led to an improved performance of the national team in the early 1990s. At the 1990 Asian Games in Beijin the Iranian team won the gold medal, which was a turning point for the sport.[126] The man who had led the national team to victory, Ali Parvin, was himself a popular former player of pre-revolutionary times, but he ran afoul of the hard-line head of the football federation, who reportedly resented the renewed ascendancy of pre-revolutionary figures, and was made to resign after a series of defeats in 1994.[127] In the second half of 1997 football fever in Iran acquired a political importance due to the openness with which the political struggle between the different factions in Iran was being carried out. The head coach of Iran's national team, Mayeli-Kohan, who was identified with the conservative faction, did not allow some of Iran's star players, who played in German *Bundesliga* teams, to join the national team. The result was a dismal performance of the team in the last qualifying games for the World Cup, where the team almost snatched defeat from the claws of victory. When Iran lost 2-0 against Qatar in Doha on 7 November, the matter became an affair of state and was discussed in parliament. Mayeli-Kohan was dismissed and replaced by the recently-arrived Brazilian head coach of Iran's Olympic football team, Valdeir Vieira, a former head coach of the Costa Rican national team. Under his supervision the team achieved two ties against Australia, allowing it to become the thirty-second and last team to qualify for the World Cup.

When the news of the 'victory' reached Iranians around the globe, there was celebration everywhere. As soon as the referee blew the final whistle, people poured into the streets in Teheran and the country's other big cities and celebrated, defying the official insistence on sombreness in public places.[128] In Ardabil, Tabriz and Mashhad people went to the homes of the parents of Iran's star players, Ali Da'i, Karim Baqeri, and Khodadad Azizi, and honoured their parents. The celebrations have to be interpreted in light of the presidential election of May 1997. By December the millions who had cast their ballot for Mohammad Khatami felt that the change they had voted for was being stymied by the political establishment, and they jumped on an opportunity to let off steam that was patriotic in nature, since joy about one's own country's success is nothing the regime could very well criticize. But the newspaper *Jomhuri-ye eslami*, ever the guardian of ideological purity, characterized the celebrations as a 'cultural fall' (*soghut-e farhangi*).[129]

From Melbourne the team flew to Dubai, where they were acclaimed by thousands of Iranian expatriates. Before the return of Iran's athletes to Iran the government asked people not to greet them at the airport, as is customary, but to proceed to the big Azadi Stadium, whither the footballers would be taken by helicopter. Except that the sexual segregation at stadiums was to be upheld: 'sisters' were asked to stay at home and watch the event on television. In spite of this, of the 70,000 fans who turned up at the stadium to greet the returning heroes, about 5,000 were women – they literally crashed the gates.[130] The mingling of the sexes at the stadium was of course a break of post-revolutionary practice, and it was reported that a few women took off their veils in defiance of the very strict dress codes that have been enforced since 1981. A football stadium, wrote Bromberger, 'is one of those rare spaces where collective emotions are unleashed …, where socially taboo values are allowed to be expressed'.[131] In the aftermath of this event, the feminist press pressed the issue of women's presence at soccer matches, arguing that women should be allowed to voice patriotic feelings as well.[132]

In January 1998 Valdeir Vieira, in spite of his popularity, was sacked, and a Croatian, Tomislav Ivic, was chosen instead to coach the national team.[133] But under the pressure of conservatives he was dismissed in May 1998 and replaced by an Iranian who had returned after a long stay abroad to coach the rising team of Teheran, Bahman.[134] The interval between Iran's qualification for the World Cup in November 1997 and the game with the United States in Lyons on 21 June 1998 was marked by intense infighting among Iran's sport functionaries. But in the end followers of President Khatami emerged victorious, and before the Cup spokesmen for the team proclaimed that they would surprise the world. The tradition of Takhti now came in: it provided a reservoir of values and attitudes embedded in traditional Iranian culture that could be called upon to correct the image of the 'ugly Iranian'. In France the Iranian players came to the grounds well groomed and clean shaven,[135] and presented their counterparts with a bouquet of flowers before each game. The United States-Iran game had been built up to a grudge match by the media, but American and Iranian officials had instructed players to be courteous, and FIFA, the world governing body of football, had declared 21 June 'Fair Play Day'. President Clinton taped a message that was broadcast before the game, a message in which he expressed the hope that the game would be a 'step toward ending the estrangement between our nations'.[136] When the big moment came, the two teams exchanged gifts and eschewed the customary pre-game team photos in favour of a joint one with the 22 players intermingled. The two teams jointly received the FIFA Fair Play award on 1 February 1999.

In Iran, people celebrated the victory of their team rather than the defeat of the United States, and public revelry was devoid of any anti-American flavour. Again, the joyous atmosphere was in direct defiance of the culture of mourning and sobriety that hardliners in the regime promoted.[137] Elsewhere in the Middle East, however, crowds celebrated the defeat of the United States, especially in the Shi'ite areas of Lebanon and in the West Bank. In the United States, the game was hardly noticed.

There was hope that this game, and others that followed, might lead to a thaw in US-Iranian relations. While in the United States, President Clinton congratulated the Iranian team on its victory, in Iran the official reaction was Janus-faced, like the government. President Khatami put the accent on sportsmanship and commented that 'what counts is the endeavor, hard work, solidarity, skill and intellect displayed by our young people', but admitted that 'of course, one feels even happier when the result of this worthy endeavor is victory'. Ayatollah Ali Khameneh'i, by contrast, likened the victory to the revolution and the war against Iraq, and stated: 'tonight, again, the strong and arrogant opponent felt the bitter taste of defeat at your hands'.[138] In the end, nothing came of 'sports diplomacy' at the state-to-state level,[139] but in Iran the celebration had a cathartic effect. For Iranian youth, Iranian participation at the World Cup meant that their pariah nation had rejoined the international community, and parallels were drawn between *Jam-e jahani* (World Cup) and *Jame'eh-ye jahani* (world society). The integration of Iranians in world society was symbolically furthered when, in the aftermath of the 1998 World Cup, many top Iranian players started playing in foreign soccer teams, mostly in Germany, where long-time Iranian residents began acting as middlemen and agents.[140] Soccer fans in Iran now had an emotional stake in the fortunes of European football teams. Conversely, some Iranian players abroad, like Khodadad Azizi, used their newly acquired wealth to fund projects at home.[141]

The soccer fever of the late 1990s undoubtedly gave a boost to national integration in Iran. Secular and religious Iranians, men and women, people from the capital and from the provinces, were all united in their support of the national team, and followed its uneven fortunes with joy and anxiety. This enthusiasm was even shared by members of the Iranian diaspora, whose relations with their home country have not always been free of tension.

In the autumn of 2001 the Iranian national team fared badly in the qualifying matches for the 2002 World Cup. Again people poured into the streets, this time to vent their frustrations. Disappointment over the team's loss mingled with disappointment over the stalled reform in Iran, and, fuelled by Persian-language radio broadcasts from Los Angeles, rumours circulated that the government had deliberately instructed the national team to lose so as to prevent a repetition of the celebrations of 1998. The demonstrations turned into riots in which a number of buildings were ransacked; hundreds were arrested.[142] In 2002, the prohibition on women attending football games was selectively lifted when the team of Ireland played Iran in another World Cup qualifying game in Teheran. On that occasion Irish women were allowed to attend, but Iranian women were not – the argument being that the fans from Ireland would not understand the foul language of the male Iranian spectators in the stadium.[143]

Violence erupted again on 25 March 2005, when the Iranian team beat the Japanese team in Teheran in a qualifying match for the 2006 World Cup. Five people were trampled to death, 40 more were injured, and 100 buses were damaged after the game.[144] That young Iranians should pour into the streets both when their team won and when it lost is not astonishing, for

> [f]ootball is full of vicarious achievement and vicarious 'frustration'. Where achievement is frustrated, the 'unjustified defeat' is usually ambiguous enough to permit further argument and redefinition, in similar style to for the ways in which religious systems have previously legitimized other hostile worlds to their adherents … Just as sects developed as 'religions of the oppressed', so football offers an attractive and exciting interlude to those whose economic or 'profane' life is dominated by lack of hope, lack of realistic ambition, and lack of any means through which they can feel achievement or fulfilment.[145]

Conclusion

As this article has attempted to show, the history of football in Iran has been intimately intertwined with politics, both domestic and international. Successive Iranian regimes have tried to use sports for internal and external legitimation. But under both the Pahlavi and the Islamic regime this effort has been hampered by the appalling state of the sports bureaucracies, which have been inefficient, corrupt, nepotistic, and riven by personal rivalries and jealousies. The rapid turnover of functionaries has made planning all but impossible. While it is perhaps exaggerated to claim that 'sports is one of the disaster areas of the Iranian way of life',[146] the fact that Iranian athletes gain any medals at all at international competitions is a minor miracle, if one compares the conditions under which they train with the facilities at the disposal of people in industrialized nations. The head of the Iranian Football Federation in 1998, summarized the woes of Iranian football as follows: the state does not provide sufficient support, there are no real clubs, and state enterprises that sponsor a club do so illegally, and their directors can be taken to task, there are far too few grass-covered playing fields, ticket prices are too low to generate any significant revenue, there are no scientific centres to help players enhance their performance, the input of the educational system is nil, and Iran has no voice at the international level.[147]

There can be little doubt that it was the Pahlavi state that created contemporary Iran's 'field of sport practices', to use Bourdieu's term.[148] But once created, a demand was generated for the products of this field that survived the demise of the monarchy. The passion for football became a sign of dissent, and its manifestations reflected the counterculture that the official puritanism generated.[149]

The privileging of team sports, especially football, was initially a deliberate act to foster the spirit of cooperation among Iranians. Durkheim recognizes that the passing of mechanical solidarity does not necessarily herald the advent of organic solidarity, and can instead lead to what he termed 'anomie'.[150] It would seem that social change in Iran has produced at least as much anomie as organic solidarity. A sports team is ideally more than the sum of its parts, but in Iran one has the uncanny impression that the team is at times less than the sum of its parts. In the 1930s an English observer wrote about football players in Kerman that while the idea of team-spirit was growing, 'on less important occasions … some men will not pass the ball'.[151] Three decades later, the American basketball coach of the national Iranian team noted in 1967 that he had to work with individuals who related atomistically. The key relationships, he reported, were not cooperative patterns of teamwork but rather competitive interpersonal relationships that extended well beyond the basketball court.[152]

Another facet of anomie is the violence all too often displayed by spectators. Conservatives have a point when they show that from the attack on the headquarters of *Nahid* to the scuffles that regularly mar soccer matches in Iran there is a long thread of violence that weaves through the history of Iranian football.[153] But even writers critical of the conservative establishment have recently become more candid about the violence that attends many games, especially those that pit the 'Reds' and the 'Blues' against each other.[154] The hostility between Esteqlal/Taj and Perspolis fans would remind one of the traditional rivalry between urban heydari and ne'mati factions in Iranian cities,[155] were it not for the fact that such hostility is endemic in the world of soccer and by no means unique to Iran. The triumph of football worldwide is a facet of the globalization of culture,[156] and by now football has conquered most of the world with the exception of the United States of America, but even there it is progressing steadily.[157] The game's persistent popularity in Iran shows that Iranians' insertion in global culture has continued unabated.

Acknowledgements

I thank Kamran Aghaie, Peter Alegi, Mehdi Bozorgmehr, Michel Chaouli, Sadreddin Elahi, Parviz Ghelichkhani, Najmedin Meshkati, Sharif Nezam-Mafi, Philippe Rochard, Leyla Rouhi, Manouchehr Sabeti, Cyrus Schayegh, Sunil Sharma, Asghar Shirazi, Amir Soltani, and Mostafa Zamani-Nia for their help and suggestions. All interpretations are mine.

Notes

[1]   *The Economist*, 13 Dec. 1997, 37.
[2]   Pickford, 'Aspects of the Psychology of Games and Sports', 285. For an analysis of how military metaphors pervade the language of football see Küster, 'Kriegsspiele – Militärische Metaphern im Fußballsport', 53–70. See also Bromberger, *Le Match de football*, chapter 15, 'Où il est question de guerre, de vie, de mort, de sexe, de l'autre'.
[3]   For a discussion of the bellicose dimension of football see Kuper, *Football against the Enemy*. For an interesting perspective on the short war between El Salvador and Honduras, see Kapuściński, *The Soccer War*, Chap. 'The Soccer War,' pp.157–84. For a study of football in Latin America see Mason, *Passion of the People?*
[4]   See Malek-Mohammadi, *Varzeshha-ye sonnati, bumi va mahalli*.
[5]   See Rochard, 'The Identities of the *Zûkhânah*'.
[6]   See Chehabi and Guttmann, 'From Iran to all of Asia'.
[7]   See Banuazizi, 'Iranian National Character'.
[8]   See for instance Harnack, *Persian Lions, Persian Lamb: An American's Odyssey in Iran*, 121–37.
[9]   Chehabi, 'Sport and Politics in Iran'. Although I tried to analyze the legend objectively, I was myself misled to some extent by the hagiographic nature of some of my sources. For an insider's account of how the legend was created by Iranian oppositionists, see Sharif, 'Az insan ta ostureh'.
[10] Lever, *Soccer Madness*, 29.
[11] See, for instance, Patrick, 'The Psychology of Football'.
[12] Buytendijk, *Le Football: Une étude psychologique*, 48–9.
[13] See Durkheim, *The Division of Labor in Society*, 31–87.
[14] Bromberger, 'Football as World-view and as Ritual', 296.
[15] Christian Bromberger, 'De quoi parlent les sports?', *Terrain*, 25 Sept. 1995, 6. See also his 'Football, drame, société', 12–19.
[16] In recent years a plethora of books has come out that document almost every single game played in Iran. See Afrasiabi, *Sardaran-e pa beh tup*; Yekta and Nurinezhad, *Tarikh-e futbal-e Iran*; Sadr, *Ruzi, ruzegari, futbal*, 15–90; and Abbasi, *Futbal-r Iran*.
[17] On Jahn see Überhorst, *Zurück zu Jahn*.
[18] On Ling, see Diem, *Weltgeschichte des Sports und der Leibeserziehungen*, 793–5 and Lindroth, 'The History of Ling Gymnastics in Sweden. A Research Survey'.
[19] Sadri, *Tarikh-e varzesh*, 138–9. Sadri calls the Russian method *zakolski*, which in all probability refers to Sokol gymnastics.
[20] See Schayegh, 'Sport, Health, and the Iranian Modern Middle Class in the 1920s and 1930s'.
[21] Sadri, *Tarikh-e varzesh*, 138–9.

[22]   'Khiyalat', 1, emphasis added. Iran was of course not the only country in which reformers associated national effeteness with insufficient taste for physical exercise. For the case of France, see Weber, *France, Fin de Siècle*, Chap. 11, 'Faster, Higher, Stronger'. For India, see Rosselli, 'The Self-image of Effeteness'.

[23]   For the text of the law, see *Ta'lim va tarbiyat*, 3, 7–8, 1 or Sadri, *Tarikh-e varzesh*, 139. For a glimpse of Ling's reception in Iran see M.M.T.T., 'Ling: sha'er va varzeshkar 1776–1839', 15–16, 58.

[24]   Sadri, *Tarikh-e varzesh*, 140, 142.

[25]   Ibid., 139 and Sadri, *Danesh-e varzesh*, 43.

[26]   On the export of football by Britain to the rest of the world, see Guttmann, *Games & Empires*, 41–70; and Walvin, *The People's Game*, Chap. 5, 'Britain's Most Durable Export', 96–117; and Mason, *Passion of the People?*, Chap. 2, 'English Lessons', 15–26.

[27]   Fişek, 'The Genesis of Sports Administration in Turkey', 626.

[28]   Sparroy, *Persian Children of the Royal Family*, 255–6. I am grateful to John Gurney for bringing this book to my attention.

[29]   See, for instance, Howard, *A Merry Mountaineer*, 82–3. I am grateful to J.A. Mangan for this reference.

[30]   Vosuq, *Dastan-e zendagi: Khaterati az panjah sal tarikh-e mo'aser 1290–1340*, 15.

[31]   In the 1930s, for instance, soccer was also the major sport at the Syrian Protestant College, later renamed American University of Beirut. Penrose, Jr., *That They May Have Life*, 286.

[32]   See J. Armajani, 'Alborz College', *EIr*.

[33]   Boyce, 'Alborz College of Tehran and Dr. Samuel Martin Jordan, Founder and President', 193–4, 198.

[34]   Jordan, 'Constructive Revolutions in Iran', 350–1.

[35]   Williamson, *In a Persian Oil Field*, 164. For the 'international' character of games between England and Scotland see Moorhouse, 'One State, Several Countries', 55–74.

[36]   This, incidentally, was also an issue in Europe around the same time. In 1913 the yearbook of the German football association carried an article complaining about the shorts worn by football players, which it deemed *sittlich empörend* (morally disgraceful), and suggested that players wear trousers that did not constrain the knees but covered the thigh muscles. Egger, '"Sportswear": Zur Geschichte der Sportkleidung', 136.

[37]   Cf. pre-modern European games in which players kicked an inflated pig's bladder around. Elias, 'Der Fußballsport im Prozeß der Zivilisation', 16.

[38]   Yekta and Nurinezhad, *Tarikh*, 19–22; *Keyhan-e varzeshi*, no.631 (1967–68), 10, as quoted in Sarvestani, 'Dastan-e varzesh-e modern'.

[39]   Sadri, *Tarikh-e varzesh*, 153. Sadri was the secretary of the association.

[40]   Safari, *Ardabil dar gozargah-e tarikh*, 240.

[41]   Abbasi, *Futbal-e Iran*, 17–23. The original police reports are reproduced.

[42]   *Akhbar*, 19 July 1998, 5. On the traditional footwear of Iran see Jamshid Sadaqat-Kish, 'Giva', *EIr*.

[43]   Abbasi, *Futbal-e Iran*, 76.

[44]   Yekta and Nurinezhad, *Tarikh*, 34–5, 41.

[45]   Ibid., 38. Apparently Reza Shah was so upset by the first British goal that he wanted to leave the game, but was deterred by an army officer who argued that the ruler's departure would discourage the players. He stayed, and the Iranians scored two goals. Sadr, *Ruzi, ruzegari, futbal*, 21–2 and 84n, 13.

[46]   The entire correspondence between various ministries is reproduced in Abbasi, *Futbal-e Iran*, 25–56.

[47]   *Keyhan-e varzeshi*, no.631 (1967–68), 10, as quoted in Sarvestani, 'Dastan-e varzesh-e modern'; and Yekta and Nurinezhad, *Tarikh*, 56.

[48]   *Keyhan-e Varzeshi*, no. 637, as quoted in Sadr, *Ruzi, ruzegari, futbal*, 24–25.

[49]   For the significance of these games for Soviet diplomacy see Peppard and Riordan, *Playing Politics*, 101.

[50]   Yekta and Nurinezhad, *Tarikh*, 78–9.

[51]   Ibid., 22–3.

[52]   Ibid., 92.

[53]   *Ettela'at*, 4 Jan. 1934, 2, as quoted in Yekta and Nurinezhad, *Tarikh*, 103.

[54]   Yekta and Nurinezhad, *Tarikh*, 106–8.

[55]   Hajj-Azimi and Azadpanah, *Tarikh-e varzesh-e Iran*, 135.

[56]   *Tehran Mosavvar*, 14 Dec. 1929, 9, as quoted in Yekta and Nurinezhad, *Tarikh*, 77.

[57]   Hajj-Azimi and Azadpanah, *Tarikh-e varzesh-e Iran*, 137.

[58]   'Akharin jashn-e mosabeqeh-ye futbal', *Ta'lim va tarbiyat*, 117. See also *Ta'lim va tarbiyat* 5, 9–10, 549–51.

[59]   Sadiq, *Yadegar-e omr: Khaterati az sargozasht*, 172.

[60]   *Tarikh-e farhang-e Azarbayjan*, 318. When the German Orientalist Walther Hinz visited Ardabil in 1938, the local director of education (representative of the ministry of education) 'proudly showed [him] photos of football teams he had created'. Hinz, *Iranische Reise: Eine Forschungsfahrt durch das heutige Persien*, 60.

[61]   For details, see Yekta and Nurinezhad, *Tarikh*, 162–250.

[62]   de Villiers, *L'Irresistible ascension de Mohammad Reza Shah d'Iran*, 69–70. See also His Imperial Majesty Mohammed Reza Shah Pahlavi Shahanshah of Iran, *Mission for my Country*, 53 and 60, where the Shah writes that he 'was very proud of winning prizes in … throwing the discus, putting the shot, throwing the javelin, the high jump, the long jump, and the 100-metres'.

[63]   'Sherkat-e valahazrat-e homayun velayat-e ahd dar mosabeqehha-ye futbal', 796–9.

[64]   Yekta and Nurinezhad, *Tarikh*, 325, 350–1.

[65]   Sadr, *Ruzi, ruzigari, futbal*, 25.

[66]   Merrit-Hawkes, *Persia: Romance and Reality*, 164–5. The practice of covering one's head made hitting the ball with the head difficult, and the author reports that at one game he witnessed the boys would 'come on the field wearing their hats, and…take them off only when they thought they could get in a hit'. Ibid., 166.

[67]   Ashna, ed., *Khoshunat va farhang: Asnad-e mahramaneh-ye kashf-e hejab (1313–1322)*, 30. According to Sadreddin Elahi, one of Iran's foremost scholars of sport, Kashani may have been thinking of a sport field that had been established on the abandoned cemetery of Emamzadeh Yahya in the Udlajan quarter of Teheran.

[68]   Sadri, *Tarikh-e varzesh*, 155.

[69]   Sadr, *Ruzi, ruzegari, futbal*, 30–1. In the end Iran did not send a delegation to these games at all, probably because Indonesia had incurred the displeasure of the International Olympic Committee by refusing to invite Israel and the Republic of China. Ru'inpur, *Iran dar baziha-ye asia'i*, 97–9.

[70]   As is well known, Calcutta is the football capital of cricket-loving India. See Mason, 'Football on the Maidan'.

[71]   Sadr, *Ruzi, ruzegari, futbal*, 31–3.

[72]   Giulianotti and Armstrong, 'Introduction: Reclaiming the Game – An Introduction to the Anthropology of Football', 12.

[73]   Reppa, *Israel and Iran*.

[74]   The football matches between Iran and Israel and their impact on Iranian Jews are discussed in greater detail in Chehabi, 'Jews and Sport in Modern Iran'.

[75]   Thaiss, 'Religious Symbolism and Social Change', 226–7. The story was confirmed to me by informants in Iran.

[76]   Lewis, *Semites and Anti-Semites*.

[77]   This conforms to a widespread pattern of football matches experienced by the spectators as substitutes for war. See Kuper, *Football against the Enemy*, especially the Introduction,

which relates Dutch reactions to the 1988 victory of the Netherlands' team against the German team, a victory that was celebrated by otherwise quite reasonable and liberal-minded people as a revenge for the German occupation of the Netherlands more than four decades earlier.

[78]   This is confirmed by the fact that when bazaar merchants collected money to buy gifts for the Iranian players after the game, they refused to accept the contribution of Jewish merchants, ostensibly on religious grounds. Thaiss, 'Religious Symbolism', 227.

[79]   On 16 September 1974 Alam noted in his diary that on the final day of the Asian Games, Iran had come second, which corresponded to the Shah's wish that in Asia there should be two developed nations, Japan in the East and Iran in the West. *Yaddashtha-ye Alam*, 197–8.

[80]   The other major football rivalry is between the teams of Bandar Anzali and Rasht, an expression of the rivalry between the two main cities of Gilan province. This sort of rivalry between two teams in the same city or region is very common, to wit the Celtics and Rangers in Glasgow, Boca Juniors and River Plate in Buenos Aires, Hapoel and Maccabi in Tel Aviv, etc.

[81]   Manouchehr Sabeti, personal communication.

[82]   I have this information from Ali Moradi, who as an Islamist militant disrupted football games in Isfahan. Personal communication, Berlin, March 1993.

[83]   This is analyzed in Mazlish, *The Revolutionary Ascetic*.

[84]   For a left-leaning analysis of Brazil's football craze see Lever, 'Soccer: Opium of the Brazilian People'.

[85]   Fátima refers to the site on which the Virgin Mary appeared to three shepherd children in 1917, and Fado is the popular music of Lisbon and Coïmbra. In Spain see Shaw, *Fútbol y Franquismo*.

[86]   Sadr, *Ruzi, ruzegari, futbal*, 29.

[87]   Ibid., 37

[88]   Alikhani, ed., *Yaddashtha-ye Alam*, 376; Ibid., vol.3, 194–5; and Ibid., vol.4, 321.

[89]   Buytendijk, *Le Football*, 17.

[90]   See Beeston, 'The Game of *maysir* and some Modern Parallels'.

[91]   See, for instance, Hoseyni, *Tarjomeh va towzih-e Lom'eh*, volume 2, 393–6.

[92]   Naciri, 'Die Einstellung des Islam zum Sport', 652–4.

[93]   Weber, *The Protestant Ethic and the Spirit of Capitalism*, 166–7.

[94]   Brailsford, 'Puritanism and Sport in Seventeenth Century England', 324–5.

[95]   *Ettela'at-e haftegi*, 23.

[96]   I am grateful to Hamid Dabashi for pointing this out to me.

[97]   Which led supporters of both teams to cover the walls of Teheran with somewhat counter-intuitive graffiti like 'death to Independence' and 'death to Victory'!

[98]   *Keyhan-e varzeshi*, No.1327, 9 Feb. 1980, as quoted in Sadr, *Ruzi, ruzegari, futbal*, 43–4.

[99]   Sadr, *Ruzi, ruzegari, futbal*, 47.

[100] *Keyhan-e varzeshi*, no.1366, 6 Dec. 1980, as quoted in Sadr, *Ruzi, ruzegari, futbal*, 44.

[101] Personal communication.

[102] *Jomhuri-ye eslami*, 19 Oct. 1983, 11.

[103] *Jomhuri-ye eslami*, 8 March 1984, 15.

[104] Sadr, *Ruzi, ruzegari, futbal*, 44–7.

[105] The events were analyzed in detail in a series of articles in *Keyhan*, 10 Oct. 1984, 19; 11 Oct. 1984, 19; 13 Oct. 1984, 23; 14 Oct. 1984, 19.

[106] Quoted in Brailsford, 'Puritanism and Sport in Seventeenth Century England', 325.

[107] Interestingly enough, nine decades earlier the government of Sultan Abdülhamit had forbidden football games played by non-foreigners in Istanbul on the same grounds, and disbanded the first Turkish football clubs (Black Stockings and Kadiköy) before the first game was over. Fişek, 'The Genesis of Sports Administration in Turkey', 626.

[108] *Jomhuri-ye eslami*, 11 Oct. 1984, 10.

[109] *Jomhuri-ye eslami*, 13 Dec. 1984, 5; and 24 Dec. 1984, 7.

[110]   It is noteworthy that Iranian adolescent POWs at an Iraqi prison camp, who had volunteered for the war, knew all about British football, and that soccer competitions were one of the main attractions of camp life. Brown, *Khomeini's Forgotten Sons*, 9, 54, 57, 74–5.

[111]   For instance two articles titled 'The Role of Politics in Football' in *Jomhuri-ye eslami*, 20 May 1986, 5; and 21 May 1986, 5, which called football an instrument of imperialism.

[112]   The similarities between attending a football match and attending a religious ritual are explored in Coles, 'Football as a "Surrogate"' Religion?'; and Bromberger, 'Football as World-view and as Ritual', 305–11.

[113]   *Resalat*, 22 Dec. 1987, 1 and 2. Khomeini merely acknowledged what is well known but not commonly talked about in the West. See Guttmann, *The Erotic in Sport*.

[114]   The article also claimed that because of these broadcasts government employees came to work tired, having stayed up all night to watch TV. *Iran Times*, 15 July 1994, 6 and 12. On that world cup see Sugden and Tomlinson, eds., *Hosts and Champions*.

[115]   Sadr, *Ruzi, ruzegari, futbal*, 50.

[116]   Paul, 'Der iranische Spitzenfußball und seine sozialen und politischen Dimensionen', 77–8.

[117]   Gilles Paris, 'Tout Téhéran vibre pour les "Rouges" du Pirouzi', *Le Monde*, 25 June 1998, III.

[118]   Paul, 'Der iranische Spitzenfußball', 79; and Bromberger, 'Le football en Iran', 107.

[119]   Women's soccer was declared to be unobjectionable by a number of senior clerics in 1998, and in 1999 the first female indoor tournament was held. But no men were allowed to attend.

[120]   This is a worldwide phenomenon and has received considerable scholarly attention. See Alan Dundes, 'Into the Endzone for a Touchdown'; Suárez-Orozco, 'A Study of Argentine Soccer'.

[121]   *Iran Times*, 15 July 1994, 6 and 12; 29 July 1994, 6 and 14.

[122]   *Pahlavan*, 29 Aug. 1995, 7.

[123]   *Iran Times*, June 1998, at a seminar on sport and spirituality.

[124]   Interview *Arzesh*, 19 July 1993, 12.

[125]   This division parallels the situation in Turkey, where football is the emblematic sport of the secularists, while wrestling is preferred by more tradition people. See Stokes, 'Strong as a Turk'.

[126]   Sadr, *Ruzi, ruzegari, futbal*, 50–3.

[127]   Morteza Qolamzadeh, 'Whatever Happened to Ali Parvin?', available at <http://www.iranian.com/Nov95/Parvin.html>.

[128]   Bromberger, 'Le football en Iran', 102.

[129]   Ibid., 103.

[130]   *The Independent*, 6 Dec. 1997, 22. This may also have been because the government had given boys' schools a day off, but not girls' schools.

[131]   Bromberger, 'Football as World-view and as Ritual', 302.

[132]   See, for instance, *Zan~n*, no. 39 (}b~n-} Oct.–Dec. 1997).

[133]   *Iran Times*, 16 Jan. 1998, 2 and 23 Jan. 1998, 1.

[134]   From 1973 to 1976 the national team had been managed by the Manchster United coach Frank O'Farrel, but those were more cosmopolitan days.

[135]   N[awid] K[ermani], 'Gut rasiert', 32.

[136]   Jere Longman, 'Diplomacy and Urgency as the U.S. Faces Iran', *The New York Times*, 21 June 1996, C2.

[137]   Elaine Sciolino, 'Singing, Dancing and Cheering in Street of Teheran', *The New York Times*, 22 June 1998, C9; and Yaghmaian, *Social Change in Iran*, 49–54.

[138]   *Iran Times*, 26 June 1998, 2.

[139]   For a more detailed account, see Chehabi, 'US-Iranian Sports Diplomacy'.

[140]   Hans-Günther Klemm, 'Traum aus 1001 Nacht', *Kicker: Sonderheft* (1998), 74 and Hans-Günter Klemm, 'Deutschland als Ziel, Daei als Pionier', *Frankfurter Allgemeine Zeitung*, 20 Aug. 1999, 39.

[141]   Bromberger, 'Le football en Iran', 108.
[142]   Nazila Fathi, 'Soccer Melees Keep Erupting in Iran, With a Political Message', *New York Times*, 26 Oct. 2001, A7.
[143]   Fozooni, 'Religion, Politics and Class', 367.
[144]   *RFE/RL Iran Report*, Vol.8, No.13 (30 March 2005).
[145]   Coles, 'Football as a "Surrogate" Religion?', 75.
[146]   Forbis, *Fall of the Peacock Throne*, 170. For a revealing aperçu of sports life under the Shah see pp.170–4.
[147]   Hashemi-Taba, *Dastan-e yek so'ud*, 102–6.
[148]   Bourdieu, 'Comment peut-on être sportif?'.
[149]   On the concept of counter-culture in contemporary Iran, see Schirazi, 'Gegenkultur als Ausdruck der Zivilgesellschaft in der Islamischen Republik Iran', 135–63.
[150]   Durkheim, *The Division of Labor in Society*, 291–309.
[151]   Merrit-Hawkes, *Persia, Romance and Reality*, 165.
[152]   Bill, 'The Plasticity of Informal Politics', 139–40, quoting Donald J. Linehan, who coached Iran's team 1966–67.
[153]   See, for instance, Sarvestani, 'Dastan-e varzesh-e modern'.
[154]   Sadr, *Ruzi, ruzegari, futbal*, 74–80.
[155]   On this phenomenon, see Perry, 'Artificial Antagonism in Pre-Modern Iran'; Perry, 'Toward a Theory of Iranian Urban Moieties'.
[156]   Guttmann, *Games & Empires*, Chap. 2.
[157]   See Markovits and Hellerman, *Soccer & American Exceptionalism*.

References

'Akharin jashn-e mosabeqeh-ye futbal.' *Ta'lim va tarbiyat 4*, no. 2 April–May 1934.
'Khiyalat.' *Kaveh* n.s. 2, no. 6 (8 June 1921).
'Sherkat-e valahazrat-e homayun velayat-e ahd dar mosabeqehha-ye futbal.' *Ta'lim va tarbiyat 6* (1936): 796–9.
Abbasi, Mehdi. *Futbal-r Iran: Tarikh-e mostanad va mosavvar*. Teheran: Selseleh, 2001.
Afrasiabi, Bahram. *Sardaran-e pa beh tup: Tarikh-e mosavvar-e futbal dar Iran az aghaz ta jam-e jahani-ye 1998 Faranseh. 2 vols.* Teheran: Author, 1998.
Ahmad Vosuq, Sepahbod, *Dastan-e zendagi: Khaterati az panjah sal tarikh-e mo'aser 1290–1340.* Teheran: n.p., n.d..
Alikhani, Alinaqi, ed. *Yaddashtha-ye Alam.* Vol. 2. N.p.: New World Ltd, 1993.
Ashna, Hesameddin, ed. *Khoshunat va farhang: Asnad-e mahramaneh-ye kashf-e hejab (1313–1322).* Teheran: Department of Research Publication and Education, 1992.
Banuazizi, Ali. 'Iranian National Character: A Critique of Some Western Perspectives.' In *Psychological Dimensions of Near Eastern Studies,* edited by L. Carl Brown and Norman Itzkowitz. Princeton: The Darwin Press, 1977: 210–39.
Beeston, A.F.L. 'The Game of *maysir* and some Modern Parallels.' *Arabian Studies 2* (1975).
Bill, James A. 'The Plasticity of Informal Politics: The Case of Iran.' *Middle East Journal 27* (1973).
Bourdieu, Pierre. 'Comment peut-on être sportif?' In *Questions de sociologie* (1980). Paris: Les Éditions de Minuit, 1984.
Boyce, Arthur C. 'Alborz College of Tehran and Dr. Samuel Martin Jordan, Founder and President.' In *Cultural Ties between Iran and the United States,* edited by Ali Pasha Saleh. N.p: 1976.
Brailsford, Dennis. 'Puritanism and Sport in Seventeenth Century England.' *Stadion 1*, no. 2 (1975).
Bromberger, Christian. 'Football as World-view and as Ritual.' *French Cultural Studies 6* (1995).
———. 'Football, drame, société.' *Sport*, no. 150: 12–19.
———. *Le Match de football: Ethnologie d'une passion partisane à Marseille, Naples et Turin.* Paris: Éditions de la Maison des sciences de l'homme, 1995.

————. 'Le football en Iran.' *Sociétés & Représentations* (Dec. 1998).

Brown, Ian. *Khomeini's Forgotten Sons: The Story of Iran's Boy Soldiers.* London: Grey Seal, 1990.

Buytendijk, F.J.J. *Le Football: Une étude psychologique.* Paris: Desclée de Brouwer, 1952.

Chehabi, H.E. 'Sport and Politics in Iran: The Legend of Gholamreza Takhti.' *International Journal of the History of Sport 12* (Dec. 1995).

————. 'Jews and Sport in Modern Iran.' In *Yahudiyan-e irani dar tarikh-e mo'aser, Vol. 4,* edited by Homa Sarshar and Houman Sarshar. Beverly Hills: Center for Iranian Jewish Oral History, 2001.

————. 'US-Iranian Sports Diplomacy.' *Diplomacy and Statecraft 12,* no.1 (March 2001): 89–106.

Chehabi, H.E. and Allen Guttmann. 'From Iran to all of Asia: The Origin and Diffusion of Polo.' In *Sport in Asian Society: Past and Present,* edited by J.A. Mangan and Fan Hong. London: Frank Cass, 2003.

Coles, Robert W. 'Football as a "Surrogate" Religion?' In *A Sociological Yearbook of Religion in Britain.* London: SCM Press, 1975.

de Villiers, Gérard. *L'Irresistible ascension de Mohammad Reza Shah d'Iran.* Paris: Plon, 1975.

Diem, Carl. *Weltgeschichte des Sports und der Leibeserziehungen.* Stuttgart: Cotta, 1967.

Dundes, Alan. 'Into the Endzone for a Touchdown: A Psychoanalytic Interpretation of American Football.' *Western Folklore 37* (1978).

Durkheim, Emile. *The Division of Labor in Society.* New York: The Free Press, 1984.

Egger, Heike. '"Sportswear": Zur Geschichte der Sportkleidung.' *Stadion 18,* no.1 (1992).

Elias, Norbert. 'Der Fußballsport im Prozeß der Zivilisation.' *Der Satz 'Der Ball ist rund' hat eine gewisse philosophische Tiefe,* edited by Rold Lindner. Berlin: Transit Buchverlag, 1983.

Ettela'at-e haftegi, no.1980 (15 March 1980).

Fişek, Kurthan. 'The Genesis of Sports Administration in Turkey.' In *Geschichte der Leibesübungen. Vol.6,* edited by Horst Ueberhorst. Berlin: Bartels & Wernitz, 1989.

Forbis, William H. *Fall of the Peacock Throne: The Story of Iran.* New York: Harper & Row, 1980.

Fozooni, Babak. 'Religion, Politics and Class: Conflict and Contestation in the Development of Football in Iran.' *Soccer and Society 5,* no.3 (Autumn 2004).

Giulianotti, Richard and Gary Armstrong. 'Introduction: Reclaiming the Game – An Introduction to the Anthropology of Football.' In *Entering the Field,* edited by Gary Armstrong and Richard Giulianotti. Oxford: Berg, 1997.

Guttmann, Allen. *Games & Empires: Modern Sports and Cultural Imperialism.* New York: Columbia University Press, 1994.

————. *The Erotic in Sport.* New York: Columbia University Press, 1996.

Hajj-Azimi, Nasrollah and General Dr Azadpanah, *Tarikh-e varzesh-e Iran.* Teheran: n.p., n.d.

Harnack, Curtis. *Persian Lions, Persian Lamb: An American's Odyssey in Iran.* New York: Holt, Rinehart and Winston.

Hashemi-Taba, Mohandes Seyyed Mostafa. *Dastan-e yek so'ud.* Teheran: Entesharat-e Nurand, 1997–98.

Hinz, Walther. *Iranische Reise: Eine Forschungsfahrt durch das heutige Persien.* Berlin-Lichterfelde: Hugo Wermühler, 1938.

Hoseyni, Seyyed Ali. *Tarjomeh va towzih-e Lom'eh. Vol.2.* Qom: Dar al-Elm, 1994.

Howard, R.W. *A Merry Mountaineer: The Story of Clifford Harris of Persia.* London: Church Missionary Society, 1935.

Jordan, Samuel M. 'Constructive Revolutions in Iran.' *The Moslem World 25* (1935).

K[ermani], N[awid]. 'Gut rasiert.' *Frankfurter Allgemeine Zeitung,* 11 July 1998.

Kapuściński, Ryazard. *The Soccer War.* Translated by William Brand. New York: Alfred A. Knopf, 1990.

Kuper, Simon. *Football against the Enemy.* London: Orion, 1995.

Küster, Rainer. 'Kriegsspiele – Militärische Metaphern im Fußballsport.' *Zeitschrift für Literaturwissenschaft und Linguistik 28* (Dec. 1998): 53–70.

Lever, Janet. 'Soccer: Opium of the Brazilian People.' *Transaction 7,* no.2 (1969).

————. *Soccer Madness.* Chicago: The University of Chicago Press, 1983.

Lewis, Bernard. *Semites and Anti-Semites: An Inquiry into Conflict and Prejudice.* New York: W.W. Norton, 1986.

Lindroth, Jan. 'The History of Ling Gymnastics in Sweden. A Research Survey.' *Stadion 19–20* (1993–94).

Malek-Mohammadi, Gholamhoseyn. *Varzeshha-ye sonnati, bumi va mahalli.* Teheran: Komiteh-ye olampik-e jomhuri-ye eslami-ye Iran, 1986.

Markovits, Andrei S. and Steven L. Hellerman, *Soccer & American Exceptionalism.* Princeton: Princeton University Press, 2001.

Mason, Tony. 'Football on the Maidan: Cultural Imperialism in Calcutta.' *International Journal of the History of Sport 7,* no.1 (1990): 85–95.

————. *Passion of the People? Football in South America.* London: Verso, 1995.

Mazlish, Bruce. *The Revolutionary Ascetic: Evolution of a Political Type.* New York: McGraw-Hill, 1976.

Merrit-Hawkes, O.A. *Persia: Romance and Reality.* London: Ivor Nicholson & Watson, 1935.

M.M.T.T. [Mohammad Mohit Tabataba'i?], 'Ling: sha'er va varzeshkar 1776–1839.' *Amuzesh va parvaresh 10,* no.2 (April–May 1940).

Moorhouse, H.F. 'One State, Several Countries: Soccer and Nationality in a "United" Kingdom.' In *Tribal Identities: Nationalism, Europe, Sport,* edited by J.A. Mangan. London: Frank Cass, 1996: 55–74

Naciri, M. 'Die Einstellung des Islam zum Sport.' In *Sport in unserer Welt: Chancen und Probleme,* edited by Ommo Grupe. Berlin: Springer, 1972.

Paris, Gilles. 'Tout Téhéran vibre pour les "Rouges" du Pirouzi.' *Le Monde,* 25 June 1998.

Patrick, G.T.W. 'The Psychology of Football.' *The American Journal of Psychology 14,* no.3–4 (July–Oct. 1903): 104–17.

Paul, Ludwig. 'Der iranische Spitzenfußball und seine sozialen und politischen Dimensionen.' *Sozial- und Zeitgeschichte des Sports 12,* no.2 (1998).

Penrose, Jr., Stephen B.L. *That They May Have Life: The Story of the American University in Beirut.* New York: The Trustees of the American University in Beirut, 1941.

Peppard, Victor and James Riordan. *Playing Politics: Soviet Sport Diplomacy to 1992.* Greenwich, CT: JAI Press, 1993.

Perry, John R. 'Artificial Antagonism in Pre-Modern Iran: The Haydari-Ne'mati Urban Factions.' In *The Final Argument: The Imprint of Violence on Society in Medieval and Early Modern Europe,* edited by Donald J. Kagay and L.J. Andrew Villalon. Woodbridge: The Boydell Press, 1998.

————. 'Toward a Theory of Iranian Urban Moieties: The *Haydariyyeh* and *Ni'matiyyeh* Revisited.' *Iranian Studies 32,* no.1 (Winter 1999): 51–70.

Pickford, R.W. 'Aspects of the Psychology of Games and Sports.' *British Journal of Psychology 31,* no.4 (April 1941).

Reppa, Robert B. *Israel and Iran: Bilateral Relationship and Effect on the Indian Ocean Basin.* New York: Praeger, 1974.

Rochard, Philippe. 'The Identities of the *Zûkhânah.*' *Iranian Studies 35,* no.4 (Fall 2002): 313–40.

Rosselli, John. 'The Self-emage of Effeteness: Physical Education and Nationalism in 19th Century Bengal.' *Past and Present, 86* (1980): 121–48.

Ru'inpur, Bizhan. *Iran dar baziha-ye asia'i. Vol.1* (1951–1970). Teheran: Keyhan, 1998.

Sadiq, Isa. *Yadegar-e omr: Khaterati az sargozasht. Vol.2.* Teheran: Dehkhoda, 1975.

Sadr, Hamid-Reza. *Ruzi, ruzegari, futbal.* Teheran: Avizheh, 2000.

Sadri, Abolfazl. *Tarikh–e varzesh.* Teheran: Vezarat-e Farhang, Edareh-ye koll-e tarbiyat-e badani, 1962.

Safari, Baba. *Ardabil dar gozargah-e tarikh. Vol.3.* Ardabil: Islamic Azad University Press, 1992.

Sarvestani, Esma'il Shafi'i. 'Dastan-e varzesh-e modern.' *Sobh 76* (Oct. 1997).

Schayegh, Cyrus. 'Sport, Health, and the Iranian Modern Middle Class in the 1920s and 1930s.' *Iranian Studies 35,* no.4 (Fall 2002): 341–69.

Schirazi, Asghar. 'Gegenkultur als Ausdruck der Zivilgesellschaft in der Islamischen Republik Iran.' In *Probleme der Zivilgesellschaft im Vorderen Orient,* edited by Ferhad Ibrahim and Heidi Wedel. Opladen: Leske + Budrich, 1995.

Sharif, Mehdi. 'Az insan ta ostureh.' *Iranian-e Vashangton 2,* no.38 (8 May 1998).

Shaw, D. *Fútbol y Franquismo.* Madrid: Alianza Editorial, 1987.

Sparroy, Wilfrid. *Persian Children of the Royal Family: The Narrative of an English Tutor at the Court of H.I.H. Zillu's-Sultán, G.C.S.I.* London: John Lane: The Bodley Head, 1902.

Stokes, Martin. 'Strong as a Turk: Power, Performance and Representation in Turkish Wrestling.' In *Sport, Identity and Ethnicity,* edited by Jeremy MacClancy. Oxford: Berg, 1996.

Suárez-Orozco, Marcelo Mariò. 'A Study of Argentine Soccer: The Dynamics of its Fans and Their Folklore.' *The Journal of Psychoanalytic Anthropology 5,* no.1 (Winter 1982).

Sugden, John and Alan Tomlinson, eds. *Hosts and Champions: Soccer Cultures, National Identities and the USA World Cup.* Aldershot: Arena, 1994.

Ta'lim va tarbiyat. 3, 7–8 (Sept.–Oct.–Nov. 1927).

Ta'lim va tarbiyat. 5, 9–10 (Nov. 1935–Jan. 1936): 549–51.

Tarikh-e farhang-e Azarbayjan. Tabriz: Farhang, 1956.

Thaiss, Gustav Edward. 'Religious Symbolism and Social Change: The Drama of Husain.' Ph.D. diss., Washington University, 1973.

Überhorst, Horst. *Zurück zu Jahn.* Bochum: Universitätsverlag, 1969.

Walvin, James. *The People's Game: The History of Football Revisited.* Edinburgh and London: Mainstream Publishing, 1994.

Weber, Eugen. *France, Fin de Siècle.* Cambridge, MA: The Belknap Press of Harvard University Press, 1986.

Weber, Max. *The Protestant Ethic and the Spirit of Capitalism.* New York: Charles Scribner's Sons, 1958.

Williamson, J.W. *In a Persian Oil Field.* London: Ernest Benn Limited, 1927.

Yaddashtha-ye Alam. Vol.4. Bethesda, MD: IBEX Publishers, n.d.

Yaghmaian, Behzad. *Social Change in Iran: An Eyewitness Account of Dissent, Defiance, and New Movements for Rights.* Albany: State University of New York Press, 2002.

Yekta, Hoseyn and Mahmud Nurinezhad. *Tarikh-e futbal-e Iran.* Teheran: Khaneh-ye andisheh-ye javan, 1999.

Split Loyalty: Football-cum-Nationality in Israel

Amir Ben-Porat

What has made sport so uniquely effective a medium for inculcating national feelings, at all events for males, is the ease with which even the least political or public individuals can identify with the nation as symbolized by young persons excelling at what practically every man wants, or at one time in life had wanted, to be good at. 'The imagined community of millions seems more real as a team of eleven named people.' The individual, even the one who only cheers, becomes a symbol of his nation himself.[1]

The close association between football (soccer) and nationality is well reported in literature.[2] Because of its popularity in almost every twentieth-century society, football has become instrumental in the creation of a national identity. Many states have made a special effort to tie football to nationalism. This proved quite effective until the second half of the twentieth century but now, with, in particular, the accelerating process of globalization and commodification of the game, the association between football and nationalism has to some extent been undone. Among other things, this change has affected the relationship of the football supporter with *his/her* club vis-à-vis the relationship of supporters with *their* national team; that is to say, what some previously saw as the natural priority of the latter, no longer remains uncontested.

Nationality is a form of collective identity – a concept much debated in historical literature. Some authors like Appaduari, Bhabha and Hall[3] add more intriguing elements to the question of collective identity. Although the concept's form and substance are contested, most of those involved in the debate over its meaning consider it a useful term, in particular in identifying collective identity in the form of nationalism and concerning its correlation with certain aspects of football. This concept is slightly elaborated in the next section of this essay.

In the 1950s and 1960s, the association between football and nationality in Israel was very close. However, by the end of the twentieth century, one could observe a split in loyalties, a split that was related to changes in the broader social context. Most important in this regard has been the process whereby Israel is becoming a capitalist society, with the inevitable commodification of soccer. This has forced some concrete changes in the orientation of club management, the players, and most notably, the fans. In effect, fans' loyalty towards their local clubs has increasingly clashed with their loyalty towards the national team.

Nationalism and Identity

Post factum, at the dawn of the third millennium, it is apparent that the twentieth century was the century of nationalism. Whilst the concept itself is still debated in academic literature, it is more or less agreed that the basic unit of collective reference was (and still is) the nation-state. With the collapse of the USSR and the Yugoslavian regimes, the number of state units has increased and, in many cases, the central position of the nation-state (as a reference point of identity) has been reinforced.[4]

Moreover, by exploring the connections between the nation, nationalism (a special embodiment of collective identity) and the state, writers have suggested that in order to survive, a state (and/or nation) requires certain 'functional mechanisms' and that the generation of national identity is one such mechanism.[5] National identification may take certain modes of expression, and football – more specifically, the correlation between football and nationalism, which works through the mediation of the supporters – is, as shown in the following passages, quite an effective mechanism through which national identity can be generated.

It is suggested here that the association between football and national identity occurs within two relatively independent spheres. The first is the heroic sphere in which the national team represents the entire population, and when 'the imagined community of millions seems more real as a team of eleven named people'.[6] Thus the heroic sphere *belongs* to the people, to men and women (and minorities), and not just to the *regular* football fans. The heroic sphere of a nation includes very few, somewhat awe-inspiring, moments such as an independence day, a memorial day and – albeit on a different scale - the kinds of victory which, even for the most successful footballing nations, occur only rarely. Certain other sporting successes, such as the winning of Olympic medals, can also be incorporated into this particular sphere.

The second sphere comprises the 'routine' or small moments, a sphere, which Billing calls the 'banal sphere'.[7] Billing argues among other things that national identification is formulated, not always intentionally, by the absorption of concepts and ideas about nationalism through certain popular modes of communication (termed 'parole'). An individual's beliefs and attitudes toward the state and nation (and other social objects) are shaped by the daily parole. Apparently, these are acquired and internalized through what seem to be routine encounters with banal events (such as football league games), which implicitly and/or explicitly, often bear certain nationalistic symbols. These repeated banal events reconstruct national identification as self-evident, as a core element of individual identity and, often, even as the natural social order.

By its cultural nature, and no less importantly by its routine practice, football is based on many repeated banal events that convey – again not always intentionally – the parole of nationalism. In routine encounters, such as league and cup games, national symbols are present, for example the anthem which is played and sung before kick-off, the gestures and comments of the spectators, and the mere (and banal) fact that football is embodied in *national* leagues. Thus, football embodies heroic and banal moments in certain situations, such as when a game is played between two rivals officially belonging to the same state, but seen to represent different nationalities, ethnicities or religions within that state. Here, the banal and the heroic may be interwoven to provide a conflict-ridden situation. The banal becomes a heroic moment, at least for some of the participants.[8]

Football and Nationalism

> More than a million people gathered on the Champs-Elysee on the night of France's victory in the World Cup of 1998. The scenes were repeated all across France as people congregated to celebrate the triumph of the French football team.[9]

Football and nationalism became acquainted with each other almost at the birth of the game; as the sport was codified and took its modern form during a stage of rapidly accelerating nationalism. The establishment of FIFA (Fédération Internationale de Football Associations) in 1904 acted as a trigger for meetings between state teams, and these events became the battlegrounds for national pride and heroic moments of national identity. Many modern states rushed to actualize the potential invested in football for empowering nationalism and identity.[10]

Initially football was a local game, played in neighbourhoods, villages, cities, regions and so forth. By definition the prime, if not exclusive, loyalty of supporters was to the local team, that is, the *we-group* identity was almost totally related to the local team, in opposition to a *they-group* identity ascribed to every other team. But when football began to cross national boundaries, for example, when a national team played in the World Cup, the state stepped forward and appropriated the sport (in its heroic moments) as an instrument for generating national identity. Football, therefore, came to be used as a way of strengthening the state's power vis-à-vis its citizens.

This association between football and nationalism is a global phenomenon. Even in those societies that appear less enthusiastic and less emotional than (to take a good example) the South Americans,[11] the state is not indifferent to events that see the national team in action, for these occasions often produce heroic and emotional moments that are controllable and usually benign. Most significantly, through certain types of manipulation by the state, or its agents, both wins and losses tend to unify the people in support of their team, the nation, the state, and also the political leadership. It has therefore been presumed that the loyalty of the fans can be channelled to maintain the national social structure; in other words, 'the state comes first'.

The Hypothesis of Split Identities

It appears that toward the end of the twentieth century the previous condition of football fan loyalty began to change, and fans started to become more concerned with their local club than with the national team. More particularly, when the interests of the local club clashed with that of the national team, the *committed* fan tended to side with the interests of his/her local club. Various types of evidence are indicative of this trend; for instance, interviews with fans who comment or complain about the burden on *their* players, because of participation in international matches.[12] The selection of club players for the national team, although it is still welcomed and seen to be prestigious, has begun to lose its uncontested status among the fans.

The hypothesis of split loyalties has some solid grounds. One may observe the phenomenon with regard to the commodification of football, a process, which has tended to undermine the national aspect of football. The Bosman Ruling is also indicative of this trend, epitomizing the marketization and de-nationalization of football. The process of globalization has, indeed, reached the realm of sport. Capital and labour are moving across national borders with increasing freedom. Related symbols, such as those that specify the association between football and nationality, are also retreating. Although football world cups, and the various continental football competitions, remain emotionally effective at the nationalistic level, it seems that they are the last bastions of *football-cum-nationalism*. There are more than a few indicators that the future of football will increasingly be centred on individual clubs,[13] and the reasons for this are located outside the football arena, in the engulfing socio-economic system.

Israeli Football and Politics

Two characteristics dominated football in Israel after the establishment of the state in 1948. From this point, the game was both political and nationalistic. As with other sports in Israel at the time, football fell under the auspices of three political centres:[14] Hapo'el, a sports federation associated with The Histadrut (the General Federation of Labor) and thus with the then dominant political parties in government; Maccabi, a sports federation associated with the bourgeois parties in the Knesset (Parliament); and Beitar, a federation associated with a right-wing political party, which was then in opposition (though at present constitutes the major party in government). These federations had already been in existence for quite a few years prior to the establishment of the state of Israel, and their power derived from their political affiliations. The state acknowledged their special status in sport and, in practice, state money allocated to sport was channelled through these federations, with each having the authority to distribute the money according to their priorities.

The influence of the federations on their local football clubs was total. First, the local club was economically dependent on its federation. Hapo'el, because of its association with the Histadrut and the parties in government, was more able to support its clubs than either Maccabi or Beitar. Yet, since soccer in Israel was not yet professional, that is players were not paid wages and were considered amateur, the upkeep of a football team was quite cheap. Consequently Maccabi and Beitar could still significantly influence their clubs through the allocation of economic resources. Besides the support of its federation, the local club had almost no other sources of finance (money from ticket sales was small and part was paid back to the federation). Thus the influence of the federation – and of politics – was indeed absolute.

The Israeli Football Association (IFA) was controlled and run by these sports federations. Formally, the constituency of the Football Federation consisted of the individual football clubs from across the country. These clubs participated in the election of the 'general assembly' of the Football Association. Practically and legally the Football Association's institutions were occupied by the representatives of the sports federations, proportional to the results of the most recent election to the general assembly. Hence, in effect, the individual club was associated to the Football Association by means of its political sports federation. It can be stated that in football, as in almost every instance of Israeli society at that time, politics reigned supreme.[15] The politicization of football had two salient effects. First, the political animosity between the federations was exported to the terraces and increased supporter tensions. When a game between two clubs from different federations took place, spectators came, of course, to watch the match, but also to demonstrate their loyalty both to their club and their political party. The terraces were filled with thousands of people, an impressive phenomenon at that time. Second, although the sports federations were politically hostile to each other, all shared a few basic ideological elements. First and foremost, they all considered themselves Zionist, and supported the newly established state, and did not contest its sovereignty.[16] At all events, loyalty to the club and to the federation was channelled into support for the state. Protests at the terraces, which accompanied many games, were aimed at the governing elite (the old guard Labor party) and not at the existence of the state itself.

Football was used to produce national identification in two different, although related, ways. First, the heroic sphere, in a form of the national team, was enacted through the direct influence of the political federations on the game. The influence of the federations, and particularly that federation associated with the party in power, was transmitted to the state. The state, as shown below, was not a passive recipient, but initiated some nationalistic heroic moments through the use of football. Second, the banal form of nationalism was enacted 'from below', with events in the football stadium frequently directed to nationalistic symbols. These banal occasions were not unadulterated either, because of the broader context of football in Israel and, in particular, the political federations' dominance of the organization of sport. As noted above, conflicts between rival crowds were kept within consensual boundaries and inadvertently reinforced participants' loyalty to the state.

The role of the state in using football in a political and ideological manner (and hence, constructing heroic moments) is exemplified by the tour of the Israeli national team to the USA in September 1948. At this time the newly established Israel, the Palestinians and a number of Arab states were at war. The team's visit was initiated by the Ministry of Foreign Affairs and organized by the Ministry of Defense. Since many of the football players served in the army, causing the football league to be suspended, the army was ordered to take responsibility for the preparation of the team for the trip. The political objective of this event was not concealed and newspapers reflected on this with some pride:

> The delegation of our warriors who will appear in the United State of America has an important role … our soldiers/sportsmen were taken from the trenches to the frontier of propaganda regarding the Israeli issue.[17]

The team played three games, two in New York and one in Philadelphia. The American teams won all three games, but playing-success was not considered central to the success of the tour more generally. Every game was played in the presence of a huge crowd largely composed of American Jews but, most importantly, with politicians and celebrities in attendance. In terms of propaganda, the tour was worthwhile.

During the 1950s and the 1960s, football became the most popular local sport in Israel. The national league was consolidated and was divided into several divisions. Almost every town had one football club, while many cities had two or three. The games of the first and second divisions attracted big crowds, particularly when matches involved teams linked to the competing political federations.[18]

Despite the political animosity between the above federations the importance accorded to the national team was higher than any other element in football. Practically, Zionism, hence nationalism, was consented by these federations. In August 1949, Israel played Yugoslavia in a World Cup qualifying competition. Israel lost both home and away matches, but the press (which, except for a very few newspapers, was attached to and financed by political organizations) was highly enthusiastic: 'Four Great Moments of the Israeli Team' and 'A Great Day for the Goalkeeper' were two typical headlines in the newspapers after the two legs. This was the first time the Israeli national team had participated in an official competition, and nationalistic spirits overwhelmed everything else.

During the 1950s, the national team played more regularly, with fixtures against, amongst others, Cyprus, Turkey, Greece, Yugoslavia and the USA ('league selection'). The climax for the Israeli team was a meeting with the Russians in a preliminary round for the Melbourne Olympic Games in July 1956. For political reasons (that is, Israel had just renewed diplomatic relations with the USSR) the return fixture in Israel became a nationalistic event with, for example, a high ranking army officer nominated as the team manager. The national stadium in Ramat-Gan was full, with almost every minister and senior official of the Israeli government amongst the crowd. Others listened to the commentary of the game on the radio and through loudspeakers that were installed in the city streets of Tel Aviv, Haifa and other cities. The Israeli press was very 'enthusiastic' in its nationalistic support.[19] Though, as expected, the Israelis lost to the Russians 1-2, given the previous playing records of both teams, this was not in any way considered a disgrace. Most accepted that the result of the game was secondary to the advancement of (state) politics, with football merely the means to this end. A heroic moment was created and cherished.

Whilst it is not possible to present supporting statistics, for there were no public opinion surveys of football fans at that time, contemporary newspaper coverage and oral history interviews indicate that the primacy accorded to the importance of the national team relative to club matches was uncontested. Though each federation lobbied for its own players to be selected, internal conflicts – which at other times disrupted league fixtures – were suspended in favour of the national team. A generally nationalistic atmosphere pervaded football, as it did almost every other aspect of life. The supremacy of state and nation was undisputed, but this was to change radically five decades later.

Split Loyalties

> First of all, you played because you loved the game, second, you played for the emblem, and if you played in the national selection, you played for the flag ... today playing football is for the dollar, not the flag.[20]

From the 1950s to the 1990s, Israeli football underwent a transformation. The change was gradual and influenced by the processes which led to Israeli society becoming capitalist,[21] the most significant element of which was privatization of the public economy (that of the state and of the Histadrut, the General Federation of Labor, that together possessed over 50 per cent of the state economy before privatization). This transformation had a critical impact on football clubs as institutions, as well as on players and the managers and administrators of football in Israel. In practice, it forced football (or to be accurate, the upper divisions of the league) to change from being essentially politically owned, to become very close to business entities. However, in order to better comprehend the situation concerning football, the following section identifies some of the more significant changes in football that have specifically impacted upon the identities and loyalties which club supporters have with regard to their respective clubs and the national team.

The Formation of a Footballers' Market

Until the 1970s, footballers were, in practice, bound to a specific club and federation. Moving from one club to another was restricted and regulated by the IFA. Only a few players travelled outside Israel to play, and indeed this tended to be to places where football was a minor or peripheral sport (for example, South Africa, the USA). Players were amateurs and economic support for individual players was rare. This situation began to change in the 1980s, when some Israeli footballers moved to play in France and Germany. The IFA attempted to regulate the migration of footballers, but failed.

Migrating players received little or no help and practically exported themselves, but their actions indicated to others that there was another way to ply one's trade.

Thus, the market for players was initiated by those players who sought professional recognition and financial remuneration. The chairmen of the clubs, nominated by local political organizations with the consent of their federation, were unable to resist and yielded to the players' requests. The federations, anxious about their clubs' positions in the leagues, turned a blind eye. As players' status began to shift from amateur to semi-professional, they started to negotiate their financial rewards and, on a few occasions, threatened to call players' strikes. Subsequently, an unofficial players' market came into effect. The IFA's initial response was to ignore the situation. It then attempted to regulate players' wages before finally conceding to market forces. By the end of the 1990s, the status of the Israeli footballer who played in the first, second, or even the third division of the league, was that of a professional, very similar to the status of his colleagues in Europe.

The Foreigners are Coming

In 1989, after a period of disagreements between the IFA and the sports federations, the IFA decided to allow non-Israeli players to play within its leagues.[22] Initially each club in the first division of the league was allowed two foreign players but this quota has subsequently been raised on a number of occasions. From 1999, each club in the top division has been allowed five non-Israeli players, with clubs in the lower divisions allowed two or three non-Israelis. The importation of foreign players indicated the beginning of a new phase in the position of the clubs. Management (still largely public) invested more money in their clubs, whilst local fans were compelled to adjust to a team that included mercenaries. The players' commitment was largely tied to their financial contracts. Eventually, the club (hence, the local team) became more central than before to the management and, most significantly, to the fans: players are coming and going but the club remains a symbol of heritage and locality – loyalty to the club was the last bastion of the fans.

Privatization of Clubs

As noted earlier, from 1950 to the late 1980s, Israeli football was run, and therefore dictated, by political bodies. Consequently, football club chairmen were political figures nominated by local or nationwide organizations. The federations supported their clubs and controlled their behaviour. For example, in addition to the IFA regulations regarding player transfers, the former instituted an unofficial clause controlling the transfer of players between clubs from different federations. On a few occasions, league games were disturbed because of a political rift between the federations (at one point, Hapo'el and Maccabi even established different leagues for their clubs only). Yet as noted above, even while they maintained a situation of animosity, the priority of the national side was uncontested. When the national team played an international fixture, the federations declared a 'truce'. Therefore, with the Arab minority under military administration practically remaining silent, the loyalty of the entire Israeli populace was centred on eleven people representing the state.

The early 1990s marked a turning point, as the commercial football model replaced the political one. Clubs (that is, in legal terms, the management rights for a definite period) were purchased by individual entrepreneurs and, in many important aspects, they became private, even though most of them retained their existing names and therefore the nuance of federation's affiliation; for example, *Hapo'el* Beer-Sheva, *Maccabi* Tel-Aviv, and *Beitar* Jerusalem. Maccabi Haifa was privatized in 1993, Hapo'el Haifa in 1994, and others followed. A few clubs in this league, those not attractive enough to find private buyers, came under municipal ownership. The reason for the privatization of the clubs is 'exogenous'. As with the entire Israeli society, the influence of the political instance (level) was decreasing as economic instance increased. Consequently, the sports federations, which had previously exploited their political connections, could no longer support their clubs to the extent that they had done before. In effect, the clubs in the two top divisions became autonomous organizations, the fate of which was invested largely in the club's own hands, that is its ownership/management – though partially but significantly in the hands of the fans.

Entering Europe

In 1992, after a long struggle, Israeli football clubs (and the national team) were admitted to play in UEFA organized events. Maccabi Tel-Aviv participated in the early round of the Champions League, and Hapo'el Petach-Tikva in the UEFA Cup competition. Since then, Israeli clubs have regularly participated in UEFA events. This has had a concrete and immediate impact on club administrators' and fans' terms of reference; that is to say, the value of the local clubs has been augmented and now fans can reach out to the world of football (that is, Europe) through their local club as well as through their national team. Clubs' events in Europe, however, have become more frequent than those of the national team. Thus fans have had more *business* in Europe than before.

These changes represent the epitome of the practice of commodification, a process, which has been identified as affecting Israeli society at large. Although, in the main, this has only affected Israel's soccer elite (clubs in the lower divisions remain relatively untouched by such processes), in the top division club management, players and supporters have all had to reconsider their priorities regarding their attachment to the local club which, with the weakening of the federations, has become the focus of the interest in football in Israel. It is assumed that, because of the privatization of clubs in the upper divisions, and the impact on Israeli clubs of participating in European events (although, participation depends on the club's achievements in local competitions), supporters experience a conflict of loyalties. But before we deal with this issue of the emerging dilemma of supporter loyalty, a few words of clarification may be needed to outline the reorientation of football club management and the players.

It is fairly obvious where the priorities of the new directors of the clubs lie. The transformation of most of the first division clubs from a political to a *business* mode of operation has had two related consequences. The first is a change in the balance of power between the clubs and IFA, with the former, which before were almost totally subjected to a federation, becoming relatively autonomous economic organizations. As administrators of relatively autonomous economic organizations, the new directors, committed to the financial viability of their local club, have sought to make their team the focus of public attention. Despite a dominant economic orientation of the premiership league in Israel at present, in reality, only very few clubs have some concrete economic power. This was evident, for example, in the (as it turned out, abortive) attempt of the chairmen of first and second division clubs during the 2000/01 season, to form an autonomous league administration (similar to the administration of the Premier League in England). The primary motive for this initiative, it was argued, was that the clubs' interests required special (financial) attention and, in particular, the interests of those clubs which qualified for participation in UEFA events needed to be given greater attention. On more than one occasion, certain club chairmen defied the IFA, claiming that the latter's mode of operation was antiquated and not suited to the new social and political context, that is, the commodification football and the transformation of clubs into corporations. For example, the chairmen of two leading clubs, Maccabi Haifa and Hapo'el Tel-Aviv, made public their dissatisfaction with the policy of IFA and, more particularly, of the IFA chairman himself, arguing for the need to recognize the interests of individual clubs, compared to the interests of the football league in general and the IFA.

Second, the Israeli players' priorities, implicit in their actions during the 1980s, became explicit in the early 1990s, with the demand to become fully professional, and thus have the freedom to sell their talents in the 'free market'. As footballers elsewhere in Europe had done, players in the top Israeli divisions strengthened their union in order to strengthen their market power vis-à-vis that of the IFA and club managers. In a few important respects the players became 'free agents', selling their assets to the highest bidder. Their interests would seem to be associated with the new era of football in Israel – with the players acting as catalysts to its emergence and consolidation. Since the 1990s, a footballer (assisted by agents and lawyers) negotiates his financial remuneration directly with the club chairman. Subsequently, because of the mobility of players between clubs, the loyalty of the former is 'contract contingent'; that is to say, it exists for as long as the contract lasts. The bottom line is that the loyalty of the Israeli football player is invested primarily in his specific trade and his 'exchange value'.

Essentially, football is a game with three major participants: club management, players and supporters (fans). The first two have a specific and defined role in the game. The third group's role is less specific but no less indispensable. In contrast to a certain post-innocence football which sees football matches as a mobile commodity, grounded in the frame of television, many scholars and football specialists[23] argue that without the presence of fans on the terraces, football would be little more than a technical, *cold* and *dry* game. For the supporters, given their emotional identification, attachment and loyalty, football is *their* cultural phenomenon, and only secondly economic and political. The fan, conceived as either supporter or consumer, is therefore an essential element of the game.[24] Yet the fans differ from both the new directors and the players with respect to their priorities.

Since the establishment of the Israeli state, Israeli football supporters related football to political and nationalistic feelings. Being engulfed by a political society, the supremacy of the national team was ensured by the authority of the IFA (which, as noted above, was political in its composition), by the hegemonic national/Zionist ideology that appreciated the instrumentality of international football competitions, and by the state (and hence the governing elite) which did not interfere in the running of football except on a few occasions (for example, when a fixture had specific political overtones). In effect, because of its predominant position, the state could manipulate support for the national side when it seemed proper to do so. For example, the (political) press was encouraged to promote the forthcoming game while government ministers, trade union leaders and high-ranking army officers announced their intention to attend. Every international match taking place in Israel was packed with ardent fans who appreciated the mere fact that the national side was playing for the state and the nation simultaneously. Even though about 10 per cent of Israel's population in the 1950s were Arabs, the national team included only Jewish players. This, consequently, led to an apparent convergence of the (Jewish) nation and state on the football pitch. From the 1970s, however, some Arab players playing for major clubs at that time were invited to join the national squad. Nevertheless, Arab support for the national team remains, for certain good reasons, ambivalent.

With the changing structure of Israeli football during the 1980s and beyond, it is possible to argue that the 1990s marked the beginning of a new era in Israel at large, and in football in particular. In accordance with this argument, it is suggested that the uncontested priority of the national selection thus started to be brought into question relative to the priorities of fans' local clubs. The outcome is the existence of split loyalty, which comes to the fore when the interests of the national selection clash with the interests of the local club. Several examples are offered here in support of this argument. In 2002, Hapo'el Tel-Aviv participated in the UEFA Cup. Because of political and security reasons, the team's home games were played outside Israel (in Cyprus, Turkey, Italy, and even as far away as Holland). Against all odds, the team won its matches against two leading European club sides, Chelsea of England and Parma of Italy, to reach the quarter-final stage. The media in Israel were excited and enthusiastic, and the achievements of Hapo'el Tel Aviv were seen to reflect positively on both the state and the nation. However, Hapo'el fans had different feelings and displayed a banner on the terraces which said, 'Hapo'el and Not Israel'. The message was clear: 'we (the fans) disagree with the nation-state appropriation of the club's success. This belongs to us alone.' In effect, the Hapo'el supporters demarcated the line between the local and the national; that is, they gave vent to their split loyalties.

Another example is provided by the recent attempts to appoint a national team coach. After a relatively poor career with the squad, the Danish coach, Richard Neilsen, resigned in 2002. The position was offered to Dror Kashtan, the highly acclaimed coach of Hapo'el Tel-Aviv. In the past, veteran Israeli players, when offered the position of national coach, had normally accepted the same. But Kashtan declined the IFA offer on the ground that it would incur a substantial financial loss if he relinquished the post of a club (team) manager. This incident, which in another context would be considered trivial, is revealing. In the near past, when football was political, such a refusal was unimaginable, for it would have provoked angry public debate with accusations about the coach's sense of *national duty*, et cetera. In the case of Kashtan, however, there was hardly any negative comment. In the 1990s, when football had become a commercialized game, the position of a national coach was clearly less attractive, and the draw of association with state and nationalism weaker. Moreover, Hapo'el Tel-Aviv fans were highly satisfied that the club's interests (and economy) took precedence over that of the national team.

The conflict of interests also occurs at the level of club chairman. For example, Eli Zino, then the chairman of Hapo'el Beer-Sheva (a club in the top division) complained in the daily newspaper about the IFA's decision that Yossi Benayoun, the club's best player, should play a national youth team fixture instead of representing the club in a critical game. 'The player first of all represents the local club', said the chairman to a reporter, 'the national selection comes second'.[25] Ultimately Eli Zino had to abide by the decision of the IFA, because of the latter's formal authority (and the threat of possible sanctions) over the individual club. Yet, what has come to be known as 'Zino's complaint', which would have been considered an aberration in the past, when the club was run by political leadership, is today accepted as a legitimate standpoint.

While reading the Israeli newspapers and listening to supporters talking about incidents like those mentioned above, one is inclined to conform to the argument, as this essay has tried to posit, that the present attitude of Israeli football fans is characterized by a split in loyalties between the clubs and the national team. For many fans, sympathies are divided three ways: between their clubs, the national team, and, due to the widespread television broadcasting of games from several foreign leagues, a club outside Israel. Famous teams from around the world, such as Manchester United, Liverpool and Real Madrid, are popular in Israel and have a relatively large body of supporters.[26] However, recent research has shown that a conflict of loyalties between the local Israeli club and what I have elsewhere called an 'overseas sweetheart' is negligible.[27] Very few Hapo'el Tel Aviv supporters experienced an inner state of conflict at the clashes between their local club and Chelsea or Milan. A conflict between loyalty to the local clubs and loyalty to the national selection is much more probable.

As part of the research, Hapo'el Beer-Sheva fans, were asked about their reaction to the following possible scenario:

> Your team is scheduled to play an important game in the league, and the national team coach demands that the club's players who have been selected to play in the national team, do not participate in this game, because they are scheduled to play the following week in an international game. What is your reaction?

A small proportion (five out of 25 interviewees) sided with the hypothetical demand of the national coach. Some (seven interviewees) refrained from expressing support for either side. The rest (13) sided strongly with their club. Responses included: 'My team is above everything'; 'Let the national team wait, our team is more important'; 'I don't care about the national team, the priority is to the local team'. Thus, a substantial proportion of the Hapo'el Beer-Sheva supporters agree with their club chairman Eli Zino that in the case of conflict, priority should be given to the interests of the local club over those of the national team. Another research by the author indicates a more generalized version/nature of this 'split loyalty' phenomenon. A nationwide survey of football fans, conducted by the author in 2003, found that over 25 per cent denoted that their primary loyalty was to their club rather than to the national side. More specifically, in a (hypothetical) situation in which club interests clash with national selection interests, the above 25 per cent sided with the club. In comparison to the situation during the first few decades of statehood, this is a new phenomenon.[28]

From the viewpoint of fans, the possibility of a clash of interests between those of the local team and those of the national side is real, although in practice such clashes are rare. The IFA tends to postpone games in the top division during the week in which the national team is scheduled to play. However, during the 1990s, some conflicts of interest did occur, and the club sides were forced to give way. Fans voiced their dissatisfaction both in stadiums and through the media.

New Balance

Football and nationalism have been companions for a long time. The priority of nationalism, or that of the state over regionalism, has been acknowledged through the formal position granted to the national team. Furthermore, when regionalism is involved in an internal ethnic or nationalistic conflict (as in Spain between the Basques and the rest of Spain, or in Scotland between Protestants and Catholics) there are appeals (by the government, the press, the Football Association) to give priority to the national side, and for supporters to (temporarily) set aside their differences. However, not all fans comply and certain disgruntled groups (such as the Basques, Catholics in Glasgow and also Arabs in Israel) have refused to support the national team. Yet, in general, the games of the national squad promote solidarity; people and groups are *required* to stand by the national flag.

Indeed, the symbolic position of the national team is strong, not just in Israel but globally. The World Cup is the best evidence of this point. With the accelerating commodification of the game, however, the growing financial investments in the local club on one hand and the growing attachment of the fans to the club on the other hand, decrease the importance of the national team in relation to the local club. In actual fact, the national side *was* supported enthusiastically during World Cup qualifying games in 2002 (which, as noted above, were played outside Israel), but the team failed to get beyond the preliminary stage. In contrast to this, a few local clubs have reached the European competitions and recorded some notable achievements. This has had a much stronger impact on the local fans and has probably reinforced their commitment to *their* club. In these cases the national side has lost some credit, while the local club has gained some credit. The traditional basis of football in Israel has thus been realigned; the primacy of politics is taken over by that of economy. The local club with a consolidated fan following is getting increasingly strong, while the national team, regarding its position with fans, is facing some question marks. Football thus reflects some major facets of the changing trends in Israeli society.

People still come in their thousands to support the national team. Many, who have no special local club, give the national side backing because it is a symbol of the nation-state. But it appears that for the *fanatic*, national selection has lost its prerogative over his local club. When 'push comes to shove' and the interests of the local club clash with that of the national selection, the fan finds him/herself involved in an awkward situation. Some hesitate, but many others have made a decision, 'my football club is "my castle" and everything else comes second'.

Notes

[1]   Hobsbawm, *Nation and Nationalism*, 143.
[2]   Archetti, 'Masculinity and Football'; Boyle, 'We are Celtic Supporters'; Cronin, *Sport and Nationalism in Ireland*; Jarvie, 'Nationalism and Cultural Identity'; Maguire, *Global Sport*; Marks, 'The French National Team'; Duke and Crolley, *Football, Nationality and the State*; King, *The European Ritual*.
[3]   Appadurai, *Modernity at Large: Cultural Dimensions of Globalization;* Bhaba, *Nation and Narration*; Hall, 'The Question of Cultural Identity'.
[4]   Hobsbawm, *Nation and Nationalism*; Hall and Held, 'Citizen and Citizenship'; Nairan, *The Break-Up of Britain*.
[5]   Smith, *The Ethnic Origin of Nations*; 'Introduction', Anderson, *Imagined Communities*.
[6]   Hobsbawm, *Nation and Nationalism*, 143.
[7]   Billing, *Banal Nationalism*.
[8]   Ben-Porat, '"Biladi Biladi"'.
[9]   Mignon, 'Fans and Heroes', 79.
[10] Archeti, 'Masculinity and Football'; Cronin, *Sport and Nationalism in Ireland,* King, 'Football Fandom and Post National Identity in New-Europe'.
[11] Mason, *Passion of the People.*
[12] Interviews with fans are available in various monthly sports magazines (e.g., the English magazine *When Saturday Comes,* The Israeli *Sham Hamis'hack* [*The Name of The Game*], etc.). FIFA offers a unified international calendar 'in pursuit of ending those tedious club v country squabbles'. Keir Radnedge, 'Commentary', *World Soccer*, Feb. (2002), 30. For more substantial information, see King, *The European Ritual.* Also, the sports section of the Israeli daily newspaper, *Ha'aretz*, published an article (13 Oct. 2001) about the early voluntary retirement of star players in Europe from their national teams. The article based on various sources of information specified that this made the players more available to their club. It seems clear that the players and their club management are happy with this move, whilst managers of national teams clearly have much to lose.
[13] Indicators include the G-14's attempt to establish their own league, the pay per view programmes of particular clubs for their fans, the growing significance of European Champions League Games. For further details on this point, see Conn, *The Football Business;* and Giulianotti, *Football: A Sociology of the Global Game.*
[14] Ben-Porat, *From a Game to a Commodity.* As in other places, football in Israel is a male-dominated game. However, about 25 per cent of the people *interested* in football in Israel are women. Moreover, about 20 per cent of the Israelis are Arabs (citizen of the state). Their attitude to the heroic sphere is, at the very least, ambivalent. Also see Ben-Porat, *Football and Nationality.*

[15]   Ben-Porat, *From a Game to a Commodity.*
[16]   Ibid.
[17]   Ibid., 134.
[18]   Ibid.
[19]   Porat and Lerer, *Sport 50.*
[20]   Interview with Meir Toviash, a former footballer at Wingate Archive, Wingate, 19 June 2000.
[21]   Ben-Porat, *State and Capitalism in Israel.*
[22]   Ben-Porat, 'The Political Economy of Soccer'.
[23]   See Note 2.
[24]   See, for example Giulianotti, 'Supporters, Followers, Fans and Flaneurs'.
[25]   *Ha'aretz,* 27 April 1998, 14.
[26]   Ben-Porat, 'Overseas Sweetheart: Israeli Fans of British Football'.
[27]   Ibid. In April-May 2002, 25 face-to-face, semi-structured, interviews with 'fanatic' fans were conducted. This was a first stage of a nation-wide study of football fans in Israel, which was completed in June 2004. Individuals were interviewed at their home. The results of the nation-wide study support the above.
[28]   See Note 15.

References

Anderson, B. *Imagined Communities.* London: Verso, 1990.

Appadurai, A. *Modernity At Large: Cultural Dimensions of Globalization.* London: University of Minnesota Press, 1996.

Archetti, E. 'Masculinity and Football: The Formation of National Identity in Argentina.' In *Games Without Frontiers,* edited by R. Giulianotti and J. Williams. Aldershot: Arena, 1994.

Ben-Porat, A. *State and Capitalism in Israel.* Wesport, CT: Greenwood Press, 1993.

———. 'Overseas Sweetheart: Israeli Fans of British Football.' *Journal of Sport and Social Issues 24,* no. 4 (2000): 35–44.

———. '"Biladi Biladi": Ethnic and Nationalistic Conflict in the Soccer Stadium in Israel.' *Soccer and Society 2,* no.1 (2001): 19–38.

———. *From a Game to a Commodity: Football in Israel 1948–1999.* Sede Boqer: Moreshet, 2002.

———. 'The Political Economy of Soccer: the Importation of Foreign Soccer Players to the Israeli League.' *Soccer and Society 3,* no.1 (2002): 54–86.

———. *Football and Nationality.* Tel Aviv: Resling, 2003.

Bhaba, H., ed. *Nation and Narration.* London: Routledge, 1990.

Billing, M. *Banal Nationalism.* London: Sage, 1997.

Boyle, R. 'We Are Celtic Supporters … Questions of Football and Identity in Modern Scotland.' In *Game Without Frontiers,* edited by R. Giulianotti and J. Williams. Aldershot: Arena, 1994.

Conn, D. *The Football Business.* Edinburgh: Mainstream, 1997.

Cronin, M. *Sport and Nationalism in Ireland.* Portland: Four Courts Press, 1999.

Duke, V. and L. Crolley. *Football, Nationality and the State.* Edinburgh: Longman, 1996.

Giulianotti, R. *Football: A Sociology of the Global Game.* Cambridge: Polity Press, 1999.

Giulianotti, R. 'Supporters, Followers, Fans and Flaneurs: a Texonomy of Spectator Identity in Football.' *Journal of Sport and Social Issues 26,* no.1 (2002): 22–46.

Hall, S. 'The Question of Cultural Identity.' In *Modernity and its Futures,* edited by S. Hall, D. Held and T. McGrew. Cambridge: Polity Press, 1992.

Hall, S. and D. Held. 'Citizen and Citizenship.' In *New Times,* edited by S. Hall and M. Jacques. London: Lawrence and Wishart, 1989.

Hobsbawm, E.J. *Nation and Nationalism Since 1870.* Cambridge: Cambridge University Press, 1990.

Jarvie, J. 'Nationalism and Identity.' In *The Changing Politics of Sport,* edited by L. Allison. Manchester: Manchester University Press, 1993.

King, A. 'Football Fandom and Post National Identity in New-Europe.' *British Journal of Sociology 51,* no.3 (2000): 419–42.

King, A. *The European Ritual.* Aldershot: Ashgate, 2003.

Maguire, J. *Global Sport: Identities, Societies, Civilization.* Cambridge: Polity Press, 1999.

Marks, J. 'The French National Team and National Identity.' In *France and the 1998 World Cup,* edited by H. Dauncey and G. Hare. London: Frank Cass, 2000.

Mason, T. *Passion of the People.* London: Verso, 1995.

Mignon, P. 'Fans and Heroes.' In *France and the 1998 World Cup,* edited by H. Dauncey and G. Hare. London: Frank Cass, 2000.

Nairan, T. *The Break-Up of Britain.* London: New Left Books, 1977.

Porat, Y. and M. Lerer, *Sport 50.* Tel Aviv: Alpha, 1998.

Smith, D. *The Ethnic Origin of Nations.* Oxford: Basil Blackwell, 1994.

Africans' Status in the European Football Players' Labour Market

Raffaele Poli

The Post 1995 Salary Explosion and the Dualization of European Football

The International Federation of the Associations of Professional Footballers (FIFPro), which groups together the unions of players from 40 countries, in existence since 1966, was not recognized by either FIFA or UEFA prior to 1995, when the Bosman law came into force. With this decree the status of players within the system of professional football was raised significantly. In the first place, while ruling that all players whose contracts have expired are free to sign a new one with another club without payment or any compensation to the original club, the Bosman law provoked a massive increase in the amount in salaries paid to players. In many cases, the money saved by the clubs in the payment of these compensations was reinvested in salary budgets in order to attract players. According to Gianpaolo Monteneri, former director of the players' status department of FIFA, 'from an economic point of view, after the Bosman law, the direction of capital flows in professional football has considerably changed. Instead of circulating between clubs, more and more money ended up in players' or the agents' pockets.'[1] Moreover, in the major European leagues, the new cash profits generated by the sale of television rights equally contributed to a strong increase in salary. In France, for example, the gross salary expenditure of the League 1 clubs almost trebled from the season 1995/96 to 2001/02.[2] During the same period, a similar growth in the total amount of wages occurred in German Bundesliga clubs, while in the English Premiership and Italian Serie A clubs the gross salary expenditure increased almost fourfold (see Figure 1).[3]

In Italy, according to the income declaration for the year 2000, 85 players figure among the 500 persons having earned the most money in the entire country. With a revenue of 12 million euro, Alessandro Del Piero, ranked thirteenth, followed closely by his former president Giovanni Agnelli, eleventh with 13.5 million, and was actually ahead of the prime minister and president of AC Milan, Silvio Berlusconi, who declared 8.3 million euro and was ranked 24th. Players of Inter Milan, Ronaldo Nazario Lima, Javier Zanetti and Christian Vieri declared more income than their president Massimo Moratti, as did the captain of AS Roma Francesco Totti when compared to the club's president Franco Sensi.[4]

According to the classification of the best paid players in the world established by the bi-weekly *France Football*, a ranking that takes into account not only the salaries and premiums paid by clubs but also the incomes generated by sponsors, the top 20

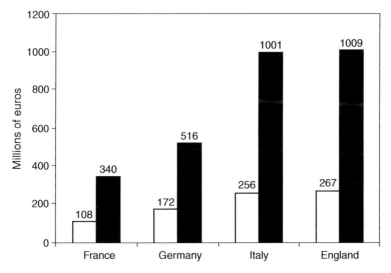

Figure 1 Gross salary expenditure growth from 1995/96 (white) season to 2001/02 (black) in French, German, Italian and English top level divisions

includes 18 players that are members of clubs belonging to the G-14.[5] These players in 2002 earned 178.7 million euro, of which 121.6 were paid by the clubs (68 per cent) and the remainder by the sponsors. In some cases, the remuneration by sponsors was higher than that of the clubs. This was notably the case of David Beckham, who earned 15.2 million euros, of which 8.4 were paid by sponsors (55.3 per cent). This type of player, who earns more by marketing their image than by playing soccer ensuring additional income to the clubs, is the exception to the rule. In many cases, the clubs, even the richest ones, pay out salaries that cannot be sustained in the long term. According to the amount published in the monthly *World Soccer*, the 20 clubs having the biggest turnover in Europe, for the season 2001/02 spent on average 58.2 per cent of their total income on the players' salaries (1.54 billion euro out of a total of 2.64). In certain cases (SS Lazio Rome, Inter Milan FC et cetera), the amount spent on salaries was even greater than the club's total income. In France, in 2001/02, an average of 69 per cent of the annual income of the first division clubs was spent on the payment of players' salaries. In Italy, this rate was 90 per cent, in England 62 per cent, and in Germany 49 per cent. In these four countries, in comparison with the season 1995/96, the ratio between the turnover of the clubs at the highest national level and the expenditures in players' salaries increased from 52.75 per cent to 67.5 per cent.[6]

On 5 November 2002, in order to deal with the increase in salaries paid by clubs belonging to the G-14, the organization concluded a kind of 'stability pact' by agreeing on the introduction of a salary cap for the season 2005/06 stipulating that the global salary budget of the clubs cannot exceed 70 per cent of the total turnover.[7] However, up until now, this decision has had little effect on the star players if we consider that the average income of the 20 best paid players in the world has risen from 7.94 million euros in 2002 to 8.93 million in 2003.[8] An ever-increasing economic gulf separates the players of the major European clubs from the vast majority of professional footballers in the world.

Players' Salaries: the Reflection of a Dual Labour Market

The average net annual remuneration by players in the top leagues for the season 2002/03 was 709,000 euro in Italy, 634,000 euro in England, 340,000 euro in Spain, 310,000 euro in Germany followed by 225,000 euro in France. In Belgium, according to an investigation conducted on 77 premier league players, the average net income per annum was situated at around 60,000 euro.[9] For a given country, the disparity existing at the same competition level is also remarkable. This is reflected in a pioneering work conducted by Jean-François Bourg in 1989 on this issue. Through the case study of French professional football, he defined the sport labour market as being 'segmented' and 'dual'. According to his study, 'a strong dispersion characterizes the distribution of income'. In fact, for the 1987/88 season, 'the highest hundred incomes account for the half of the total amount of distributed salaries, while representing only 15 per cent of the total number of team members'. As a consequence, 'the players of the lowest ten percent receive only 3 per cent of the total salary mass'.[10] The calculation of the 'inequality coefficient', measured by the division of the total amount of the 10 per cent of the highest salaries by that of the 10 per cent of the lowest ones, indicates, by 1987 already, the existence in the football players market of a gap (13.33) twice as great as the one existing in the male working population in France as a whole.

With the explosion of the top salaries and the stagnation of the lower ones, the gap characterizing the employment market in football increased year by year. In Italy, the players of the fourth competition level, the C2, earned on average for the season 2001/02 more than ten times less than their colleagues playing in Serie A (see Figure 2).

According to the statistics given by clubs, the five most important teams of Serie A during the 2003/04 season spent on salaries more than double the amount spent by the other 13 clubs (421 million euros against 186.9).[11] The gulf separating the best paid players from the lowest paid ones, as well as the absence of a 'middle class' of player, is clearly illustrated by the next graph produced from data provided by the Italian Football League. In fact, 34.4 per cent of the footballers employed by Serie A clubs were situated in the lowest salary class, while 29.6 per cent were situated in the highest one, which implies that 64 per cent of the players occupied positions belonging to these two extremes (see Figure 3).

With regard to the second level of competition, the graph representing players' salaries takes a more linear form. Indeed, in Italian Serie B a restricted number of footballers earn a very high salary, while a majority of players belong to the lower salary classes (see Figure 4).

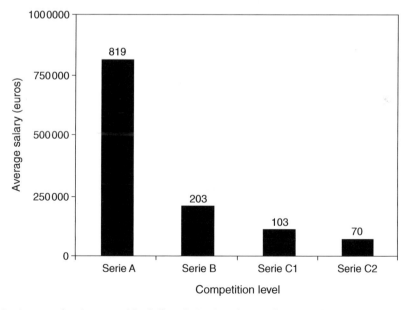

Figure 2   Average salary in euros of footballers playing in Italy according to level of competition (2001/02).
Source: Calcio 2000, no. 65, May 2003

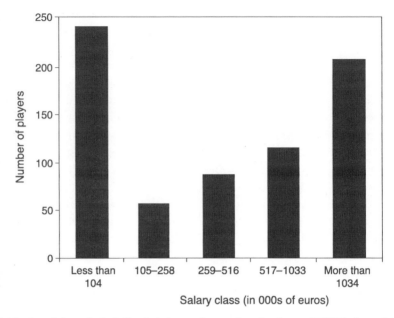

Figure 3   Number of players in the Italian Serie A according to salary class (season 2001/02). *Source:* Italian Lega Calcio

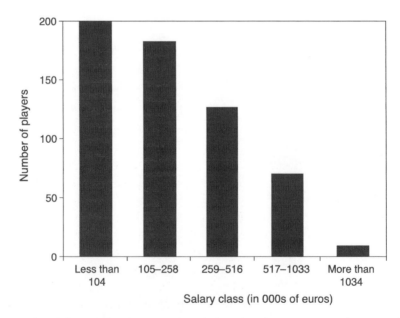

Figure 4   Number of players in the Italian Serie B according to salary class (season 2001/02). *Source:* Italian Lega Calcio

Everywhere in Europe, over the past few years, the number of players without employment increased in a spectacular manner. In England, at the end of the season 2002/03, 586 players did not have a contract for the following season. The head of the players' Union, Gordon Taylor, declared, 'our job is to help them all to find a club, but I would be happy to find a job for even two thirds of them'.[12] According to Jean-François Bourg, since 1974, the creation of football academies in France is a strategy devised by the clubs 'to increase the supply of workers in order to influence negatively the labour price'.[13] According to him, 'the surplus amount of workers is not a simple conjectural imbalance, it is, rather, necessary to the smooth running of the sport system which needs a constant circulation of players'.[14]

Outside Europe, the situation is even more dramatic. The vast majority of African clubs find themselves unable to pay their players' salaries and thus are not in a position to stop them migrating. For example, players of Coton Sport Garoua, one of the best-managed clubs of Cameroon, which have won the Cameroon championship four times since 1997, earn less than 400 euros per month.[15] In Latin America, the situation is no less critical. In 2002, Chilean players organized a general strike reclaiming payment of their salaries. After three weeks during which competition were stopped, the Confederation of South American Football Associations (CONMEBOL) lent $250.000 to the Chilean Federation, which was then distributed to the clubs. In 2001, in order to restart the championship, the Argentinean Federation had to intervene to reimburse, by means of 18 monthly payments, the $50 million of salary backlog due to the players.[16]

The International Migration of Footballers in UEFA Countries: A Quantitative Approach

In a previous statistical analysis, I studied the squads of 78 professional and semi-professional leagues affiliated to the UEFA in order to determine the number of foreign players having been recruited by the 1,358 teams taking part in these championships.[17] It thus transpired that 5,334 players moved internationally 'with the ball' and found themselves abroad during the 2002/03 season.[18] This figure refers only to players based outside their country of origin whose migration is directly linked to a recruitment operated by a foreign club.

Concerning the geographical origin of these migrants, the footballers from Eastern European countries were the most represented abroad in the UEFA federations (1,586, 29.7 per cent), followed by Western Europeans (1,532, 28.7 per cent), Africans (1,046, 19.6 per cent) and Latin Americans (902, 16.9 per cent). The main exporter country was Brazil, which, with 509 footballers playing for European clubs, contributed 9.5 per cent to the total amount of the migrants 'with the ball' in UEFA countries. After Brazil, we find players from Serbia Montenegro (275), from France (259), from Argentina (244), from Nigeria (193), from Ukraine (145), from Croatia (136) and from Cameroon (125). Regarding the receiving countries, most of the foreign professional players were based in England: 718 migrants 'with the ball' played in clubs from the Premiership to the Third Division in 2002/03 season, which

Table 1   Foreign players per team in the most 'abroad orientated' top European leagues (season 2002/03)

League	Number of clubs	Number of foreign players	Foreign players per team
English Premiership	20	320	16.00
German Bundesliga	18	239	13.28
Russian Professional FL	16	196	12.25
Scottish Premier Division	10	118	11.80
Belgian Jupiler League	18	212	11.78
Portuguese Super Liga	18	210	11.67
Greek Ethniki Katigoria	16	147	9.19

represents 13.5 per cent of the total amount of foreign players in UEFA leagues. Behind England, the most internationally orientated professional leagues were German (510), Italian (374), Portuguese (349), Belgian (306), French (305) and Spanish (195) ones. In terms of the rate of foreign players in squads, Premiership clubs, with on average 16 footballers recruited abroad per team, had the highest score (see Table 1).

In order to measure the importance of foreign players' presence according to the competition level, a correlation was measured between UEFA ranking position of countries and the rate of players having moved internationally 'with the ball'. A positive correlation between these two variables exists, which indicates that the recruitment of players abroad is directly linked to the level of teams and championships (see Figure 5).

Nevertheless, if we take into account the variable of players' origin, it appears that the regression is not always linear, such as in the case of Africans. It is to this perplexing question to which I shall turn in the remainder of the article.

African Players' Situation: An Over-representation in less Well-off Leagues

If the total amount of players recruited by professional clubs outside their country of origin diminishes according to the level of competition, the degree of this decrease differs depending on the continent of origin of the players. For example, from a five level hierarchy of European leagues elaborated from the UEFA ranking,[19] it appears that, in contrast to Latin American counterparts, for example, whose relative percentage presence diminishes constantly from 24 per cent in the first level to 11 per cent in the last one, players recruited in Africa are comparatively more numerous in the last four levels of competition than in the first one (see Figure 6).

The relative over-representation of African players in the last four levels of European competition indicates the need of less well-off clubs to recruit 'low cost' players abroad. This occurs also in the context of a strategy based on speculation, in which financially weak and middle-ranged European clubs aim to buy young footballers in Africa in order to resell them at a higher price to richer clubs.

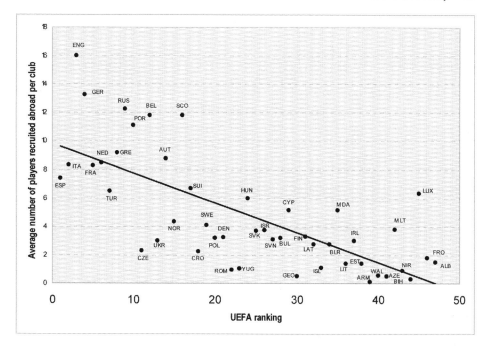

Figure 5   Correlation between UEFA ranking country position and abroad recruitment of players

The comparison between the following two maps shows geographically the over-representation of Africans in less well-off European football leagues, such as in Eastern European ones, in comparison to the total amount of players recruited abroad.

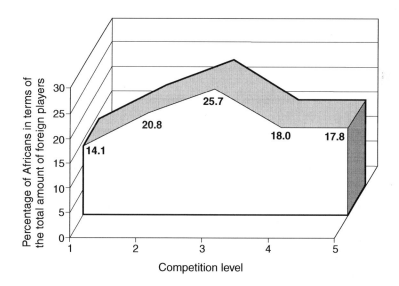

Figure 6   Percentage of African migrants in terms of the total amount of foreign players according to the level of competition (season 2002/03)

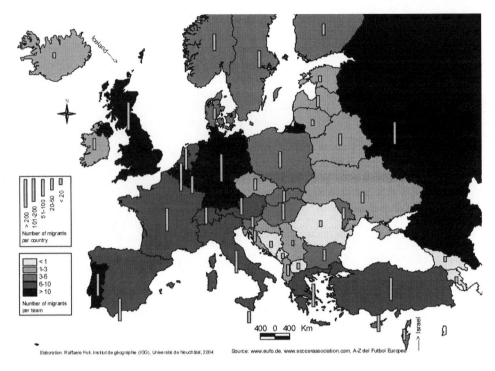

Figure 7   Number of players recruited abroad per team in UEFA countries (top national division) and total amount of migrants

The relative over-representation of African players in less well-off European Leagues such as in Romania (53.3 per cent of the players recruited abroad came from Africa), Malta (52.6 per cent), Belgium (43.4 per cent), Switzerland (33.7 per cent) or Albania (33.3 per cent), supports the hypothesis of the rule of 'low cost' labour force filled by players of this origin. The interviews carried out with eight Cameroonian players[20] playing professionally for Swiss clubs during the 2002/03 season confirmed that African players at the start of their career very often suffer from different forms of discrimination. The first type of discrimination intervenes in labour market access because of the frequent existence of quotas limiting the presence of non-communitarian players in European clubs while the second kind of discrimination is situated at the level of labour stability. In fact, African footballers are very often pushed to sign short-term contracts allowing European clubs to separate themselves easily from players if they do not find satisfaction with them. Discrimination has been also observed in terms of payment of salary. Timothée Atouba, for example, received from the first European club for which he played, Neuchâtel Xamax, only a third of the sum stipulated in the contract that he signed. Only after one year, could he manage to obtain two thirds of the sum, almost 3,300 euros per month. During this year, the club officials and his agent met his complaints with threats to send him back to Cameroon.

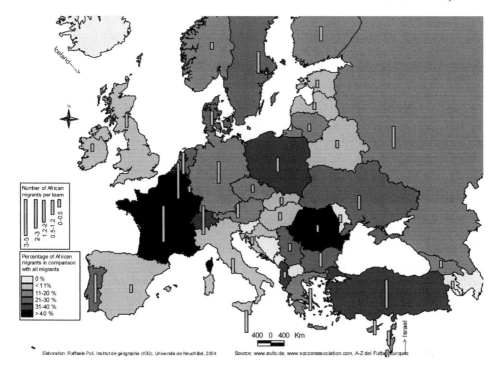

Figure 8   Percentage of African migrants in terms of the total amount of foreign players according to country (top national divisions) and total amount of African migrants 'with the ball'

Comparison between the Six Most Represented African Countries: Different Degrees of Poor Integration

Regarding the six African countries that provide the most players to European clubs,[21] different models of migration exist according to the competition level in which these footballers play. At one extreme, the Nigerian migrants are very numerous in the lower divisions, while at the other extreme Moroccans migrants are concentrated in the higher divisions. Economic criteria in the country of origin must be taken into account if we wish to understand these divergences. While Nigerian players wish to play abroad whatever the cost, Moroccans prefer to stay at home if the recruiting club does not offer acceptable conditions. Among the other nationalities, the Cameroon footballers tend to follow the Nigerian model being well represented at all levels of competition, while the Senegalese, Ivorian and Ghanaian migrants are situated in between these two models while being comparatively more concentrated at the inter-mediary level. A significant correlation has been measured between the GDP per capita of the countries of origin of the migrants and the level of competition of the clubs by which they are employed (see Figure 9).

An even stronger correlation exists between the GDP per capita and the average age of African players in Europe, which indicates that the migration is directly linked to the

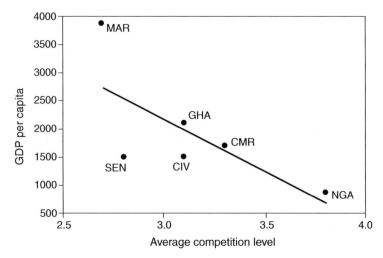

Figure 9   Correlation between the average competition level of migrants from the six most represented African countries and their GDP per capita

economic situation of the country of departure. The poorer a state is, the younger are the players going abroad seeking better living conditions (see Figure 10).

Among the six cases analysed, Moroccans represent an exception. In fact, their average age of migration is higher than that of the footballers of the other countries. Two arguments explain this difference. On the one hand, the Moroccan professional clubs, in contrast to the vast majority of Sub-Saharan ones, have the potential to offer good wage conditions to the best players, which does not generally encourage them to leave at a very young age. On the other hand, the cost to transfer Moroccans players is

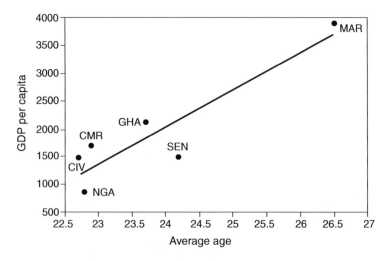

Figure 10   Correlation between the average age of migrants from the six most represented African countries and their GDP per capita

also higher, which means that the European clubs prefer to recruit them once that they have acquired enough experience, rather than to suppose on a hypothetical future progression, as is very often the case of players coming from Sub-Saharan countries.[22]

Conclusion

This essay underlines the importance of economic criteria to explain the general poor status of African footballers in the European players' labour market. Indeed, comparatively more clubs of lower divisions, which cannot afford to pay high salaries, employ African players in Europe. Moreover, they are very often transferred with the intention to be consequently re-transferred to a bigger club in order to make a profit. In this speculative strategy, stimulated by the increasing gap separating the rich clubs of the major leagues from the rest of the teams, Africans players are very sought after because of their reiterative commercial value. At the same time, to fully understand the dynamics leading to the development of the recruitment of African players we have to go beyond the economic criteria, taking into account historical and social reasons. In fact, to make African players' migration possible, European clubs and players' agents groups needed to set up transnational networks. These are very often indebted more to socio-historical criteria than to financial ones. For example, if Kolo Touré was transferred from the Ivory Coast to Arsenal, it was because of the personal links existing between the manager of the English club, Arsène Wenger, and Jean-Marc Guillou, who owns the football academy in which Kolo Touré has been trained. Besides, it was not a coincidence if the Frenchman Guillou chose the Ivory Coast, a former French colony, to realize his project.

Another reflective example showing that economic criteria do not explain all mechanisms of the recruitment of African players is furnished by the Romanian case. As mentioned, Romania is the UEFA country where Africans are relatively the most represented in terms of the total amount of players recruited abroad 'with the ball'. If we deepen the analysis, we discover that most of African footballers playing in Romania come from Ghana. A further investigation indicates that a former Ghanaian national team coach, Petre Gavrila, is Romanian. This makes possible the transfer of Ghanaian players from Africa to Eastern Europe. Indeed, after his time in Ghana, Gavrila became a player agent and he created a 'Euro-African' training centre in the Romanian town of Busila.

Like Gavrila or Arsenal, a greater number of European clubs and players' agents groups are interested in creating or financing football academies in Africa, or in concluding partnership agreements for player transfers with African clubs or academies. The transnational networks set up for the training, recruitment and transfer of African players are almost always controlled from 'above'[23] and serve the needs of the European football economy more than the African one.

Under these conditions, as John Bale and Paul Darby have pointed out, the African 'muscle exodus' inhibits the development of African football or, at best, creates dependent development. This is a situation that we usually find in other economic sectors.[24]

The functioning of the football players' transfers system in the 'global sports arena'[25] has many similarities with the export of raw materials from Southern to Northern countries, which largely benefits the latter. As in the world economic system in general, the unfairness of the mechanism regulating African players' migrations is manifest, but nobody has shown any real urge to change this. Though FIFA introduced rules to prevent the transfer of players under 18 years old and elaborated a mechanism of solidarity to protect the work of nursery teams through the payment of fees, it did not give itself the financial means to effectively enforce the juridical changes.[26] European football federations and Governments want to protect national players and make access to the national players' labour market difficult for Africans by quotas limiting their presence. European clubs want to save money by salary dumping or generate profits by continuous player transactions. For a variety of reasons, as argued in the essay, African players lend themselves perfectly to these kinds of speculation strategies.

On the other side of the Mediterranean Sea, African clubs hope to improve their conditions by partnership agreements with European clubs or players' agents and, in the fight for their financial survival, accept the worst terms of exchange. Moreover, African football federations and Governments see players' exodus as a possibility to reintegrate more competitive players in national teams in order to obtain top international results. Because of that, they tend to favour the migrations instead of supporting local development of the game. The price that is being paid has been the personal failure of a very important number of young players. Most of them come to Europe 'with the ball' but are unable to integrate themselves into the professional football circuit. Thus, they end up by finding themselves in very precarious situations.

Notes

[1]   Interview with Gianpaolo Monteneri, 29 July 2003.
[2]   *France Football*, no.2978, 6 May 2003, 13.
[3]   *Deloitte & Touche Annual Review of Football Finance* (hereafter *DT Football Finance*), July 2003, 14.
[4]   *La Gazzetta dello Sport*, 18 Jan. 2003, 12.
[5]   *France Football*, no.2978, 6 May 2003, 6–10.
[6]   *DT Football Finance*, July 2003, 14.
[7]   *World Soccer*, July 2003, 21.
[8]   *La Lettre du Sport*, no.275, 9 May 2003, 4.
[9]   *DT Football Finance*, July 2003; *France Football*, no.2978, 6 May 2003, 13; *Sport/Foot Magazine*, no.26, 25 June 2003, 26.
[10] Bourg, 'Le marché du travail sportif', 150–1.
[11] *La Gazzetta dello Sport*, 29 July 2003, 12.
[12] *France Football*, no.2984, 17 June 2003, 46.
[13] Bourg, 'Le marché du travail sportif', 156.
[14] Ibid.
[15] *Cameroon Tribune* (Yaoundé), 21 Nov. 2003.
[16] *FIFA Magazine*, Feb. 2003, 42–3.
[17] Poli, *Les migrations internationales des footballeurs*, 157. Main sources used are Internet sites <www.eufo.de> and <www.soccerassociation.com>, and the annual review *A-Z del Futbol Europeo*. This review, edited in Spain, contains a large number of statistics on players' career paths.

[18]   Lanfranchi and Taylor, *Moving with the Ball*, 273.
[19]   The first level of the hierarchy includes top divisions of England, Spain, Italy, Germany and France. In the second level, we find top leagues of the Netherlands, Portugal, Russia, Turkey and Greece. Inferior leagues of the countries mentioned above are ranked from the third to fifth level, as well as top divisions of the countries that have not been inserted in the first two levels.
[20]   Players interviewed included Timothée Atouba and Hervé Tum (FC Basle), Augustine Simo (FC Zurich), Jean-Pierre Tcheutchoua (FC Aarau), Armand Deumi (FC Thun), Samuel Ojong (Neuchâtel Xamax FC), Achille Njanke (SR Delémont) and Frédéric Ayangma (FC Bulle).
[21]   Players from Nigeria, Cameroon, Ghana, Senegal, Ivory Coast and Morocco represented in the 2002/03 season 58.7 per cent of the footballers recruited by European clubs in Africa.
[22]   Poli, 'Des migrants à qualifier. Les footballeurs africains dans quatre pays européens', 143–64.
[23]   For further details on this point, see Smith and Guarnizo, 'The Locations of Transnationalism', 3–34.
[24]   Bale and Sang, *Kenynan Running: Movement Culture, Geography and Global Change*, 229, and Bale, 'African Footballers and Europe: Migration, Exploitation and Postcolonialism', 14; Darby, *Africa, Football and FIFA.*, 236, and 'The New Scramble for Africa', 217–44.
[25]   Bale and Maguire, *The Global Sports Arena*, 289.
[26]   Amadu, Chamas and Noemi, 'Kids never came back', 175.

References

Amadu, Musa, Joseph Chamas and David Noemi. 'Kids never came back. High Hopes, Harsh Realities', unpublished manuscript. Neuchâtel: CIES, 2003.

Bale, John. 'African Footballers and Europe: Migration, Exploitation and Postcolonialism.' (unpublished manuscript, 2001).

Bale, John and Joseph Maguire. *The Global Sports Arena: Athletic Talent Migration in an Interdependent World.* London: Frank Cass, 1994.

Bale, John and Joe Sang. *Kenynan Running: Movement Culture, Geography and Global Change.* London: Frank Cass, 1996.

Bourg, Jean-François. 'Le marché du travail sportif.' In *Economie politique du sport*, edited by Wladimir Andreff. Paris: Dalloz, 1989.

Darby, Paul. *Africa, Football and FIFA. Politics, Colonialism and Resistance.* London & Portland: Frank Cass, 2001.

———. 'The New Scramble for Africa: African Football Labour Migration to Europe.' In *Europe, Sport, World: Shaping Global Societies,* edited by J.A. Mangan. London: Frank Cass, 2001.

Lanfranchi, Pierre and Matthew Taylor. *Moving with the Ball: the Migration of Professional Footballers.* New York & Oxford: Berg, 2001.

Poli, Raffaele. *Les migrations internationales des footballeurs. Trajectoires de joueurs camerounais en Suisse.* Neuchâtel: Editions du CIES, 2004.

———. 'Des migrants à qualifier. Les footballeurs africains dans quatre pays européens.' In *La mobilité internationale des compétences,* edited by Mihaela Nedelcu. Paris: L'Harmattan, 2004.

Smith, Michael and Luis Guarnizo. 'The Locations of Transnationalism.' In *Transnationalism From Below,* by Michael Smith and Luis Guarnizo. New Brunswick: Transaction Publishers, 1998.

Review Essay on Peter Alegi, *Laduma! Soccer, Politics and Society in South Africa*

Chris Bolsmann

With the readmission of South African football into the international fold in 1992, a new phase began in the nation's sporting history. In football, the euphoria continued with the national team winning the 1996 African Cup of Nations and participating in two World Cups in France in 1998 and Japan and South Korea in 2002. In addition to staging the 1996 African Cup of Nations, the most important football competition, the FIFA World Cup will be held in the country in 2010. Despite the above-mentioned successes, relatively few studies have focussed on South African football. Mark Gleeson, South Africa's foremost football writer and commentator, notes in his forward to the book *Laduma! Soccer, Politics and Society in South Africa* that 'a general apathy with regard to the history of sport and its role in the development of South African society has ensured that this country does not possess a formal history of its football [and that] *Laduma!* will inspire others to add to this rich tapestry of our sporting heritage'.[1] Recent popular works amongst others on football in South Africa include: Friedman's biographical account of two of South Africa's most popular modern day players, Mark Fish and Lucas Radebe; Auf Der Heyde's journalistic account of reporting on football in Africa; Raath's richly detailed documentation of the history of the game and many of the clubs and Mazwai's glossy pictorial account of the last 30 years of the sport.[2] These contributions certainly fill important gaps in documenting a variety of aspects of the game more generally. However, Alegi's *Laduma!* is significant as it represents a richly detailed academic account of the historical development of football in South Africa. In addition, the author's analysis is intersected by the broader political and social issues often neglected in some of the other accounts. Alegi's contribution is part of an increasing body of academic work concerned with football in South Africa. Moreover, it contributes to the social history of sport in the country.

The author sets out to investigate the history of football in South Africa by examining the specific role the game plays in the social lives of black South Africans. The timeframe of analysis spans the years 1910 to 1976, that is, until the Soweto uprising. Alegi considers how football, a British and colonial game, was transformed into the most significant form of urban popular culture and was able to overcome class and generational differences. In addition, 'it examines the creation and maintenance of a sphere of social action that influenced class and generational divisions, shaped masculine identities, and served as a mobilising force for neighbourhood, township, and political organisations'.[3] Finally, Alegi suggests that 'the social history of football sheds new light on key themes in the modern historiography of South Africa'.[4]

Theoretically, Alegi builds on the social history of sport and leisure in South Africa and further discusses struggles over space in colonial and capitalist contexts. Tim Couzens' pioneering work on the history of football in South Africa represents an important contribution that discusses the development of the game in the cities, on the mines and in villages.[5] Building on this, *Laduma!* draws on and extends the work of Atkins, Cooper, Martin and Thompson who argue that workers contest and negotiate capitalist and colonial attempts to control their lives.[6] Significantly, Alegi drawing on Couzens' notion of 'moralizing leisure time'[7] argues that sport became a site of struggle in South Africa between African players on the one hand, and 'white missionaries and philanthropists, government officials, and employers'[8] on the other. These sites of struggle over space are central to the study of South African history due to state attempts to racially segregate all spheres of life. Moreover, *Laduma!* documents the Africanization of football whereby black South Africans are able to determine their own histories in terms of sport and leisure.

The book comprises eight thematically and chronologically arranged chapters. Alegi lays the foundation for his analysis in Chapter 1 by locating the importance of physical ability in pre-colonial South Africa through stick fighting, cattle raiding, racing and hunting, and competitive dancing. The author highlights the parallels in sporting laws in pre-colonial societies, as sporting codes were open to negotiation, yet they shared similarities with the fixed rules of modern sport. Thus the British were not responsible for the introduction of sporting laws and rules into South Africa. Alegi demonstrates how nineteenth-century South Africa enjoyed numerous sporting and leisure activities. Drawing on scholarly work on Kenyan athletics,[9] Alegi suggests pre-colonial sporting traditions embodied modern principles of fitness, performance and competition. Moreover, 'indigenous sporting traditions were elaborate public spectacles of fitness and physical prowess, technical expertise, strategy, and tactics'.[10] Therefore, the existence of indigenous games and leisure activities allowed British sport to be successfully transplanted into the colony.

In Chapter 2, Alegi traces the origins of colonial football in South Africa during the latter part of the nineteenth century. Football was brought to the country by missionaries, traders, sailors and soldiers. The author suggests 'what is perhaps the earliest documented football match in Africa in Cape Town'[11] was played between colonial administration employees and soldiers on 23 August 1862. However, Raath suggests 'South Africa's first recorded match appeared in Port Elizabeth's *Eastern Province Herald* on 23 May 1862'.[12] With the discovery of diamonds and gold in 1867 and 1886 respectively, the large-scale migration of blacks to the mines occurred and sport became increasingly popular and central to the lives of migrants. The Anglo-Zulu War

(1879) and the South African War (1899–1902) brought large number of British soldiers to the country, further popularizing the game. As Alegi points out, 'black South Africans' acceptance of British football fostered a perception of soccer as plebeian and black and rugby as patrician and white'.[13] During this period, separate football organizations were founded for Africans, Indians and whites. The author notes that the first South African team to play in England in 1898 was the Orange Free State Bantu Football Club based in Bloemfontein and states that 'virtually nothing is known about this group'.[14] However Raath, drawing on English newspapers, the *Newcastle Daily Journal, Bolton Evening News*, and *Reading Standard*, suggests a team out of depth on tour, playing and losing 37 matches, bar one draw and conceding over 200 goals in 1899.[15] The popularity of soccer amongst black South Africans meant the game 'was transformed into a sphere of action where expressions of African modernity could be forged, tested, and negotiated'[16] and this forms the focus of the following two chapters.

Chapters 3 and 4 represent case studies of the development of football in Durban and the Witwatersrand respectively. Alegi documents the period in which football developed into a black male working-class pastime in tandem with its broader institutionalization. The 1920s and 1930s were characterized by high rates of urbanization and capitalist expansion intersected with increased segregation. The author traces the emergence of the *kholwa*, a small class of Zulu-speakers, made up of landowners, those who attended mission schools and white-collar professionals who were largely responsible for the development of the game in Natal. Durban soon became an important centre for South African football with teams also emerging from the ranks of blue-collar workers. In 1916, the Durban and District Native Football Association (DDNFA) was founded with Douglas Evans playing a leading role. This role, however, became problematic when emerging African nationalism objected to 'white stewardship'[17] in the game. Alegi demonstrates how nationalism in racial and interracial terms leads to an uneasy existence with cooperation and confrontation taking place. The period under review highlights the neglect on the part of the white authorities in providing adequate facilities for the development of the game. As a result, games were played in informal spaces that were not victim to police harassment and control. Struggles over playing facilities ultimately highlighted the linkages between sport and politics in South Africa. However, the town council did begin to provide facilities for the game in an attempt to 'depoliticize African popular cultural expression'.[18] In addition, football also offered the town council an avenue to generate income. Significantly, Alegi argues that white involvement in the game brought about an increase in African political consciousness as was manifested in replacing 'Native' with African in the Association name. Moreover, the involvement of political leaders such as Albert Luthuli along with trade unionists and members of the African National Congress (ANC) provided African elites with a vehicle to overcome class divisions within communities under the banner of 'race-conscious populism'.[19] At the same time control of the game remained in the hands of the *kholwa*. The argument follows that football played the role of 'asserting changing black masculine identities'[20] as players could affirm and express themselves rather than succumb to extreme racism and oppression, and thus African men were able to negotiate their identities.

In Chapter 4, Alegi discusses the development of football on the Witwatersrand and in Johannesburg in particular. Football became formally organized after the First World War while the Witwatersrand and District Native Football Association (WDNFA) was established in 1917. White managers on the mines approved these developments and saw them as opportunities 'to curb militancy, increase discipline and production, and improve health'.[21] After the 1920 mineworkers' strike, football was encouraged by mining bosses as a means to bolster production and morale. In Durban, white officials were involved in the organization of the game to 'defuse growing political unrest, win converts, and moderate the effects of severe economic deprivation'.[22] Resentment to white involvement also emerged and this was articulated in the black press. In addition, 'Native' was replaced by African in the name of the Association. At the national level, the South Africa African Football Association (SAAFA) was established in 1932 and the rival South African Bantu Football Association (SABFA) in 1933. As early as 1892 the white South African Football Association (SAFA) was established with associations for Indians in 1903 and Coloureds in 1933.

Chapter 5 traces the Africanization of the game, which included 'religious specialists and magic, various rituals of spectatorship as well as indigenous playing styles'.[23] Throughout the country, football teams were employing the services of diviners and healers to improve their performances on the football field. In Durban, Evans and some of the *kholwa* opposed the use of magic in football, however, they were unable to stop 'this powerful and creative indigenous adaptation'[24] still prevalent in the modern game. Alegi contends this practice meant the de-colonization of football occurred, which in turn, resulted in the growth and expansion of the game during the 1930s. As the popularity of the game grew, spectator numbers increased and, significantly, football spectatorship was not only a male activity with women also attending and reporting on games. Alegi provides further evidence of the Africanization of the game through the use of praise names for players adopted from the Zulu and Sotho traditions. Often these nicknames were bestowed on players according to their capabilities and skills. Moreover, this practice further linked the football fan to their sporting icons. Occasionally football violence also occurred. The increased popularity of football meant that white business attempted to profit from the commercial prospects offered by the game by sponsoring trophies amongst others. The Africanization of the game was not only manifested outside the field of play but significant changes on the field in terms of playing styles occurred. *Marabi* represented the fusion of traditional and modern music 'that dominated lower-urban class black leisure between the wars'.[25] In football terms, because of the increased popularity of street football, individual skill and flair that was entertaining and flexible developed representing *marabi* football. In contrast, Motherwell as a playing style was developed after the tours during the early 1930s by the Scottish team of the same name. The style of ground passing and positional play outclassed all South African opposition and was eagerly adopted by local teams. Football's ability to overcome the ever-increasing segregation along racial, class and gender lines amongst others was noted by ANC leaders. Indeed, a fund raising match was arranged between the rival black football associations in 1944 to raise funds for the ANC. After the Second World War, football's popularity was unrivalled in South Africa and this was closely linked to the broader socio-political changes brought about by industrialization and urbanization.

Arguably South Africa's most popular and successful football club, Orlando Pirates is the topic of discussion in Chapter 6. Drawing extensively from Maguire's[26] interview data with Orlando Pirates officials, Alegi documents the emergence of a football club established by a group of schoolboys in 1937 strongly rooted in the community. A number of other teams emerged in Soweto during this period, yet none had the longevity of Orlando Pirates and this is attributed to the close community ties that were forged along with loyalty and identification with the team. Officials of the club stressed the importance of not only playing football but being part of the broader community and the establishment of a burial society bears testimony to this point. Within 20 years, Orlando Pirates became popular throughout the country not only due to their success on the field, but also due to the changing context brought about by apartheid in 1948. Alegi also discusses the emergence of another Soweto team, Moroka Swallows, who were able to challenge the dominance of Orlando Pirates.

Chapter 7 documents the emerging struggle against apartheid and for playing facilities, in conjunction with the increasing popularity of the game for entrepreneurs as an outlet to retail goods from sporting equipment through to alcohol and tobacco. The author notes that during the 1950s football was able to connect across racial, economic and political lines, amongst others.[27] The South African Soccer Federation (SASF) was established in 1951 by African, Coloured and Indian officials. No one was barred on racial grounds and the organization became the largest of its kind in the country and importantly was a 'multiracial umbrella body opposed to apartheid in football'.[28] This political position adopted by the Federation was part of the broader political developments in the country whereby racially exclusive organizations adopted multiracial positions as in the case of the Congress Alliance. In Durban, the success of Bush Bucks Football Club during the 1950s brought into practice 'hidden professionalism'[29] even though from the early 1920s, the game offered commercial incentives and possibilities. Durban emerged as the most important football centre in the country and this reputation was further enhanced with successful foreign tours to neighbouring African states by teams selected from the city and region. Moreover, Alegi remarks that these tours 'bolstered the game's links to wider processes of industrialisation, urban migration, cultural change, and the construction of social identities throughout southern and central Africa'.[30] During the 1950s, while inter-racial football matches became increasingly popular, the Pretoria regime opposed this.

In the final substantive chapter, Alegi outlines the emergence of professional football and the onslaught by the apartheid state to segregate sport. In 1956, the first apartheid sports policy emerged. According to this policy, inter-racial competitions were not permitted and teams made up of different racial groups should be avoided. In addition, black sporting organizations were discouraged from seeking international recognition. It was maintained that this should take place through existing white structures. Indeed, the SASF sought recognition from the world governing body FIFA in 1954. The white SAFA had already been accepted in 1952. Also, the SASF's proposed merger with the SAFA was rejected. Soon SAFA was renamed the Football Association of South Africa (FASA) and was able to attract local black associations and 'this paternalistic touch of trusteeship ideology divided black sport'.[31] This co-option delayed the inevitable suspension of FASA by FIFA in 1961. In the same year African, Coloured and Indian administrators established the South African Soccer League (SASL) two years after the establishment of a league for white teams. In contrast to the white league, the SASL struggled to secure financial backing and facilities for the game and accordingly 'this underlies the profound connections between sport and the political economy of apartheid'.[32] In tandem with the establishment of a league, supporters clubs emerged which were not exclusively restricted to men. New identities and relations developed across gender and class lines amongst others, as was manifested in the formation of mutual aid societies. In addition, by the early 1960s there were attempts to form women's playing teams. For Alegi, 'the SASL's firm ideological commitment to non-racial sport strengthened the democratising impulse in football'.[33] At the same time, alcohol consumption, gambling and violence became more frequent. The final blow to the SASL was dealt by the white federation which successfully lobbied to bar the league access to playing fields, in an attempt to attract black fans to the white league, control domestic football and finally have their suspension from FIFA lifted.[34] The league ceased to exist by 1966.

In the short Epilogue, Alegi claims to have briefly highlighted 'the most important developments in the domestic game between 1971 and 1992'.[35] However, justice is not done to an important period in South African football history. After meticulous and detailed observations and analysis in the previous chapters, the epilogue is disappointing. Indeed, this period deserves a fuller and more detailed investigation and analysis due to the social and political changes both on and off the field.

In sum, *Laduma!* can be described as a significant contribution to the social and political history of football in South Africa. Alegi makes use of comparative analysis by considering the urban centres of Cape Town, Durban and Johannesburg and rightly points out that a 'fiercely local approach that dominates South African urban historiography'[36] exists and *Laduma!* aims to transcend this. It offers a synthesis able to overcome regional differences while simultaneously maintaining a richly detailed narrative. Alegi successfully synthesizes the histories of the three different metropolitan areas. Moreover, the study locates the development of football in South Africa in relation to other colonial societies. Alegi comes up with an analysis not constrained by either imperial cultural connections or dominant power relations. The work instead puts 'an emphasis on indigenous African initiatives, including open accommodation, selective adaptation and active resistance'.[37] His use of extensive documentary and oral evidence deeply enriches the analysis as is evident in his detailed notes and the use of photographic illustrations throughout the text. Notwithstanding some discrepancies and a disappointing epilogue, *Laduma!* thus fills an important gap in the historiography of South African sport. However, the period from the 1970s onwards needs further detailed examination and analysis. The 2010 FIFA World Cup is not only an opportunity for the country to stage the most important football contest, but also for further research and analysis to be undertaken.

Notes

[1]   Alegi, *Laduma!*, x–xi.
[2]   Auf Der Heyde, *Has Anybody Got a Whistle?*; Friedman, *Madiba's Boys*; Mazwai, *Thirty Years of South African Soccer*; and Raath, *Soccer Through the Years 1862–2002*.
[3]   Alegi, *Laduma!*, 1.
[4]   Ibid.
[5]   Couzens, 'An Introduction to the History of Football in South Africa'.
[6]   Atkins, *The Moon is Dead!*; Cooper, 'Urban Space, Industrial Time, and Wage Labour in Africa'; Cooper, 'Colonizing Time'; Martin, *Leisure and Society in Colonial Brazzaville*; and Thompson, 'Time, Work-Discipline, and Industrial Capitalism'.
[7]   Couzens, 'Moralizing Leisure Time'.
[8]   Alegi, *Laduma!*, 147.
[9]   Bale and Sang, *Kenyan Running*.
[10] Alegi, *Laduma!*, 14.
[11] Ibid., 15.
[12] Raath, *Soccer Through the Years*.
[13] Alegi, *Laduma!*, 16.
[14] Ibid., 18.
[15] Raath, *Soccer Through the Years*.
[16] Alegi, *Laduma!*, 20.
[17] Ibid., 27.
[18] In la Hausse de Lalouvière, 'The Cows of Nongoloza'.
[19] In Halisi, *Black Political Thought in the Making of South African Democracy*.
[20] Alegi, *Laduma!*, 35.
[21] Ibid., 39.
[22] Ibid., 42.
[23] Ibid., 49.
[24] Ibid., 50.
[25] Ibid., 57.
[26] Maguire, 'The People's Club'.
[27] Alegi, *Laduma!*, 87.
[28] Ibid., 107.
[29] Ibid., 94.
[30] Ibid., 100.
[31] Ibid., 114.
[32] Ibid., 119.
[33] Ibid., 129.
[34] Ibid., 133.
[35] Ibid., 137.
[36] Ibid., 148.
[37] Ibid., 149.

Book under review

Alegi, Peter. *Laduma! Soccer, Politics and Society in South Africa* (Scottsville: University of Kwazulu-Natal Press, 2004). Pp. xv + 221, 24 illustrations/photographs, bibliography. £18.99, ISBN 1869140400.

References

Atkins, Keletso. *The Moon is Dead! Give Us Our Money! The Cultural Origins of an African Work Ethic, Natal, South Africa, 1883–1900.* Portsmouth, NH: Heinemann, 1993.

Auf Der Heyde, Peter. *Has Anybody Got a Whistle? A Football Reporter in Africa.* Manchester: The Parr Wood Press, 2002.

Bale, J. and J. Sang. *Kenyan Running: Movement Culture, Geography and Global Change.* London: Frank Cass, 1996.

Cooper, Frederick. 'Urban Space, Industrial Time, and Wage Labour in Africa'. In *Struggle for the City: Migrant Labor, Capital and the State in Urban Africa,* edited by F. Cooper. Beverly Hills, CA: SAGE, 1983.

Cooper, Frederick. 'Colonizing Time: Work Rhythms and Labor Conflict in Colonial Mombasa'. *Colonialism and Culture,* edited by B.D. Nicholas. Ann Arbor: University of Michigan Press, 1994.

Couzens, Tim. 'Moralizing Leisure Time: The Transnational Connection and Black Johannesburg, 1918–1936'. In *Industrialisation and Social Change in South Africa,* edited by S. Marks and R. Rathbone, 1982.

Couzens, Tim. 'An Introduction to the History of Football in South Africa'. In *Town and Country-side in the Transvaal,* edited by B. Bozzoli, 1983.

Friedman, Graeme. *Madiba's Boys: The Stories of Lucas Radebe and Mark Fish.* Claremont: New Africa Press, 2001.

Halisi, C.R.D. *Black Political Thought in the Making of South African Democracy.* Bloomington and Indianapolis: Indiana University Press, 1999.

la Hausse de Lalouvière, Paul. '"The Cows of Nongoloza": Youth, Crime and Amalaita Gangs in Durban, 1900–1936,' *Journal of Southern African Studies 16,* no. 1 (1990): 79–111.

Maguire, R. 'The People's Club: A Social and Institutional History of Orlando Pirates Football Club, 1937–1973'. B.A. Hons. thesis, University of the Witwatersrand, 1991.

Martin, P. M. *Leisure and Society in Colonial Brazzaville.* Cambridge: Cambridge University Press, 1995.

Mazwai, T., ed. *Thirty Years of South African Soccer.* Johannesburg: Mafube Publishing, 2003.

Raath, Peter. *Soccer Through the Years 1862–2002.* Cape Town: Peter Raath, 2002.

Thompson, E. P., 'Time, Work-Discipline and Industrial Capitalism.' *Past and Present 38* (1967): 56–97.

'Le Sénégal Qui Gagne': Soccer and the Stakes of Neoliberalism in a Postcolonial Port

Michael Ralph

Playing with Slavery, Navigating Neoliberalism

> The oughtness of Atlantic slavery's memory and the justness of excavation reside in refusing to efface through forgetfulness the historical complicity and contemporary failures of Western liberal democracies.[1]

Bineta, one Senegalese commoner, told the author that on the eve of George Bush's visit to Gorée Island they were taken to a soccer stadium and locked inside. That's all she would say about it. To learn more, I was forced to conduct my own investigation.

According to those interviewed on the morning of 7 July 2003, US military personnel arrived on Gorée Island around 4.00 a.m. accompanied by bomb-sniffing dogs. Residents were evacuated from their homes as soldiers conducted their investigations.

As soon as they were finished, the island's entire population was hoarded onto Gorée's sandlot soccer field.[2] Once the field was packed to capacity, people were sealed in by a barricade, trapped on a barren field, beneath the Senegalese sun, without any shade.[3] The satchels of water distributed haphazardly provided little relief for the crowd during the eight hours some of them spent in that spot – from nearly 6.00 a.m. to 2.00 p.m. – though the visit, which lasted less than two hours, took place between 11.00 a.m. and 1.00 p.m. All cell phone communication was disabled during this time.

'They cornered us like sheep', said a teenage soccer player visibly outraged at the treatment he had received from the US soldiers. Others, with whom I spoke, articulated a stronger sentiment. From female market vendors and restaurant owners, I noticed, a single Wolof phrase recurred consistently in interview transcripts: *Da fa mélni Diaam mo gna watt* which, when translated into English means, 'It was like slavery had returned'.

How are we to understand this discourse on slavery more than 150 years after it was officially abolished in French territories? Why did it surface during this particular event, as Senegal hosted a delegation from the United States? If the epigraph above is any guide, perhaps the memory of slavery is linked to democracy's 'failure' to take root in 'Western liberal democracies'? But which 'Western' nation? France? The US? And if only 'Western … democracies' experience these contradictions, why is this narrative emerging in Senegal at present? In what ways has Senegalese democracy 'failed'? What was *its* aspiration?

Who designed the security measures taken for Bush's visit? If someone from the US, why did the Senegalese government comply? Under what conditions? These laconic strictures seem to contradict the political congeniality that exists between George W. Bush and Abdoulaye Wade. On several occasions, Wade has received praise from the US Commander-in-Chief for being the most democratic of the world's Islamic countries. Since the last quarter of 2001, Senegal has become a veritable foil for suspected terrorist nations everywhere as Bush urges others to take notice and follow suit.

But shouldn't Senegal, in turn, have noticed *these* events? Is the high esteem with which it is regarded by its Western comrade relevant only to certain occasions, under specific conditions? Is US *amitié* reserved only for the national leader? Bush arrived at the island on board Wade's presidential yacht. There is but one way to enter and exit Gorée. What exactly was security personnel concerned about? Did this community of people on a small island off the coast of Senegal really constitute a threat to US national security? If not, how might we explain these events? How do they register in the Senegalese political imagination, if at all?

What does it mean that a soccer field was the setting upon which African bodies faced the coercive presence of US power on Senegalese soil? In recent times, Senegal has gained international notoriety as a soccer powerhouse, especially after its upset victory over France in the 2002 World Cup. The domain of sport has suddenly become a key vehicle through which Senegal has worked to distinguish itself – even assert its potential – to the world of nations. This realm has attracted so much support that, in 2000, Wade broke the Ministry of Youth and Sports into two separate Ministries, so each could receive adequate attention. There is a consensus among government officials that in the past, as one cabinet member put it, 'Le sport a dominé le jeunesse' ([Matters of] sport dominated youth [concerns]) though, of course, in this instance 'sport' meant soccer. The main problem was that the Minister of Youth and Sports had been so busy marketing, funding and promoting the national soccer team in competitions abroad, he had little time for domestic issues.

In the way soccer is tied to Senegal's international image, it is as if the government wants to suggest that, given the right resources and under the right conditions, it can perform as well politically and economically as the nation's footballers have performed athletically with the resources given them.

Casting a critical eye toward this ideology of sport, this article explores the way sport is implicated in Senegal's effort to recast itself as a democratic nation – one increasingly removed, geopolitically, from the Islamic world – and reposition itself as an ally of the United States, which connects it to an international political framework that does not assign the same privilege to the nation's relationship with France which has been, until now, Senegal's most powerful ally.

In this effort, sport emerges as a tool through which Senegal renegotiates its relationship with other nations. This aim is embedded in the ethnographic events and historical developments this essay seeks to untangle by paying close attention to the main issues highlighted: the shifting shape of Senegalese geopolitics and the country's fascination with representing itself through sporting successes. To do this, I dribble back and forth between a series of overlapping events tied to Senegal's response to the tragic events of 9/11, and the country's aggressive 2002 World Cup bid and its Cinderella-esque victory over defending champions France in the opening round. After exploring these two distinct trajectories, I show the way they yield political anxieties that collapse clumsily into President George W. Bush's 2003 visit and become intensified through the way that moment is represented. I focus specifically on the trope of 'slavery' as it emerges in local discourses since, as I will show, it is a key narrative device for interpreting Senegalese subjectivity at this crucial historical juncture.

'Le Sénégal sur la liste des terroristes'

This headline from the Senegalese daily *L'info 7* is misleading. At first blush, it implicates Senegal in a global terrorist network. The sentiment being expressed, instead, is quite different. This article indicates Senegal has been listed as one of the potential targets of a terrorist plot. It is not immediately clear why Senegal might be thought to obstruct terrorist aims – whatever they happen to be. Senegal is itself an Islamic nation, making this situation all the more curious.

Yet if it is true, as this targeting suggests, that Senegal somehow provoked the wrath of terrorists-at-large, it probably had to do with the dramatic turn of events that characterized the nation's new geopolitical agenda in the immediate aftermath of 9/11. Before the World Trade Center attacks were even ten days old, Wade had already

formed an African coalition to fight terrorism. This was not the only coalition in operation. The most well known is what would become the 'War for Enduring Freedom', a
military operation directed primarily, if not exclusively, by the United States. Senegal
had little to offer the United States and its allies in the way of arms. But what the
nation lacked in firepower, it made up in enthusiasm. Speaking not simply for himself
but for African Heads of State more generally, Wade affirmed on 20 September 2001
that African nations condemned the terrorist acts committed against the United States
nine days previously ('Les pays africains ont individuellement condamné les actes
terrorists commis contre les Etats-Unis le 11 septembre') and declared that, following
the lead of the global coalition of Western nations fighting terrorism, he would create
a committee of seven African nations dedicated to the same cause ('J'ai proposé … la
création d'un comité de 7 chefs d'Etat … contre le terrorisme'). Why exactly African
participation needed a separate channel along which to proceed was not altogether
clear from the *L'Info 7* article that carried Wade's remarks. Crystal clear, however, was
the President's commitment to forming the collective in which he expected to include,
at least, the Nigerian, South African and Algerian heads of state. And, although he had
not yet heard back from them, Wade assured the world he would do his part to ensure
no African nation would finance or otherwise enable terrorist activities. This he
considered not simply a Muslim affair; in fact, it was, in many ways, not a Muslim
affair at all because the President remained convinced there were no terrorist activities
of this sort operating in Senegal although the country is more than 90 per cent
Muslim.[4]

Early on, Wade made it clear he wanted his coalition to include Presidents Thabo
Mbeki of South Africa, Olesugun Obesanjo of Nigeria, Abdelaziz Boutéflika of Algeria,
and acting President of the Organization of African Unity, Frederik Chiluba of Zambia.
By the time Wade's summit was convened on 17 October in Dakar, it boasted 15
African heads of state.[5] Based on deliberations taking place during this time, the
countries assembled created a Déclaration de Dakar ultimately signed by 27 nations
which acknowledged the gravity of the actions initiated by terrorists on September 11,
2001, affirmed the solidarity of these African countries with the United States of
America, expressed its conviction that Africa remain free of all terrorist activity
whether motivated by political, philosophical, ideological, racial, ethnic or religious
concerns, considered the guidelines of the United Nations and the Organization of
African Unity/African Union to offer the best protocol for fighting terrorism, and
recommended that the Pact Against Terrorism, proposed and coordinated by Senegal,
be ratified through official protocol. The document concludes by congratulating
Abdoulaye Wade for taking the lead among African Heads of State to promote peace
and security throughout the Continent.[6]

Senegal's leadership in this regard was acknowledged by many, including the United
States. *Le Soleil*'s front page article from the day the Pact first convened shows the then
US Secretary of State Colin Powell clasping Wade's right hand affectionately. Thirteen
days later, George W. Bush would publicly affirm his appreciation for Africa's efforts
at the Forum for African Economic and Commercial Cooperation.[7] In remarks from
the same day, Bush announced he would put up 200 million dollars toward private

investment for countries in sub-Saharan Africa and was ready to offer American corporations certain protections against risk to encourage investment in the region.[8]

The role these African nations agreed to play in fighting terrorism could be considered a basic humanitarian reflex. It does not, by itself, signal a particular relationship with the United States. But the key role Senegal played in organizing the Pact, it seems, requires further examination when one considers the fact that it is an Islamic country *and* that, by creating a pact against terrorism, this African nation automatically – if indirectly – joined the United States as part of the coalition that would expand the purview of freedom through militaristic campaigns organized against those nations it considered to be complicit with global terrorism. Besides, as the *L'Info 7* article mentioned above indicates, not only did Wade explicitly invoke this agenda when describing his Pact's *raison d'être*, it was implied as well in his statement that his alliance was designed to complement the efforts of 'Western nations' already organized for this effort.

It bears mentioning, too, that Wade's determined position on the matter was not reflective of the nuanced exchanges taking place in Senegalese popular media. Critical of the way Bush's coalition was driven by what seemed to many as a divine right to fight, Cheikh Bamba Dioum published an article in *Le Soleil* entitled, 'God bless the USA … *And* Afghanistan'.[9] Malick Ndiaye, Leader of the Collective Social Forces for Change, instead declared that he supported 'neither Bush nor Ben Laden' in his *L'info 7* piece.[10]

In trying to understand why Wade considered it to be so important that Senegal provide immediate assistance to the US, it is worth noting relations between the countries are significantly better than they have been historically.[11] Available documentary evidence demonstrates the latter's increased role regarding political support and financial assistance.[12] The US is such an important benefactor for Senegal, in fact, that French President Jacques Chirac recently held talks with President Wade to 'remind' him which country has historically been his greatest ally.[13]

Still, even if one believes that Senegal's crusade against terrorism was at least in part motivated by the effort to build closer ties with the United States, it is not altogether clear whether its 2001 geopolitical strategies were indicative of the extent to which that bond had already been solidified, or whether it was an effort to more fully secure one. Bush's response seems to have created a powerful incentive in any case. However much the 200 million dollar investment fund was the deliberate result of US enthusiasm about Africa's anti-terrorism effort, it sent a message that the superpower nation approved and was prepared to offer its support both rhetorically and financially. To the extent that African nations are frequently expected to demonstrate their commitment to democracy as a precondition for receiving foreign direct assistance, this act could be taken as a sign that fighting terrorism is one way of producing democratic governance. In this fight, Bush believed one either supported the cause or sabotaged it. In various international arenas, he worked to recruit allies. These domains did not have to be explicitly political either. He threatened to boycott US participation in the 2002 World Cup, for instance, if other nations did not demonstrate a satisfactory commitment to fighting against the encroachment of global terrorist networks.

Ultimately, however, Bush must have been pleased he decided not to do so because the US national team performed exceptionally well during the tournament competition and reached the quarter-finals. This was the subject of a friendly conversation with another world leader whose team had also done surprisingly well. As they met in June 2002 to discuss politics and, among other things, how exactly each country was planning to fight terrorism and promote democracy in the world, George W. Bush and Abdoulaye Wade 'dreamed' about the possibility that, if both teams continued to excel in their respective divisions, the US and Senegal would meet in the World Cup Championship.[14] At the same time, soccer was becoming increasingly significant for Senegalese subjects at the local level.

'Il faut travailler…'

Thus it seems, even as Senegal was proving itself increasingly democratic by leading the African war against terror, it was pursuing another course of action partially aimed at improving its national image. This leads back to the query posed earlier about why soccer became ensnared in horrified accounts of the Bush visit. Is it significant that Goréans experienced slavery again for the first time on the island's only soccer terrain? If so, what implications does this have for Senegalese politics?

The answers to these questions lie in the events surrounding Senegal's World Cup bid and details concerning the 'successes' it achieved. Evaluating these means we must revisit key moments in the Presidency of Abdoulaye Wade since the extent to which he has been able to combat postcolonial problems serves as the point of departure for understanding the propensities of contemporary political operations.

In 2000, Abdoulaye Wade finally moved from the Senegalese opposition into the role of Head of State for a nation that had seen Senghor's rule from independence in 1960 until 1981 followed by the subsequent direction of his former Prime Minister Abdou Diouf for another 19 years. Many hoped that the country had finally received leadership that could breathe new life into a stagnant economy. One of the reasons Wade's 2000 Presidential bid was so successful – when measured against his adversary's and his own previous efforts – was that he managed to secure the participation of Senegal's most powerful and disaffected constituency: the youth. In a nation where more than 50 per cent of the population is under the age of 20 and where urban youth constitute more than 40 per cent of the total 48 per cent unemployed population,[15] the youth labour problem *is* the nation's most significant economic obstacle. Previously, youth had been more often an object of political discourse than a subject of political change and transformation. With the 2000 election, many believe, this began to change. Using the Wolof word *Sopi*, meaning 'Change' as his campaign mantra, Wade summoned the nation's resources of regeneration in a concerted effort to displace the political world Senghor created in favour of one that would, he argued, assign youth the important role they deserve in Senegalese political and social life.

As indicated in his inaugural address, Wade specifically intended for Senegalese youth to become the engine of national productivity – and production, more precisely.

His inaugural speech, in which he referred to this constituency as the country's most valuable 'resource', builds to a crescendo that closes with the motto for which Wade would subsequently become famous. It is a phrase that links various seemingly disparate aspects of the President's political philosophy: 'There is no secret [to success]: you should work, work some more, work a lot – work forever.' ('Il n'y a pas de secret: il faut travailler, encore travailler, beaucoup travailler, toujours travailler'.) Wade's words were memorialized and resurface in a number of popular *mbalaax* songs throughout Senegal. 'Il faut travailler, beaucoup travailler, encore travailler, toujours travailler…' is always the refrain. The most popular of these songs was made by the group Pape et Cheikh. But as the song ends, the chorus changes, the most significant word in the mantra being transformed by the writers' efforts to index what they no doubt hope will be the outcome of all this hard work, 'Il faut gagner, encore gagner, beaucoup gagner, toujours gagner' ('You should win, win some more, win a lot, always win').[16]

Le Sénégal qui gagne

> While Africa pours talent into European football, it has yet to benefit from the economic and social development that could be generated by professionalizing this sport.

Isabelle Saussez[17]

Senegal prepared to qualify for the 2002 World Cup amidst a general sense that this historical moment was unprecedented. Sports enthusiasts praised the team for its talent, poise and conditioning. As the team marched straight through the qualifying matches, few were surprised, and with each additional victory, national enthusiasm increased. Even former coach Claude Le Roy, now in France, spoke in glowing terms about the great squad he had left behind in Dakar. By his estimation, the team stood a great chance to win big at the previous World Cup, but an administrative error had prevented it from competing.[18] Now, it seemed, they would perform to the best of their tremendous abilities on an international stage. That outsiders emphasized their support for the Senegalese side only intensified domestic pride for their achievements.

Little wonder, then, that when the team finally qualified for the World Cup an impromptu parade commenced as Senegalese peoples floated downtown Dakar in celebration of this momentous achievement. For his part, President Wade cut short an official trip to France so he could party with the national team at home: 'At this time, it's the most important thing that could happen to any country and I will join the team and the nation in celebrating by reducing the amount of time I was expected to stay in Paris.' He offered, as well, his sentiments about the importance of this moment, 'My deepest congratulations go to the courageous Lions who have *made history* for Senegal'.[19] The President resurfaced in Senegal wearing the jersey of striker El-Hadji Diouf and joined the 'madness' that characterized local celebrations, according to one spectator. A few days later, the President held a special ceremony and concert at the Presidential Palace, where each team member was presented with a bonus of 10 million FCFA (then $15,000).[20] Senegal's qualification was made sweeter by the fact that, at that moment, the team was officially ranked 14th in Africa and only 70th in the world.

Yet, it was only one of four African teams admitted to World Cup competition that year. Immediately, Senegal received a flurry of invitations asking the team to compete in various matches, including one each against Japan and South Korea – co-hosts for 2002 World Cup action – and a match expected to be Brazilian soccer star Ronaldo's 'welcome back' game after recovering from an injury.[21]

Entering World Cup competition was such a big deal for Senegalese soccer enthusiasts that star striker El-Hadji Diouf felt like 'People in Senegal were as happy as if the team had already 'won the World Cup'.[22] By the time World Cup play actually approached the following year, the entire nation was fighting back nervous excitement. As Senegal prepared quietly, political officials, fans and journalists affirmed the importance of the victory for a nation only now earning a reputation as a major contender among the world's elite football teams. The drama was intensified by the fact that Senegal was slotted to battle its former colonial master, France. This athletic contest was saturated by its world-historical significance. As long-time supporter Souleman Soldi Goliathe indicated, 'Senegal-France is an historic match. Our matches against Denmark and Uruguay are important, but France is the one that really matters ... This is the European country that colonized us. And, God willing, we will beat them.' The government, in its effort to galvanize support for the team, promoted the slogan that the *Lions de Teranga* – as the team is affectionately called – hail from 'Le Senegal qui gagne' ('The Senegal that wins'). Where the slogan came from is not altogether clear, but in the days, weeks and months leading up to the match against France, the motto littered fliers, posters and signs across the country. *Le Sénégal qui gagne*. Once emblazoned across the nation, the phrase stuck. El-Hadji Diouf, arguably the team's best, but certainly it's most controversial, player, seemed profoundly to understand the political consequences of this postcolonial drama. As the team had swept through qualifying competitions on the strength of his eight goals, he found himself catapulted into the position to command the Senegalese forces for this important battle. 'It's like being the leader of a country', he once said when asked to explain his feelings about this historic encounter.[23]

So when Senegal pulled off the 1-0 upset victory, few could contain their adulation. Pape Mbaye, a 28-year-old supporter who found himself screaming his support for the team in an impromptu parade outside the Presidential Palace, was not sure whether the event officially constituted a national holiday or not but, as far as he was concerned, 'It might as well be, because everyone is out on the streets'.[24] Once again, supporters crowded the innermost streets of Dakar, gravitating, significantly, around Le Place de l'Independance and the Presidential Palace. Red, yellow and green Senegalese flags, hats, scarves, t-shirts and African-style boubous, were the only acceptable attire to commemorate the occasion.

These circumstances nevertheless reveal a paradox. Many of the Senegalese players are arguably as European as they are African. At the very least, most of them have honed their skills overseas. Further, to the extent that they spend most the year playing for European club teams – in France, Switzerland, and England – they are hardly ever in the country.[25] Yet they are its emissaries on important diplomatic missions, such as this one. This seeming contradiction actually exposes a more significant and widespread feature of Senegalese social life: whether one is speaking of professional athletes, musicians, students, politicians, merchants or professors, the persons occupying the highest ranks of power and wealth are those who spent some period of time 'absent' from the nation. Socio-economic mobility in this context, in other words, means moving out to move up.

Despite this, the power of the win was impossible to deny. And suddenly, *Le Sénégal qui gagne* referred not simply to a nation with the ability to win, but one that had proved it could and was destined to do so. Supporters delivered the chant when welcoming the national team back home. Abdoulaye Wade was careful to use it in speeches. It was a slogan that, when offered, immediately invoked the euphoria attached to this victory. The motto followed the national team through World Cup competition.

As might be expected, the team's success cast a favourable impression on the President, who was quick to associate himself with this turn of events. Immediately declaring a national holiday in honour of the team's victory, Wade appeared at the national parade in a vehicle with the top open so everyone could see him juggling a soccer ball to commemorate this important event.

Having been in office only two years at that point, Wade's presidency had coincided with Senegal's eruption onto the world scene as a soccer team of renown. Making public note of his undying emotional and financial support for the squad, especially after this victory, made him into a national hero of sorts even as it provoked criticism from his opposition who remained disgusted at what they considered to be vulgar opportunism. 'Of course, our president is trying to capture this performance of the Senegalese boys, but I think it is very childish, painful I think [*sic*], because it is not the result of his football policy', said Amath Dansokho, leader of the Independence and Labor Party, part of Wade's opposition.[26]

Senegal would win again before tying a match and losing another to finally exit World Cup competition. But they had already 'made history', affirming a place in the spotlight for themselves and their national leader.

What is to be made of the team's success and of its ability to cast a positive spin on Abddoulaye Wade's tenure at the nation's helm? Indeed, as a result of this athletic spectacle, many people ignored the concerns of rural agriculturalists who'd seen their peanut returns diminish steadily from the moment independence was achieved in 1960, when Senegal was one of the world's leading producers of the crop. What of the government's inability to cope with recurring energy shortages, or the fact that it had not yet found a way to replace the countless jobs lost to agricultural stagnation or quell the escalating numbers of young men who had been crowding urban areas for the past few decades in search of work as a result?

Dansokho's remarks are telling. Without even offering an elaborate treatment of the gender issues under consideration, he indexes them by referring to the national team as 'boys' and condemning Wade's appropriation of their hard work. After all, one of the most prominent features of Senegalese neoliberalism has been the way it valorizes masculinity in projects imagined as being the most economically viable and successful. From the exploits of Murid traders overseas, which contribute overwhelmingly to the remittances which now constitute one of the largest incomes for Senegalese families, to the athletes such as soccer and, increasingly, basketball players, Senegalese success stories frequently privilege male subjects with access to foreign capital. And why

shouldn't they? In a country with few economic options, and hardly any local industries of note, is that not the only way the economy can be saved?

Certainly from one vantage point, Senegalese politics has been characterized, during
the past several decades, by increased reliance on structural adjustment, donations
from other nations, and revenues derived from the increased privatization of industries. This includes granting amnesty to Murids who make valuable donations to the
government in return for tax leniencies. In this way, their holy city of Touba can even
be considered, to a large extent, privatized. But whether this is the most fruitful political
course to pursue remains to be seen. Just as privatization has increased, so has the
intensity of the nation's employment slump. Meanwhile, the repertoire of alternatives
that might effectively remedy this predicament has all but dissipated.

It seems one should, therefore, be critical of the assumptions underlying this intense
adherence to neoliberal schemes despite the growing body of evidence that such a strategy, by itself, will likely yield few positive long-term results. Taking my cue from the
way this ideology is entangled with the nation's commitment to highlighting sporting
successes, I have tentatively called this set of political commitments *gagnism. Gagner* is,
of course, the French verb meaning 'to win'. Concerning Senegalese politics, the
government is presently proceeding as if it believes neoliberal capitalism furnishes a set
of rules that, when followed, will automatically yield the desired results. This is the
same idea promoted in athletic competition, that a proper disciplinary regime automatically translates into victory. For that reason, the parallels are startling.

Yet the ideology of gagnism is rather more elaborate than Senegal's commitment to
winning by pursuing this particular formula. To carry the analogy further, athletic
competition always presumes an idealized subject, imagined to be most well suited for
sporting contests. Just as firms try their best to select athletes most capable of achieving
the desired results, a key aspect of Senegalese neoliberalism involves convincing potential donors that it has achieved a form worthy of their investment. Each country is
expected to fit a particular profile: democracy according to a particular definition, for
instance. Otherwise, it is considered unfit for sponsorship and is, in these instances,
disqualified from competition altogether.[27] NEPAD (the New Partnership for
Africa's Development), after all, 'calls on African leaders *to put their houses in order* in
exchange for foreign direct investment' (Owusu, emphasis added).

Or one might consider one of the World Bank's most recent poverty reduction
efforts in Africa, the CDF or Comprehensive Development Framework. Soon after he
was appointed President of the Bank in 1995, James Wolfenson created the CDF as a
development framework that would not focus solely on macroeconomic factors but
would also consider the social, political, cultural and environmental aspects of social
empowerment. These measures were taken with the understanding that Structural
Adjustment Programs (SAPs) had been ill-conceived and seldom successful. It is
nevertheless difficult to distinguish definitively between the two different kinds of
programmes because, while SAPs are marked by what Owusu calls 'a coercive conditionality', and CDFs promote autonomy for countries receiving assistance, this does
not mean they do not have their own measures for assessing that certain conditions are
met. CDFs, in fact, often contain a selectivity predicated on the presence of a 'good

policy environment' which is so ambiguously defined it tends to undermine the programme's expressed guarantee of country self-direction, constraining it under more clandestine forms of conditionality which translates into the persistence of rigorous modes of subject-management at the level of the nation-state.

The extent to which *gagnism* is an appropriate analytic for evaluating contemporary Senegalese politics remains to be seen. For the moment, it only bears mentioning that it constitutes a specific idea about the salvific capacity of male-managed foreign capital and a sense that the nation's hopes for success depend in large part on its ability to prove it can assume the form idealized as being most appropriate for achieving positive results, according to the firms that broker the capital exchanges from which Senegal expects to benefit.

This male-focussed image of 'success', portrait of potential overseas exchange(s), and emphasis on foreign investment accompanied by the corporate sponsorship of agencies located elsewhere, all provide clues that might help explain why a soccer field was the site for the staging of this neoliberal spectacle. But to make sense of local discourses that index the horrors of slavery in the midst of Senegal's quest toward economic and political liberalization, one must devote critical attention to the circumstances surrounding 'the visit' that provoked comparisons with the legacy of this region's most inhumane traffic in human commodities.

Though American publications spoke of Bush's address as one directed at Senegalese peoples,[28] most of them were too busy (fighting heat exhaustion) and too far removed (from the Gorée Island museum) to hear the address. The speech is nevertheless important to analyze because it had a purpose *and* an audience. Determining how each of these might be understood based on the way these events could be read from the vantage of Senegal's new relationship with the US, is the primary analytic objective in the next section.

A Heartbreaking Speech of Staggering (Ir)relevance

> Ships at a distance have every man's wish on board.
>
> Zora Neale Hurston, Their Eyes Were Watching God

According to those interviewed, Bush arrived on Gorée Island around 11.00 a.m. US State Department records indicate his remarks began promptly at 11.47 a.m.. Almost immediately, the US President situated his remarks in the context of the history of Trans-Atlantic slavery, which serves as the backdrop for this important speech event.

> At this place, liberty and life were stolen and sold. Human beings were delivered and sorted, and weighed, and branded with the marks of commercial enterprises, and loaded as cargo on a voyage without return. One of the largest migrations of history was also one of the greatest crimes of history.
>
> Below the decks, the middle passage was a hot, narrow, sunless nightmare; weeks and months of confinement and abuse and confusion on a strange and lonely sea. Some refused to eat, preferring death to any future their captors might prepare for them. Some who were sick were thrown over the side. Some rose up in violent rebellion,

delivering the closest thing to justice on a slave ship. Many acts of defiance and bravery are recorded. Countless others, we will never know...

Here Bush endorses resistance as a feasible strategy for Africans who refuse to accept their own captivity. Perhaps Bush believes that, when faced with a 'crim[inal]' and tyrannical regime people ought to pursue their freedom by any means necessary.

And yet, Senegal became an important US ally at this historical juncture because of President Wade's expressed disdain for Islamic jihads waged by Muslims who see the United States as an imperial regime. These adversaries would likely position themselves against the superpower as its victims, like the Africans who were objectified as part of 'commercial enterprise'. But Bush certainly was not speaking of *them*. The 'War for Enduring Freedom' was about identifying 'terrorists' associated with the axis of evil, not commending people who decide to declare themselves revolutionaries in the face of a political superpower. This phraseology, then, applauds a nebulous sense of resistance that does not correspond to any particular historical actors or events. Perhaps this explains why no specific personages or sites of struggle are named, though Bush would be more specific at other moments in his speech:

> In the struggle of the centuries, America learned that freedom is not the possession of one race. We know with equal certainty that freedom is not the possession of one nation. This belief in the natural rights of man, this conviction that justice should reach wherever the sun passes leads America into the world.

> With the power and resources given to us, the United States seeks to bring peace where there is conflict, hope where there is suffering, and liberty where there is tyranny ... Africans have overcome the arrogance of colonial powers, overturned the cruelties of apartheid, and made it clear that dictatorship is not the future of any nation on this continent. In the process, Africa has produced heroes of liberation – leaders like Mandela, Senghor, Nkrumah, Kenyatta, Selassie and Sadat. And many visionary African leaders, such as my friend, have grasped the power of economic and political freedom to lift whole nations and put forth bold plans for Africa's development.

Armed with the appreciation for truth and justice achieved through the activism of African-descended peoples in the US, who worked alongside concerned whites, the United States government is apparently now using its 'power and resources' to introduce 'peace' and 'end conflict' in ways that are especially beneficial to African people.

Bush's haste to link African people to the American quest for 'freedom' forced a grammatical miscue. Instead of saying that 'African people are now writing "their" own story of liberty' he says 'African people are now writing *your* own story of liberty...' And this is a narrative that features most prominently the African 'fathers' of independence, which include the first Senegalese President Leopold Sedar Senghor and someone Bush refers to as his 'friend', who remains unnamed although he is most likely referring to current Senegalese President Abdoulaye Wade whom he commends for having 'grasped the power of economic and political freedom to lift whole nations and put forth bold plans for Africa's development'. He is speaking of NEPAD, the New Partnership for Africa's Development, an initiative that 'support[s] neoliberalism and sees global integration as the key to Africa's development'. Wade was one of the main architects of the proposal and is one of its biggest supporters in Africa.

> Because Africans and Americans share a belief in the values of liberty and dignity, we must share in the labor of advancing those values. In a time of growing commerce across the globe, we will ensure that the nations of Africa are full partners in the trade and prosperity of the world ... We know that these challenges can be overcome ... There is a voice of conscience and hope in every man and woman that will not be silenced – what Martin Luther King called a certain kind of fire that no water could put out. That flame could not be extinguished at the Birmingham jail. It could not be stamped out at Robben Island Prison. It was seen in the darkness here at Gorée Island, where no chain could bind the soul. This untamed fire of justice continues to burn in the affairs of man, and it lights the way before us. May God bless you all.

According to this view Africa's descendants overseas are, by now, American and therefore no longer need to be separated out. Instead, Bush focuses on outlining the way their shared 'belief in the values of dignity and liberty' link up with the need to make Africa 'full partners in the trade and prosperity of the world'. The alternative – not being 'full partners ... in ... trade' – is linked, in this discourse, to all manner of social problems, including the spread of AIDS and civil wars – both infectious diseases that, apparently, run rampant in Africa. Not to 'move in [this] direction', too, is to fuel the efforts of 'merciless terrorists' and Senegal's historic mission would not allow it to do that, given the way its present geopolitical projects dovetail with the spirit that sustained both Martin Luther King, Jr. in his Birmingham jail and Nelson Mandela in his Robben Island cell. These leaders endured these forms of incarceration to awaken a sense of 'hope' that dwells in the 'human heart' of every 'man and woman'.

Bush, apparently, was not the only one concerned with where 'hope' lies. The French equivalent (ESPOIR) was scrawled on the wall of the Gorée Island site where the local population was detained. This word had a special significance for me, based on my travails in Senegal. Invariably, friends would ask if I could somehow help facilitate their career pursuits. The word 'espoir' was always used to articulate their aspirations. My friend Lamine for instance, a sculptor, once asked if I might be interested in going into business with him. If I could front the money for him to make a major purchase of wood from Mali, he suggested, he could produce a number of sculptures in bulk and split the profits with me. He knew it was more of a long-term investment, but he was sure we both stood to gain. 'I know it's a lot to ask, Michael', he conceded, 'But you're my last hope [*dernier espoir*]'.

Some months after my first visit to Senegal in 2002, I received a letter from Pierre, a security guard for the home where I had stayed. He was writing to ask if I knew of any security or law enforcement opportunities in the US for which he might be suited. As the letter drew to a close he, too, made sure to indicate that I was his *dernier espoir* [last hope]. Significantly, I think, the phrase of note was *dernier espoir* – always in French, even for my friends who communicated almost entirely in Wolof and acknowledged they were barely literate in the nation's official language.

This term, *espoir*, as an index of desperation stood opposite another which was used to articulate the prospect of prosperity: *gagner*. Lamine and Pierre (who don't know each other) both used to say they needed my assistance because, in Senegal, it was *difficile à gagner quelque chose* (difficult to find something). A former basketball player I once interviewed expressed the same distress. 'In Senegal', Ibrahim told me in Wolof,

'It is difficult to find [*gagner*] a job unless you are well-placed [*bien placé*].' The phrase *difficile à gagner quelque chose*, though relatively simple, resists translation. The sense being communicated here is that it is 'hard to find something' or 'difficult to find work'. But the word *gagner* was usually deployed by interviewees to speak about prospects for *earning* money. They hoped this or that opportunity would enable them to 'earn' an income. *Gagner*, then, means at once to 'find', 'win' or 'earn' revenue. And, like *espoir*, it is a sentiment that, for whatever reason, made more sense to communicate in French than through a Wolof equivalent.

It is in this context that being imprisoned on Gorée Island during a visit from the world's foremost superpower reminded Senegalese citizens of the extent to which they are 'trapped' in a particular marginal economic and political position, just as it led others to the conclusion that, although it was 'unjust', it was something the country 'needed' if it is to gain stature in the world of nations.

In this time of economic desperation, moments like the Bush visit crop up as opportunities for the nation to attract the kind of capital commitment that could, potentially, reverse its economic course. But what is the significance of this event at Gorée Island and why does the theme of 'enslavement' speak so profoundly to Senegal's historic place in an Atlantic economic formation and the role to which it aspires in the contemporary incarnation of this triangulation? The victims of the 'enslavement' that characterized the 2003 visit might be sceptical of the message being promoted but, in the current political climate, a message need not be well received to achieve a meaningful transformation between two collective entities. Increasingly, in fact, it is the 'abortive rituals' that subjects enact that help them 'erase' past actions so these do not undermine present pursuits.

Qui gagne?: The Neoliberal Subject in Senegal

> We are never so steeped in history as when we pretend not to be.
>
> Michel-Rolph Trouillot[29]

During a visit to Paris on 18 November 2002, President Abdoulaye Wade met with Senegalese students in a conversation he used to defend his image against widespread public scrutiny regarding his negligible impact on the nation's most pressing social problems. Undaunted, the Head of State Wade claimed his presidency had in fact been responsible for numerous 'successes', which included the national team's victory over France in the World Cup a few months prior.

But why should the performance of the national team be viewed as a victory for the Presidency? Why was it mentioned alongside other aspects of domestic policy? What is the position of sport in the Senegalese political imagination, and how has that role been shaped by the political initiatives promoted under Wade?

Framing these questions in the context of such political manoeuvring leads right back to Senegal's new relationship with the United States. In thinking through the events that transpired at Gorée, one is inclined to wonder why George W. Bush mentioned the events of the Trans-Atlantic Slave Trade in his speech at all. The precise motivations driving the production and reception of this political performance are difficult to discern, but it should be noted – as the work of Michel-Rolph Trouillot indicates – this kind of narrative has become more frequent in recent years. As he explains, 'Collective historical apologies are increasing worldwide … these rituals of apology create pastness by connecting existing collectivities to past ones that either perpetrated wrongs or were victimized'. Citing, among other examples, the Reconciliation Walk where participants marched throughout Europe along the same path as that of Christian warriors involved in the Crusades to apologize for the destruction wrought by their religion, Trouillot outlines the conditions of possibility in which some collective subjects feel compelled to address others, creating a complex relationship to history in the process since, often times, who inhabits these collectivities is not altogether clear. Frequently, the events to which these 'apologies' refer have taken place several centuries before. It is not always evident, then, to whom the addressers are referring, or which addressees are being targeted. Yet, given that the point about such claims may be less what they assert than the fact of their assertion,[30] it might be in the structure of these illocutions that we discover their true significance for the actors involved, 'As transformative rituals, apologies always involve time … [t]hey mark a temporal transition: wrong done in the past is recognized as such, and this acknowledgement itself creates or verifies a new temporal plane, a present oriented toward the future'. Indeed, from the ethnographic evidence marshalled above, it seems subjects from both Senegal and the United States were interested in using evidence of a 'wrong done in the past' – in this case, the tansatlantic traffic in human beings – to erect 'a present oriented toward' a mutually beneficial future.

But though Trouillot's important work on these kinds of illocutionary rituals helps us to understand what is at stake in these speech acts, his term for them – 'historical apologies' – is something of a misnomer in this case. After all, Bush did not actually apologize for slavery during his visit to Senegal. For the second time in fact, the US President faced criticism for not apologizing for the nation's participation in this cruel exchange, an admission many people feel is long overdue. Ultimately, if we review the transcript from George W. Bush's speech above, it is possible to chronicle the intricate lyrical gymnastics he undertook to elaborate some of the horrors of the slave trade *without* actually offering an apology. If indeed, as Trouillot suggests, apologies are used to create 'pastness' between the perpetrator and recipient of a 'wrong', perhaps this sheds light on the reasons why the United States has never been able to offer a formal apology for slavery, neither at the United Nations Conference on Racism where the US delegation left early,[31] nor on this fateful day at Gorée. Maybe there is something about the historical trajectory of US political and economic ambitions that renders slavery inhumane but prevents it from being considered 'wrong'.[32] Maybe, even beyond the widely acknowledged point that slavery and freedom are conditions of each other's possibility, it is true that slavery is a form of economic extraction difficult to disentangle from the structure of capitalism, although the latter is usually imagined as having successfully moved beyond it.

Sadly, many Goréeans may not be able to move beyond the trauma associated with Bush's visit to the island, despite the fact that, for many of them, slavery had previously been a distant notion even as they inhabit an island whose traffic in that legacy provides its primary revenue. Ironically, as this essay has shown, the consequences of this seeming paradox were spelled out most explicitly during Senegal's attempt to court amiable relations with a potential political ally and financier. All this suggests neoliberal economic transactions have complex constitutions: they provide not merely moments of contradiction amidst what can seem like exploitative behaviour but a sense that such hardship is a necessary part of the process one must undergo to reconstruct one's image – and, by extension, improve one's chances of achieving 'success'.

Notes

[1]   Hesse, 'Forgotten Like a Bad Dream', 165.

[2]   Interviewees explained to me that on 7 July 2003 – the day George W. Bush visited Dakar, Senegal at the outset of his African tour – people were prohibited from going to work so the roads would be completely clear when the Presidential cavalry passed through. In order that security could ensure safe passage, apparently, hundreds of baobabs were cut down. This infuriated many Senegalese citizens of all ages, occupations and classes. The baobab is a national symbol of strength and solidarity. These trees represent wisdom and are, above all else, timeless. What did it mean that they could be decimated so casually, in exchange for a few hours with the US President? The account of what transpired at Gorée, though, was more intense. According to Bineta, the entire population of the island was taken to a soccer stadium and locked inside. I later learned it was a sandlot soccer field, barricaded to prevent escape. Yet the way the image was transformed into a solid fortification as the story circulated suggests that participants conveyed a sense of being physically confined to that spot. In the popular imagination, the makeshift barriers became concrete enclosures.

[3]   Some people insist even Senegalese law enforcement officials were trapped in the soccer terrain. Others claim unarmed local police were on hand to assist the American military, who brandished rifles. Either way, very few people were spared the humiliation of being hoarded onto the playing field, pinned against friends, neighbours, colleagues and comrades. Fewer still missed the profound irony that all this was taking place a few feet from the historic *Maison des Esclaves* (Slave Houses or Slave Dungeons), responsible for the tourism that usually provides this island economy's primary revenue.

In recent years, some scholars have raised an eyebrow about Gorée's historical legitimacy as a central port in the Trans-Atlantic Slave Trade. Recent work suggests the current site of the *Maison des Esclaves* served primarily as a private residence for one Anne Pépin (the *signare* of French governor Stanlisas-Jean, Chevalier de Boufflers) and her family, tenants, servants and slaves. Scholarship suggests that although Pepin sometimes engaged in various minor forms of overseas exchange and occasionally held enslaved Africans in the basement of the residence, the *Maison* was not the pivotal site of Atlantic dispersion it is often imagined to be. Given all this, the slavery discourses that emerged in the aftermath of 7 July 2003, seem at best curious, at worst, unjustified.

The Bush visit, though, ultimately hinges on a profound historical irony: the technique of coercion used to subdue Senegalese peoples in that moment was a more reliable reproduction of the way enslavement occurred on Gorée Island than any event that has ever occurred at the *Maison des Esclaves*, for slavery in this locale typically did not proceed through dungeons and warehousing. Instead, enslaved Africans were usually hoarded together and bound in open-air 'captiveries', awaiting placement onto ships that would send them across the Atlantic. For more on this, see Samb, *Gorée et l'esclavage*.

[4]   See 'Pour la création d'un Pacte africaine contre le terrorisme', *L'info 7*, Thursday 20 Sept. 2001, and 'Le président Wade propose un "Pacte africaine contre le terrorisme"', *Soleil*, Thursday 21 Sept. 2001.

[5]   'Les chefs d'État réaffirment l'engagement sans faille de l'Afrique', *Le Soleil*, 18 Oct. 2001, 3.

[6]   Ibid.

[7]   'Nous sommes reconnaissants de soutien offert par l'Organisation de l'unité africaine et par de nombreuses organizations régionales africaines', was the translation of Bush's commentary published by *Le Soleil* in the article, 'Bush remercie le continent africain pour son soutien [Bush thanks the African continent for its support],' 30 Oct. 2001.

[8]   Ibid. 'M. Bush également annoncé la création d'un fonds de soutienb des investissements privés dans la region … des garantie et une couverture du risque politique pour leurs projets en Afrique sub-saharienne.'

[9]   'God Bless the USA … and Afghanistan', *Le Soleil*, 12 Oct. 2001 (emphasis added).

[10] 'Les partisans du "Ni Bush ni Ben Laden" remittent ça aujourd'hui,' *L'info 7*, 7 Nov. 2001.

[11] Close ties between the US and Senegal, it must be noted then, constitute a recent occurrence. While Senegal has operated differently from many socialist nations in its reluctance to align itself with other socialist or communist countries, it was never intimate with the United States either. Sheldon Gellar argues, for instance, 'Senegal's ties with the United States have been primarily economic. Senghor's pro-French orientation, Senegal's policy of not taking sides in superpower conflicts, and the willingness of the United States to give France a free hand in francophone West Africa were all factors working against Senegal's developing close ties with the United States.' At the same time, for more than two decades there have been trends suggesting 'the two countries [might] very well develop close political ties'. Writing 23 years ago, Gellar noticed that, 'With its adamant opposition to any Soviet influence in Africa, the Reagan administration sees Senegal, which has sharply criticized Cuban and Soviet involvement in Angola and Ethiopia, as a friend and potential ally'.
Senegal's relationship with the United States, however, grew slowly during the past few decades. This alliance really only became significant economically and politically during the Clinton administration. Experts have long noticed that while Senegal is 'clearly closer to the West than to the Soviet Union and Eastern Europe in its political and economic outlook … [w]ithin the West Senegal looks more toward Western Europe than toward the United States'. And 'although Senegal may be moving somewhat closer to the United States', as a pragmatic way to secure financial assistance, a few decades ago it still seemed 'unlikely that the country [would] abandon its policy of nonalignment and openly take the side of the United States in the Cold War between the superpowers'. The War against Terror, on the other hand, seems to have offered Senegal the occasion to do so.

[12] See 'Les Etats-Unis renouvellent leur engagement en Afrique [The United States renews its relationship with Africa]', *Linfo 7*, 18 Feb. 2000 and 'Nous avons d'excellentes relations avec les Etats-Unis d'Amérique [We have a great relationship with the United States]', an article from *Le Soleil* that features this quote from Cheikh Tidjane Gadio, Minister of Foreign Affairs, 30 March 2001.

[13] Lara Pawson, 'France tackles Senegal's U.S. Trend', *BBC News*, 19 Feb. 2004.

[14] 'Bush et Wade rêvent d'une finale Sénégal-USA', *Le Soleil*, 19 June 2002. The front page headline translates as 'Bush and Wade dream of a Senegal-USA final match'. The article heading itself, on the newspaper's interior, carries a similar sentiment, 'Bush et Wade souhaitent USA-Sénégal', or 'Bush and Wade wish for a USA-Senegal final'.

[15] Recent statistics provided by the United States Central Intelligence Agency. See www.ciaworldfactbook.com/senegal.

[16] The term 'gagner' offers a semantic ambiguity that is useful to ponder. It could either mean 'to win' or 'to profit', in this phrase.

[17] 'Africa on the sidelines of world football', *The Courier ACP-EU*, July-Aug. 2002.

[18] 'We had a great team ten years ago, but unfortunately the chairman of the federation forgot to register us for qualification for Italia, so we missed out … The team today is even stronger and they will create a big surprise in Japan and Korea … in terms of quality of players, they have all it takes to put up a good performance at the World Cup.' See 'Le Roy backs Lions to reach q-finals', *BBC Sport*, 24 July 2001, <news.bbc.co.uk/sport/hi/english/football/Africa/newsid_1454000/1454984.stm>.

[19]   See 'Senegal celebrates Cup heroics', *BBC Sport*, 21 July 2001, <news.bbc.co.uk/sport/hi/english/football/Africa/newsid_1450000/1450680.stm> (emphasis added).

[20]   'Senegal back to heroes welcome', *BBC Sport*, 22 July 2001, <news.bbc.co.uk/sport/hi/english/football/Africa/newsid_1451000/1451800.stm>.

[21]   Ultimately, however, Senegal could not make the match and was replaced by Nigerian club champion Enyimbe. 'Invitations flood in for Senegal', *BBC Sport*, 11 Aug. 2001, <news.bbc.co.uk/sport/hi/english/football/Africa/newsid_1486000/1486387.stm>.

[22]   'Lions players rule in France', *BBC Sport*, 13 Aug. 2001, <news.bbc.co.uk/sport/hi/english/football/Africa/newsid_1488000/1488932.stm>.

[23]   'Senegal in fever over World Cup debut', *BBC Sport*, 14 May 2002, <news.bbc.co.uk/sport/hi/english/football/Africa/newsid_1986000/1986835.stm>.

[24]   'Football fever hits Senegal', *BBC Sport*, 12 June 2002, <news.bbc.co.uk/sport/hi/english/football/Africa/newsid_2040000/2040841.stm>.

[25]   'The whole of the Cameroonian squad plays abroad, along with 22 Senegalese, 21 Nigerians, 16 South Africans, and nine Tunisians.' Isabelle Saussez, 'Africa on the sidelines', *The Courier ACP-EU*, July-Aug. 2002.

[26]   'Senegal's success story', *BBC Sport*, 16 June 2002, <news.bbc.co.uk/sport3/worldcup2002/hi/team_pages/Senegal/default.stm>.

[27]   Taylor, *NEPAD*; NEPAD, *Annual Report*.

[28]   Scholars have, as yet, not devoted much attention to the Bush visit or its historical resonance with the Trans-Atlantic Slave Trade, either in the Senegalese popular imagination, or based on the constitutive features of this momentary captivity. Despite the fact we are now in a rather different historical epoch, a good deal remains to be learned, I think, from the infrastructure(s) through which capital—symbolic and economic—continues to circulate in trans-Atlantic circuits, and the political networks that make these forms of exchange possible.

To the extent that this was a moment captured, negotiated, and processed at length by Senegalese subjects, one ought to examine it to see what might be revealed about the character of Senegal's relationship to the U.S. and the neoliberal aspirations this political circuit seems to signify.

[29]   Trouillot, *Silencing the Past*, xix.

[30]   Ibid., xvii.

[31]   'Mixed emotions as Durban winds up', *BBC News*, 8 Sept. 2001, <212.58.226.40/hi/English/world/Africa/newsid_1530000/1530976.stm>.

[32]   Ibid. 'European countries agreed to apologize for slavery as a "crime against humanity"' (notably not the United States, although Bush would use the exact same phrasing two years later in his speech at Gorée). They, along with the United States, had been keen to make sure the wording would not make them liable for reparations. EU spokesman Koen Vervaeke, said: 'In the way [the UN resolution on racism] is drafted now, there *can't* be any legal consequences' (emphasis added).

References

Hesse, Barnor. 'Forgotten Like a Bad Dream: Atlantic Slavery and the Ethics of Postcolonial Memory.' In *Relocating Postcolonialism*, edited by David Theo Goldberg and Ato Quayson. Oxford: Blackwell Publishers, 2002.

NEPAD. *NEPAD Annual Report*. Midrand, South Africa: NEPAD Secretariat, 2002–03.

Samb, Djibril, ed. *Gorée et l'esclavage: Actes du Séminaire sur 'Gorée dans la Traite atlantique: mythes et réalités.'* Dakar: IFAN, 1997.

Taylor, Ian. *NEPAD: Towards Africa's development or another false start*. Boulder: Lynne Reinner, 2005.

Trouillot, Michel-Rolph. *Silencing the Past*. New York: Beacon Press, 1995.

Sports and Development in Malawi

Sam Mchombo

Introduction

The dominant view of development has, traditionally, been presented in terms of economic programmes. These reflect advances in the improvement of basic amenities in the lives of the people as well as provision of means for the attainment of those luxuries that contribute towards the improvement of the quality of life. While economic development may dwell on attraction of increased investments, production and marketing of material goods, the development of the infrastructure requisite for trade, both nationally and internationally, contributing to a healthy balance of payments, the programme of national development normally includes more. National development includes determination of the means by which the society regenerates itself, improves the production capabilities of the populace through the education and improved health of its youth, the diversification of its economic base, improved agricultural methods to guarantee food security, technological innovation and its integration into the cultural heritage of the people, adaptation of cultural practices to altered circumstances or change, et cetera. Thus, the programme of national development encompasses more than just improved living conditions.

This is significant because in the third world countries the idea of development tends to be driven by efforts to attain and adapt the achievements of the more developed countries, comprising what used to be known as the first or second world. The efforts to emulate the developed countries has, not entirely unexpectedly, been beset by difficulties leading to frustrations and, unfortunately, insurmountable national debt to international financial lending institutions such as the International Monetary Fund (IMF) or the World Bank. The debts incurred with those institutions have, ordinarily, been in addition to debts from individual developed nations under 'bilateral agreements'. Normally, loans secured under such bilateral agreements have included conditions that, effectively, contribute directly to the improvement of the quality of life in the lending nations. For instance, capital for the development of specific projects, such as the construction of a rail line, or of a factory, may be accompanied with the requirement that the raw material either be supplied by the borrowing country, not always possible, or be secured from the lending nation. This reduces the loan to a means to making the receiving country a client to companies in the lending country, effectively guaranteeing employment of the workforce in those companies, improving further the lending country's development. Additionally, the conditions that the lending institutions, specifically the IMF and the World Bank, have normally stipulated to ensure that the debts incurred are serviced, known as 'structural adjustment programs', have resulted in further erosion of the whole agenda of development, as third world governments have been forced into currency devaluation, elimination of government subsidies for the very programmes calculated to improve the lives of the people, and the forced adoption of a market economy of the developed world. The difficulties for the third world nations emanate from the fact that the economic and political bases that stimulated development in the developed nations are incommensurate with the conditions in the 'developing' countries. Worse, international aid has contributed as much to some aspects of development as it has to the further under-development of third world countries.[1]

Inevitably, the poor nations sometimes begin to seek alternative strategies to development or to re-define the concept of development. This amounts to relativization of the idea of development so that the notion captures what should count as improved conditions in the welfare of the populace relative to prevailing conditions and available resources. For instance, when the first president of Malawi, the late Hastings Kamuzu Banda, decided to move the country's administrative capital from the city of Zomba in the south, to Lilongwe in the centre, he made it explicit that he would strive for something that was 'simple but dignified'. In other words, it was not to be a replica of the capital city of some developed nation.

Development in Africa has also been adversely affected by other factors. These include chronic famine and the emergence of HIV/AIDS. The pandemic has had a devastating effect on the economic performance of African countries in that it has decimated the able-bodied and economically active and productive segment of society. The loss of youth has not only translated into economic stagnation but, given

the identification of the pandemic with sexual activity, it has contributed to curtail-
ment of the means of procreation and regeneration of society. This has forced a
review of the notion of national development. Under the circumstances, development has come to include not just the education of the youth but, rather, efforts to
save them, restore their health and, given the scarcity of financial resources, determine ways in which the youth can be encouraged to channel their energy and vigour
to the development of the country and its admittedly modified notion of development. It is the aforementioned conditions that have, in recent times, exploited the
youth's love of sports as a means to development. We turn to this aspect in the next
section.

Soccer in Malawi

It is something of a truism at this juncture that soccer is the most popular sport in
Africa. Indeed, its popularity is attested by the inordinate amount of meagre resources
allocated to it in most countries, far outstripping other sporting activities. The national
soccer leagues, affiliated to the Fédération Internationale de Football Association
(FIFA) through a local national Football Association, are probably the most organized
of all sporting activities at the national level. The soccer clubs participating in the
national leagues provide more than mere entertainment. Guilianotti and Armstrong
note that 'there is obviously more to the game than a collection of naked facts regarding
teams, results, and championships'.[2] Soccer provides one dimension of identity or of
political activism, as evidenced in recent efforts to promote peace in Mexico with the
Zapatistas, or to stamp out racism in and through sports. In fact, recently, on 29
November 2005, a team comprising Palestinians and Israelis, organized by the Foun-
dation of Shimon Peres, played a 'match for peace' against the leading Spanish club of
FC Barcelona, soon after the crowning of Ronaldinho, a player for FC Barcelona, as the
Ballon D'Or star (Europe's best player of the year). Soccer has also been featured in the
promotion or restoration of international understanding or relations, as when Team
USA, the men's national soccer team of the United States, hosted the national team of
Iran in Oakland, California, in 2001. The contest assumed greater significance in light
of the nadir reached in Iran/USA relations after the taking of American hostages in Iran
in 1979, later released in 1980.

Given the ethnic heterogeneity that characterizes African countries, sometimes
leading to civil or internal strife, national soccer teams participating in international
tournaments have achieved more in fostering national identity, albeit temporarily,
than political efforts may achieve. In some cases, such as in the Olympics or the
World Cup tournaments, African teams that qualify effectively unite the continent.
For instance, Giulianotti and Armstrong observe that '[W]hen Nigeria defeated
Argentina to win the football (or soccer) tournament at the 1996 Olympic Games,
that victory was no single victory for one nation over another. For most Africans
with an interest in football, Nigeria's triumph was a continental rather than a
national success.'[3] It has even been claimed that fútbol unites Latin America. As
McDaniel-Keith points out:

Football is a sport with more geo-political significance than most of us imagine. Since the Argentina-England war over the Falkland Islands and Argentina's World Cup win over England in 1986, meetings of the two teams have been referred to as 'blood matches'. The fact that these are football teams, not armies, is often lost in the bloody shuffle. The team becomes the country.

Football defeats can crush a country's hopes and self-image. When Argentina's economy crashed in 2001, many observers hoped that a win in the 2002 World Cup could restore national pride and dignity. When their team was eliminated in the first round, it was insult on top of injury: the two blows – economic and athletic – were inextricably linked in the national imagination.[4]

Part of the appeal of soccer is that, relative to other sporting activities, it is cheap. The basic equipment required is a ball, and this could be made of rags or plastic paper tied up, if a regulation ball cannot be secured. It also provides a means of socialization into cooperative ventures though participation in a team sport. The dynamics of such team sport include learning to cooperate with others and work together to achieve a special goal, viz., winning the game or overcoming the opposing team in concert. In addition, there is the development of individual skills and the improvement of motor skills, coordination of perceptual and motor skills, and improvement of personal physical health. The logic of attainment of defined and definable goals through cooperative work in a team is central to the exploitation of the sport to achieve ends other than the immediate ones of overcoming the opposing teams. Specifically, the ends could be redefined such that they include contribution to national development, appropriately determined, and the sport becomes a means to the achievement of those ends. Naturally, the redirection of the sport to serve as means to ends that are nebulous and removed from the immediate concerns of game results requires some incentives, as well as directors who determine the ends for which the sport can serve as the means. Indeed political candidates in some third world countries, for instance, in Malawi, have routinely exploited soccer during campaign seasons in order to woo votes. They supply soccer balls to youths, especially in impoverished rural areas, to gain popularity. In any case, part of the rationale behind the exploitation of sports, specifically soccer, in the service of national development in the east African nation of Malawi derives from the redefinition of the goals for which the sport is a means, and satisfaction of the requisite incentives to gain the support of the youth involved.

The Youth and National Development in Malawi

Besides the existence of the Ministry of Education, many African countries reflect their concern for, or interest in, youth involvement in national development through the creation of a Ministry of Youth and Sports. Sometimes 'culture' is included in that ministry when it is not part of the ministry of education. In general, the activities of such a Ministry rarely affect the majority of the youth who, in general, reside in rural areas. Low on the list of immediate needs, the budget for such a ministry cannot compete with that of health, agriculture or defence. Effectively, the Ministry has little more than token value. The youth cannot hope to be assisted in essential ways from the ministry, a fact that is aggravated by the fact that sporting activities in rural areas lack organization, sponsorship or even basic facilities. In Malawi, although other sporting activities get some support through the terms of reference of the Malawi National Council of Sports, the focus on sports remains largely on soccer. There, the attention goes to the teams (or clubs, to use the term most common in Europe) that participate in the national league. A number of those clubs have sponsorship. It is in the effort to provide the needed assistance to the sidelined youth and to motivate them to focus on more than the sporting activity that other youth development programmes have evolved. A specific example can be gleaned from ongoing activities in Malawi, to which I now turn.

In July 2002, I spent a few days in Ndirande, near the city of Blantyre in Malawi, waiting to return to my professional duties in the United States. Ndirande is a bustling 'township' that grew as people who moved into the Blantyre area seeking employment, continued to put up 'temporary' shacks et cetera. Englund provides an apt characterization of Ndirande. He notes that 'Ndirande, "the Soweto of Malawi", [is] a densely populated and predominantly poor township where migrants from all the districts of Malawi began to outnumber local villagers from the 1940s onwards'.[5] The current image of Ndirande remains far from attractive, as some accounts make evident. Thus, writing in *The Malawi News* of 27 September–3 October 2003, the Sports Reporter Pilirani Kachinziri, describes Ndirande in the following unflattering terms:

> Blantyre's sprawling slum of Ndirande is believed to be a den of criminals, drug traffickers and prostitutes.

> A bare 10-minute drive from city centre, this stretch of shanty township has most of its buildings made of card boards, corrugated iron sheets, mud and grass.[6]

It was in these surroundings that one afternoon, while waiting for my host to return from work, I spotted 10-year-old boys playing soccer in a small clearing by the roadside edge of a corn field with part of the uncultivated section serving as a make-shift trash dump. They were kicking a ball of wrapped plastic sheets. Lacking other pressing demands, and as a licensed referee of the United States Soccer Federation, I decided to pass the time with the kids. My offer to referee them was met with incredulity, but the sight of a regulation ball that I offered to lend them transformed their disbelief into joy. The dynamics of the game immediately altered and there was heightened interest of the on-lookers. Indeed, even a kids' game using a ball of plastic wrappers, played on an afternoon of a workday, could still command an audience.

At the end, one of the spectators, a teenager who introduced himself as Rafiki Makata, approached me for assistance in obtaining a soccer ball. He and other teenagers from the area played recreationally, but they lacked the most essential piece of equipment, a ball.

Mtaya Football League in Nkhotakota

My initial response to the request was decidedly negative. At that time I was involved in assisting the youth in Nkhotakota, my district of origin. Located along the central shores of Lake Malawi, Nkhotakota's claim to fame is that it is one of the places where in the nineteenth and early twentieth centuries, an era characterized by Arab slave trade in Malawi, slaves were collected for transportation by boat north to Tanzania and the Arabian Peninsula. Eventually, as the British sought to end slavery and establish colonial rule, it is the place where 'a deal was struck between the British and the local slave-trade agent Jumbe, to desist from further slave-trade. A treaty was signed between Jumbe and Sir Harry Johnson in 1889. The tree under which the treaty was brokered remains as an historical monument, a few yards away from the main center of Anglican missionary activity in Nkhotakota.'[7]

While passing by the village school of Chombo in 1997 I was treated to the sight of children having classes in the open, under trees. This was a consequence of lack of physical structures to hold classes in. Subsequently, I was appealed to for a soccer ball because the school, of which I am an alumnus, did not have a soccer ball. Eventually, I donated two balls only to find myself appealed to further for soccer outfits. The potential of converting me into the supplier of soccer equipment and more, through exploitation of the image of 'the local boy who made it good in California', was plainly evident. It was a ploy that, to all intents and purposes, was destined to make for a dependency relationship where the hardships of the school would be exploited to gain assistance, eventually to degenerate into the appearance of entitlement. I surmised that it would not be an apt means of aiding either the school or the local community. Rather, it was going to foster the illusion that there is a benefactor who will remedy the woes of the school and the community through the happenstance of being a local boy resident and working in the United States. Encouraging such an illusion would be a disservice to the community. In trying to determine ways of making a positive impact in the community, I resolved to make donations of sports equipment contingent on the recipients' willingness to contribute to their local communities through engaging in community service. These would include helping the elderly in their agricultural work to improve chances of increased food security, contributing to the maintenance of the health care facilities or clinics, of places of worship, clearing the cemeteries, increased commitment to their educational programmes, et cetera. In order to ensure that the conditions attached to the assistance did not undermine the authority of the school's principal, the project was conducted outside of the strictures of school administration. I organized youth soccer teams in the villages.

In 1999 I purchased two sets of soccer jerseys and shorts, and soccer balls. These were given to two teams. One, Kapanga Blades, was based in my village of Chombo, while the other, Chalunda Chizito Chiefs, was based some 50 km north, at Liwaladzi Health Center. This location was the residence of my aunt, Mrs Lilian Bai, and her husband, Mr Joseph Bai. The youth readily consented to focus on community service. Following on a suggestion made by Nancy Kendall, then a graduate student at Stanford University in California, focusing on public health issues in Malawi, I resolved to include heightened awareness of HIV/AIDS as part of the project.

The two teams that were organized in Nkhotakota would have constituted the extent of my involvement in youth development or my contribution to the local community. Alterations to the plan were a consequence of unforeseen subsequent developments. As a faculty member of the Berkeley campus of the University of California, my regular pursuits of teaching and research had distracted me from sports. However, in 1998 I got involved in soccer in my residential city of San Pablo, as a coach for Under 7 boys in the San Pablo United Youth Soccer Club. In the fall semester of 1999, subsequent to the donation of soccer gear to the teams in Malawi, I met Kim Brown, then a student in my Swahili class. She played for the campus women's team. When she learned about my efforts to engage the youth in Malawi in projects that would contribute to their local communities, she deemed it a worthwhile project and proceeded to discuss the matter with the Head Coach of Women's soccer, Kevin Boyd, and the assistant coach, Jennifer Thomas. They immediately noted a way to dispose of their unused or no longer useful equipment by donating it to an apparently good cause. The project immediately received support through donations of jerseys, shorts, shin-guards, balls, et cetera. In 2000, I increased the number of teams to four, the additions being the Yamikani Eagles in my home village, and the Ng'ombe Chargers at Liwaladzi. Further, I encouraged the youth to form a village league, the Mtaya Football League, through which the idea of community service and increased awareness of HIV/AIDS would be spread. Each team participating in the league and securing assistance through it would be required to engage in community service and contribute towards heeding warnings about HIV/AIDS. The contribution of the University of California at Berkeley (Cal) equipment made for increased involvement with the youth in Malawi and the project had decidedly taken on a life of its own. It also began to attract unwanted and unwarranted attention and concerns from political aspirants or incumbents. This called for the inclusion of explicit statements about the non-partisan and a-political nature of the programme.

Besides the contribution from Cal soccer, other soccer clubs in the East Bay and North Bay of the San Francisco Bay area also made contributions when the news spread. Donations of jerseys and cleats came from the San Pablo United Youth Soccer Club, El Cerrito Youth Soccer Club, Real Marin Soccer Club, et cetera. The youth interest grew as participation in the league and the call to community service were viewed as means to receiving soccer equipment. Of course a central aspect of all this was to contribute to improvement in the youth's physical health, in their technical skills in soccer playing, and in the provision of entertainment in areas still lacking basic amenities such as running water or electricity, which hampers delivery of entertainment provided by the electronic media. Further, traditional modes of entertainment, such as traditional dances, are seasonal.

Mtaya Football League was intended to be an effort at grass-roots level in a rural community to motivate the youth to engage in community service and heed warnings about HIV/AIDS. The teams participating in it were spread over a stretch of 50 kilometres. Using local rivers as convenient boundaries, the league was located in Nkhotakota district in the area bounded to the south by Kaombe River and to the north by Dwangwa River. It comprised two zones, one demarcated by Kaombe River to the south and Bua River to the north, and the other by Bua River to the south and Dwangwa River to the north. To promote interaction, each zone had an all-star or select team. The two teams, Mtaya Astros for the Kaombe-Bua zone, and Mtaya

Mavericks for the Bua-Dwangwa zone, would have periodic contests, providing occasion for the two communities to interact. The first contest was held in 2001 for which I served as the referee. A trophy that I had purchased in Mexico was presented to the winning team which was, on that occasion, the Mtaya Mavericks.

The contest provided a unique opportunity to reiterate the goals and objectives of the league. These included promotion of awareness among the youth of the AIDS pandemic and reinforcement of preventive measures, such as abstinence or the proper use of condoms; the use of sports as a means to encourage the youth to focus on education for self-empowerment, as well as their physical and mental development; and, to promote discipline and heighten a sense of responsibility among the youth.

It was also stressed that the league would remain a strictly non-political organization and would strive to maintain neutrality with regard to religious affiliation. In fact, emphasis was placed on promotion of tolerance with regard to political orientation or religious affiliation, and the youth were encouraged to be of service to their various places of worship, that included both churches and mosques.

On AIDS and Development in Malawi

The incorporation of AIDS awareness or education into the project is more than a matter of mere convenience or pandering to current interests or politically appealing issues. The pandemic has not merely been a calamity that has claimed lives but, as a consequence, it has had disastrous effects on development in African countries. The first publicized cases of AIDS may have been in California, initially identified with the gay community, but the disease has had its major impact in the countries of the sub-Saharan region of Africa. In those countries it is 'those people who have been groomed to lead the nation into the future who are dying at the highest rates. In South Africa's Natal Province, which suffers one of the highest AIDS rates anywhere, the epidemic has led to a self-perpetuating public health nightmare.'[8] The public health nightmare indicated here is one that has profoundly affected economic development and complicated in non-trivial ways strategies or content of national development. Economically, the decimation of the most productive segment of the population, teachers, police, medical personnel, the civil service, the military, et cetera, has translated into scarcity of work-force, resulting in deterrence of investment as apprehension grows concerning the rate of returns from the investment. In addition, industrial productivity has been adversely impacted by the preponderance of funerals, always disrupting normal duties or work routine. Further, the decimation of the able-bodied segment of the society has resulted in altered and highly skewed demographics where the countries seem to, noticeably, comprise the very old and the very young. This raises important issues about the education and training of those children, besides the more immediate issue of caring for them. The lack of personnel available to transmit skills and values, to provide care, or guarantee a future for the nation can only be viewed as constituting a tragedy. When compounded with chronic famine and scarcity of nutrition, and an international community whose response to such problems in fringe countries like Malawi is niggardly, one would be excused for expressing despair or growing despondence about the future of Malawi or Africa in general.

The economic stagnation brought about by the impact of AIDS has also contributed significantly to a negative evaluation of democracy. The shift to democratic practice in many African countries occurred, by sheer coincidence, during the era that AIDS took hold or became noticeable and evident as the greatest health issue of modern times, even viewed as undermining or negatively impacting aspects of national security.[9] The disease of AIDS has simultaneously impacted economic activity, as the able-bodied and productive members of the society have been the primary victims, and affected the government's ability to provide essential services needed for development or improvement of infrastructure as the need to treat and combat the disease has increasingly commanded or influenced budget allocations. For instance, in May 2000, responding to queries about his purported overtures to critics of HIV as a source for AIDS, President Mbeki of South Africa pointed out that there was need for re-evaluation of the approach to AIDS especially in light of the exorbitant prices of the available drugs. In South Africa, AIDS treatment reduced to the requirement that the whole entire budget for the Ministry of Health be devoted entirely to it exclusively. Clearly the issue of the costs associated with AIDS treatment, as well as means of containing the disease and saving the lives of, especially, the youth, have pre-occupied many African countries.[10] The absence of real signs of alleviation of the hardships engendered by the pandemic makes the task urgent. The situation is exacerbated by the fact that the spread of the disease is identified with the most intimate of human relations – sex.

Efforts to control the transmission of the disease, ordinarily transmitted through 'vaginal sex',[11] have called for major shifts in both the lifestyles of the population, especially the youth, and cultural perspectives of the African society. Culturally, both in Malawi and other African communities, open and candid discussion of sexual matters is considered taboo. Addressing the issue of AIDS demands a relaxation of that attitude, which will allow for, and accept, discussion of sex in polite parlance. This remains difficult. Mtenje, in his inaugural lecture delivered in 2002 at Chancellor College, University of Malawi, noted ruefully how instructions about the proper use of condoms were explicit in English, not always readily accessible to the majority of Malawians, but were couched in idiomatic and metaphorical language when expressed in the local language of Chichewa. Commenting on the locally publicized messages on HIV/AIDS prevention, he notes that,

> The English versions of the messages are direct and clear. They talk about the role of condoms in the prevention of sexually transmitted diseases. On the contrary, the Chichewa messages, which are intended for the Malawian with average education, are cryptic, vague, un-instructive and misleading at best.[12]

Language is important to national development[13] and more so in the aspect of development that is concerned with saving the youth of the nation. The proper exploitation of language to achieve those goals is essential. Yet under the circumstances, cultural practice appears to constitute a serious barrier to the attainment of those goals. This is one area where modification of cherished cultural habits as reflected in linguistic practice is warranted.

Further, in Malawi, as elsewhere, there is emphasis placed on procreation. Consequently, the most encouraged methods of controlling the spread of AIDS, namely abstinence or the use of prophylactics, are both viewed as having a negative impact on that goal. Overcoming these obstacles is essential to the preservation of the youth, the resurgence of positive economic activity, and the articulation of a national development programme. And, as indicated, the prevalence of AIDS during the period of transition to democratic practice, loosely translated as the acceptance of multi-party politics, accompanied by privatization and liberalization of the economy, leading to removal of government subsidies and, as has been the general case, to higher levels of unemployment as market forces make themselves felt, has made for a negative evaluation of the benefits of democracy. The success of democratic practice in Malawi is dependent upon positive economic performance. To achieve this, AIDS education, awareness, prevention and cure inevitably constitute necessary conditions. This becomes a pre-requisite to any putative formulation of the agenda of national development.

Enter SM Galaxy Football Club in Ndirande

In 2002, when Rafiki Makata approached me about assisting the youth in Ndirande, the Mtaya Football League in Nkhotakota already had in excess of 16 teams participating in it. Many were still waiting for their turn to receive material support. This was proving difficult because the donations, when obtained, needed to be transported. The most reliable means of getting the material there was simply as my luggage when I visited. Air travel to Malawi from California is not cheap, and paying for excess baggage limits further the amount that can be transported. My reluctance to extend my involvement through assisting the youth of Ndirande, based as they were in the major commercial city of the country, keen to look the part eventually, was not entirely unreasonable or baseless.

It is somewhat ironic that the youth that have turned into a show-case of what can be achieved for the community through sports and youth activity are the ones whose request for assistance had been met initially with rejection. The change of heart occurred on the same day that I had been approached. Ms. Sandra Phiri, my host in Ndirande, was aware of the project in Nkhotakota. She made a suggestion regarding the request from the Ndirande youth, viz., that they should be assisted but held to comparable conditions. Extending the project to Ndirande would not merely contribute toward a restoration of pride and hope among them, but their contribution would be a real boon to the community. Besides, their activities might attract the attention of the local media. That would make for wider publicity of the goals and objectives of the project, potentially acquiring national significance. Her suggestion altered the course of events. The youth were contacted and were given the conditions attached to any assistance that they would receive to promote their participation in soccer. They readily consented.

I decided to have the team properly constituted and recognized. The team accepted the name of SM Galaxy, partly inspired by the professional soccer team based in Los Angeles, called the L.A. Galaxy, one of the two teams in California that play in Major League Soccer. They were furnished with jerseys that I had purchased in Hong Kong and Mexico during my visits there for teaching duties or conferences, jerseys donated by Cal soccer, and Bay Oaks T-shirts donated by Scott Lambert of Piedmont, California. He became aware of my work in Malawi through an encounter when I refereed for the Bay Oaks tournament. He decided to help.

Coaching the team as well as offering guidance fell to Aubrey Nankhuni. A resident of Ndirande, he had played in the national league, but currently serves as the Assistant Coach of the national league team sponsored by the Electricity Supply Corporation of Malawi (Escom). He has not only taken to working with the youth with enthusiasm – highly commendable given that it is purely voluntary – but he has ensured that community service remains top of the youth activities. As anticipated, SM Galaxy caught the attention of the local press, which has publicized their charitable work.

The exploitation of soccer as means to youth development, community service, the fight against HIV/AIDS through heightening awareness about the dangers of unprotected sex, began to boost the profile of the youth playing for SM Galaxy. They acquired the status of catalysts for increased dissemination of the goals of the programme. Greater publicity of the project was to be achieved through meeting yet another request from the team – they wanted to join the Southern Region Football League of Malawi, the southern conference of the national league, managed by the Football Association of Malawi (FAM), the local affiliate of FIFA. My hesitation in consenting to this request was, again, understandable. It was no longer going to be a matter of equipping the youth with material, most of which was donated anyway but, this time, there would be need for capital expenditure to meet registration and operating costs. The reluctance that had underlain my original response to them now seemed to be vindicated. Yet, this was indeed the means by which other youth could get the message and might feel attracted to contribute in comparable ways. Somehow this was indeed a means to the even greater goal of potential nationwide adoption of the ideas behind the project.

Equipped with some of the press reports of the charitable work that SM Galaxy had done, I appealed to colleagues at a Linguistics workshop in Berlin, Germany, in November 2003. The response was generous. Donations that amounted to over 200 Euros, added to my own modest contributions, got SM Galaxy into Division 1 of the league. It was made clear to the team that its participation in the league owed a lot to the assistance from the international community, rendered to cheer them in their exemplary commitment to the objectives of the project. The message was clear that any future assistance from the international community, hence their continued participation in competitive tournaments, would be predicated on their unwavering commitment to community service, to combating HIV/AIDS through observation of the recommended preventive measures, and their contribution to national development.

To facilitate accountability and transparency in financial affairs, I advised the team to appoint a committee of office bearers who would manage the affairs of the club. The team has an administrative structure, and a constitution that mandates the Coach, the

Trustee Member, currently Ms. Sandra Phiri, whose residence also serves as the team's official meeting place, and the treasurer, currently one of the players, Mr. Bright Sissero, to manage the team's finances. The team elected me to serve as Patron. The team was advised to have a bank account that would be operated in a manner consistent with management of an organization's finances. I opened an account for them, in the hope that it would also facilitate future donations, allaying apprehension about misuse of funds if channelled through me or other individuals. Further, I urged the team to secure a mailing address. To that end I paid for a post office box for the team.

It is very likely that the degree of support that the team found itself commanding contributed tremendously to improvement of the team's self-esteem as well as the team's performance in the league. It also underscored for them the importance of keeping their end of the bargain. SM Galaxy has been exemplary in community work. It was a major victory for the team that in its first season in Division 1 of the Southern Region Football League of Malawi the team finished off tied for position 3 in points, but dropped to position 4 on goal differential, with real prospects of promotion to the next division up, the Premier Division. The youth's charitable contributions to society have included visiting the sick – especially the children – at Queen Elizabeth Central Hospital in Blantyre City, cutting the grass at, and mopping the floor of, the historical St Michael's Church of the Central African Presbyterian (CCAP) of Blantyre Synod, as well as clearing trash that had piled along the road in their residential area of Ndirande New Lines, an obvious health hazard. During a recent visit in January 2005 the team requested me to donate, on their behalf, two soccer balls to the inmates of Chichiri Prison in the City of Blantyre. All this has captured the interest of the local media. This has provided a major boost to the project as more youth have got interested in participating, obviously with an eye toward securing comparable assistance.

Boost from International Interest

This youth development project, centred around the exploitation of the passion for soccer and sports has, in no small measure, benefited from my occupation as a faculty member of Linguistics at the University of California, Berkeley. The occupation and the location have made for a degree of ease in soliciting assistance from Cal soccer programmes. My involvement with the Alameda Contra Costa Youth Soccer League (ACCYSL) of the California Youth Soccer Association, primarily as a soccer referee, has contributed greatly to the formation of networks that have been advantageous to the Malawi Youth Soccer Project. A number of Youth Soccer Leagues and Soccer Clubs in northern California have become aware of the needs of the youth in Malawi and the activities that they are engaged in as a condition for assistance. SM Galaxy has turned out to be the salient feature of the youth programme in Malawi because of the press coverage that the team has had. This is significant because press coverage of sports in Malawi normally focuses on the sponsored teams in the top division of the league, the Super League of Malawi. That is the division that provides the players to the Malawi National Team (called The Flames). Naturally, this is not surprising. Soccer contributes to the international visibility of countries that, otherwise, would remain obscure.

This is comparable to the role that the inter-collegiate athletics programmes play in American academe. As noted by Hannah Perot[14], in the United States sports programmes enhance the prestige of academic institutions besides comprising a significant aspect of the overall education of the youth that includes physical education and the inculcation of such valued qualities as discipline, team spirit, patriotism and physical health that derive from organized sports. In fact, some academic institutions owe their national visibility to their sports programmes without which their profiles might not have extended beyond their local communities.

In 2004, I learned that there is, at last, a women's national team in Malawi. The players held some of their training sessions with SM Galaxy. During a visit over the winter break of December 2004 to January 2005 I met the players. The team literally lacked basic facilities, which is comprehensible. Soccer around the world has been a men's sport for a long time, even more so in Africa since its introduction there. The exception has been in the United States, where the women have been central to the current growing popularity of the sport. Naturally, with men's soccer clubs barely surviving despite the heated passion that the sport generates, investment in women's participation requires massive lobbying. However, recent trends to multi-party politics and the accompanying adoption of democratic practice in many African countries,[15] regardless of the actual implementation of ideals of democracy, have made for review of certain practices and re-examination of apparently entrenched beliefs. This has included the issue of gender equality. The women have seized the moment to overhaul the prevailing views relating to gender roles and to push for equality.[16] The advent of women's soccer in Malawi fits into that discourse.

The full integration of women in the political economy and national development clearly enhances democracy. The view of democracy adopted here is the one articulated by Noam Chomsky. In his book, *Deterring Democracy*, Chomsky points out that,

> A society is democratic to the extent that its citizenry play a meaningful role in managing public affairs. If their thought is controlled, or their options are narrowly restricted, then evidently they are not playing a meaningful role.[17]

Conceived in these terms, an urgent question for emergent democracies in Africa relates to the role of women in advancing democratic ideals. If the pronouncements that the education and health of the family and, consequently, of the nation, are computed in terms of the investment the nation makes in its women, are to be more than merely politically-correct rhetorical devices, then it argues for the full integration of women into the political and economic arenas. Their inclusion in development through sports is consistent with the pursuit of democracy. Put differently, the full extension to women of educational opportunities, political and economic involvement, and the unconstrained latitude for them to 'play a meaningful role in managing public affairs' should constitute a necessary condition for the growth and maintenance of democratic practice in Africa. This includes participation in the sports arena, definitely one aspect of national development.

Significantly, the gender issues also provide a unique opportunity for the incorporation of women into the programme of community service and in the fight against HIV/

AIDS through sport. The latter cannot be downplayed. As AIDS continues to afflict African countries, there is a view developing among some males that, in order to avoid infection, they should have sex with young girls. The stigma that is associated with having sex with minors is somewhat diminished by the retention in some African cultures, including Malawi[18] of the practice of marrying prepubescent girls. Although the practice may have thrived in European culture in the past[19] it is one that is no longer current in light of the legal characterization of a 'minor' and proscription of sexual intercourse with minors. Whatever the subterfuge, the practice in the modern era is tantamount to further aggravation of a difficult situation. Encouraging participation in organized sports not only contributes towards the improved physical health of the young women, and enhances self-esteem but, as a consequence, it contributes to the avoidance of such victimization. As noted by Ruth Okubo[20] 'athletics is a valuable tool in which to direct and guide children in all aspects of their development'. She notes, further, that this is vindicated by events in the United States where, 30 years ago, there was a 'very high rate of teenage pregnancy'. However, the situation changed radically with the institution of Title IX in 1972. With its institution there was a 'decline in those numbers of teenage pregnancy. By creating opportunity for women to play in sports, that rate of teenage pregnancy has been reduced by about 30%. It has been shown that women playing sports tend to have a higher self-esteem, are less likely to get pregnant and use drugs.' Clearly extending the scope of women's participation in sports, especially the incredibly popular sport of soccer, will pay major dividends in the country's efforts to reclaim a healthy citizenry and plan for the future.

In Malawi, the dire straits of the women's team, worse than the boys, invited an extension to them of the logic employed to exploit soccer for community service and youth development. When I met the women's team I donated a set of Cal jerseys that the Cal women's soccer team had given me, as well as shin-guards provided by the youth of Piedmont Community Church in California. Recently, the women's national team in Malawi has received some recognition and secured modest assistance from the vice-president of the country. This became imperative in light of the team's expected participation in an eight-nation tournament of the Cosafa Castle Cup hosted by Zambia during the month of November 2005. While the problems faced through lack of sponsorship remain acute, as noted by Dorothy Kasito, the chairperson of the Malawi National Women Football Committee, the realization that women's soccer deserves support is now evident and it is beginning to make an impression on society. According to the Malawi paper, *Nation Online* of Wednesday 2 November 2005, the current president of the Football Association of Malawi, Walter Nyamilandu, is quoted as admitting that the women 'deserve to be assisted because women's soccer is growing not only in Malawi but also in the region and it is ideal and better for us to be growing together with the other countries'.

Currently, there is a women's league in Malawi, called Chiukepo Mhango Women Football League, from which players for the national squad will, in future, be identified or selected. This is certainly a step forward despite the reality of the women's league which, like other sports, remains overshadowed by the men's Super League of Malawi. Still, the prospect of travelling to Zambia for the regional tournament encouraged the vice-president of Malawi, Cassim Chilumpha, to make a financial contribution of approximately $2,000 and to donate '30 balls, two sets of uniforms, boots, and two first aid kits for the cause'.[21]

Subsequent to a discussion of the issues of language, politics and development in Malawi with some of my students, one student, Anna Key, a goalie of the Cal Women's soccer team, indicated to me her desire to visit Malawi. An undergraduate enrolled in Peace and Conflict Studies, whose experience of Third World conditions did not go beyond images presented through media portrayals, she seemed to have become curious about the role that her sport of soccer was allegedly playing in dealing with societal ills or in enhancing aspects of national development. She was also keen to get affiliated with an orphan care facility and volunteer her services. She travelled during the month of May 2005, and remained there for three weeks.

Anna Key's trip was opportune. For a start, SM Galaxy members introduced her to the women's team and to the orphanage that had been arranged to host her. She donated Cal soccer equipment to the women's team. The significance of her trip was two-fold. On the one hand, it got the youth of SM Galaxy to realize that their existence, hence their activities, had gained increased familiarity among segments of the international community. Therefore, they needed to sustain their work as proof of the claims made about the role of soccer or sports in youth development as an aspect of a national development programme. On the other hand, the reality of third world conditions that constitute normal living for the people, their efforts to overcome poverty, to fight HIV/AIDS, et cetera, so overwhelmed Anna Key that she returned with a determination to help those orphans in every way possible, help the women's soccer team to the extent possible, and contribute towards heightening awareness about the plight of the less economically fortunate. Further, she resolved to gear her educational career towards attainment of employment that would sustain her efforts to contribute to the improvement of life and conditions in places such as Malawi. She has already indicated her desire to return to Malawi. Her stated goals and objectives got a boost from a reasonably detailed article about her visit that appeared in the 11 October edition of *The Contra Costa Times* newspaper in California, eventually reproduced in other papers of the Alameda Group. This served as a catalyst for at least one charitable organization, Child 2 Child, based in Santa Rosa, California, to approach her to be a spokesperson. Child 2 Child is a non-profit organization whose mission, according to Steven Falk, the founder, is to 'provide simple and direct opportunities that enable children to help other children around the world'.[22] Steven Falk envisions a project called 'Cool to Care' with Anna Key as the spokesperson, spreading the word to her peers.

The visit by Anna Key was followed in the following month of June, by that of a youth group from the Piedmont Community Church (PCC), a visit that put SM Galaxy yet again at the centre of international interest. Piedmont Community Church in Northern California has an active outreach programme that has involved its youth in development projects in, *inter alia*, Mexico. The Church is also involved in development projects in Malawi. These are centred at Kafita CCAP Church. Located in the Kawale area within Lilongwe, Malawi's capital city, Kafita CCAP Church has sister relations with PCC. The latter has been involved in projects at the sister church as well as at other locations. These include an orphan care facility, The Ministry of Hope located at Mponela, and a hospital at Embangweni in the northern part of Malawi. Following an initial visit to Malawi in 2003 by some members of PCC, led by the pastor Rev. Bill McNabb, two of the delegation, Ms Sara Hirsch and Dr John White, resolved to lead a youth delegation to Malawi as part of the outreach programme. They both had heard about SM Galaxy and had expressed a desire to learn more about the team's activities and meet with the team members. In June 2005, a 16-person delegation from PCC that included 12 youths visited Malawi.

During my December 2004 to January 2005 visit to Malawi, I had been encouraged by friends and family members to consider extending the project to Lilongwe. The location, called Area 49 but popularly referred to as Dubai, was identified as an ideal site for extension of the project. A youth team was organized, to become the focal point of bringing the goals of the project to the capital city. The team accepted the name of Chalunda Earthquakes. Like SM Galaxy, the name was partly inspired by the professional team in Major League Soccer and based in Northern California, the San José Earthquakes, and also in part by the youth team that I have been involved with in San Pablo, called The San Pablo Earthquakes. Equipped partly with soccer jerseys donated by the Stanford University soccer programme, the Chalunda Earthquakes will provide friendly rivalry to SM Galaxy. While the rivalry on the soccer field will be more evident, and the provision of a trophy is bound to add to the excitement, the major idea is to foster rivalry in their contribution to community service, the fight against HIV/AIDS and to national development. The visit of the youth group from PCC provided the occasion for the inaugural contest between SM Galaxy and Chalunda Earthquakes.

The meeting with SM Galaxy made enough of an impression on John White that he decided to contribute to the effort. Approached to serve as a church elder for Chiombamwala Church, a congregation not far from Kafita CCAP Church, he resolved to see the activities of SM Galaxy extended to Chiombamwala. He has expressed interest to have a youth team organized there, to be called Chiombamwala Highlanders, that will be guided by the same principles and ideals of service to church and community, promotion of God's work, awareness of the dangers of HIV/AIDS, et cetera, that have suffused the outlook and ethic of SM Galaxy soccer team.

In September 2005, PCC collected soccer equipment from the Piedmont Soccer Club to send to the youth of Malawi. Covering the PCC collection of soccer equipment for Malawi the local paper *The Piedmont Post* of 7 September 2005, noted that,

> Piedmont soccer outreach is joining an enormously successful program originated by Dr Sam Mchombo, born in Malawi and now Associate Professor of Linguistics at the University of California, Berkeley. Through donations from private sources as well as the university, Dr Mchombo has helped provide uniforms and gear for nine teams in his native country.

> What's really innovative is the requirement that each Malawian team receiving donations from the US must commit to significant ongoing community service. So far that has included assistance to the elderly, cleaning areas around their cities, visiting the sick in hospitals, and promoting awareness of the dangers of HIV/AIDS.[23]

The paper also carried a brief account of the game between SM Galaxy and Chalunda Earthquakes, mainly reflecting the impressions of the PCC youth of the conditions they perceived.

Soccer and Development in Africa

Soccer is a very popular sport in Malawi and in Africa in general. In some limited cases it has provided the route out of poverty for those players who, eventually, managed to develop into professional players playing for rich clubs in Europe, the Middle East or Asia. The appeal that soccer has on African society can even be gauged from recent political events. In Liberia the candidacy of George Weah for the presidential election of 2005 derived its credentials from his international image as a soccer player who, in 1995, was voted the Ballon D'Or star. It was significant that as his candidature gained momentum with prospects for ascendancy to the presidency, questions arose concerning the impact that his lack of academic training might have on his duties as head of state and of government. Effectively, his achievements on the soccer field more than made up for any perceived shortcomings in educational qualifications.[24] Soccer seemed to have conferred on George Weah recognition comparable to that derived from wrestling that gave Jesse 'The Body' Ventura the credentials to become Governor of Minnesota or from film acting that gave the late Ronald Reagan the credentials to become Governor of California, eventually President of the United States or Clint Eastwood to become Mayor of Carmel in California.

The popularity of soccer and the scarcity of financial and material resources in Africa combine to make the sport susceptible to exploitation for the attainment of various goals. The goals can vary widely. Thus, just as soccer can be exploited to secure votes in political campaigns, or unify people, it can equally be used to solidify ethnic rivalries or promote bigotry. The claim that the Malawi Youth Soccer project is geared towards youth development and contributes to national development is coherent only to the extent that the concept of development is made explicit. It was indicated above that the notion of development is one that may have been relativized to countries and prevailing conditions. Under the current circumstances the claim that sports in general, but soccer in particular, is exploited for developmental ends, reduces to the subterfuge of linking soccer to activities in society whose subjective evaluation is positive, and whose overall estimation does not conflict with goals of national development, to the extent that these are clearly articulated. As such, it remains an open question as to whether those activities comprise aspects of national development or whether, by fiat of policy decision, such activities are, at best, indifferent to development programmes of the nation. Nevertheless, it could be argued that, after all, common to all human societies is the need to train children and youth to become responsible adults and citizens. This is achieved primarily through organized instruction, either in the form of apprenticeship or, as is the case in modern times, in the form of elaborate instruction through educational institutions which feed into the economic growth of society. Educational institutions provide most of the trained and skilled workforce required for industry just as some industries have had their genesis in research activities conducted on academic campuses. The literacy acquired through learning itself feeds into other enterprises and contributes to the political development of the nation.[25]

To the extent that investment into healthy youth impacts the future as those youth gain improved chances of survival and receive the training to assume responsibility for the future political direction and economic advancement of their country, the effort to achieve that through sports can indeed be subsumed under the rubric of national development.

Conclusion

While the exploitation of soccer in Malawi for community service, to combat HIV/AIDS through increased awareness and education, to contribute to gender equity, et cetera, originated independently, comparable programmes have occurred elsewhere. In Kenya, the Mathare Youth Sports Association had its origins and goals determined in a fashion somewhat parallel to that presented here.[26] As it turns out, the model sketched here about the Malawi Youth Soccer Project is one that has begun to inspire people from, or working in, other African countries. Within Malawi, the project has gained momentum from the activities of the SM Galaxy Coach Aubrey Nankhuni. He has used the team as a launch pad into increased youth activity in other locales within the country. A trip to the United Kingdom in September 2005 to participate in a three-week programme of youth soccer coaches bolstered his resolve to remain involved in youth activities. The programme is steadily assuming a national presence as it begins to spread to other parts of the country with increased diversification of the sports activities encouraged and supported. For instance, the Cal Basketball programme (through the Head Coach of Men's basketball Ben Braun, and Women's basketball) has made donations to contribute to the on-going efforts. This is very welcome and speaks of the degree of confidence generated among members of the larger community with regard to achievement of the goals of youth development through sports.

The ideas have also gained ground among those assisting youth in other countries. For instance, Steve Isaacs of Orinda, California, has got his teenage children and other youth from the area involved in helping the youth in a village in Southern Kenya. Their work received coverage in *The San Francisco Chronicle* newspaper. The youth have been involved in the construction of a school library as well as collection and supply of books to the school, helping the children with school equipment and financial means for education, as well donating soccer gear to the youth of the village where their activities are focused. After reading about my work with the youth in Nkhotakota that appeared in the Berkeley campus paper *The Daily Californian* of 14 February 2001, Steve Isaacs has decided to adopt the idea of linking the assistance to community service and HIV/AIDS awareness among the youth in that Kenyan village. In El Cerrito, California, Ruth Okubo a teacher at Stege Elementary School in Richmond, California, upon being apprised of the project in Malawi, has decided to collaborate with her daughter, Tiffany, a Peace Corps volunteer in Cameroun, to adopt and adapt the programme there. It would appear that whatever notion of youth development or national development is deemed fit, the outlined activities inspired by the exploitation of the passion for soccer are either a subset of the concept or intersect with it in a very significant way.

Acknowledgements

I am deeply indebted to Martha Saavedra for providing the stimulus to focus on this issue, and for her constant support to my intellectual pursuits. I thank Al Mtenje for insights on sports in Malawi, and Ruth Okubo for comments on earlier drafts of the paper. I am grateful to Kunjilika Chaima, Richard Chinansi, Sam Chunga, Sam Fleming, Will Jones, Pilirani Kachinziri, Andrew Tilimbe Kulemeka, Scott Lambert, David Mason, Stuart Mbolembole, David Mchombo, Aubrey Nankhuni, Southwood Ng'oma, Walter Nyamilandu, Sandra Phiri, and Tony Scullion for their constant interest in, and encouragement of, youth development through sports in Malawi. I owe a special debt of gratitude to Brad Agoos, Kevin Boyd, Kevin Grimes, Jennifer Thomas and Maite Zavala of Cal Soccer Program, Ben Braun, Sarah Holsinger, of Cal Basketball Program at the University of California, Berkeley, to Steven Morrison of Berkeley High School, to Janet Ceja-Orozco and the San Pablo United Youth Soccer Club, Stuart Levine and Mark Thieme of Benicia Youth Soccer League, Berkeley Adult Co-ed Soccer League, John Schuster of Stanford University Soccer Program, as well as Piedmont Community Church, for support in various ways. Thanks to Scott Kail, Ariana Killoran and Christopher Lee, for carrying equipment to Malawi. My most heart-felt gratitude goes to the youth of Malawi, especially those participating in Mtaya Football League in Nkhotakota, SM Galaxy Football Club in Ndirande, Blantyre, and Chalunda Earthquakes Football Club in Area 49, Lilongwe, for their response to the call for service to the community and for indulging me in my passion for soccer.

Notes

[1]   For relevant discussion see Susan George's *A Fate Worse than Debt. The World Financial Crisis and the Poor*, or Jeffrey Sachs' observations on the problems of Bolivia in his recent book *The End of Poverty. Economic Possibilities for Our Time*.

[2]   Guilianotti and Armstrong, 'Drama, Fields and Metaphors: An Introduction to Football in Africa', 1.

[3]   Ibid.

[4]   McDaniel-Keith, 'GOOOAL! Football and Nationalism in Latin America', 1.

[5]   Englund, 'Winning Elections, Losing Legitimacy', 173.

[6]   Pilirani Kachinziri, 'Galaxy Shines Brighter', *The Malawi News*, 27 Sept.–3 Oct. 2003 (Blantyre, Malawi), 19.

[7]   Mchombo, 'Religion and Politics in Malawi', 8.

[8]   Weinstein, 'The Effect of AIDS on Southern Africa', 2

[9]   Mchombo, 'Impact of AIDS on Economic Development in Malawi', *Znet* (2000).

[10] Mchombo, 'Rounding up Hookers in Malawi', *Znet* (2000).

[11] This was made explicit in a spring 2001 Jim Lehrer News Hour report by Elizabeth Farnclough on AIDS in Malawi, aired on the Public Broadcasting System television in the United States.

[12]   Mtenje, 'The Role of Language in National Development', 17.
[13]   Mchombo, 'National Identity, Democracy, and the Politics of Language in Malawi and Tanzania.'
[14]   Personal communication.
[15]   Mchombo, 'Democratization in Malawi: Its Roots and Prospects'.
[16]   Brady and Khan, *Letting Girls Play*; Mchombo, 'Women and the Building of Democracy in Africa', *Znet* (1997).
[17]   Chomsky, *Deterring Democracy*, 6.
[18]   See LaFraniere, 'Forced to Marry Before Puberty, African Girls Pay Lasting Price'.
[19]   In Act I Scene II of William Shakespeare's play Romeo and Juliet, Capulet tries to fend off Paris' proposal for Juliet's hand in marriage with the observation that she had not yet 'seen the change of fourteen years'. He persuades Paris to 'let two more summers wither in their pride ere we may think her ripe to be a bride'. To this Paris responds with the observation that 'younger than she are happy mothers made'. Taking Paris' comment literally, it hints at the prevalence in Shakespearian England of 'minors' getting married.
[20]   Personal communication.
[21]   *The Malawi National Newspaper*, 2 Nov. 2005.
[22]   *The Contra Costa Times*, 11 Oct. 2005, B2.
[23]   *The Piedmont Post*, 7 Sept. 2005, 12.
[24]   Although George Weah got the majority vote in the first round of the polling, he did not get enough to be declared the winner. In the run-off election, his opponent, Ellen Johnson-Sirleaf won the majority vote, becoming the first elected female president in Africa.
[25]   Mchombo, 'The Role of Media in Fostering Democracy in Southern Africa'.
[26]   Hognestad and Tollisen, 'Playing Against Deprivation: Football and Development in Nairobi, Kenya'.

References

Brady, Martha and Arjmand Banu Khan. *Letting Girls Play. The Mathare Youth Sports Association's Football Program for Girls,* New York: The Population Council, Inc., 2002.

Chomsky, Noam. *Deterring Democracy.* London and New York: Verso, 1991.

Englund, Harri. 'Winning Elections, Losing Legitimacy. Multi-Partyism and the Neo-patrimonial State in Malawi.' In *Multi-party Elections in Africa,* edited by Michael Cowen and Liisa Laakso. New York: Palgrave and Oxford: James Currey, 2002: 172–86.

George, Susan. *A Fate Worse Than Debt. The World Financial Crisis and the Poor.* New York: Grove Weidenfeld, 1990.

Giulianotti, Richard and Gary Armstrong. 'Drama, Fields and Metaphors: An Introduction to Football in Africa.' In *Football in Africa. Conflict, Conciliation and Community,* edited by Gary Armstrong and Richard Giulianotti. New York: Palgrave Macmillan, 2004: 1–24.

Hognestad, Hans and Arvid Tollisen. 'Playing Against Deprivation: Football and Development in Nairobi, Kenya.' In *Football in Africa. Conflict, Conciliation and Community,* edited by Gary Armstrong and Richard Giulianotti. New York: Palgrave Macmillan, 2004: 210–26.

LaFraniere, Sharon. 'Forced to Marry Before Puberty, African Girls Pay Lasting Price.' *The New York Times CLV,* no.53, 27 Nov. 2005.

McDaniel-Keith, Kaitlin. 'GOOOAL! Football and Nationalism in Latin America.' Unpublished seminar paper, University of California, Berkeley, 2004.

Mchombo, Sam. 'The Role of the Media in Fostering Democracy in Southern Africa.' *The Journal of African Policy Studies 3,* no.2 & 3 (1997): 1–22.

———. 'Democratization in Malawi: Its Roots and Prospects.' In *Democratization in Late Twentieth-Century Africa. Coping with Uncertainty,* edited by Jean-Germain Gros. Westport, CT: Greenwood Press, 1998: 21–40.

————. 'National Identity, Democracy, and the Politics of Language in Malawi and Tanzania.' *The Journal of African Policy Studies 4,* no.1 (1998): 33–46.

————. 'Religion and Politics in Malawi.' Institute for African Development Occasional Papers Series, 2004, *Issues in Political Discourse Analysis* 1, no. 2 (2005).

Mtenje, Al D. 'The Role of Language in National Development: A Case for Local Languages.' Professorial Inaugural Lecture, University of Malawi, 2002.

Nation (Malawi) Online, <www.nationmalawi.com>, 2 Nov. 2005.

Sachs, Jeffery. *The End of Poverty. Economic Possibilities for Our Time.* New York: The Penguin Press, 2005.

Weinstein, Matt. 'The Effect of AIDS on Southern Africa.' Unpublished seminar paper, University of California, Berkeley, 2000.

An Opportunity for a New Beginning: Soccer, Irish Nationalists and the Construction of a New Multi-Sports Stadium for Northern Ireland

David Hassan

Introduction

As Bairner observes, the 'history of football in Northern Ireland has witnessed some remarkable achievements, not least the performances of the national team at the World Cup Finals of 1958 and 1982'.[1] For a country with a population of barely 1.5 million people the success gained by both international and club sides representing Northern Ireland has arguably been disproportionate to its size. Indeed, Northern Ireland also qualified for the World Cup Finals held in Mexico in 1986, although it failed to progress past the initial group stages of that tournament. If the sport is viewed on an island-wide basis, an 'Irish' team has contested the latter stages of the FIFA World Cup on five of the last six occasions. The resurgence of the Republic of Ireland soccer team as an international force has been reflected in its presence at the 1990, 1994 and 2002 finals. Northern Ireland has also produced some of the finest exponents of the game, amongst them Pat Jennings, Martin O Neill and, most noteworthy, possibly one of the greatest players the world has ever seen, George Best. Yet, for all this, soccer in Northern Ireland has, certainly from the late 1960s, been synonymous with sectarian division and ethnic conflict. That this remains the case is of course lamentable, albeit not surprising given the political maelstrom in which the sport has sought to exist.

The relationship between sport and national identity in Northern Ireland has been the subject of academic inquiry for some time.[2] The study of soccer has been central to such research and the role the game plays in portraying various shades of political opinion in the country is a common aspect of such scholarship.[3] On occasion, however, this work has failed to offer adequate explanation concerning the exact motives or levels of (dis)engagement by those who utilize soccer in this way. A related, but no less significant, factor regarding the volume of research that has taken place in this field is the fact that very few people actually attend soccer matches in Northern Ireland. According to a recently published report by the Department of Culture Arts and Leisure (Northern Ireland) (DCAL), this figure is as low as 3 per cent of the total population.[4] On the whole it is the Catholic minority (nationalists) who choose not to engage with soccer in the country.[5] As a result this essay will focus on some of the reasons why this is the case. In part it will also examine the decision of the British government to construct a new multisports stadium on the outskirts of Belfast, Northern Ireland's capital city. The stadium requires a tripartite arrangement between the Gaelic Athletic Association (GAA), the Ulster Branch of the Irish Rugby Football Union (IRFU) and soccer's governing body in Northern Ireland, the IFA. Whilst the two issues may at first appear unrelated, the fact is that only by encouraging (and facilitating) more Catholics to attend soccer matches in Northern Ireland will the IFA avoid very obvious criticisms concerning its moral, ethical, social and financial role in safeguarding the long term viability of any new stadium.

In January 2004 the British government began a consultation process to ascertain the feasibility and levels of support that existed for the construction of a new 42,000 fully seated stadium in Northern Ireland.[6] Whilst this is a development broadly welcomed by those involved with sport in the country, others question the level of investment needed for a stadium of this size.[7] This is particularly the case when measured against a shortage of funds for health, education and a failing transport infrastructure throughout Northern Ireland. Furthermore, there has been a tendency in some quarters to refer to this project as the 'national' stadium, which has been a cause of some concern for northern nationalists.[8] Most controversial of all is the decision to locate the new stadium on the site of the former Maze Prison, on the outskirts of Belfast. In this case the Maze, also referred to as Long Kesh, has a unique symbolic resonance for nationalists and republicans as it was here in 1981 that ten republican prisoners died whilst on hunger strike in protest at the failure of the British government to grant them political status.[9] Whilst these are legitimate reservations, equally there is a sense that with the dawn of a new political dispensation in Northern Ireland, nationalism in particular must demonstrate its commitment to a more settled future in the country. This is in line with undertakings it gave as part of The Belfast Agreement signed in 1998. If northern nationalists are to shed the image of themselves as a community fundamentally opposed to any form of reconciliation with the unionist people of Northern Ireland, or of the institutions of the state, it is self-evident that they will have to come to terms with the source of such recalcitrance.[10]

With this in mind, and by way of explaining the attitudes of northern nationalists to soccer and what it represents in Northern Ireland, this essay further proposes that The Belfast Agreement has failed to properly address the issue of sectarianism in the country. In its place an irrational unwillingness to accede to the wishes of unionism and an intolerance of those sympathetic to the link with Britain has been perpetuated. This is based around a determination on the part of nationalists to prevent their historical subjugation in Northern Ireland from continuing. Put simply, some northern nationalists are indisposed to support the new 'national' stadium for Northern Ireland because of the involvement in the project of the IFA. Many in this community view the organization as culturally British and embodying a sense of positive indifference to the nationalist people of Northern Ireland.[11] However, this essay argues that on the whole such opposition is irrational, unfounded, outdated and portrays the nationalist people in a regrettable light. Of course this is not to suggest that the genuine grievances nationalists and republicans in Northern Ireland have had with the British State or with loyalist paramilitaries should simply be cast aside. The many years of discrimination suffered by nationalists have made them understandably wary of becoming overly acquiescent to the wishes of unionism or any more inclined towards the new political order in Northern Ireland. However, whereas their continued reluctance to move forward, to be progressive and embrace a new beginning might well be based on genuine cases of injustice, it is questionable whether such disinclination remains as valid at the beginning of the twenty-first century.

Many of these questions will be discussed in much greater depth throughout the course of this essay. However, in the case of nationalist's lack of engagement with soccer in present day Northern Ireland, for example, they can begin to demonstrate their willingness to move forward by proving more receptive to the promptings of the IFA.[12] One of the fundamental problems of life in any divided society is a reluctance to step outside clearly demarcated boundaries of what is considered acceptable behaviour for fear of criticism from within. Yet on a simple issue like attending Northern Ireland home international matches, nationalists appear resistant to change.[13] This resistance notwithstanding, for sport and society to develop in Northern Ireland and for initiatives such as a new national stadium to be a success, both parties – the IFA and the minority nationalist community – require the support of each other. It would be entirely regrettable if potentially very positive developments of this kind were lost through a simple unwillingness to compromise. This said there have been significant movements in this direction in the past few months. The GAA, which is essentially an organization patronized by Irish nationalists, appears to be more inclined to support the development of a new multi-sports stadium for Northern Ireland than at any other time in the past. Nevertheless it is still unclear if this support is conditional upon either the size or location of any new development and thus whether this backing would evaporate should claims to downgrade the overall capacity of the stadium be upheld. However, before these matters are explored in more detail it is necessary to say something about the contemporary political situation in Northern Ireland. It is clear that despite the emergence of a supposed period of sustained peace in the country the divisions that affected life there for over 30 years still remain. Unfortunately this has meant that sectarian attitudes and negative perceptions of 'the other' community in Northern Ireland continue to exist amongst large sections of the country's population.[14]

The New Political Realities of Life in Post-Agreement Northern Ireland

The Belfast Agreement, which was signed on 10 April 1998 by a cross section of constitutional parties in Northern Ireland, was designed to bring about a new political order in the country. In the light of almost three decades of continuous sectarian violence, it was an ambitious goal on the part of the co-signatories to the accord, amongst them the British and Irish governments. It is not necessary to provide a comprehensive overview of the genesis of inter-community hostility in Northern Ireland for, as Harris correctly observes, it is one of the most thoroughly researched and written-about conflicts in the world.[15] Instead, it is sufficient to state that throughout the latter part of the twentieth century, in this most westerly outpost of the United Kingdom, relations between the majority Protestant community (and hence politically unionist) and the minority Catholic population, most of who continued to promote an unreconstructed form of Irish nationalism, were at best strained.

Since 2002 the Northern Ireland Assembly has been in suspension. The majority unionist population remain sceptical of the commitment of the Irish Republican Army (IRA) to abide by its claim to have put all its weapons beyond use and to cease other activities that together place a question mark over it willingness to change. This view remains despite an independently verified act of decommissioning on the part of the paramilitary organization in September 2005. In contrast Sinn Fein, the widely regarded political wing of the IRA, has suggested that the unwillingness of the British government, as well as that of the pan-Unionist establishment, to agree to the full implementation of The Belfast Agreement has been the main obstacle to a suitable resolution of the impasse.[16] In some respects, this dispute, which shows no immediate signs of resolution, is an indication of the depth of mistrust that still remains in post-Agreement Northern Ireland. This suspicion is largely borne out of an enduring problem of sectarianism in the state, a situation that has remained largely unchanged despite the birth of a supposed period of normalization. In fact The Belfast Agreement had very little to say about sectarianism and although it promised a series of commissions to arbitrate on matters of justice, equality and policing, on the whole it offered very little by way of practical resolutions to this problem. As Tonge remarks: 'The unstated assumption was that the resolution of the constitutional conflict would result in the normalisation of society and the eventual eradication of societal sectarianism.'[17] Of course this analysis, in view of the ongoing disputes that still exist between the two main communities in Northern Ireland, has since proved to be short-sighted.

Of greater significance for the future of Northern Ireland are poll results that suggest that in the seven years since the signing of the accord, rather than an expected move towards a more liberal centre ground by Northern Ireland's electorate, it has instead reverted to the extremes. According to Harris, 'An analysis of the pattern of vote transfers in the 1998 Assembly elections indicated they showed possibly the most "communal" (meaning staying entirely with one's "own side") voting pattern since the re-introduction of PR (Proportional Representation) into Northern Ireland in 1973.'[18] At the most recent Westminster elections in 2005 the depth of division in the Province was more apparent than ever. Of the 18 seats available, nine were claimed by Rev. Ian Paisley's Democratic Unionist Party (DUP) and five by Gerry Adams' Sinn Fein. Both are to be found at diametrically opposed ends of the political spectrum in Northern Ireland as the extent of political and societal divergence in the country has, it seems, never been greater. At present six out of every ten people who choose to vote in Northern Ireland do so in support of one of the two aforementioned parties, compared to slightly over four in every ten in 2001. This again highlights the inherent flaw in the logic underpinning The Belfast Agreement – that somehow peace and harmony would flourish despite there being no fundamental difference in the way people in Northern Ireland lead their lives. Rather, in the three years since the return to direct rule in the country opinions, on the face of it, have become more polarized than ever.

Perhaps one of the main reasons why this situation developed is that the Belfast Agreement made a very limited attempt to accommodate civil society, undoubtedly one of its fundamental failings.[19] In fact it was left to one of the minor parties, the Northern Ireland Women's Coalition, to propose the formation of a Civic Forum, comprising a total of 60 members plus one chairperson. Those in support of a forum of this type saw considerable potential in developing cross-community consensus and overcoming some of the misguided stereotypes and myths that continued to exist between the two communities in Northern Ireland. They were to be disappointed as not only did the Civic Forum fail to achieve any meaningful results, those invited to sit on it were largely middle-class professional people and thus less likely to be acquainted with the reality of Northern Ireland's continuing difficulties. Commenting specifically on the political logic underpinning the founding of the Civic Forum, Tonge believed: 'it risked being a collection of the unelected and the unelectable, devising alternative forms of non-communal, inclusive politics'.[20] Of course this aspiration in itself has considerable merit, albeit there is a broad acceptance that such a position still remains some way off. Instead, the Belfast Agreement legitimizes and encourages the celebration of two equal communities and their cultural traditions. This in turn has led some commentators to suggest that, by taking this to its logical conclusion, the accord ultimately confirms sectarian division in Northern Ireland by facilitating ongoing separation between two distinct ideological positions.[21] Interestingly one of the few areas of life in Northern Ireland that has shown any progress towards reconciliation is sport. In particular the GAA has demonstrated its commitment to a new beginning on the island by agreeing to the removal of Rule 21 and the temporary repeal of Rule 42. The former had previously prevented members of the British army and police personnel in Northern Ireland from joining the organization. It was removed in November 2001 despite the overwhelming opposition of GAA members in Northern Ireland. Similar objections were expressed when a decision to permit the interim repeal of Rule 42 was taken at the organization's annual congress held in April 2005. The existence of this rule had meant that sports such as association football and rugby union were not allowed to be played at GAA grounds. Certain GAA supporters continue to view soccer, in particular, as an anathema because of its close association with England. Nevertheless their determination to oppose both decisions was largely indicative of an abject unwillingness to countenance change in Northern Ireland.[22]

Soccer in Northern Ireland

Soccer has a long and illustrious history on the island of Ireland. It is broadly accepted that the game was introduced to the country by the British from 1652 onwards and it was their influence that was central to its growth, especially in the north-east of the country.[23] In contrast there was a less direct transference of football to other parts of Ireland. In fact by the mid-nineteenth century the game was being played only in certain private schools within the Dublin region, amongst them Montpellier, St Helen's and Chapelizod being most prominent. Thus the diffusion of the game followed different routes to different places; and the consequences were also different. These differences reflected many universal aspects of the development of soccer, such as being considerably more popular in urban rather than rural areas. That said it was also more readily received in those parts of the country that retained support for the union with Britain and less so amongst advocates of Irish national independence movements, including those that had developed in the country around the turn of the twentieth century. Of course this was the period when the game grew still more popular as, now in codified form, it began to assume an unparalleled global significance.

To address the growing importance of the sport in Ireland a national governing body, the IFA, was formed in Belfast on 18 November 1880. As other governing bodies, including the IRFU (1874) and the GAA (1884), began to organize themselves more coherently it soon became clear that the IFA was the only major sporting body to have its headquarters in the north of the country. In time this was to have a major influence on how the sport was organized and administered on the island. As political developments in Ireland spawned a more resolute approach to the issue of national sovereignty, all aspects of life in the country assumed added importance by either supporting or resisting movements towards Irish independence. Consequentially by 1890 the first problems began to surface for the IFA in attempting to govern a sport that was segregated along religious, ethnic, political and geographical lines. Over time the partition of Ireland became inevitable as the gap between the predominantly nationalist south and unionist north grew ever wider. By 1 June 1922, in accordance with the political separation of Ireland, which resulted in the six counties located in the most north-easterly part of the country breaking away to form Northern Ireland, a new governing body for soccer in the Irish Free State was formed.[24] This organization was known simply as the Football Association of the Irish Free State (FAIFS). At present soccer in what is now the Republic of Ireland reflects a progressive, multi-cultural and forward-looking nation. In contrast the game in Northern Ireland remains a much more resolute symbol of Britishness, or more accurately non-Irishness, for the predominantly Protestant support base it now commands.[25]

Nevertheless, this situation has developed considerably over the last decade and it is now no longer appropriate to view soccer in Northern Ireland as the sole preserve of a small group of hard-line loyalists or even a setting where nationalists continue to be unwelcome. Despite the continued practice of young northern nationalists declaring their allegiance to Republic of Ireland international sides in preference to Northern Ireland, these remain the exception rather than the rule.[26] It is now expected that such individuals would choose to play for Northern Ireland, provided they are sufficiently talented and inclined to do so. In contrast many nationalists who are not given the choice of which team to play for continue to support the Republic of Ireland side. This is a direct result of feeling marginalized in the context of Northern Ireland and is, in particular, a reaction to the sectarian abuse directed at prominent Catholic players, amongst them Glasgow Celtic midfielder Neil Lennon.[27] Thus whilst the reticence of nationalists to become involved with soccer in Northern Ireland may have been understandable in the past, especially prior to the mid-1990s, the very positive work of the IFA's Community Relations Officer, Mr Michael Boyd, has made the atmosphere at games significantly more inclusive. In doing so he has received the backing of the Official Northern Ireland Supporters Club, a most welcome development and a further indication of how times have changed. Whilst the environment around Windsor Park, not to mention elements of the game itself, remains problematic for northern nationalists it would be wrong to suggest that things have not improved significantly. Today the atmosphere at matches is some way removed from when Windsor Park was regarded as 'a Protestant place for Protestant people … (and where) Catholics must require special dispensation to be there'.[28] In the light of an evolving climate both inside and outside soccer, it represented an opportune time for the Government to examine the future direction of the sport in Northern Ireland and decide how best to allocate an estimated £8 million of new investment. However, in the absence of any quantifiable data indicating the levels of interest that existed in the game, this was to prove a difficult task. Thus, in January 2004 DCAL commissioned the consultancy firm PriceWaterhouseCoopers to undertake the first major study into the attitudes of people in Northern Ireland to soccer.[29]

The Level of Interest in Soccer throughout Northern Ireland

Of the 1,101 households surveyed as part of the investigation, and after weighting the data for gender imbalance, three categories of respondents emerged. In total some 62 per cent stated that they were 'not interested' in soccer, 35 per cent described themselves as 'armchair fans' whist only 3 per cent stated that they attended domestic soccer matches in Northern Ireland on a regular basis. In the absence of any comparable data for the rest of Ireland it is difficult to state convincingly whether these figures are representative of football fans as a whole throughout the island. However, by any standards, the numbers of people physically attending games is remarkably low. Indeed the fact that almost two thirds of those surveyed had no interest whatsoever in the game should be a timely reminder to sports administrators in Northern Ireland about the level of apathy many have towards their activities. Indeed those who claimed they were 'not interested' in soccer had not attended a match in the previous 15 years and had not watched a game on television at any point during the preceding two years. Perhaps not surprisingly 43 per cent of those who fell into this category were female and were also over 60 years of age. They were more likely to be Catholic (nationalist) and living in a district council area without a recognized senior soccer team. In contrast, of the 38 per cent who did express either an active or passive interest in the game, the overwhelmingly majority were male, Protestant (unionist), single and from a lower-working-class background.[30]

Some 68 per cent of 'armchair' fans had never or rarely attended a domestic soccer match in Northern Ireland and approximately the same number had been similarly absent from international matches at Windsor Park, the home stadium for Northern Ireland games. Of these more than 4 out of 10 said that a reduction in bigotry/sectarianism would encourage them to return. However in most cases, and across several socio-economic sectors, a poor standard of play was cited as the main reason why fans had chosen not to attend matches. Interestingly those who support Northern Ireland by attending games at Windsor Park on an intermittent basis tend to be over 60 years of age and Protestant. In contrast one third of 'armchair' fans claimed to support the Republic of Ireland international soccer team, rather that their northern counterparts. It is safe to conclude that these individuals emanate from the nationalist community and in most cases claim they are either not interested in soccer in Northern Ireland (24 per cent) or have difficulty with the sectarian nature of certain aspects of it (27 per cent). Viewed in their entirety the figures also reveal that a majority of Catholics surveyed (52 per cent) felt that there were insufficient opportunities for members of their community to become involved with soccer in Northern Ireland in any capacity.[31]

Finally, of the very small numbers who do attend soccer in Northern Ireland on a regular basis, one in every three can be defined as male, between 30 and 59 years of age, Protestant and married. Interestingly over 75 per cent of these individuals had been attending soccer matches in Northern Ireland for more than 15 years. This would suggest that little has changed over this period in terms of supporter demographics and confirms the image of soccer in Northern Ireland as a sport dominated by those sympathetic to the union with Britain. This report, alongside two others published simultaneously, which focussed on the experiences of 'armchair' fans and attendances at Northern Ireland matches, provided objective data on the actual appeal of soccer in the country, in line with recommendations from the 'Creating a Soccer Strategy for Northern Ireland' document published in 2001.[32] This was the latest attempt to provide a strategic direction for the game in the country, albeit the first time the Government had become directly involved in drawing up proposals for the future of soccer in Northern Ireland.

In October 2000, Michael McGimpsey, Member of the Legislative Assembly (MLA), then Minister for Culture, Arts and Leisure in the Northern Ireland Assembly, established an advisory panel to consider how the local game could move forward. Drawing upon his personal involvement with the panel, Bairner outlines in some detail its remit, including some of the issues it attempted to address. At the heart of the panel's deliberations and seemingly central to all other concerns was the issue of governance for the sport in Northern Ireland. For example, Bairner highlights two groups, which according to the figures are subject to social exclusion from the local game: Catholics and Women. In both cases he claims that such a state of affairs can 'be linked to concerns about governance'.[33] On the whole there was more than a little unease expressed about how the sport had descended into such a poor state, as well as agreement amongst the panel members that a more coherent, professional and forward thinking administration was necessary to take the game into the new millennium. To this end the IFA has recently appointed its first ever Chief Executive Officer, Mr Howard Wells, who brings considerable experience to the post. Whilst Mr Wells has thus far avoided the critical issue of how to encourage more nationalists to attend international matches, he is mindful of the need for the IFA to become more commercially aware. This in itself will be absolutely crucial if the IFA is to play a full and equal role in ensuring the success of any new multi-sports stadium in Northern Ireland.

The 'National' Stadium

In January 2004 Angela Smith, Parliamentary Under Secretary for State with responsibility for sport, instructed Mr Tony Whitehead, Strategic Advisor with the Strategic Investment Board (SIB), to investigate the feasibility of building a new multi-sports stadium in Northern Ireland. The SIB, which was set up to advise on Northern Ireland's infrastructure, was itself a product of the Reinvestment and Reform Initiative (RRI) announced by the British government in 2002. This initiative, amongst other aims, was designed to identify strategic military bases and security sites which, in a post-conflict Northern Ireland, could be redeployed for the economic and social regeneration of local areas. By January 2005 Angela Smith was able to announce that three locations had been short-listed for the site of the proposed £85 million stadium.[34] These were the Maze Prison site, the North Foreshore of Belfast Lough and the so-called Titanic Quarter in east Belfast. Of greater significance was the assertion by Smith, supported by Tony Whitehead, that any new stadium would have to be commercially viable. Aside from private sector investment, in the form of sponsorship and retail space, what was ultimately being proposed was a sharing agreement between the three main team sports in Northern Ireland, association football, rugby union and Gaelic games. Whilst the plan was enthusiastically supported by the IFA and welcomed by the Ulster Branch of the IRFU, at that time the response of the Ulster Council of the GAA was typically non-committal. That said its secretary, Mr Danny Murphy, in an interview with the main evening newspaper in Northern Ireland, *The Belfast Telegraph*, did initially suggest that his organization would be supportive of such a development. When it quickly became apparent that this may not be an entirely accurate reflection of the views of 'grassroots' members, Mr Murphy issued a robust 'clarification', which amounted to a failure to either support or reject the new proposals. In fact it was yet further evidence of an uneasy accommodation the GAA has reached with association football in Ireland.[35]

In May 2004, Mr Whitehead outlined the key aims of the feasibility project for the stadium, which was designed to position Belfast as a major force on the sporting landscape amongst similar sized countries throughout Europe:

As part of the business plan exercise, all three sports bodies have played their full part, in terms of opening up their books and agreeing sets of assumptions. By that I mean realistic sets of assumptions on likely attendance, tickets prices etc. If we do move to the next stage and are asked to find the most appropriate site, quite clearly the number one criteria for that will be acceptability to all three sports bodies, both in terms of neutrality for the three sports bodies and also the fan base of the three sports bodies.[36]

The plan for a new stadium has been discussed in various settings for some considerable period of time. Two bodies have been at the forefront of these deliberations, the Sports Council for Northern Ireland (SCNI) and the IFA. Whilst the aspirations of the SCNI cannot be questioned, the motives of the IFA are primarily driven by the dilapidated condition of Windsor Park. In contrast the Ulster Branch of the IRFU has successfully hosted major rugby matches at its home ground of Ravenhill in south Belfast whilst the GAA, an essentially amateur sporting organization, remains the envy of many of its professional counterparts on account of its array of impressive stadia. Thus whilst the need for a new stadium has clear support in certain sectors, other sporting bodies appeared less convinced.

In an overall sense, the RRI, of which the proposed stadium is but one aspect, was introduced to address the substantial backlog of major capital investment projects necessary, in the opinion of the Government, to provide Northern Ireland with a first-class infrastructure for the twentieth-first century. Central to the urban regeneration component of the RRI strategy are a series of proposals based around the development of certain areas of Belfast that have traditionally been overlooked when it comes to public sector investment. There remain many parts of the capital city and its surrounding hinterlands that are significantly underdeveloped when measured across a range of societal markers. This was a point highlighted in 1999 by the then Parliamentary Under Secretary of State Mr John McFall when the issue of a new stadium in Northern Ireland was first debated in the House of Commons. Referring to a working party that he had formed to conduct a preliminary examination on the possibility of a new multi-sports stadium, he said: 'It (The working group) has an important contribution to make in taking forward the concept of a national stadium. It is an important issue in the development of sport in Northern Ireland. Such a stadium has been missing. It is certainly an issue that I take seriously.'[37]

Nevertheless, it was not until 30 March 2005, almost six years after the matter was first raised, that the Government was in a position to announce the former Maze prison site in County Antrim as the only viable option for the new sports stadium. The stadium would be constructed on the site alongside an International Centre for Conflict Transformation, a zone for industrial development, an arts centre and an international equestrian centre in a total redevelopment estimated to require £1 billion of public and private investment. The IFA has been a long time supporter of the concept of a national stadium for Northern Ireland, whilst proposals contained within the aforementioned report *Creating a Soccer Strategy for Northern Ireland* also suggested such a development should take place. Recommendation R14.1 of the document stated that: 'A national stadium, which would provide a neutral and welcoming environment and meet international standards for football, should be established.'[38]

This suggestion fell short of requesting a stadium for the sole use of soccer, perhaps mindful that on its own the game is not sufficiently well supported to guarantee the financial viability of such a project.

However, before this situation can be realized, several difficulties, many informed by historical grievances concerning actual or perceived acts of injustices against the minority nationalist community, remain to be resolved. One of the initial problems concerns the level of cooperation between the IFA and the other national governing bodies (the GAA and the Ulster Branch of the IRFU) thought necessary to ensure the success of the project. To be financially viable the Government requires the three main national governing bodies in Northern Ireland to commit to the use of the stadium in a proportionate manner. In other words, because the GAA attracts many thousands of followers to its games it is envisaged that it will only be required to play a small number of its matches at the new development. In contrast it is understood the Ulster Branch of the IRFU has suggested it is prepared to play a total of 30 matches over a given season to ensure its commitments are met. At the time of writing it is still unclear the precise number of games the IFA has said it is willing to play at the new stadium. This has created a fair degree of scepticism within the ranks of the other two organizations, especially the GAA, who fear they may be asked to effectively subsidize the IFA's involvement in the stadium. This would be ironic, as neither the GAA nor the IRFU has any immediate need for a new stadium and it is only the IFA that appears to be actively campaigning in this regard.[39]

The other main problem is the proposed site of the new stadium. This is an issue which has been the source of often heated debates between different shades of political opinion in Northern Ireland. The controversy relates directly to a suggestion that the stadium be built on the site of the former Maze Prison, situated near Lisburn, some seven miles south-west of Belfast. It is a decision that has angered members of the republican and nationalist communities who consider the proposal insensitive, as the Maze Prison was the site of the hunger strike campaign by Irish republican prisoners in 1981. The death of ten inmates following their failure to accept food in protest at the refusal of the British government to grant them political status served to galvanize Irish nationalism in a most profound manner. The prison is therefore thought to have much wider significance for this community, one the latter wish to preserve in memory of those whom they consider made the ultimate sacrifice in the face of perceived British intransigence. Of additional concern for nationalists and republicans is the fact that one of the key advocates of the scheme remains the IFA and that the new multi-sports stadium is being increasingly referred to as the 'national' stadium. This is because on the one hand the IFA has a less than enviable record in dealing with sectarian elements amongst its supporter base (although, as has already been stated, it has made considerable efforts to correct this in recent years), whilst for republicans in particular the term 'national' has clearly defined parameters and, in their eyes, is certainly not coterminous with Northern Ireland. With the redevelopment of Wembley Stadium in London, the widely regarded Millennium Stadium in Cardiff and the excellent Hampden Park in Scotland, each of the other so-called 'home' nations has stadiums that compare favourably with any others throughout Europe. It is perhaps only to be expected therefore that Northern

Ireland would wish to follow suit, albeit that in the other three previous examples the status of the nation itself is not in question. In the case of a country where large sections of the population appear to have difficulty with symbols that would imply broad acceptance of how the nation is presently constituted, an unwillingness to agree to future developments of this kind is perhaps not entirely unexpected.

Conclusion

In terms of active participation in soccer northern nationalists are to be found in roughly proportionate numbers on the playing fields of Northern Ireland. For them the sport carries broadly the same level of interest as it does their unionist counterparts. Instead their opposition to it manifests itself at a more ideological level. In this respect, the IFA constitutes but one further example of unionist hegemony amid a wide range of bodies similarly sympathetic to the link with Britain. Indeed, there is an argument that with the demise of other identifiable symbols of Ulster Protestantism, the IFA, and the game of soccer itself, has been encouraged to fill this sizeable void. Whilst this may be to overstate the importance of the IFA there is little doubt that many nationalists continue to harbour some degree of resentment towards it for what they consider to be past indiscretions. Perhaps understandably, therefore, many nationalists wish to have little involvement with the organization or what it stands for. One of the main themes of this essay has been to suggest that such an approach is not only regrettable, it is also arguably outdated and not a true interpretation of soccer in present day Northern Ireland. Problems certainly remain and there will always be small sections that remain positively indifferent to the activities of the IFA and thus may be only too pleased to see its problems continue. As such what is required in the current climate is a certain amount of goodwill on all sides, including on the part of northern nationalists, to help shape a better future for Northern Ireland generally. The proposed construction of a new multi-sports stadium on the outskirts of Belfast provides one such opportunity for all sides to work together to help secure the long-term viability of the project. To do so the IFA will have to continue, and further enhance, its ongoing efforts to encourage more nationalists to attend soccer matches in Northern Ireland. For their part northern nationalists will have to recognize their responsibilities in proving receptive to such initiatives. The satisfactory resolution of such difficulties could represent one positive step towards a more settled and peaceful society for all concerned.

Notes

[1]   Bairner, 'Creating a Soccer Strategy for Northern Ireland', 30.
[2]   Bairner, *Sport, Nationalism and Globalisation*; Sugden and Bairner, *Sport, Sectarianism and Society in a Divided Ireland*; Cronin, *Sport and Nationalism in Ireland*; David Hassan, 'A People Apart: Soccer, Identity and Irish Nationalists in Northern Ireland', 65–83.
[3]   Bairner and Darby, 'Divided Sport in a Divided Society'; Sugden and Bairner, 'Ireland and the World Cup'; Bairner, '"Up to their Knees?"'; Bairner and Walker, 'Football and Society in Northern Ireland'.
[4]   *Soccer Interest in Northern Ireland*. Department of Culture, Arts and Leisure (Northern Ireland).

[5]   Hassan, 'A People Apart'.
[6]   Department of Culture, Arts and Leisure (Northern Ireland), Minutes of the DCAL Executive Team Meeting on 22 Sept. 2004. Available from <http://www.dcalni.gov.uk/contman/includes/upload/file.asp?co>. Accessed 20 June 2005.
[7]   Available from <http://www.sferson.jervhost.com/stadium4belfast/supporters_say.shtml>. Accessed 22 June 2005.
[8]   BBC News, 'NI stadium "needs support"', available from <http://newsvote.bbc.co.uk/mpapps/pagetools/print/news.bbc.co.uk/1/hi/northern_ireland>. Accessed June 6 2005.
[9]   O'Malley, *Biting at the Grave*.
[10] Staunton, *The Nationalists of Northern Ireland, 1918–1973*.
[11] Hassan, 'A People Apart'.
[12] Available from <http://www.irishfa.com/index/articles.php?id=1106&page=Cross+Community>. Accessed 12 June 2005.
[13] Hassan, 'Sport and National Identity in Northern Ireland'.
[14] Liechty and Clegg, *Moving beyond Sectarianism*.
[15] Harris, 'The Evolution of Consociationalism in Northern Ireland'.
[16] Gerry Adams, Presidential Address to 2005 Sinn Fein Ard Fheis in Dublin. Available from <http:// sinnfein.ie/peace/speech/39>. Accessed 20 June 2005.
[17] Tonge, *The New Northern Irish Politics?*, 14.
[18] Harris, 'The Evolution of Consociationalism in Northern Ireland', 38.
[19] Tonge, *The New Northern Irish Politics?*
[20] Ibid., 204.
[21] Ibid.
[22] Hassan, 'The Gaelic Athletic Association, Rule 21, and Police Reform in Northern Ireland'.
[23] Hassan, 'A People Apart'.
[24] Bairner, 'Creating a Soccer Strategy for Northern Ireland'.
[25] Magee, 'Football Supporters, Rivalry and Protestant Fragmentation in Northern Ireland'.
[26] Bairner, 'Creating a Soccer Strategy for Northern Ireland'.
[27] Hassan, 'Sport, Identity and Irish Nationalism in Northern Ireland'.
[28] Bairner and Shirlow, 'Loyalism, Linfield and the Territorial Politics of Soccer Fandom in Northern Ireland'.
[29] *Soccer Interest in Northern Ireland* (DCAL).
[30] Ibid.
[31] Ibid.
[32] *Creating a Soccer Strategy for Northern Ireland*, (DCAL).
[33] Bairner, 'Creating a Soccer Strategy for Northern Ireland', 31.
[34] BBC News, 'Maze site "approved" for stadium', available from <http://news.bbc.co.uk/1/hi/northern _ireland/4395105.stm>.
[35] Hassan, 'The Gaelic Athletic Association, Rule 21, and Police Reform in Northern Ireland'.
[36] Available from <http://news.bbc.co.uk/1/hi/northern_ireland/3726165.stm>. Accessed 18 May 2005.
[37] *House of Commons Hansard Debates* for 16 March 1999 (pt 46). Available from <http://www.publications.parliament.uk/pa/cm199899/cmhansard/vo990316/debtext/90...>. Accessed 6 June 2005
[38] *Creating a Soccer Strategy for Northern Ireland*, (DCAL), 74.
[39] BBC News, 'NI stadium "needs support"'.

References

Bairner, Alan. '"Up to their Knees?" Football, Sectarianism, Masculinity and Protestant Working-class Identity.' In *Who are 'the people?' Unionism, Protestantism and Loyalism in Northern Ireland*, edited by P. Shirlow and M. McGovern. London: Pluto, 1997.

————. *Sport, Nationalism and Globalisation. European and North American Perspectives.* Albany, New York: State University of New York Press, 2001.

————. 'Creating a Soccer Strategy for Northern Ireland: Reflections on Football Governance in Small European Countries.' *Soccer and Society 5,* no.1 (2004): 27–42.

Bairner, Alan and Paul Darby. 'Divided Sport in a Divided Society: Northern Ireland.' In *Sport in Divided Societies,* edited by J. Sugden and A. Bairner. Aachen: Meyer and Meyer, 1999.

Bairner, Alan and Peter Shirlow. 'Loyalism, Linfield and the Territorial Politics of Soccer Fandom in Northern Ireland.' *Space and Polity 2,* no.2 (1998): 163–77.

Bairner, Alan and Graham Walker. 'Football and Society in Northern Ireland: Linfield Football Club and the case of Gerry Morgan.' *Soccer and Society 2,* no.1 (2001): 81–98.

Creating a Soccer Strategy for Northern Ireland. Belfast: DCAL (Northern Ireland), 2001.

Cronin, Mike. *Sport and Nationalism in Ireland: Gaelic Games, Soccer and Irish Identity since 1884.* Dublin: Four Courts Press, 1999.

Harris, Cecilia. 'The Evolution of Consociationalism in Northern Ireland.' Ph.D. diss., UC Cork, 2002.

Hassan, David. 'A People Apart: Soccer, Identity and Irish Nationalists in Northern Ireland.' *Soccer and Society 3,* no.3 (2002): 65–83.

————. 'Sport and National Identity in Northern Ireland: The Case of Northern Nationalism.' Ph.D. diss., University of Ulster, 2001.

————. 'The Gaelic Athletic Association, Rule 21, and Police Reform in Northern Ireland.' *Journal of Sport and Social Issues 29,* no.1 (2005): 60–78.

————. 'Sport, Identity and Irish Nationalism in Northern Ireland.' In *Sport and the Irish. Histories, Identities, Issues,* edited by Alan Bairner. Dublin: UCD Press, 2005: 123–39.

Liechty, Joseph and Cecelia Clegg. *Moving beyond Sectarianism: Religion, Conflict and Reconciliation in Northern Ireland.* Dublin: Columba Press, 2001.

Magee, Jonathan. 'Football Supporters, Rivalry and Protestant Fragmentation in Northern Ireland.' In *Sport and the Irish. Histories, Identities, Issues,* edited by Alan Bairner. Dublin: UCD Press, 2005: 172–90.

O'Malley, Padraig. *Biting at the Grave: The Irish Hunger Strikes and the Politics of Despair.* Belfast: Blackstaff, 1990.

Soccer Interest in Northern Ireland, Department of Culture, Arts and Leisure (Northern Ireland). Belfast: HMSO, 2004.

Staunton, Enda. *The Nationalists of Northern Ireland, 1918–1973.* Dublin: Columba Press, 2001.

Sugden, John and Alan Bairner. *Sport, Sectarianism and Society in a Divided Ireland.* Leicester: Leicester University Press, 1993.

————. 'Ireland and the World Cup: "two teams in Ireland, there's only two teams in Ireland…".' In *Hosts and Champions: Soccer Cultures, National Identities and the USA World Cup,* edited by J. Sugden and A. Tomlinson. Aldershot: Arena, 1994.

Tonge, Jonathan. *The New Northern Irish Politics?* Basingstoke: Palgrave Macmillan, 2005.

National Sports and Other Myths: The Failure of US Soccer

Sandra Collins

By many measures, soccer in the United States is doing well. On the tenth anniversary since the establishment of Major League Soccer in 1996, there are numerous statistics that support the claim that American soccer at the recreational, professional and international levels is in fact successful. US Youth Soccer Association claims that there are over 3.2 million registered players with the world's largest coaching and volunteer network of 800,000 people in 2004.[1] Even more telling, the Sporting Goods Manufacturers Association (SGMA) of America claims that as of 2002, 1.3 million more kids played soccer than Little League Baseball.[2] American youth are choosing soccer over the national pastime. Furthermore, the SGMA reveals that in 2001 over 19 million Americans were playing soccer, a 23.8 per cent increase from 1987.[3] Of the 19 million Americans playing soccer, 8,775,000 are from ages 6–11; 6, 197,000 from 12–17; 1,640,000 from 18–24; 911,000 25–34; and 1,519,000 35+.[4] This phenomenon is not

restricted to either the East or West coast, as regional participation is evenly distributed: Northeast, 3,944,000; North Central 5,781,000; South, 5,788,000; and West,
3,529,000. Soccer has become the second largest participation team sport in the US
after basketball, leading the SGMA to declare, 'American soccer participation ... will
never again be labeled a fad. Soccer is an integral part of America's sports landscape.'[5]
According to the SGMA, 'Soccer is the "hot" team sport,' with an increase of 41 per cent
of frequent players.[6] The greatest driver of the increase in American soccer participation is the growth in women playing soccer. American Sports Data research reveals that
female players now comprise 55 per cent of frequent players in 2000, compared to only
28 per cent in 1987.[7] At the college level, soccer is the most popular sport for women
on NCAA teams.[8] With increased player participation, the corporate support and
media attention to professional soccer cannot be far behind.

   In fact, professional soccer is slowly emerging as a major force in the sporting landscape with international success at World Cup tournaments and the Olympic Games
by the men's and women's teams. The establishment of men's First Division professional league (MLS) and the recently disbanded league for women which may or may
not be re-launched, the Women's United Soccer Association (WUSA), have made
many in-roads into the American sporting landscape. Despite the fact that experienced
US World Cup stars, such as Bobby Convey and DaMarcus Beasley, are playing for
foreign teams, the league is dominated by young players such as, Clint Dempsey, Eddie
Gaven, Eddie Johnson, Freddy Adu, Brian Carroll, Josh Gros and Alecko Eskandarian,
which will help the long-term development of the league in the US.[9] In April of 2005,
Landon Donovan returned to MLS with the LA Galaxy after a three-month stint with
Germany's Bayern Leverkusen. His return bodes well for challenging the strict salary
caps for players of American soccer clubs that has been the mainstay of the conservative
economic model promoted by the MLS. In a league with an average salary of $30,000
per year, Donovan renegotiated a five-year, $4.5 million deal revealing that the MLS is
willing to compete with European clubs for specific American soccer stars.[10] MLS
refused a $4 million transfer offer by Portuguese club Benfica in 2005 and a $3 million
bid from Spain's Real Mallorca in 2004 for FC Dallas star Eddie Johnson.[11] In
addition, MLS recently allowed for the increase of senior international players from
three to four.[12] According to American Soccer Leaders, creating successful teams
with visible soccer stars is critical to the long-term viability of American soccer. It is the
success of quality teams that will bring the American masses around, as Francisco
Marcos of USL quips 'America loves a winner and will support nothing else'.[13] Paul
Kennedy, managing editor of *Soccer America Magazine*, further validates this by
claiming, 'The biggest impact the success of the United states – and most important,
the visibility for young American starts – will have is if they lead to an infusion of new
money into MLS for player development. That means more money to keep young stars
such as Landon Donovan in MLS and more money to entice other young players to join
MLS at a young age.'[14]

   MLS has responded to this advice in launching both its Project 2010 and U-Programs
to create alternative channels to develop young American soccer stars. The 2004
recruitment of Freddy Adu, the youngest player in the MLS at age 14, is a sign of these

programmes' success. Criticisms of the expedited green card given to Ghana-native Adu ring hollow given Adu's incredible year with the D.C. United team which ended with their fourth MLS cup title.[15] FC Dallas forward Eddie Johnson is also a product of U-17 programme, through which at the age of 15 he received a scholarship to the US Soccer Federations' under-17 residency programme at the IMG Soccer Academy in Bradenton, Florida. At 17 years of age, Johnson was selected by Dallas in the second round of the 2001 MLS draft.[16] Both Adu and Johnson symbolize the promise of developing young, black American soccer stars that will be critical in attracting the next generation of sport spectators and players.

In 2004, two new league teams, Real Salt Lake (which is based in Salt Lake City, Utah and is backed by former NBA and Madison Square Garden executive Dave Checketts) and Club Deportivo (CD) Chivas USA (which is based in Los Angeles, California and is financed by Mexican mogul Jorge Vergara), have had strong stadium ticket sales and expanded the league to 12 teams in 2005.[17] There may be further expansion of the league in 2007. MLS/Soccer United Marketing claim there are an estimated 80 million soccer Americans supporting the growth of American soccer, with 22 million fans attending MLS matches during the league's first eight seasons of 1996–2003.[18]

In addition, soccer-specific stadiums which are smaller in size and are actively championed by the MLS were recently built: in 1999 Columbus, Ohio for the Crew and in 2003, the Home Depot Center in Carson City, California for LA Galaxy and CD Chivas USA.[19] There are plans for a FC Dallas team stadium in Frisco, TX and a $70 million, 20,000-seat stadium in Bridgeview, Illinois for the Chicago Fire. These soccer specific stadiums will bolster additional revenues from luxury boxes and restaurant concessions.[20] Ultimately, these soccer-specific stadiums signal the long-term investment in professional American soccer.[21]

American soccer has also secured long-term and lucrative corporate sponsorship deals that may have seemed elusive ten years ago. In the fall of 2004, MLS achieved an exclusive 10-year partnership agreement with Adidas-Salomon AG as the sole official athletic sponsor and licensed product supplier for the US Division professional league, worth an estimated $150 million.[22] The partnership agreement is unprecedented and grants Adidas the official athletic sponsor and licensed product supplier for the United States Division 1 professional league. 'The partnership incorporates every aspect of the game, from product creation, to grassroots, television rights and retail distribution.'[23] In addition to its 10-year sponsorship deal, Adidas will help start a reserve league for developmental players for the MLS. The Adidas sponsorship deal, according to Erich Stamminger, a board member of Adidas, was to 'increase their 50 percent stranglehold on the football market in the United States.'[24] Adidas had already secured sponsorship deals with the Kansas City Wizards, D.C. United and Columbus Crew of MLS.[25] Don Garber, the Commissioner of MLS and CEO of Soccer United Marketing claims that this deal is 'a clear indication of the League's position on the global sports landscape and its prospects for the near future'.[26] This deal, however, may conflict with the US Soccer Federation's contract with Nike which was extended until 2014 for an estimated $100 to $150 million.[27] Nike was also involved in the MLS-USSF joint initiative to identify top prospects and sign them to professional contracts within the MLS, called Project-40 programme. Although conflicts between the reserve league and the Project-40 were initially not specified, according the USSF spokesman Jim Moorhouse, recently the Generation Adidas group has replaced the Nike Project-40 programme and given roster exemption to players who leave college early or skip it to commit to professional soccer.[28] Nonetheless, two lucrative corporate sponsorships are also signs of the profitability of the American soccer market.

Furthermore, American national television coverage of soccer is more prominent than ever. ABC/ESPN/ESPN 2, Telemundo and Univision have continued to televise soccer. US Soccer programming is a core investment for Univision Networks given the 35 million viewers it attracted during the 2002 World Cup.[29] In 2002, MLS struck a landmark four-year television agreement with ABC, ESPN and ESPN2. In 2003, HDNet joined in the soccer market and in February 2005, Fox Sports World announced that it would now be named the Fox Soccer Channel during its coverage of Super Bowl XXXIX. MLS Chief Operating Officer Mark Abbott remarks, 'This year's lineup calls for 26 games on ESPN2; three on ABC Sports; 25 to 30 on Fox Soccer Channel; 28 on HD Net, 11 or 12 on ESPN Deportes; and 20–30 on Fox Sports in Espanol.'[30] These developments have led to Soccer United Marketing to declare that 'Nearly 95 per cent of MLS Games can now be viewed on live television, a startling accomplishment for such a nascent league'.[31] Although American ratings have been small, they are increasing. ESPN2's 2004 season average was 0.2, an 18 per cent rise in delivery to 180,872 households, and ESPN's TV ratings were about 200,000 homes per game in 2002.[32] These television networks have made commitments to the MLS given their belief in the business viability of American soccer. In terms of average attendance per game, Major League Soccer is often on par with the National Basketball Association.[33]

According to these statistics of increased participation, stadium attendance, corporate sponsorship and national television contracts, David Sternberg, Executive Vice-President and General Manager of Fox Soccer believes 'MLS could become the fourth major pro league in the US'.[34] Yet, after ten years, MLS has failed to make an impact on the national sports landscape, confesses MLS Commissioner Don Garber.[35] 'I think we still are focused on the soccer audience first and the general sports fan second', Garber said. 'All of the US Soccer Federation's research has shown that there are 50 million people who are connected with the game, and obviously there are not 50 million people who are coming to our games and watching our games on television. We still have a lot of work to do to get closer to the soccer-involved person in this country, and that's really what we're going to focus on the next couple of years.'[36]

Despite the laudable achievements in participation and professional soccer in the United States, the failure of soccer to emerge as a popular spectator sport is often explained away by the unexamined American myth of what constitutes its national sports. The Big Three of football (not futbôl), baseball and basketball are unabashedly hailed as American, while soccer is not. What exactly makes these sports American? Anecdotally, Americans are often ahistorical when they analyze why soccer continues to be dismissed by the popular American imagination. A rare historical and political exploration into the failure of soccer as an *American* sport was completed by Andrei S.

Markovits and Steven L. Hellerman in their book, *Offside: Soccer and American Exceptionalism*.[37] Despite the percentages of Americans who participate in soccer, Markovits and Hellerman define sports culture as what people talk about and follow as opposed to what they do. Specifically, Markovits and Hellerman state that they are 'interested in what we call "hegemonic sports culture", meaning the sports culture that dominates a country's emotional attachments rather than its callisthenic activities'.[38] The hegemonic sports culture is represented through various outlets of popular culture, such as newspapers, magazines, films, television shows and literature. Despite the meteoric participation rates of American soccer, Markovits and Hellerman argue that the failure of soccer in America has historical and political cultural factors that continue to operate in contemporary America.

In the era between 1870 and 1930 when most industrialized and modernized nations were also developing sports cultures, America's dominate sports culture 'developed sufficient differences and indigenous peculiarities to create a sport space that can be justifiably labeled singularly American'.[39] The most significant factor in the development of what has come to be identified as 'American' sports (football, baseball and basketball) is the self-imposed isolated global position of the United States at the turn of the nineteenth century. As Markovits and Hellerman argue:

> Whereas the British bourgeoisie derived much of its pride and self-legitimation from being part of the centre of the global empire, its American counterpart attained much of its identity precisely from having spurned this very empire and – in contrast to its Canadian and Australian cousins – in having established a successful 'frontier' republic in wake of its opposition to this empire. This strong ambivalence toward Great Britain in particular (and Europe more generally) – manifesting itself in a clear affinity fostered by a common language and culture on the one hand, and a disdain for the old colonial master and its ways on the other – greatly influenced the development of public discourse in the United States during the latter half of the nineteenth century. This 'special relationship', marked by both admiration and rejection, proved particularly significant for the development of American sports. *As such, this American ambivalence toward things British and European and the attempt to create a cultural niche in line with – yet independent of – British and European culture, constitutes an integral part of American exceptionalism.* (emphasis in original)[40]

As such, from the 1870s to the 1930s when the sports space was being established in many nations, it was this cultural drive to 'Americanize' sports imported from, or influenced by, sports in Great Britain or Europe that ultimately crowded out soccer in the United States. Markovits and Hellerman painstakingly trace the early history of baseball, basketball, football and soccer in America to conclude that 'By the time Britain's own mass sport, soccer, had been successfully exported all over the world, America's sport space was already occupied by former British imports now converted into genuine American sports plus an indigenous American invention that was to prove vastly popular in the cramped quarters and indoor activities of America's newly arrived immigrants and their American-born children.'[41] The popularity of baseball at the turn of the twentieth century, the influential role of American universities in popularizing sports and the invention of basketball, Markovits and Hellerman contend, restricted the draw of soccer in the United States. In addition, the early history of soccer in the United States was also plagued by various institutional and organizational mishaps that further weakened any chance American soccer had of developing into a major sport in the US.

The central tenet of Markovits and Hellerman's argument revolves around their notion of American exceptionalism in the global order and how this exceptionalism also influences the sport space in America. For Markovits and Hellerman, American sports have a very different relationship to nationalism than that of soccer played by most of the world. It is this sense of a 'self-contained nationalism acting apart from the rest of the international arena' that characterizes America's top three sports of baseball, basketball and football. The rivalries, Markovits and Hellerman argue, in America's top three sports are 'not attached to national entities as in the world of soccer, but almost exclusively to subnational ones'.[42] The national teams of soccer repeatedly engage in international competitions and underscore soccer's 'deeply anchored nationalism'. American exceptionalism has fomented not only much of America's international political and economic identity, but also its sporting culture. Markovits and Hellerman conclude by stating:

> While soccer fosters highly national sentiments and identities, it also offers an inter-national language of communication and an international cultural code that is truly binding and bonding. None of the hegemonic American sports offers either of these sentiments. American sports neither engender a deep sense of nationalism nor provide a genuine forum for internationalism. They remain confined to a world all their own.[43]

Through the thorough analysis of Markovits and Hellerman, the failure of soccer to emerge as a major sport in the United States has deep historical and cultural roots that are revealed in a comparative context to other industrial, modernized nations. Marko-vits and Hellerman contend that despite how global the culture of industrial modernity has become, much of American culture is characterized by local aspects that separate it from the 'norm elsewhere'. The accelerated flows of globalization have not erased the peculiar differences that render America exceptional, and this difference also defines the American sports space. Supported by detailed historical analysis, Markovits and Hellerman demarcate two trajectories for the future of soccer in America, both its success and failure, and their conclusion is disappointedly non-committal to either.

Yet, Markovits and Hellerman's thesis bears much weight upon understanding the historical and contemporary failure of soccer in the United States. There is validity in the self-proclaimed provincialism and exceptionalism of American culture and recent foreign policy decisions: America may be in the World, but the World is not in Amer-ica. That is to say, the flows of global culture may emanate from the United States, but rarely do the flows from abroad make a deep impact in the psyche of American culture. The globalization of American culture has exported McDonald's, Starbucks, Levi's, Nike and even the television show *Baywatch* to much of the world. It is hard, however, to identify other forms of foreign culture that has made prominent in-roads into Amer-ican culture. Franklin Foer, a staff writer for the *New Republic*, explores the circuits of globalization by using soccer as a metaphor in his recent book, *How Soccer Explains the World: An Unlikely Theory of Globalization*.[44] Despite the promise of globalization and its attendant prosperity to all, Foer uses soccer in different national locales to muse why globalization has failed: 'Why have some nations remained poor, even though they had so much foreign investment coursing through them? How dangerous are the multinational corporations that the Left rails against?'[45] Foer remarks that the promise of globalization was to erase local institutional differences and render them homogeneous, but his travels and research revealed just the opposite, that 'globalization had failed to diminish the game's local cultures, local blood feuds, and even local corruption'.[46] Soccer in Serbia, Scotland, Hungary, Great Britain Brazil, Ukraine, Italy, Spain and Iran are written about with such interesting insight and with careful explorations of how both positive and negative aspects of the local persist and failed to be erased by soccer (aka globalization). Soccer in the United States is briefly discussed, and in spite of any in-depth analysis, Foer mirrors much of Markovits and Hellerman's arguments regarding American exceptionalism. In fact, the American culture wars of the 1980s and the split during the 2004 Presidential election are signs for Foer not so much of the difference of American culture vis-à-vis the world, but of the difference of globalization in the United States. Soccer bashing in the United States – the vehement and prolific sports writing against soccer – is a manifestation of the phobia of globalization in America. As Foer remarks, 'Globalization increasingly provides the subtext for the American cultural split'.[47] Here, Foer demarcates those cosmopolitan Americans who hold a worldview (aka 'liberals') against those of 'American exceptionalism' who hold that America's unique legacy and position render it above international law (aka 'conservatives').[48] The debates within America over soccer and globalization are part and parcel of life in a global world, Foer concludes. The future of soccer, he implies, is dependent upon whether America continues to define the choices within globalization as a strict either/or proposition between one side and another instead of the diversity within the range of both sides.

The tenets of American exceptionalism proposed by Markovits and Hellerman and the divisive globalization of Foer provide some insight not only into the struggle of American soccer but also into the attendant anxieties of America in the global world of today. In their analysis of soccer, however, both Markovits and Hellerman and Foer should have further explored their concepts of exceptionalism or globalization. Recently, Harry Harootunian, an eminent historian of Japan and modernity at New York University, addressed the concept of 'new imperialism' which has informed much of contemporary global life in a post 9/11 world in a small book, *The Empire's New Clothes: Paradigm Lost, and Regained*.[49] For Harootunian, America's new imperialism of rational achievements reframed the pre 9/11-notion of globalization which was an extension of the Cold War modernization project.[50] The former promise of the globalization of prosperity everywhere is actually a historical extension of the promise of modernization to 'make all societies look alike'. Here, Harootunian quotes extensively from Kristin Ross, a historian of modern France, about the promises of modernization, '[T]he most important promise made by modernization: its evenness. Modernization is even because it holds within itself a theory of spatial and temporal convergence; all societies will come to look like us, all will arrive eventually at the same state or level, all the possibilities of the future are being lived now.'[51]

Markovits and Hellerman employ the notion of exceptionalism that characterizes much of America's culture and practices to analyze soccer, but fail to explore how in the history of capitalism and modernization there is no model which defines America as unique vis-à-vis the world. In other words, each nation is unique in the sense that the local inflection of the globalization of capitalism is unique to that nation; no nation resembles one another. While there are similarities and differences, there is no benchmark of an industrial, modern nation which renders America uniquely exceptional in comparison to any other nation. Despite the American propensity to fuse capitalism and democracy together as an end-goal for the global order, Harootunian contends, 'capitalism always generates unevenness and forms of unequal exchange'.[52] As such, the world order will never deliver the type of globalization that both Markovits and Hellerman and Foer describe. It is not enough to identify that America is different, exceptional or unique in the global order, either in real socio-economic-political terms or in perceived cultural terms. Markovits and Hellerman cites that America has historically defined itself as isolated from the world, and yet this is not exceptional. China, Japan, Finland and many other nations will claim national difference in the wake of a global order. Markovits and Hellerman's argument would have been strengthened if he accounted for how these inequalities function in America and what the socio-economic-political payoffs are. Some may be easy to posit: the unique role of America in occupying Iraq; the continuation of many myths about American life as being classless and racially integrated; or the provincialism in contemporary American society which only fuels the uniqueness of baseball, football and basketball to reign supreme in America despite their lack of international competition. In Foer's work, a quick survey of academic work on the tensions between the local and the global would have added analytical depth to his insights into the continued presence of the local in a global world. In fact, the term *glocal* ('glocalization') was coined to describe the very process of local responses to global challenges that Foer's work could have benefited from.[53] Nonetheless, both Markovits and Hellerman and Foer provide commentary and further insights into why American soccer continues to struggle.

Perhaps the failure of soccer to capture the popular imagination of America lies also in the fact that it is a diverse sport and represents a cross-section of America, in terms of both the players (from 31 countries around the globe) and the fan base who range from stereotypically white suburbanites to urban Latinos. If the top three spectator sports (baseball, football and basketball) are primary dominated by the middle class and working poor in contrast to the white, suburban affluence of soccer (with the exception of the Latino population), then class and race are definitely issues that inform the failure of American soccer to capture the imagination of popular America. Class and race continue to be problematic categories of experience within contemporary America, which the 2005 *New York Times* explored in a series of articles entitled 'Class Matters'.[54] Contemporary America has not come to terms with the reality of its twenty-first century life – class and race still continue to be plague Americans in ways that contemporary America has failed to seriously address. In terms of race, Major League Baseball has continued to change, incorporating Japanese and other national players from around the globe; American football has continued to be associated with the champions of every American hometown; and basketball is the dreamscape of many black inner-city urban youth. And Soccer? If the MLS stated goal is to 'reflect inclusiveness and diversity', perhaps its failure and continued difficulty is precisely because its goal – in the current sociological and political climate of modern America – is an ephemeral one, one that the government, media and masses are struggling to define in a post-9/11 world.

Notes

[1]   Statistics available from US Youth Soccer Association website <www.usyouthsoccer.org>.
[2]   Foer cites this statistic in his work, *How soccer Explains the World*, 244.
[3]   Basketball has some 38,663,000 million participants. This data is available from 'Soccer in the USA 2002–2003,' 4.
[4]   Ibid., 5.
[5]   Ibid., 4.
[6]   The SGMA report cites American sports Data, Inc. as source for the statistics. In 1990, 2.7 million Americans played soccer 52 or more times; in 2000, it was 3.8 million. For further details, see 'U.S. Trends in Team Sports', 4.
[7]   American Sports Data, cited in ibid., 14.
[8]   National Collegiate Athletic Association cites 18,188 women players on 811 teams in 2000, a 168 per cent increase over 1990 (6,781 women on 318 teams), See ibid., 15, 25.
[9]   John Haydon, 'Plenty to be grateful for in MLS (Sports)', *The Washington Times*, 27 Nov. 2004.
[10] Grant Wahl, 'Eddie Makes This Game Look Cool'.
[11] Ibid.
[12] Haydon, 'Plenty to be grateful for in MLS (Sports)'.
[13] 'Ask Francisco: USL commissioner Francisco Malcos answers questions from SoccerTimes readers', *SoccerTimes*, 29 Jul. 2000, <www.soccertimes.net/proleagues/usl/2000/jun29.html>
[14] 'Soccer in the USA 2002-2003,' 7.
[15] Gus Martins, 'Soccer Notes; there was much Adu; Heralded teen makes gains in MLS (Sports)', *The Boston Herald*, 2 Feb. 2005.
[16] Grant Wahl, 'Eddie Makes This Game Look Cool'.
[17] Two teams from Tampa and Fort Lauderdale teams were dissolved in 2004.
[18] http://www.sumworld.com/properties/mls/index.php?set-0.
[19] 'Constructed on the campus of California State University, Dominguez Hills, at a total cost of $150 million, the 27,000-seat soccer stadium is the centerpiece of a massive multi-sport facility. Also at The Home Depot Center are a 13,000-seat tennis stadium, a 20,000-seat track and field facility and a 2,500-seat indoor velodrome. Volleyball, baseball, softball, basketball and other sports can be accommodated at The Home Depot Center's state-of-the-art facilities.' Jonathan Nierman, 'Home Depot Center voted top venue', 20 May 2005, MLSnet.com.
[20] Mike Reynolds, 'Kicking soccer ever higher: as MLS celebrates its 10th anniversary, soccer coverage is more prolific than ever'. (Special report: sports programming), Multichannel News, 21 March 2005.
[21] Haydon, 'Plenty to be grateful for in MLS' (Sports).
[22] The deal was publicized on 10 Nov. 2004. 'The partnership incorporates every aspect of the game, from product creation, to grassroots programs, television rights and retail distribution. Among the highlights of the deal, Adidas and MLS plan to work with the soccer community on a developmental league that will provide opportunities for future soccer stars.' See Soccer United Marketing website<htpp://www.sumworld.com>. Also see, 'Adidas deal with MLS contains plans for reserve league', *AP Worldstream*, 10 Nov. 2004.

[23]   'Adidas, Major league Soccer and Soccer United Marketing Sign Landmark Sponsorship Agreement', *PR Newswire*, 10 Nov. 2004.

[24]   'Adidas sign MLS sponsorship deal', *Agence France Presse English*, 5 Oct. 2004.

[25]   'MLS and adidas announce long term partnership', *MLS Communications*, 10 Nov. 2004, <www.mysoccer.com/mls4/mls1110.phtml>.

[26]   'Adidas signs 10-year deal with MLS'. *AP Worldstream*.

[27]   'Adidas deal with MLS contains plans for reserve league'.

[28]   Alan Pearce, 'Rapids Rush to Spark Scoring Striker Deal Adds to Defensive Draft', *Denver Rocky Mountain News*, 15 Jan. 2005 and 'Adidas deal with MLS contains plans for reserve league'.

[29]   Kevin Downey, 'Look who's talking: usually reticent Univision finally starts to tell its story' (Hispanic Television Special Report) (Univision Networks), *Broadcasting & Cable*, 13 June 2005.

[30]   Reynolds, 'Kicking soccer ever higher'.

[31]   <http://www.sumworld.com/properties/mls/index.php?set-0>.

[32]   Howard Fendrich, 'ABC, ESPN to air 2002, 2006 World Cups', *Associated Press*, 3 Jan. 2002.

[33]   Sean Fredrick Brown, 'Can European Football Spur Interest in American Soccer? A Look at the ChamptionsWorld^{TM} Series and Major League Soccer', 52.

[34]   Reynolds, 'Kicking soccer ever higher'.

[35]   Pete Grathoff, 'X marks the spot as Major League Soccer kicks off its 10th season', the *Kansas City Star* (via Knight-Ridder/Tribune News Service), 2 April 2005.

[36]   Ibid.

[37]   Markovits and Hellerman, *Offside*.

[38]   Ibid., 10.

[39]   Ibid., 15, 39.

[40]   Ibid., 40.

[41]   Ibid.

[42]   Ibid., 46.

[43]   Ibid., 49.

[44]   Foer, *How Soccer Explains the World*.

[45]   Ibid., 4.

[46]   Ibid., 4–5.

[47]   Ibid., 244.

[48]   Ibid., 245.

[49]   Harootunian, *The Empire's New Clothes*.

[50]   Ibid., 5.

[51]   Ibid., preface.

[52]   Ibid., 122.

[53]   The literature is vast on local and global studies. One of the most cited sources, however, remains, Martin Shaw, 'The Global Transformation of the Social Sciences', from the Centre for the Study of Global Governance in London. For the term *glocal*, see <http://webdata.soc.hawaii.edu/fredr/GSfesto.htm>.

[54]   The *New York Times* writes of the series: 'A team of reporters spent more than a year exploring ways that class – defined as a combination of income, education, wealth and occupation – influences destiny in a society that likes to think of itself as a land of unbounded opportunity.' See 'Class Matters: A Special Section', the *New York Times*, <http://www.nytimes.com/pages/national/class>.

References

Brown, Sean Fredrick. 'Can European Football Spur Interest in American Soccer? A Look at the ChampionsWorld™ Series and Major League Soccer.' *Soccer and Society 6*, no.1 (March 2005): 49–61.

Foer, Franklin. *How Soccer Explains the World: An Unlikely Theory of Globalization.* New York: HarperCollins, 2004.

Harootunian, Harry. *The Empire's New Clothes: Paradigm Lost, and Regained.* Chicago: Prickly Paradigm Press, 2004.

Markovits, Andrei S. and Steven L. Hellerman. *Offside: Soccer & American Exceptionalism.* Princeton and Oxford: Princeton University Press, 2001.

Shaw, Martin. 'The Global Transformation of the Social Sciences'. In Mary Kaldor, Helmut Anheser and Marlies Glasius, eds., *Global Civil Society Yearbook 2003,* Oxford: Oxford University Press, 2003, pp. 35–44.

'Soccer in the USA 2002–2003.' In *Sports Participation in America 2003, Sporting Goods Manufacturers Association,* Washington D.C.: SGMA, 2004.

'U.S. Trends in Team Sports.' In *Organized Youth Team Sports Participation in the U.S., 2001, Sporting Goods Manufacturers Association,* Washington D.C.: SGMA, 2001.

Wahl, Grant. 'Eddie Makes This Game Look Cool: When a kid from the Florida projects like Eddie Johnson scores goals in bunches, it gets the attention of the world's top soccer clubs – and young African-Americans (Soccer).' *Sports Illustrated,* 30 May 2005.

Women's Soccer in the Republic of Ireland: Some Preliminary Sociological Comments

Katie Liston

Following its launch in 2000, *Soccer and Society* has aimed to cover all aspects of soccer globally from anthropological, cultural, economic, historical, political and sociological perspectives. Since 2000, however, with the exception of Jinxia and Mangan's discussion of women's soccer in China and Majumdar's research on women's soccer in India, fewer contributors have dealt explicitly with what has come to be commonly known as 'women's soccer'.[1] In a similar way, with the exception of Clayton and Harris's work on the role of footballer's wives in the construction of idealized masculinity, fewer contributors have dealt explicitly with aspects of the soccer-gender nexus.[2] In this essay, I shall attempt to address this dearth of research by focusing on aspects of the sport-gender nexus in the Republic of Ireland with specific reference to the formal emergence and development of women's soccer since 1973. The academic sub-discipline of the sociology of sport in Ireland is in its relative infancy, though a number of male sociologists including Bairner, Hassan, Magee, Fulton and Tuck have made valuable contributions to our understanding of aspects of the sport-national identity nexus in Ireland.[3] By comparison, with the exception of the author's doctoral research, the sport-gender nexus is relatively under-researched. This essay should be seen, then, as 'one symptom of a beginning';[4] that is to say, it should be seen as an attempt to develop a more adequate sociological model for the subject matter in question, in this case, females' increasing involvement in a traditionally associated male sport like soccer in Ireland. In this connection, I shall draw on empirical data gathered for a doctoral research project,[5] aspects of which have been discussed in detail elsewhere.[6] For the purposes of this discussion, I will focus more specifically on data from in-depth interviews and data gathered during my elite-level involvement as a player in women's soccer since 1995.

One of the few publications on women's soccer in Ireland is Bourke's (2004) work on 'Women's Soccer in the Republic of Ireland: Past Events and Future Prospects'.[7] In her chapter, Bourke outlines the main developments in women's soccer since the formal establishment of the Ladies' Football Association of Ireland in 1973, which, according to her, include:

> the growth in the number of domestic leagues; Ireland's initial involvement in international competition; the initiation of development plans; and the appointment of a women's development officer by the FAI.[8]

Bourke also examines some of the current organizational issues pertinent to women's soccer and attempts to draw on the figurational sociological perspective to argue that 'the football figuration is defined and utilized as the basis for identifying the factors and parties that have both enabled and constrained the development of women's soccer in Ireland'.[9] For the purposes of the present essay, I do not propose to outline these historical developments in detail. However, I shall engage with some of Bourke's arguments in order: (i) to suggest a more fruitful application of the figurational sociological approach; and, (ii) to understand better the consequences of increasing interdependence between the sexes in Ireland, one aspect of which includes the increasing participation of females in traditionally male-associated sports such as soccer since the 1970s.[10]

A Brief History of Women's Soccer in the Republic of Ireland

Bourke correctly points out that the emergence and development of women's soccer clubs in Ireland in the 1970s was not a coordinated process. Similar to the codification of modern sports in Britain and Ireland in the late 1800s and early 1900s, the existence of clubs – in this case, women's soccer clubs – predated the formal establishment of national sports associations such as the Ladies' Football Association of Ireland (LFAI). In the early 1970s, a number of Gaelic football and Association Football (soccer) clubs were established for females and these tended to be organized by people involved in large companies and firms, including the civil service, banks and manufacturing companies, as well as by existing men's clubs. The emergence of these teams/clubs contributed to increasing social pressure for the establishment of central governing bodies for women's soccer and ladies' Gaelic football. The Ladies' Football Association of Ireland (now the Women's Football Association of Ireland) was established in 1973. To digress briefly, it is significant that the title of the association was changed from 'Ladies' to 'Women' in 2001 and this coincided with the affiliation of the association with the Football Association of Ireland (FAI). The LFAI cited their desire to capture a more modern ideal as one of the main reasons for this change, alongside the prioritization of women's football within the FAI. Bourke describes the emergence and early development of the LFAI as a 'humble beginning' and this was reflected in 'teams and clubs emerging on an *ad hoc* basis'.[11] A more adequate figurational sociological explanation of these *ad hoc* developments would describe them in terms of blind social processes as this concept reflects the ways in which, as people, we are unaware of our mutual interdependence, and processes of change (which no one has planned) generate consequences which we could not foresee. In this way, the emergence of women's soccer clubs in the early 1970s can be explained in terms of the intended and unintended consequences of purposeful action by particular groups of people over time. Similarly, a more adequate figurational sociological explanation for the emergence of women's soccer in the 1970s would also point to females' increasing participation in body-contact sports more generally around this time and: (i) the position of sporting disciplines such as soccer in the overall status hierarchy of sports in Ireland (including 'Irish' sports); (ii) male and female athletes' positions within these sports; (iii) the consequences of social relations for changing self-conceptions of masculine and feminine habituses; and, (iv) the ways in which changes in the self-images and social make-up of male and female athletes are inextricably bound up with changes in the social structure of gender relations in the wider society.

In the past 20 years in particular, females in Ireland have increased their participation in what have been seen as traditionally male-associated sports such as Gaelic games, soccer and rugby (see Table 1). It is important here to clarify that the estimates of females' and males' participation in sports such as Gaelic games (Gaelic football, hurling and handball), rugby and soccer are based on data from respective national sports associations. These figures refer to those adults (and youths) *registered* or *affiliated* with a national governing body such as the Women's Football Association of Ireland (WFAI) in any one year. However, it has yet to be established if, and how, *registration* or *affiliation* with a particular sports association translates into *regular participation* in a sport such as women's soccer though, not surprisingly, leading officials of the WFAI and other national sports associations place strong emphasis on these estimates as indicators of progress over time.[12]

It is also important to note that gradual increases in the size and status of the two female football organizations mentioned in this essay – the WFAI and the LGFA – have occurred concomitantly with the increasing participation of females in these male-dominated sports. These changes, aspects of which I have outlined elsewhere, have not resulted in a *substantial* shift in the balance of power between males and females in

Table 1   Current estimates of adult male and female participants in selected sports

Sport	Male and Female Players	Total players	Year of formation
Rugby	18,000 (M)		IRFU – 1879
	900 (F)	**18,900**	IWRFU – 1991
Gaelic games	Hurling and Football	**416,880[13]**	GAA – 1884
	Camogie (F) – 80,000		CCnG – 1904
	Football (F) – 80,000	**160,000**	LGFA – 1974
Soccer	162,500 (M)		FAI – 1921
	6,500 (F)	**169,000**	WFAI – 1973

M = Male, F= Female (Taken from Liston, 2005)

sport in Ireland. The field of sports in that country can thus be characterized as a 'male preserve' such that the dominant ideological characteristics associated with team and contact sports include, though not exclusively, the display of physical strength and aggression, competitiveness, physical confrontation, a team ethic and a culture of risk.

Gaelic football is generally regarded as the fastest growing sport for females in Ireland at the moment, though few commentators have provided an empirical analysis of this claim.[14] The Ladies Gaelic Football Association (LGFA) was established in 1974 and has approximately 80,000 current members. In the past ten years, attendances at the finals of their premier competition – the All Ireland championship – have increased over six-fold from an estimated 5,000 spectators in 1993 to 30,000 spectators at the 2003 championship finals, while the average television audience for the duration of the 2003 Junior and Senior championship finals was estimated by Nielsen Media Research to total approximately 564,000 people. These increases represent an obvious growth in the wider popularity of ladies' Gaelic football as well as increasing media coverage and the incipient commercialization of the game (for example, TG4 sponsorship).[15] As I have said previously, the Women's Football Association of Ireland (then the Ladies' Football Association of Ireland) was established in 1973, one year prior to the establishment of the LGFA. The WFAI currently organizes women's soccer competitions from schools to under-age and international level. Approximately 6,500 females are currently registered to play women's soccer in 17 domestic leagues, and according to the WFAI, this figure represents an almost 100 per cent increase on playing numbers since 2000. Based on current estimates, females comprise approximately 3 per cent of registered soccer players in Ireland. By comparison, one quarter of all UK football players are female.[16] Currently, the WFAI is affiliated to, and primarily funded by, the Football Association of Ireland (FAI).

The LFAI entered teams in senior international competitions between 1974 and 1992. Following their withdrawal from international competition for three years in order to improve the national playing base, the LFAI re-entered international competition in 1995, and the Republic of Ireland has qualified for the top tier of European competition in the 2005/06 season. During this time, the WFAI have also expanded their participation in international competitions to include youth competitions (for example, under 15s and 19s), the UEFA Women's Cup and the World Student Games. In the past three years, the FAI have established a post with the responsibility for developing women's soccer, and there has been a slight though tangible shift in attitudes within the FAI towards the 'women's game'. For example, leading FAI officials have been more involved than they used to be in publicly supporting the WFAI, and this public support has been translated into their increasing involvement in coaching and advising female footballers. A full-time senior national women's coach has been appointed in 2005 by the FAI while the public profile of women's soccer has also been increasing, though not to the same extent as that of ladies Gaelic football. Evidence for this can be seen in the hosting of their premier competition – the WFAI Cup – at Lansdowne Road in 2004, for the first time alongside their male counterparts, and the WFAI Cup has received increasing television and print media coverage.

While women's soccer in Ireland is administered by the WFAI and their respective provincial, university and regional councils, the WFAI is affiliated to the FAI and it is primarily funded by that organization. The appointment of Fran Rooney as Chief Executive Officer of the FAI in 2003 meant that women's soccer received a higher media profile (for example, Rooney was proactive in including women's soccer in his discussions, and journalists tended to ask him a number of questions about women's soccer as a result of his former involvement as manager of the women's senior international team).[17] In addition, the restructuring of the management structure of the FAI on the back of the Genesis Report (following the 2002 World Cup) mirrored (and reinforced) a process of change concerning the organization and marketing of soccer in Ireland more generally. The Genesis Report was published following Roy Keane's departure from the World Cup squad in 2002 and an evaluation of the organizational structures of the FAI. Perhaps one of the most salient sociological points to emerge from this report was a concern with the persistence of amateur values in the field of soccer in Ireland. It might be argued that a concern with amateurism is/was a consequence of relative underdevelopment in Ireland until recent years, and therefore the concern with amateur values in sports like soccer and Gaelic football is unlikely to be sustainable for long, particularly in relation to those sports which facilitate international matches and competitions. While Houlihan argued that soccer in Ireland can be seen as part of a process of 'engagement with the world and [is] symbolic of Ireland's confidence',[18] this argument requires further empirical verification, and it is probably more applicable to the men's game given the relative size, status and popularity of the men's and women's associations, and the differential resources available to both.

While changes such as an increase in the numbers of females registered with the WFAI and the affiliation of the WFAI to the FAI are important in terms of the relatively small community of players and administrators of the game in Ireland, the numbers of players who compete regularly in women's soccer have not changed *significantly*, and past and present managers of the senior international women's team have encountered difficulties in their attempts to strengthen the national playing base. Having said that, FAI Development Officers are becoming more proactive in integrating younger females into their coaching and development programmes, and it seems likely that this will have some positive consequences for women's soccer

Table 2   Recent migration of international Irish female soccer players

International match	Squad size	Irish-based players	English-based players	US-based players
Ireland v Croatia	18	5	6	7
Ireland v Bosnia	17	3	11	3
Algarve Cup	20	5	11	4
Greece v Ireland	18	2	9	7
Ireland v Greece	18	2	9	7
Bosnia v Ireland	17	3	7	7
USA v Ireland	17	2	10	5
Romania v Ireland	17	4	6	7
Croatia v Ireland	18	5	6	7
Total	**160**	**31 (19%)**	**75 (47%)**	**54 (34%)**

in the future. It is also not sociologically surprising that the migration patterns of leading Irish male footballers to England and elsewhere is mirrored in the migration of some leading Irish female footballers outside the country. For example, a number of leading Irish female international soccer players currently hold soccer scholarships in the US and a number currently play for leading English teams (see Table 2). In addition, former Irish internationals have played professionally in Italy, Germany, Japan and France. Men and women have played a key role in establishing these international opportunities and enabling female footballers to 'ply their trade abroad'. The nucleus of the current Irish women's senior international squad consists of players who have played the game in Ireland (typically as youth players) and subsequently secured university scholarships or playing contracts (semi-professional or otherwise) elsewhere, generally in the UK and the US. In Table 2 above, those players listed as 'US-based' are currently registered as scholarship players with universities and colleges including Hofstra (New York), Franklin Pierce College (New Hampshire), Christian Brothers University (Memphis), Long Island (New York) and Central Connecticut State University. Those players listed as 'English-based players' are currently registered with clubs including Arsenal, Bristol Rovers, Charlton, Leeds and Fulham.[19]

While these players have undoubtedly benefited from competing at a higher level, further empirical work is needed to establish the overall effects of player migration on the standard of women's soccer in Ireland. This migration trend has had a number of likely consequences including an increase in the skills and fitness levels of those players who compete professionally and semi-professionally, and a related concern about the potential impact of a 'skills drain' on domestic women's soccer. An analysis of those female footballers involved in nine international women's soccer squads prior to 2004 (Table 2), reveals that most were playing in competitive leagues outside Ireland, a trend comparable to that of players involved in the Irish men's senior international squad. It is also possible that the gradual diffusion of women's soccer throughout Ireland and the migration of players outside Ireland in the past ten years (particularly to England and the US) have contributed to more 'outward-looking' ideas about women's sports, though this claim needs to be tested empirically.

It is commonly accepted that the US women's team has been one of the leading women's teams worldwide over the past ten or so years. One of the contributory factors to the relative acceptance of women's soccer in the US, and the relative empowerment of women there, has been the implementation of Title IX legislation for equal funding of high school and college sports since the 1970s. One of the consequences of this legislation was an (intended) increase in females' participation in high school and college sports. However, there has also taken place an unintended and disproportionate creation of employment opportunities for males in the sports and leisure field.[20] Thus, claims concerning the unequivocal success of Title IX and similar programmes vis-à-vis gender equality in sport need to be tested further for their empirical adequacy. Similarly, Williams' claim that a consensus exists and that the 'increased commercialism and professionalism [of women's soccer] is desirable and bound to happen' needs to be tested further.[21] She also argues that such a consensus is 'neither historically accurate nor inevitable' due to the limited integration of women's sports within the field of male-dominated sports and 'the widespread devaluation of women's sport, particularly of women football players'. Irrespective of the perceived ideological desirability of the integration of women's sports within the organizational structures of so-called 'men's sports', it is clear that one of the consequences of increasing interdependence between the sexes in the field of sport in Ireland (as elsewhere) has been that females have been enabled to become increasingly involved in traditionally associated male sports by virtue of wider social changes, including changes in thresholds of violence and repugnance and a corresponding equalizing trend in gender relations.[22] According to Dunning and Maguire:

> the Western European 'civilizing process' has involved, on the normative level, an accumulation of controls and taboos, for example, against males striking females, and, on the level of habitus and personality, a lowering of the 'threshold of repugnance' regarding violence and aggression.[23]

Dunning and Maguire further suggest that developments in technology (including the emergence of more effective means of contraception and the tampon) have contributed to a decrease in family size and the proportion of women's lives spent pregnant and nursing infants. In a similar way, developments in household technology have made housework easier. Taken together, these developments have contributed to a reduction in the power chances derived by men from their physical strength and ability as hunters, fighters and more recently, athletes. Correlatively, females have been enabled to become more involved in sports like women's soccer, and for longer periods of time, by virtue of blind social developments including, in Ireland, a decrease in the average size of families, decreasing birth and mortality rates since the 1970s, the introduction of birth control and various household technologies, the removal of the civil service marriage ban which prohibited females from continuing to work in the civil service following marriage, the relative demise of the Catholic Church and Ireland's entry into the European Economic Community (now the European Union), to name a few. These developments, which were neither intended nor controlled by any one person or group of people, have contributed to equalizing tendencies in power relations between males and females, such that females have been relatively enabled to become more involved in 'former' male preserves such as the field of sport. However, andrarchal social structures continue to remain dominant in Ireland (as in the USA and Britain) in the social field of sports.

Women's Soccer: Some International Comparisons

Data from in-depth interviews and a survey conducted for this study suggest that the profile of women's soccer in Ireland is lower vis-à-vis other women's sports, and sports more generally. Dunning's hypothesis that 'the sporting involvement of females may have been somewhat easier to accomplish in the USA than Britain partly on account of a degree of male support'[24] also seems relevant to Ireland in relation to those males who have been involved in the organization, administration and development of women's soccer there. Such males have tended to be relatively less established in comparison to males involved in the organization and administration of men's soccer, Gaelic games and rugby, and in the overall status hierarchy of sports generally. Indeed, research which investigates the motivations and experiences of those males who become involved in the development of women's sports, and the consequences of this for their self-conceptions as males, is an area that remains relatively under-researched in men's studies. One elite female soccer player argued that women's soccer in Ireland has 'been the poor relation of men's football for years. I mean in terms of the financial and social investment in the game. Sure women can't play football anyway, they can't kick the ball long enough and they can't head the ball hard enough!' (Moira).

In a similar way, a second female soccer player interviewed for this study felt that women's soccer in Ireland continues to be devalued, particularly by male referees. In her words:

> Even going down in a tackle, it's a fair shoulder or whatever and you fall over, you haven't been fouled or anything like that. It's just a physical game and the referees will stop play and ask if you're alright. This kind of thing. Treating us different because we are women … there was one occasion in particular when there were two girls tackling each other and they ended up pulling each others hands and torso. And the ref shouted 'oh you're jogging now' which is a local phrase for being sexual with someone. He did a running commentary throughout the match and treated us as if we were a bunch of dolls who were afraid to break our nails. I can remember another occasion when a ref wanted to stop a game early because he wanted to watch a premiership game on Sky and we were being beaten 5-0. He actually said this to our captain. We threatened to lodge a complaint unless he finished the game. We still lost but that wasn't the point really. (Sue)

We can see, then, that the emergence of women's soccer in Ireland parallels developments elsewhere, allowing for temporal and spatial differences as well as Ireland's physical location at the westernmost tip of Europe. Women's soccer is also becoming increasingly popular in some continental countries, for example, Germany, Norway and Sweden. More recently, it has grown in popularity in England, too. The relatively recent interest in women's soccer in the Western Isles in particular – that, England, Ireland, Northern Ireland, Scotland and Wales – has mirrored the increasing involvement of national organizations such as the FA and the FAI in the organization of women's soccer. In this regard, the English model of 'dispersed voluntary recreational' activities and 'competitive participation and centralized elite development'[25] is comparable to the organizational structures of women's soccer in Ireland. As it stands, it would seem that the Irish model is less centralized but there is a movement towards more centralized elite development, for example, the increasing involvement of the National Coaching and Training Centre in coaching accreditation and the emergence of national FAI coaching and development schemes. The emergence of more central- ized organizational networks of people involved in women's soccer also reflects increases in rates of participation and, by implication, a correlative increase in organi- zational patterns. This increased pressure towards a centralization of the organization of women's soccer is one consequence of the increased involvement of groups of people with conflicting interests. This has been a feature of developments in sports in Ireland more generally since the 1970s, that is to say, we do not necessarily see evidence of a clear and common purpose in the actions of powerful groups of people in the field of sports that would provide evidence for what is currently presented, by the Irish government, as a 'rational' and 'coherent' vision for the development of sports in the country. While Williams also claims that there has been an 'unbroken tradition of communities of teams, clubs and leagues, playing in periods of concen- trated and more interrupted, distributed participation' in Britain, at the same time she argues that 'the vast majority of English women will not play football during their lifetime'.[26] Given the current estimates of registered adult females in the WFAI, and correlative developments in ladies' Gaelic football, camogie and women's rugby, it is not unreasonable to suggest that Williams's statement could apply, perhaps more strongly, in the Irish case, though the adequacy of this claim needs to be tested further over time.

In her outline of the emergence and development of women's soccer in the UK, Will- iams also argues that women's soccer was an activity initiated by women for women.[27] In figurational terms, this broad statement would be regarded as an oversimplification of more complex social developments. It is the case that male and female members of organizations such as the FAI, the FA and their respective regional and local clubs have played, and continue to play, an important role in the national and international development of women's soccer. It is also the case that males were involved in, and supported, the initial codification of women's soccer in England, Ireland and elsewhere. Indeed, there is empirical evidence to suggest that some males played a key role in the establishment of the LFAI in 1973, and males continue to play a key role in the devel- opment of women's soccer currently. For example, Myles Kelly has played a leading role in the establishment and organization of women's soccer in third level colleges and universities since the late 1980s and he is currently assistant manager of the senior inter- national women's squad, while Denis Power played a central role in the establishment of a civil service women's soccer team known as Castle Rovers in the 1990s. He continues to play a key role in this club which is now known as Shamrock Rovers, and is one of the most successful women's soccer clubs in Ireland to date. Moreover, the extent of male support (in the broadest sense) for women's soccer requires further empirical research above and beyond feminist-informed research studies which place women's emancipation at the forefront of their research.

Williams, Hargreaves, Lopez[28] and others are correct to point out that, historically, male-dominated football organizations have sometimes excluded (or banned) women's soccer. However, more recent developments in women's soccer including its increasing popularity in Ireland, England and elsewhere have meant that national organizations in some countries have been constrained to extend their organizational structures to include the WFAI and the WFA as affiliate members. For example, in England, the FA has now subsumed the former Women's FA within its organizational structures and a similar development has occurred in Ireland. However feminists argue that the male-dominated governing bodies of soccer have adapted their structures at a superficial level such that we have seen the 'pseudo' inclusion of women's soccer within existing male-orientated structures. Within feminist literature, Scraton *et al.* argue that one of the key obstacles to the development of women's soccer is:

> the association of football with male sports that contains the conventional stereotypes of hegemonic masculinity in Western culture. For women to enter the powerfully male-defined and controlled world of football, they have had to challenge dominant notions of 'appropriate' female sport.[29]

It is important to acknowledge that, since the 1970s, feminist-informed analyses of sport have made a valuable contribution to an increasing awareness and understanding of gender relations in the field of sport. More importantly, feminists have made an important contribution to a greater understanding of female athletes' narratives. Since then, self-proclaimed 'male feminists' like Messner and Sabo have extended this research to include analyses of males' experiences in sport, particularly sports in America. While feminist-informed research has contributed to an increasing awareness of gender-related issues in the development of women's sports, one of the problems with this approach has been the tendency to separate the experiences of females in sport from wider social contexts in which they have increasingly begun to participate. This raises an important issue in that the conceptualization of females as a 'complete' and homogeneous group of people in and of themselves has led to a narrow and dichotomized focus on the sporting experiences of females. The same can also be said of some research into men's sports experiences. For example, to present the groups of people involved in men's and women's soccer as powerful and powerless respectively, is to oversimplify a more complex reality in which some men have played more limited, but nonetheless, important roles in the development of women's soccer, as coaches, fathers, spectators, bus/coach drivers, referees and so on. Similarly, to present those people involved in women's soccer as relatively powerless is to negate the complex social relations between the groups of people involved in sport generally, and in the organization of women's soccer in particular. More importantly, if we present women as a homogenous group more-or-less subordinate to men, we ignore the complexity of men's and women's everyday lives and the ways in which we relate to, and interact directly and indirectly with, males and females in most aspects of our lives. In other words, if we are to attempt to offer more adequate sociological understandings of the functional interdependence of the sexes, it becomes necessary to explore the ways in which males and females are bonded to each other.

In Ireland, changing attitudes towards women's soccer and gender relations more generally as well as changes in the organizational structure of the FAI have contributed, in part, to the emergence of so-called independent women's soccer clubs (for example, Rathfarnham WFC) and those clubs associated, to a greater or lesser degree, with men's clubs. For example, clubs such as Shamrock Rovers (Premier League) and Templeogue United (Premier A) have emerged from Castle Rovers and Shelbourne WFC respectively. Prior to the movement of a group of female players from Shelbourne to Templeogue United in 1999, Shelbourne WFC emerged from Wellsox FC which had existed relatively independently of any men's soccer club, that is to say, Wellsox was not associated, either formally or informally, with a men's club and it was organized largely by females. Following a number of national cup successes in the mid 1990s, Wellsox was invited to become involved with one of Ireland's leading men's football clubs. Following its integration with Shelbourne FC, the club was administered mainly, though not exclusively, by women on a voluntary basis and it received financial contributions from Shelbourne FC towards the cost of purchasing playing attire and equipment as well as for meeting laundry expenses. Following subsequent cup successes and a change in managerial and coaching staff, Shelbourne WFC disbanded and a core group of players moved to Templeogue United to merge with an existing girls' team run by this men's club. Previously, I have outlined the central involvement of Denis Power in the establishment of a civil service team in the 1990s – Castle Rovers – which, similarly to Wellsox, affiliated with a leading men's soccer club, Shamrock Rovers, in the mid 1990s. While these two examples are brief outlines of the organizational changes which have taken place in two women's soccer clubs in Ireland since the 1990s, it can be seen from this that the relationships between those people involved in men's and women's soccer is more complex than has been suggested by some analysts. While some female players have felt that they were 'the poor relations' of men's soccer, they have also benefited from increasing involvement with men's soccer in terms of improvements in facilities, increasing organizational capacities, access to greater spectator support, the appointment of (voluntary, part-time or full time) coaches, medical staff and physiotherapists and crucially, the opportunity to challenge existing attitudes towards the women's game. It is accordingly more fruitful to analyze the power relations *between* and *among males and females* in traditionally male-associated sports in terms of shifts in the balance of power between the sexes over time. A more adequate explanation of the development of women's soccer in Ireland would point out that women's soccer has continued to develop alongside the formal inclusion (and integration) of women's soccer within the FAI, and within the context of increasing interdependence between the sexes in the field of sport. However, women's soccer continues to rely largely, though not exclusively, on voluntary networks of people who organize matches, attend administrative meetings, coach and develop young players and so on. A similar pattern of voluntary provision is evident in the organization of men's junior and youth football in Ireland currently.

Females' Footballing Identities

According to Williams, 'the multiplicity of, and discontinuity in the responses [of female footballers to questions about gender] indicate that players are performing and negotiating shifting identities, of which gender is itself a plastic element'.[30] By focusing solely on females, it is not surprising that Williams found that female identities are characterized by discontinuities given that the arguments she presents draw on the comments of her subjects, all of whom were female. One of the features of the figurational perspective is a focus on the relational nature of human social relations and the ways in which individual people's beliefs, values and ideologies are reflected in the dynamics of social relations generally.[31] Elias argues that people have both an individual habitus and a variety of collective ones. In this way, people's individual and social habituses are a function both of the more immediate and longer term social networks (or figurations) into which people are born and socialized. It follows that the ways in which female and male athletes express their identities as soccer players are more adequately understood in the context of the following: their positions as individuals in the social networks or figurations specific to soccer; the position that soccer occupies in the overall status hierarchy of sports (in this case in Ireland, and including 'Irish' sports like Gaelic games); and the ways in which the balance between fixity and change in the self-images and social make-up of male and female athletes is inextricably bound up with the character and patterns of changes in the wider structure of gender relations in the society in which they live. For example, the elite female footballers involved in this study associated their young female identities as 'tomboy' with positive attributes such as physical activity, competitiveness and independence. These identities changed over time to include personality characteristics that could be generally described as 'sporty chick', that is, a sporty feminine athlete. For Scraton *et al.*, female footballers' 'identities as gendered sportswomen became more problematic in adulthood',[32] and this could be related to Williams' identification of discontinuities in females' identities over time. In contrast to Scraton *et al.*'s interviewees, the soccer players interviewed for this study did not specifically articulate any significant problematic experiences in relation to their transition from young female to teenager and adult female athlete. They were, however, aware of hegemonic ideals of femininity and masculinity and, by implication, they negotiated their identities as females and footballers (amongst other identities) in the transition from teenager to adulthood. As one of them expressed it:

> Oh yeah, I knew exactly what was expected of me as a woman and what I wasn't supposed to do. And I just ignored all that. I loved sports and there was no way that anyone was going to stop me from playing football. I suppose I must have found a

happy balance somewhere because I feel that I'm a successful female footballer. (Nicola)

While Scraton *et al.*'s footballers also felt that they had to negotiate many obstacles to their participation in soccer (for example, in terms of access, facilities and gendered ideologies), they did claim to 'incorporate their own meanings into their activities'. As Scraton *et al.*, have suggested:

> Women play with aggression, skill, determination and competition; yet they also articulate a central concern for co-operation, support, connectedness, and fun. It is these values that the women [in their study] stressed almost unanimously during the interviews and were most significant to them.[33]

In a similar way, while the female footballers involved in this study also articulated their concerns for fun and sociability, they also emphasized the attributes required to compete successfully in contact sports at an elite level. In this study, a striking characteristic of the athletes was their achievement motivations. This can be explained, in part, by their elite status. Given this, further analysis of the similarities and differences between females' experiences of leisure/recreational soccer and elite-level soccer is required to assess more adequately Scraton *et al.*'s contention that there is a 'female football culture' which exists 'across national boundaries'. Similarly, the contributors to Hong and Mangan's edited collection[34] highlight some similarities and differences in females' soccer-related experiences throughout the world, but more adequate cross-cultural analyses are required to assess any claims associated with the emergence of an 'international female football culture'.

All 12 of the interviewees involved in this study (five of whom identified themselves as footballers primarily) clearly articulated their shared belief that contact and team sports are 'a male preserve'. While they generally agreed that, as Áine put it, 'attitudes [towards females' participation in contact sports] are probably more negative than positive in Ireland to be perfectly honest', their participation in these sports also provided a central source of meaning in their lives. Sue articulated the ways in which she became sensitized to the perceived gender-appropriateness of sports from a young age. In her words:

> the school was divided into the girls' section and the boys' section and from what I can remember the big playing pitch was down in the boys' end and we never went down there. And there was a hall area in the middle of the school – indoor – and the only exercise we [the girls] got was to be taken there to do Irish dancing. And that was sport for the girls. There was a bit of PE, running around a small bit but I don't remember any ball games like soccer or Gaelic football. The girls didn't go down to the boys' end of the school. You'd see the boys down there doing sports because they had male teachers.

I have used the term 'sensitization' here to describe Sue's increasing awareness, as she matured, of the acceptance (or lack thereof) of her interest and participation in sports and physical activities. This 'sensitization' to the gender-appropriateness of sports and physical activities was reinforced in other interviewees' experiences of participation in female-inappropriate sports, including soccer, as they matured into adults. In this study, it was clear that a pattern of parental influence in females' sports participation, particularly the role of fathers and male role models, was significant for a number of reasons, not least in terms of the ways in which female footballers negotiated their transition from teenagers to adult athletes. Burton-Nelson and Dowling[35] indicated that fathers are less likely to encourage their daughters to be actively involved in sport. However, data from the present study indicate that fathers and male role models played an influential role in enabling the group of females that I interviewed to become involved, and regularly participate in, traditionally male-associated sports like soccer. For example, the five athletes primarily involved in soccer (two of whom had represented Ireland in international competitions) agreed that males (for example, their fathers, brothers, grandfathers or male friends) had played a key role in encouraging them to become involved in soccer from a young age. Similarly, female interviewees involved in an international comparative study of women's soccer recounted the role that their fathers and grandfathers played in encouraging them to 'step into this "boys" space'.[36] In other words, their positive identification with 'tomboy' behaviour was enabled and complemented by positive reinforcement from males.

Evidence from the interviews here also challenges the assumption in psychological and quantitative research generally that personality traits remain relatively stable over time, that individual human beings are 'fully' informed about the social and non-human forces that shape their lives, and that they are able to control these forces. For example, a number of interviews were characterized by contradictions between the actions and words of interviewees and the group of females seemed to apply retrospective rationalizations for their choices regarding which sports clubs to join, why they behaved in particular ways and how they responded in various ways to dominant gendered ideologies in sport. Interviewees also encountered difficulties in explaining their own gendered perceptions of other women's sports and in articulating 'fully informed' decisions. Elias argues that, in the increasingly 'civilized' societies of the West, individual human beings have relatively less control over the social forces that shape their lives and this change is mirrored in increasing levels of direct and indirect contact with other individuals and groups as well as increasing reliance on others to meet the 'conditions for human survival' and the 'conditions for human existence'. As de Swaan put it:

> The necessary conditions for the continued existence of societies are thus directly related to the conditions for (the) survival of individual people, but the two sets of conditions are not exactly the same. For a society is not simply 'a huge number of people', nor is it a sort of 'giant human being'. A society is a configuration of people in certain patterns of interdependence.[37]

Given this, it is difficult to assess the sociological reliability of the reasons cited by interviewees for their participation in contact and team sports, notwithstanding the importance that interviewees attached to these choices. Williams found that women's motivation for participation in soccer included: sporting sociability but not at the expense of the quality and frequency of competition; the accumulation of honours; and physical and intellectual skill.[38] These findings mirror the data from this study. The motivations of the elite athletes, including the footballers, I interviewed included what Dunning has referred to as:

an interest in obtaining the sorts of 'mimetic', 'sociability' and 'motility' satisfactions that can be obtained from sports by men, together with the sorts of gains regarding identity, self-concept, self-assurance and habitus (for example, greater feelings of security in public spaces and greater ability to defend themselves against physical attack) which can accrue in that connection.[39]

For example, Fiona said 'I play Gaelic 'cos I enjoy it, it's my outlet. I was always good at it.' Similarly, Áine emphasized the stress-relieving benefits that she felt she gained from her involvement in sports. In her words:

I adore being fit. I think I'm a bit obsessed about being fit, number one. It's a brilliant stress-relief as well. I find you just go out and you do … you could be in the shittiest form ever. I presume I can curse. You don't feel like doing anything and you go out and you walk away and you feel so much better in yourself. And I suppose it gives you high energy levels and you know, it's like when I look at people in work and I can fit in so much and I'm always in good form and people are so stressed in there. But if I'm stressed I'll come out of the meeting and I'll just go into the pool for an hour and then I'll come out and I'll feel fantastic. And rather than take it out on everybody else and wreck my own head, I'll just go out and plough through the pool and come back … So it's a mental thing as well, it's mental really.

Other interviewees also stressed enjoyment, sociability and the feeling of being physically fit. While Mary's working role was intensive and demanding, she felt that 'once you get out you'd feel so much better for it. And you meet so many people. Particularly around Dublin there's a phenomenal amount of people that play'. Similarly Sue said:

I feel good after it. I just enjoy doing it. Just fun, I really enjoy it. I like feeling fit. I feel good. It's a physical and an emotional thing. Something like squash is a great stress buster as well. I just go in and smack a ball and it's great because I work at home all day and, depending on the research that I'm in, and you're either stuck in a dusty library or you're in manuscripts somewhere or you're working at home stuck in front of the computer which is also in my bedroom, so I spend three quarters of my life in my bedroom. So it's great to actually get out, it's important for me.

Helen emphasized the health and fitness benefits of her participation in sports generally as well as what she referred to as 'social aspects'. In her words:

I like the fact that you're actually fit. The feeling of being fit is just really good. I like that. I like the healthy aspect it gives you, I feel so much better myself. And I really like the social aspects, you develop a real camaraderie from training with a group of women for three or four times a week.

In contrast, Betty was more explicit about her competitive motivations and desire for achievement. In her words, she was always 'striving to be the best'. She continued:

I hate being a beginner at anything. It's like I have to be the best, it's terrible. I'm not the most talented athlete you'd ever meet in your life but I work incredibly hard and I do … I train incredibly hard to try and achieve, to be better. And my motto is always 'the day that you think you are the best, you should give up because you should always strive to be the best every day'. Like every day that you train, you should learn something new or push yourself a little bit harder. I suppose it is, it's striving to be the best. It's competitiveness.

Q: So you don't like losing?
Betty: No, but I think I'm getting better at it because I play for Ireland!

Similarly to Williams's interviewees, the elite female soccer players interviewed in this study were more likely to reduce their involvement in soccer significantly (if not entirely) when they retired or when their priorities changed in line with family or career commitments. Indeed, a number of Irish women's sports associations have recently raised concerns about the relatively small number of female athletes who remain involved in sports following their retirement from elite competition.[40] All 12 interviewees' everyday experiences and personal investments in sports (for example, financial, social and emotional investments) also contradicted the commonsense idea that women are not interested in sport. Submissions to a recent Dáil Joint Committee report indicate that the developmental strategies of the members of women's sports organizations are broadly similar in terms of their experiences of exclusion on the basis of gender. That is to say, they are seeking increasing financial resources, increased media coverage, increasing support from their male counterparts and the Irish Sports Council, and the greater inclusion of their respective sports as economically viable and culturally acceptable sports in and of themselves. This recent Dáil report also shows that women's national sports organizations are competing against one another and against men's sports organizations to raise participation rates and the profiles of their respective sports. For example, members of the WFAI are competing with other associations such as the LGFA, the Irish Women's Rugby Football Union and the Camogie Association (Cumann Camogaíochta na nGael) for registered adult and youth players, as well as for the expansion of their respective sports.

Conclusion: the End of the Beginning

Given the dearth of sociological research on the sport-gender nexus in Ireland which was identified at the outset of this essay, I argued that this discussion should be seen as an initial contribution to an emerging body of sociological knowledge about sport in Ireland. I also argued that there was little or no research on women's soccer in Ireland with the exception of the author's doctoral research and Bourke's recent chapter. In this conclusion, I shall return more specifically to some of Bourke's arguments and, in doing so, I shall also try to suggest some future directions for what I think would be more adequate sociological research on women's soccer in Ireland and elsewhere.

In general, it can be said that the emergence and development of women's soccer in Ireland can be more adequately understood within the context of the 'feminization' of sports generally, and traditionally male-associated sports in particular. The feminization of soccer, that is, females' increasing participation in soccer and the consequences of this for the self-conceptions of females *and* males, requires much more theoretical and empirical work in relation to what Bourke refers to as 'the football figuration'.[41] She defines this figuration as 'the webs of interdependencies that link and both *enable* and *constrain* the actions of individuals'.[42] She also draws on Clark's [sic] football figuration[43] to suggest that the women's soccer figuration in Ireland is comprised of: schools/colleges; FIFA/UEFA; the government; clubs; sponsors; parents; scouts; 'women soccer players'; leagues; media; coaches/managers; FIFA/WFAI and other sporting bodies.[44]

Given that Bourke has attempted to apply the figurational sociological approach in her discussion, her use of terms such as 'factors' and 'parties' is confusing given that she defines these along the lines of national and organizational cultures, the lack of a top-down professional culture in women's soccer and the lack of media exposure, for example. These 'factors' are also presented in 'rational choice' terms and do not reflect the depth, complexity and breadth sought in the figurational sociological approach to sport as well as the centrality in it of the concept of power. However, given the lack of research on women's soccer in Ireland, Bourke's discussion should be acknowledged as an informative contribution to this expanding area of research. Taken together, Bourke's discussion and this paper can be seen as what Elias might have called 'a symptom of a beginning' in relation to a greater sociological understanding of the soccer-gender nexus in the Republic of Ireland. Throughout this essay, I have sought to employ a figurational sociological approach to the research question in order to suggest that an analysis of changes in the power relations between the sexes over time can help us to understand better the ways in which changes in the self-conceptions of male and female footballers go hand-in-hand with wider changes in the social structure of gender relations. Moreover, further socio-historical research is required (for example, on the emergence and development of modern sport in Ireland since the late 1800s and related to this, on aspects of the sport-gender nexus) in order to understand more adequately the emergence and development of women's soccer (as well as other women's sports) within the context of the longer-term social developments which have contributed, intentionally and unintentionally, to present-day social practices in the field of sport. One aspect of this is the increasing participation of females in traditionally male-associated sports like soccer.

Central to the figurational sociological approach are a number of concepts including: (i) blind social processes or the ways in which longer-term historical social changes have intended and unintended consequences for present-day social developments. This can be seen, for example, in the enabling and largely unintended consequences of increasing interdependence between men's and women's soccer clubs in Ireland which include improvements in facilities, increasing organizational capacities, access to greater spectator support, the appointment of (voluntary, part-time or full time) coaches, medical staff and physiotherapists and crucially, the opportunity to challenge existing attitudes towards the women's game; (ii) lengthening interdependency chains or figurations, and one of the possible consequences of this – equalizing tendencies – for power relations between the sexes; and (iii) individual and social habitus which is a useful concept in understanding the curvilinear relationship between fixity and change in people's self-images. The latter also allows us to move away from postmodern and poststructuralist tendencies to overemphasize the rate and impact of social change, and to underestimate the relative fixity, in the longer term, of patterns in the wider structure of gender relations in the field of sport and elsewhere. I have sought to use these concepts implicitly to argue that, notwithstanding the enabling consequences of increasing interdependence between the sexes in sport in Ireland, the social field of sport in Ireland can be described as 'a male preserve', particularly in relation to those sports that continue to be widely (though not exclusively) regarded as more suitable for males, for example, soccer rugby, and Gaelic football to a lesser extent. Alongside this, I have also argued, contrary to other research in this field, that changes in the self-images and social make-up of male and female athletes are inextricably bound up with changes in the social structure of gender relations in the wider society.

Notwithstanding some questions arising from the empirical reliability of self-proclaimed increases in the numbers of females participating in certain sports, we have seen some important developments in women's soccer in Ireland, for example, affiliation with the FAI, the appointment of a fulltime national coach of the women's senior team, changes in the rates of participation in women's soccer, a relative increase in print and television coverage of this sport, and increasing provision, by the FAI, for further development of women's soccer in that country. Further empirical research will be required to assess the impact of these developments on a more 'outward looking' soccer community in Ireland and changes in the position of women's soccer in the overall status hierarchy of sports in that country. Future research might also continue to explore a number of themes including: the narratives of female athletes involved at recreational and elite levels in sport; an evaluation of the intended and unintended consequences of gender equality programmes in sport; cross-cultural analyses of the experiences of those people involved in women's soccer, and related to this, any evidence that may support the emergence of an 'international women's football culture'; further explorations of equalizing tendencies in power relations between the sexes and the consequences of this for the self-images of male and female athletes; and, an exploration of the motivations and experiences of males involved, in various capacities, in women's sports, and women's soccer in particular.

Notes

[1] The term 'women's soccer' or 'women's football' has become increasingly popular in academic research in the past five years. There are two possible meanings of this term. On the one hand, it could refer to the game of soccer played by women, which differentiates it from the same game played by men. On the other hand, the term is also used to suggest that 'women's soccer' is significantly different from 'men's soccer'. A more adequate sociological term is probably soccer/football played by females. For the purposes of this paper, I will use the commonsense terms – women's and men's soccer – to refer to those females and males who participate in association football in the Republic of Ireland.
[2] See Jinxia and Mangan, 'Ascending then Descending'; Majumdar, 'The Politics of Soccer in Colonial India, 1930–1937'; Clayton and Harris, 'Footballer's Wives'.
[3] See Bairner (ed.) *Sport and the Irish* for a recent example of work in this regard.
[4] Elias, *What is Sociology?*
[5] This includes the author's elite-level participation in women's soccer in Ireland since 1995; 12 in-depth interviews with elite female Irish athletes (two were elite footballers and three had participated in soccer as a 'secondary' interest); and, a survey of 300 young people's attitudes towards the gender-appropriateness of sports and physical activities.
[6] See Liston, 'Sport, Gender and Commercialisation'; 'The Gendered Field of Irish Sport'; 'Some Reflections on Women's Sports in Ireland'; 'Sport and Gender Matters'; 'Established-Outsider Relations between Males and Females in the Field of Sports in Ireland'.

[7]   Bourke, 'Women's Soccer in the Republic of Ireland'.

[8]   Ibid., 163.

[9]   Ibid.

[10]   In their responses to a questionnaire on the gender-appropriateness of sports and physical activities, 300 young adults (52 per cent of whom were female and 48 [per cent were male) categorized soccer as a male-appropriate sport.

[11]   Bourke, 'Women's Soccer in the Republic of Ireland', 164.

[12]   There are some debates concerning the accuracy of some of these dates. Abbreviations of sports associations refer to the Irish Rugby Football Union, the Irish Women's Rugby Football Union, the Gaelic Athletic Association, Cumann Camogaíochta na nGael (camogie), the Ladies Gaelic Football Association, the Women's Football Association of Ireland and, the Football Association of Ireland, respectively.

[13]   This figure refers to estimates of adult and youth players of Gaelic football and hurling, some of which may include females. The Gaelic Athletic Association (GAA) is currently unable to provide a breakdown of adult male participants in specific sports. In 1997, the GAA estimated that 16% of its playing and non-playing members were female.

[14]   See Liston and Corry, 'Chicks without Sticks', for a sociological analysis of the accuracy of estimates of the number of females registered with the LGFA since 1974.

[15]   TG4 is a television channel that transmits most, if not all, programmes through the Irish language.

[16]   Williams, *A Game for Rough Girls*.

[17]   Rooney resigned from this position in November 2004.

[18]   Houlihan, *Sport, Policy and Politics: A Comparative Analysis*.

[19]   Defined according to the Irish, English or U.S club/university to which players were registered at the time of research.

[20]   Acosta and Carpenter, *Women in Intercollegiate Sport*.

[21]   Williams, *A Game for Rough Girls*, 146.

[22]   Dunning and Maguire, 'Process-Sociological Notes on Sport, Gender Relations and Violence Control', 314.

[23]   Ibid., 307.

[24]   Dunning, *Sport Matters*, 234.

[25]   Williams, *A Game for Rough Girls*, 148.

[26]   Ibid., 186.

[27]   Ibid., 31.

[28]   Hargreaves, *Sporting Females*; Lopez, *Women on the Ball*.

[29]   Scraton, Fasting, Pfister and Bunuel, 'Its Still a Man's Game? The Experiences of Top-level European Women Footballers', 101.

[30]   Williams, *A Game for Rough Girls*, 71.

[31]   See Liston, 'Revisiting the Feminist-figurational Sociology Debate'.

[32]   Scraton *et al.*, 'Its Still a Man's Game?', 105.

[33]   Ibid., 107.

[34]   Hong and Mangan, eds., *Soccer, Women and Sexual Liberation*. This collection includes a chapter on women's soccer in Ireland which is informative but lacking an adequate sociological framework.

[35]   Burton-Nelson, *The Stronger Women Get, the More Men like Football*; Dowling, *The Frality Myth*.

[36]   Scraton *et al.*, 'Its Still a Man's Game?', 102.

[37]   de Swaan, *Human Societies: An Introduction*, 15.

[38]   Williams, *A Game for Rough Girls*.

[39]   Dunning, *Sport Matters*, 231.

[40]   Joint Committee on Arts, Sport, Tourism, Community, Rural and Gaeltacht Affairs, *Women in Sport*, 2004. The author of this paper co-edited this report with the chairperson of the 'Women in Sport' task force established in the late 1990s.

[41] Bourke, 'Women's Soccer in the Republic of Ireland', 175.

[42] Ibid., emphasis in original.

[43] Clarke, 'Figuring a Brighter Future'.

[44] Some notable omissions from this figuration include spectators and male soccer players, amongst others.

References

Acosta, L. and L. Carpenter. *Women in Intercollegiate Sport: A Longitudinal, National Study Twenty Seven Year Update 1977–2004.* Available from www.nagws.org.; INTERNET.

Bairner, A, ed. *Sport and the Irish: Histories, Identities, Issues.* Dublin: University College Dublin Press, 2005.

Bourke, A. 'Women's Soccer in the Republic of Ireland: Past Events and Future Prospects.' In *Soccer, Women, Sexual Liberation: Kicking Off a New Era,* edited by Fan Hong and J. Mangan. London: Frank Cass, 2004: 162–82.

Burton-Nelson, M. *The Stronger Women Get, the More Men like Football: Sexism and the American Culture of Sport.* New York: Harcourt Brace, 1994.

Clarke, A. 'Figuring a Brighter Future.' In *Sport and Leisure in the Civilizing Process,* edited by E. Dunning and C. Rojek. London: Macmillan, 1992: 201–21.

Clayton, B. and J. Harris. 'Footballers' Wives: The Role of the Soccer Player's Partner in the Construction of Idealized Masculinity.' *Soccer and Society 5,* no.3 (2004): 317–35.

Dowling, C. *The Frailty Myth: Redefining the Physical Potential of Women and Girls.* New York: Random House, 2000.

Dunning, E. *Sport Matters.* London: Routledge, 1999.

Dunning, E. and J. Maguire. 'Process-Sociological Notes on Sport, Gender Relations and Violence Control.' *International Review for the Sociology of Sport 31,* no.3 (1996): 295–317.

Elias, N. *What is Sociology.* London: Macmillan, 1978.

Hargreaves, J. *Sporting Females: Critical Issues in the Sociology and History of Women's Sports.* London: Routledge, 2004.

Hong, Fan and J. Mangan, eds. *Soccer, Women, Sexual Liberation: Kicking Off a New Era.* London: Frank Cass, 2004.

Houlihan, B. *Sport, Policy and Politics: A Comparative Analysis.* London: Routledge, 1997.

Jinxia, D. and J. Mangan. 'Ascending then Descending: Women's Soccer in Modern China.' *Soccer and Society 3,* no.2 (2002): 1–18.

Joint Committee on Arts, Sport, Tourism, Community, Rural and Gaeltacht Affairs. *Fifth Report: Women in Sport.* Dublin: Government Publications Office, 2004.

Liston, K. 'Sport, Gender and Commercialisation.' *Studies 90,* no.359 (2001): 251–66.

———. 'The Gendered Field of Irish Sport.' In *Ireland Unbound: A Turn of the Century Chronicle,* edited by M. Corcoran and M. Peillon. Dublin: Institute of Public Administration, 2002: 231–47.

———. 'Some Reflections on Women's Sports.' In *Sport and the Irish: Histories, Identities, Issues,* edited by A. Bairner. Dublin: UCD Press, 2005: 206–24.

———. 'Established-Outsider Relations between Males and Females in the Field of Sport in Ireland.' *Irish Journal of Sociology* 14, no.1 (2005): 66–85.

———. 'Sport and Gender Relations.' *Sport and Society* 9, no. 4 (2006).

———. 'Revisiting the Feminist-Figurational Sociology Debate.' *Sport in Society.* Forthcoming (2006).

Liston, K. and M. Corry. 'Chicks without Sticks: The Emergence and Development of the Ladies Gaelic Football Association.' Under review.

Lopez, S. *Women on the Ball: A Guide to Women's Football.* London: Scarlet Press, 1997.

Majumdar, Boria. 'The Politics of Soccer in Colonial India, 1930–1937: The Years of Turmoil.' *Soccer and Society 3,* no.3 (2002): 70–87.

Scraton, S., K. Fasting, G. P. Fister and A. Bunuel. 'It's Still a Man's Game? The Experiences of Top-Level European Women Footballers.' *International Review for the Sociology of Sport. 34,* no.2 (1999): 99–113.

Swaan, A. de. *Human Societies: An Introduction.* Cambridge: Polity Press, 2001.

Williams, J. *A Game for Rough Girls.* London: Routledge, 2003.

Critical Events or Critical Conditions: The 1999 Women's World Cup and the Women's United Soccer Association

Sean Brown

On 10 July 1999, the United States women's soccer team played a tense and exciting (if sloppy) World Cup Final against highly regarded China. After two gruelling hours of scoreless soccer, the game was eventually decided on penalty kicks, won by the United States 5-4. Two things about the final stand out: first, the game drew a crowd of over 90,000 at the Rose Bowl in Pasadena, California. Second and even more remarkable was the 11.4 television rating, which was simply phenomenal for that or any other time.[1] It rated much higher than any men's national team game or any game that the MLS had offered on network television up to that point. To this day, it is the highest rated soccer match ever shown on American television. It was hoped by organizers that the momentum built by and for women's soccer would carry on to the creation of the WUSA

(Women's United Soccer Association). While the league averaged 8,100 fans per game in its first year, attendance faltered in the ensuing years. Additionally, television ratings were abysmal, and the league ceased operations after only three years.

The paradox of the success of the women's national team juxtaposed against the failure of the professional league adds another layer of mystery to the other lingering questions surrounding the failure of soccer to catch on in the United States at the spectator level.[2] It was thought that the 1999 World Cup final would be a critical event in the life of women's soccer in the United States. Indeed, the organizers of the event specifically planned the event as both proof of the viability of women's soccer and as a springboard to future women's soccer ventures; the culmination of which was the WUSA.[3] Jere Longman, in his book chronicling the team and the tournament, eloquently describes the essence of the importance of the match when describing assistant coach Lauren Gregg's feelings just before the match was decided on penalty kicks, 'Six months of training, of logging every penalty kick in practice, a whole career of judgment and instinct, the entire World Cup, maybe even the future of a women's professional league, came down to this, 10 names submitted on a piece of paper.'[4]

Thus, for the WUSA, it was crucial that the 1999 World Cup be successful. In addition, it would certainly benefit from an American victory in the final. The media latched onto the tournament as it progressed, and build-up towards the final match was enormous.[5] The highly successful television broadcast only added to the specu- lation that women's soccer had arrived in this country. The sport was driven by extremely likeable and marketable personalities such as Mia Hamm, Julie Foudy, Joy Fawcett, Kristine Lilly and Brianna Scurry, to name a few. The contest was in fact immortalized when, upon burying the winning shot during the penalty kick phase of the match, Brandi Chastain threw off her shirt, revealing a Nike sports bra and an extremely muscular and sculpted female body.[6] That moment survives in popular culture to this day, and it kept that match in the forefront of American consciousness long after the match itself had ended.

Unlike Major League Soccer (MLS) on the men's side, the WUSA had very limited competition throughout the world. It was assured that the best talent in the world of women's soccer would be playing in the United States, and certainly all of the top American players would be playing domestically, unlike the significant number of top American men's players that are still choosing to play in Europe (for example, Tim Howard, DeMarcus Beasley and Landon Donovan). Given these factors, it seemed that a women's professional league stood a real chance of enjoying success at or near the level of the Women's National Basketball Association (WNBA). So, why did it fail?

The remainder of this essay will attempt to reconcile the enormously popular 1999 World Cup Final and the failure of the WUSA. It also intends to explore the 1999 Cup final in terms of critical events. Doubtless the event failed to spur long-term interest in women's professional soccer. In that light, the event was distinctly *not* critical. It will also attempt to establish that the WUSA made critical mistakes in the establishment and marketing of women's professional soccer. Had these mistakes been avoided, the WUSA might have avoided its ultimate fate, and the 1999 final might now be known as *the* critical event in women's soccer, or even American soccer. Given the continued rise in the status and popularity of women's sports and certain telling circumstances of the match itself which will be discussed below, the match may still serve as a critical event in women's sports, though not in the way organizers had hoped and planned. It is hoped that this essay will contribute to the continuing attempt to answer questions about the nature of sport spectatorship in the United States, and whether the ideas of American Exceptionalism vis-à-vis soccer continue to be viable given this event analysis. I shall first try to elaborate the idea of critical events and their relation to sports, then take a look at the legacy of the 1999 Women's World Cup, the WUSA. Finally, it will be worth a discussion attempting to determine the ultimate classification of the 1999 World Cup Final. Is it simply another event, potentially world-changing but ultimately forgettable, or might there be something else, a glimmer of an enormous symbolic success, if coupled with ultimate material failure?

Critical Events and Sport

When dealing with the idea of critical events, or evenemential history, Marshall Sahlins in *Apologies to Thucydides* uses two comparative cases in baseball which will be useful for our own purposes here as well. They illustrate the developmental and evolutionary history versus histories defined by specific events:

> The history of the '39 Yankees pennant was developmental, where that of the Giants was evenemential. The first was evolutionary, the second a kind of revolutionary *volte-face*. The Yankees dominated the 1939 season from beginning to end, April to October, steadily pulling away from the second-place team. The Giants won at 3:58 P.M. (EDT) on 3 October 1951 when Bobby Thompson hit the famous home run that defeated the Brooklyn Dodgers in the last half of the last inning of the final game of a three-game playoff for the title – the teams having been tied at the end of the regular season.[7]

The 1999 World Cup had its own parallel. The China semi-final match with Norway was similar to the 1939 Yankee team. The Chinese dominated the game from start to finish, and it cannot be pinpointed exactly when victory was assured. Surely as the game wore on and the Chinese continued to score, the outcome was clear long before the final whistle. However, it cannot compare to the evenemential nature of the final. Viewers of the China-US match knew the exact moment when the match was over; the exact moment when Brandi Chastain buried the final penalty kick, the match and the World Cup were all over in an instant far more definitive than any referee's final whistle could be. It is this type of evenemential history that the organizers were trying to make with the 1999 World Cup. That the game itself was decided in a moment only added to the excitement. It was hoped that the tournament and the final game would be moments unto themselves, but for very specific purposes, discussed below.

As well, the periodization of the tournament and the game itself share structure with the 1951 National League pennant race, which (as Sahlins mentioned) was decided on the final pitch in the final inning in the final game of a playoff, which was only necessary because the New York Giants and the Brooklyn Dodgers were tied at the end of a 154 game schedule. In his essay 'The Rhetoric of History', Hexter examines the periodization of the season, not even beginning the story until August (the Major League Baseball season begins around the first of April). As the story progresses towards an inevitable but by no means predictable end, individual events acquire increasing importance. Thus, whereas Hexter begins in August with a day-by-day representation (he illustrates the periodization graphically), the final game of the three-game playoff is further expanded into an inning-by-inning account. Finally, during the final half of the ninth inning, the storytelling is switched to pitch-by-pitch, leading to the ultimate critical event, Bobby Thompson's home run to win the game and the pennant.[8]

When telling the story of the 1999 Women's World Cup, similar devices of historiography can be employed, and are to some extent by Jere Longman in *The Girls of Summer*. Longman's story centres on the final game of the tournament, with references to the other games played by both teams. As the final match progresses, the individual events again acquire increasing importance, until the second overtime still has not produced a winner. The tempo of the story again shifts into ever shorter periods of time, until Longman takes the reader through a kick-by-kick account of the shootout, which culminates in the quintessential moment when Chastain struck the final ball of the World Cup, and the champions were crowned. Like Thompson's home run, one can pinpoint the exact moment when the contest was decided, when history was made. What transpired after this moment will be the focus of this investigation, but it does not diminish the critical nature of the moment of victory or the implications of the game itself. The Chastain kick was *the* critical moment in the contest and the World Cup as a whole, just as Thompson's home run was *the* critical moment of the 1951 National League pennant race in baseball.

Thus, a critical event can be understood as 'an event *par excellance* because it instituted *a new modality of historical action* which was not inscribed in the inventory of the situation'.[9] At the very least, organizers of the 1999 World Cup hoped that the event would prove once and for all that women's sporting events could be financially viable and culturally relevant, which would have definitely represented a new mode of historical action.[10] At best, they hoped that the event could be used to launch a new women's professional soccer league in the United States. Marla Messing was the chief organizer for the 1999 World Cup, and her vision for the event leaves little doubt as to the method of organization and the goals of the tournament:

> In everything we did, we treated it as a major event. Our choices in this country are stadiums with 5,000 or 10,000 seats, or stadiums with 50,000, 60,000, or 80,000 seats. Once you decide on 5,000 or 10,000 seats, the image of what you are selling is second class. Putting it in small stadiums would have sealed the fate of the tournament. You had to sell the image of a major *event*. Right away it was major because it's at Giants Stadium and the Rose Bowl.[11] (emphasis added)

Thus, the parameters for the tournament were laid out before tickets were even made available or their demand even known. It was an enormous gamble by tournament organizers, as they risked the embarrassment of empty stadiums and financial disaster. Their gamble paid off, however, and attendance for the tournament topped 600,000, which was more than double the previous record for attendance at a women's sporting event in the United States, formerly held by the 1999 women's college basketball tournament.[12] The turnout told only part of the story. The television ratings for the event were also very healthy throughout the tournament. With the wild success of the event, it seemed that the organizers had proven their point: women's soccer could sell in the United States. Having shown that, plans began for the forming of the professional league, and the WUSA was launched in April 2001.

What is interesting about the planning of the World Cup is that it is an instance of a planned critical event. The organizers essentially drew up a script that the tournament was to follow, which it did. This was not the first instance in sport where critical events had been planned. Nearly 60 years earlier, Branch Rickey and Jackie Robinson had shown that African American baseball players belonged on the field with their white counterparts. Upon comparative examination of these two events, interesting similarities emerge. This is certainly not to say that the two events are moral equivalents. The women's national team did not face discrimination of any sort like African-Americans in the 1940s in the United States. However, in the planning, execution and acceptance of the events, these parallels remain. Where the two events take diverging paths is even more interesting.

The first similarity the two events share is the sense that those responsible were attempting to use sports to achieve ends that would ultimately have ramifications outside of the sporting world. The integration of baseball was not simply about the reorganization of baseball, but of the reorientation of race relations in general. Kelly, in an article detailing Jackie Robison's integration of 'organized baseball', makes the point that Jackie Robinson was representative of something much larger than baseball or sports, 'This is the thesis for this essay: that the critical event of Jackie Robinson breaking the color line was *the* test of strength for a new, post-war, Pax Americana modality of US citizenship, and citizenship generally.'[13] It is important to note that Jackie Robinson integrated baseball nearly two decades before the Civil Rights Act was signed into law by President Johnson. Jackie Robinson in some ways prefigured the Civil Rights movement. It was in the area of sport, where events are often dismissed as mere diversions or leisure, where real social change in race relations began.[14]

In some ways, the 1999 World Cup was an inversion of the Jackie Robinson case. Whereas Robinson and the integration of Major League Baseball predated the laws which would have forced the same result, the US Women's national team was made possible by changes in the law. In 1972, legislation now known as Title IX was instituted, which outlawed the vast funding discrepancies plaguing high school and college campuses nationwide. The additional funding made all sorts of women's sports possible, of which soccer is one of the largest beneficiaries: 'Soccer has become the fastest growing sport in the country in both high school and college. From 1981 through 1999, the number of women's collegiate soccer teams grew from 77 to 818, propelled by Title IX.'[15] The 1999 Women's World Cup, despite taking place 27 years after the passing of Title IX, was in effect a validation of the principles behind it. It proved that women's sports deserved the attention that it was getting, not simply because of some equality principle, but because it could stand up in commercial venues such as stadiums and television and hold its own with men's sports. The organizers of the event were keenly aware that in order to be a success, the tournament must be financially and commercially viable, as discussed below, and they planned accordingly.

As such, we can claim here that sometimes history does not simply happen. It is at times the result of meticulous planning, and the events can be scripted, even if sometimes the actors stray from the vision of the directors. John Kelly speaks of the integration of the major leagues in terms of its planning by Branch Rickey,[16] 'the Jackie Robinson story was set to follow a particular vision of possible progress. I don't mean this abstractly'.[17] Branch Rickey, when formulating his plan to integrate the Brooklyn Dodgers, knew that his efforts were absolutely critical in the determination of his ultimate success. This brings to mind the debate whether people can know the history that they are making, or whether structures determine history and people are without agency, floating through history, their actions never truly their own. While that debate will rage on long after today, it is clear from the actions and intentions of Branch Rickey that he was in fact attempting to make his own history. Kelly supports this idea: 'Each (Tambiah and Sahlins) sees histories constituted by agents acting within the possibilities and limits of specific social structure: people making the kinds of history they know how to make, when and where they can'.[18] As detailed above, this is similar to the actions of the organizers of the 1999 Women's World Cup, who knew that the future of women's soccer generally, and any thoughts of a professional league specifically, rested on the ability to pull off a successful and popular tournament.

Additionally, in the planning of the critical events, both the organizers and those involved with 1999 World Cup and Branch Rickey were quite conscious of the consequences of their possible failures. Refer to the above quote from Longman that detailed the thoughts of the women's assistant coach responsible for the choosing of the shoot-out participants for a reminder that those involved in the tournament and the game knew just what was at stake during that final game, and those final penalty kicks. Branch Rickey knew as well what was at stake, and the consequences of failure. He compared it to another movement close to his heart, the temperance movement:

> The mismanaged prohibition of alcohol by force had thrown the temperance movement back a century. If managed wrong, Rickey thought, 'the introduction of a Negro into baseball even without force, might similarly throw back their cause of racial equality a quarter century or more'.[19]

The (successful) breakthrough of Robinson into the major leagues was *the* event that propelled the overall integration. It was hoped that the successful world cup would propel women's professional soccer into commercial viability. Longman notes that the women of the national team in 1999 knew the history that they were making, and the risks they were taking:

> the women on the American soccer team were faced with all the Spindletop possibility and stock-market risk of speculators. They were pioneers, they made their own tradition. They began the team in anonymity, and, now, they had not only to play the game, but they had to build the World Cup's public awareness and to secure its financial viability. If they failed, not only the team, but the World Cup and the professional viability of the sport, might fail.[20]

The women of that team, like Rickey and Robinson knew not only that they had a script, but they knew what the script was and what the consequences of failure were. It is here that the events diverge. While the events surrounding Robinson followed the script (though not without unintended consequences, as we shall see) and baseball slowly became integrated, women's soccer, despite its auspicious beginnings, ultimately diverged from its script. Again, however, the unintended consequences of the event are important. Before delving into the unintended consequences of the comparative events, it will be important to detail just what happened with the WUSA, both how it failed and some possible explanations as to why.

The WUSA

Even before the league was formed, a crucial mistake was made, a golden opportunity missed. While the World Cup ended in July of 1999, the WUSA did not play its first game until April of 2001. It was thought that the demands of training for the 2000 Sydney Olympic Games necessitated the delay of any professional league until those games were complete. History was repeating itself, and not everyone was surprised at the final outcome. Soon after the 1999 final was complete, Bob Foltman, in a *Chicago Tribune* commentary, saw the potential problem, 'If a women's league is going to happen, it better happen next season. Many people within the sport say that MLS shot itself in the foot by not riding the wave of goodwill after U.S. '94 with a league in 1995'[21] (MLS did not start play until 1996). It also deserves note that the 2000 Sydney Games were not especially conducive to building on the 1999 World Cup momentum. With the large time differential (Sydney is 15 hours ahead of New York City), the women's matches could never achieve the reach of the World Cup matches. Additionally, the American loss to Norway in the final, while not enough to kill the goodwill towards US Women's soccer, was a definite letdown.

Despite the lag and the disappointment of the 2000 Olympics, when the Bay Area CyberRays and the Washington Freedom opened the WUSA's inaugural season at RFK stadium in Washington DC, 34,148 fans attended.[22] In fact, for the initial season, the WUSA as a whole averaged 8,103 fans per game, a respectable total to say the least.[23] Additionally, the league had secured television coverage via a contract with TNT, a very prominent cable outlet. The future seemed bright for the league. However, it lasted only two more seasons. TNT dropped the league after 2001, and the league was forced to seek a new deal. Though they eventually signed with another outlet, it was with PAX TV, a small and very limited outlet without the significant reach or public awareness that TNT possessed. Ratings dropped significantly in 2002, and remained steady through 2003.[24] Meanwhile, attendance for the 2002 season fell to 6,969, and remained approximately steady in 2003, with average attendance at 6,667 and the league ceased operations after the 2003 season. See Figures 1 and 2 for ratings and attendance data.

On the surface, the league was felled by three types of issues: temporal, spatial and financial. Temporally, the WUSA, by beginning their season in April, ultimately could not compete with the crowd of major sporting events during the time. During the

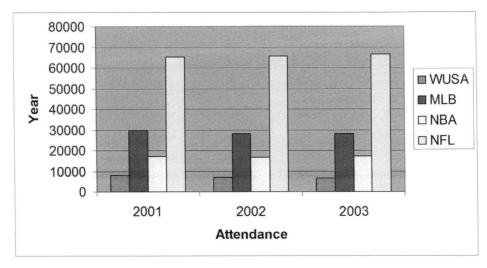

Figure 1   Average Attendance 2001–2003

month of April, Major League Baseball begins its season to much fanfare, the National Hockey League begins its playoffs (perhaps the only time when hockey can be considered a force in the American sporting landscape, albeit still a small one), and the National Basketball Association is nearing the end of its regular season, where playoff positions are sorted out of often very tense and tight races. Despite its target demographic of families (as opposed to the sports mentioned above, which generally target males from 18–54), it is quite probable that the sports calendar was simply too crowded at the beginning of each season for the WUSA to build its audience. By the end of the season, once hockey and basketball had ended their respective seasons, baseball

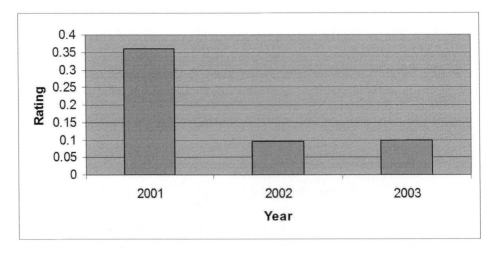

Figure 2   WUSA Television Ratings 2001–2003

was beginning its stretch drive and American football teams were in their training camps, leaving the WUSA very little room in which to operate.

These temporal circumstances are tied closely to notions of space in sport. It is generally conceded that each nation possesses a limited amount of 'space' for which many sports compete.[25] Once that space is filled, it is almost impossible to alter. The American sport space is currently dominated by three or four major entities, the National Football League (NFL), Major League Baseball (MLB), and the National Basketball Association (NBA). There is also evidence to suggest that the National Association for Stock Car Automobile Racing (NASCAR) has claimed a place in the limited sport space, taking the place of the National Hockey League (NHL). Without a niche audience of extremely loyal fans, the WUSA faced virtually impossible odds in gaining a wide audience in the long term, because soccer has had an extremely difficult time muscling its way into the limited American sports space as a legitimate and viable spectator sport, likewise with its male counterpart. The MLS has yet to turn a profit and still struggles with its image as a league playing with mostly inferior talent. It has also mostly failed to alter soccer's image as foreign or 'other'.

Despite all of this, perhaps the most crucial mistakes by the WUSA organizers may have been made at the financial level. Specifically, one could point out three overlapping areas where the league made significant and interrelated financial mistakes: franchise locations, an over reliance on corporate sponsorships, and the attempt to establish a professional league by fiat, thus forgetting the history of professional sports in the United States.

In looking at the locations that organizers chose for the league's maiden franchises, one is immediately confronted with the crowd of major professional sports teams in those areas. If one only looks at franchises from the NFL, MLB, NBA and NHL, it becomes obvious that these cities and areas had too many choices for any realistic expectations for success. A brief glance shows the following existing franchises in each WUSA market:

- Atlanta Beat – Atlanta Hawks (NBA), Atlanta Falcons (NFL), Atlanta Braves (MLB), Atlanta Thrashers (NHL)
- Bay Area CyberRays[26] – Golden State Warriors (NBA), Oakland Raiders (NFL), San Francisco 49ers (NFL), San Jose Sharks (NHL)
- Boston Breakers – Boston Celtics (NBA), New England Patriots (NFL), Boston Red Sox (MLB), Boston Bruins (NHL)
- Carolina Courage – Charlotte Bobcats (NBA), Carolina Panthers (NFL), Carolina Hurricanes (NHL)
- New York Power – New York Knicks (NBA), New York Giants (NFL), New York Jets (NFL), New York Mets (MLB), New York Yankees (MLB), New York Rangers (NHL), New York Islanders (NHL)[27]
- Philadelphia Charge – Philadelphia 76ers (NBA), Philadelphia Eagles (NFL), Philadelphia Phillies (MLB), Philadelphia Flyers (NHL)
- San Diego Spirit – San Diego Chargers (NFL), San Diego Padres (MLB)
- Washington Freedom – Washington Wizards (NBA), Washington Redskins (NFL), Washington Nationals (MLB), Washington Capitals (NHL)

By placing the franchises in large cities with full arrays of professional sport choices, the WUSA added unnecessary obstacles to an already difficult proposition of building a league that was not only a female league, but a soccer league as well. Each of these elements would have presented difficulties on their own, so the organizers of the WUSA could not afford to make any mistakes in their planning. Their choices in city selections for the franchises were crucial.

The WUSA began operations with a $40 million operating budget. This was intended to last the league five years. In addition, the league sought extensive corporate sponsorship in attempting to keep the league afloat. When the league folded, the chairman of the WUSA board of governors, John Hendricks, blamed the lack of corporate support for the failure of the league, 'If we only had six or seven CEOs in America that had stepped forward in the past year', said John Hendricks, chairman of the WUSA board of governors. 'An independent women's professional league can survive – if it has corporate support.'[28]

The enthusiasm of the corporate sponsors began to wane along with league attendance and television ratings. As the third year came around, the league had already run through its initial $40 million investments and could not convince sponsors of the long-term viability of the league. Gary Cavilli, the former commissioner of another pioneering women's league, the American Basketball League, summed up the attitudes of the sponsors, 'Year Three seems to be the year that the patience of the investors runs out. Year One is like having a baby. Year Two, there's usually a bit more optimism about the long-term future. Year Three has high expectations, but if it's still tough to get in the black after Year Three, there's a lot of questioning.'[29] Without a significant television audience or growing attendance, the main source of league revenue dried up, leaving the league with no other options.

What is left is why the league had such a difficult time building an audience that would satisfy the corporate sponsors that were funding it. The answer to this question leads to the tautology that the league organizers could never get around. Simply put, professional leagues do not spring fully formed out of nothing. The league organizers, in their desperate attempts to achieve legitimacy on par with the other major professional leagues, completely ignored those leagues' own long and rich histories, histories that in some ways prefigured the beginnings of the WUSA. Comparisons between the first season of the WUSA and previous attendance figures for the NFL and NBA are revealing. According to Barra, the NFL only averaged 8,200 fans per game in 1934, the first season in which attendance figures were kept (but not the first year of the league). Similarly, the NBA did not achieve first-year WUSA attendance figures until the 1973–74 season. In 1952, average NBA game attendance was only 3,200 (see Figure 3). Major league baseball also did not achieve these attendance levels until well into the league's existence.[30]

These leagues were able to survive by building their sports gradually, at the ground level. They were not able to even conceive of their leagues attracting the type of attention that the WUSA seemed to require to stay afloat. Had the league been grown instead of created 'fully formed', 8,100 fans per game would have been a figure about which league organizers would have been ecstatic. Barra goes on to point out that minor league baseball flourishes in many towns and small cities all over the United States,

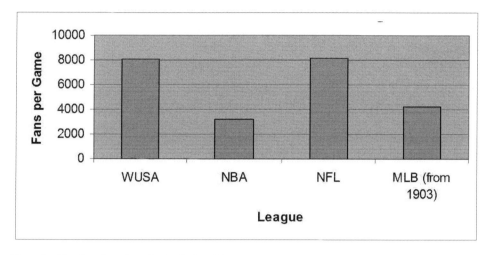

Figure 3   First Year Attendance for Professional Games

where 8,100 fans would result in a packed stadium and not disappointment. Instead of looking at the NBA, NFL and MLB as models, the WUSA would have been better off looking to a model along the lines of the Arena Football League (AFL). By locating in smaller cities with fewer sporting options, the AFL grew a large enough audience over time that it has since expanded into larger markets, and even has a network television contract with NBC. Instead, the WUSA attempted to position itself in the same area as the three major leagues in American sports, and while the fans were clearly interested in the product, they were simply not numerous enough to fulfil the completely unrealistic expectations and demands of WUSA organizers and the corporate sponsors that held all of the real power. Given these critical mistakes in a situation where mistakes could not be absorbed, it was not difficult to see the demise of the league coming far in advance, and certainly no surprise when it came.

Legacy of 1999 World Cup

The 1999 Women's World Cup and its legacy are filled with contradictions. If one simply studied the event in comparison to women's sporting events preceding it, then there is no question that the event was an enormous success on any level, not least the commercial and financial level. The tournament was profitable for the organizers, sponsors and players, who received bonuses for winning the tournament.[31] Attendance as well as television ratings were healthy throughout the tournament, and (as noted above) beyond all expectations for the final.

However, given the weight placed on the shoulders of the tournament, and the expectations in the afterglow of the tournament – namely a women's professional league that was commercially viable – the historian cannot simply base a complete judgment of the tournament on anything but the tournament plus all that followed, namely the WUSA. As detailed above, the WUSA was doomed almost from the start for a number of reasons. It was never able to build on the success of 1999, and folded after only three years.[32]

Where does this leave 1999 in terms of the critical events in sports that it was built to be? It will be useful to return to the Jackie Robinson comparisons built earlier both as a contrast, but also in the commonalities that exist between the two events. When one takes a close look at the Jackie Robinson case, on the surface it looks as though the event went according to Rickey's script, which it did to a certain extent. Despite the hardships Robinson endured, the taunts, the hatred both on and off the field, and the indifference that he often felt amongst his teammates, Robinson's entrance into Major League Baseball opened the gates, and the game was fundamentally altered and enriched by the influx of African-American players, as well as the further influx of foreign-born players that began to move more freely as a result of Robinson's presence in the league.[33] This is not to say that Robinson solved the problem of race in the United States. Nor did he even break all of the stereotypes surrounding black athletes. The logic of stereotypes is not easily defeated in the minds of those who hold them as true. For as Robinson emerged, so did new stereotypes, in two different directions. First, the myth of the African-American as genetically superior to white athletes persists in the United States today. Second, it was believed that African-American athletes, while able to play on the same field as whites, could only occupy certain positions because they lacked the intellect to play the more mentally demanding positions. This stereotype also persists.[34]

Given these circumstances, while the Jackie Robinson experiment was a success, it was not a complete one. One could say that it both was and was not successful. It was, however, still critical. It is *the* event that has gained the most credit, and deservedly so, for the integration of American professional sports. That it was not responsible for the elimination of all stereotypical thought about black athletes is irrelevant. A similar argument can and should be made about the 1999 Women's World Cup; only the circumstances are inverted. The 1999 World Cup did not follow its intended script. This does not preclude its inclusion as a critical sporting event. As Kelly writes:

> sometimes the plans work better than others, sometimes the focalization and transvaluation of events follow the lines of the blueprints better than others, sometimes the story gets changed more, or the number and intentions of actors, audiences and stakes conflict more than others. Then, the Jackie Robinson story, for the US audience, would be an extreme kind of critical event: one that followed the plan of deliberate instigators of a critical event.[35]

That the World Cup did not succeed as the catalyst for the WUSA is only moderately important. I have attempted to show that it was not the event that failed the WUSA, but the organizers of the WUSA, through a seemingly complete lack of understanding of the machinations of how to build a professional sporting league in the United States. However, the 1999 World Cup still stands very tall in the country as an affirmation of the precepts of Title IX, and as proof that, given a stage, women's sports in the United State can captivate a nation, even if only ephemerally, especially when on the international level. Given its success, it must be thought of as a critical event in women's sports. It represented a moment when the country cared more about women's soccer (a term which encapsulates two individual words normally anathema to the American sports fan) than its own national pastime, baseball.

One final commonality between our two comparative critical events will also help understand the symbolic acceptance of the two protagonists, and will also serve to underscore just how important these events are in American sporting history. It involves the tangible moments when the athlete goes from being one of 'them' to one of 'us' in the eyes of the fans, which for Kelly represents, 'the core of the critical event, fully accomplished, when it becomes unconscious, when Robinson's standing as one of "us" becomes wholly natural'. For Jackie Robinson, it happened when Red Barber, legendary voice of the Brooklyn Dodgers, began calling Robinson by another name. Kelly writes, 'one day, casually, spontaneously, Red Barber started calling Jack Robinson by a nickname in his radio broadcasts, not "Jackie" but "Robbie". Barber gave his own nicknames to his players.'[36]

For the women's national team, Jere Longman provides a similar, and possibly more striking, moment:

> Inside (the Rose Bowl), girls wore their Title IX grease-paint, their faces laminated red, white, and blue like some Betsy Ross Halloween, Mia Hamm's No. 9 and her name scrawled on their arms as gender-equity tattoos. College boys wrapped themselves in flag sarongs, while young boys joined young girls in wearing Hamm's jersey, swept up in this acceptable moment of cultural cross-dressing.[37]

Mary Ullmer made a similar observation in a *Chicago Tribune* commentary debating whether the World Cup deserved the amount of coverage that it was receiving.[38] In this instance, the transformation of the national team from the Women's soccer team to the American soccer team was completed for a few young boys. That the triumph of the moment and the transcendent quality of that team was able to trump fairly strict gender identity, especially in young boys, was a testament to just how important the women's team was to this country's sporting public. Truly it was a moment where the transformation from 'them' to 'us' became unconscious, at least for some fans. If this is truly the critical event fully realized, then there can be no other way to view the 1999 Women's World Cup Final match at a critical event in American sport history, and especially women's sport and soccer in the United States. Its impact cannot be measured by how much money a professional league made, or whether it was even successful or not. Its impact was more subtle, and perhaps more far-reaching and significant. After the 1999 World Cup, Brandi Chastain served as an assistant coach for the women's soccer programme at Santa Clara University, which went undefeated and won a national championship in the fall of 1999. The experience during that year of the athletic department at Santa Clara University is a fitting way to conclude. It is worth quoting at length, as Longman writes:

> Women's soccer was the biggest sports draw in 1999. It outdrew men's soccer by more than 2-1. A total of 15,716 spectators had come to see the top-ranked women's team, compared to 6,256 to see the men's team, which would unexpectedly reach the national championship game. A crowd of 4,000, the size of Santa Clara's student body, had seen an early season match against Stanford.

> Attendance increased 50 percent overall, gate receipts had doubled. There was something else, too. (Marlene) Bjornsrud (Santa Clara's athletic director) was getting more calls from women in their thirties and forties, interested in careers in sports administration. Doors seemed to be opening, roles seemed to be reversing. Male athletes were approaching her, asking why the women were getting all the attention.[39]

While this is certainly not the case at colleges around the country, it shows that the US/China match has had long-term effects not only on the prospect of women's soccer, but in the relationship between women and sport in general. Now that the men's national team has begun to catch up, finishing with an impressive quarter-final showing in 2002, soccer in the United States may be showing signs that the youth participation explosion that has been observed for years may be paying off with tangible results. If soccer in the United States does finally take off, as many have predicted that it inevitably will, American fans will have to acknowledge their debt to the 1999 Women's World Cup final match as one of the critical events in American soccer history.

Notes

[1]   'Attendance Numbers for USA 1999 set new marks'. Retrieved 10 May 2005 from the World Wide Web: http://www.soccertimes.com/worldcup/1999/jul11.htm. The television rating of 11.4 means that 11.4 per cent of all television households in the United States watched some part of the game. Ratings from Neilsen. It has been estimated that the game was watched by 40 million people in the United States.

[2]   The success of soccer at the youth and recreation level complicates the issue rather than simplifying it, but it will not be covered here, as it is outside the scope of this paper.

[3]   The Women's United Soccer Association, launched in 2001

[4]   Longman, *The Girls of Summer*, 11.

[5]   In the days between the semi-final matches and the final, the *Chicago Tribune* ran an average of three stories a day on the China/US final match. Television coverage was also quite prominent.

[6]   It speaks to the marketing viability of the team that some people attempted to explain Chastain's gesture as merely a marketing ploy, hatched by Nike. Given the progression of the match, this position is completely untenable.

[7]   Sahlins, *Apologies to Thucydides*, 128.

[8]   Hexter, 'The Rhetoric of History'.

[9]   Das, *Critical Events*, 5. In this definition, Das is summarizing the work of François Furet, who dealt with evenemential history in the context of the French Revolution. See Furet, *Interpreting the French Revolution*.

[10]   While some may argue that the mode of historical action represented by a women's professional sports league already exists in the form of the Women's National Basketball Association (WNBA), the fact remains that the WNBA has yet to become profitable, and is still highly subsidized by the NBA.

[11]   Longman, *The Girls of Summer*, 31.

[12]   Ibid., 13.

[13]   Kelly, 'Baseball Black and White', 2, (emphasis in original).

[14]   This is certainly not unique to baseball or to the United States. Boria Majumdar, for example, has detailed the use of cricket in India as a means of colonial resistance and as a tool for nationalist movements. Sport is an ideal site for the seeds of real social change, if only because they are so easily dismissed by those who would not take it seriously. For more on cricket and nationalism, see Majumdar, *Twenty-Two Yards to Freedom*.

[15]   Longman, *The Girls of Summer*, 17.

[16]   For a thorough and unparalleled look at the story of Jackie Robinson, see Jules Tygiel, *Baseball's Great Experiment*.

[17]   Kelly, 'Baseball Black and White', 7.

[18]   Ibid., 7. The pieces Kelly references in this passage are: Sahlins, *Apologies to Thucydides*, and Tambiah, *Leveling Crowds*.

[19]   Tygiel, *Baseball's Great Experiment*, 54.

[20]   Longman, *The Girls of Summer*, 22.

[21]   Bob Foltman, 'MLS Could ride wave of women's soccer' *Chicago Tribune*, 18 July 1999, 18.

[22]   Joseph White, '"A Great Day for Soccer": Women's league kicks off with pride, pageantry.' *Chicago Tribune*, 18 April 2001, 7.

[23]   http://www.kenn.com/soccer/wusa.html. As a comparison, the 2004 average attendance for the Women's National Basketball Association, a far more established league with financial backing from the men's arm of the league, averaged only 8,589 fans per game (from http://womensbasketballonline.com/wnba/attendance/attendance04.PDF).

[24]   In 2003, the All-Star game and the league championship game were picked up and broadcast by ESPN2.

[25]   For more on the concept of sports space, see Pierre Bordieu, *In Other Words: Essays Towards Reflexive Sociology*, and Markovits and Hellerman, *Offside: Soccer and American Exceptionalism*.

[26]   The CyberRays played in San Jose, California, but the major markets of Oakland and San Francisco are both within 50 miles (approximately 83 km) from San Jose, so those franchises are included.

[27]   Additionally, the New Jersey area has the New Jersey Nets (NBA), and the New Jersey Devils (NHL). These franchises are also relevant, as both the Giants and the Jets play in New Jersey, which illustrates the very close proximity of the areas.

[28]   Allen Barra, 'What doomed the WUSA?', *Opinion Journal* (online), http://www.opinionjournal.com/la/?id=110004049. It is interesting to note the irony of Hendricks' statement of an independent league being dependent on corporate support. This statement is indicative of the lack of perspective that the WUSA organizers had in organizing and promoting the league, which will be discussed below.

[29]   Darren Rovel, 'Still a Business, Not a Cause' (online), http://espn.go.com/sportsbusiness/s/2003/0915/1616775.html.

[30]   Barra, 'What Doomed the WUSA?'

[31]   Though, as Longman writes, the disparity in monies handed out to the women's and men's teams is startling. Longman writes that the top women's players made only $40,000 in 1999 while the top men's players were making $135,000 in 1994. Disparities also exist in coaches' salaries, despite the overwhelming success of the women's team in direct comparison to the men.

[32]   A look at the WUSA website makes it clear that those involved have not given up on reigniting the league. Committees have been formed, and a new commissioner has been appointed to help resurrect the league. Fans are also asked to pledge their financial support of the league, in hopes that enough pledges to buy tickets for a defunct league will generate sufficient interest from sponsors to start it up again. It is not clear from the WUSA website whether the lessons of 2001–04 have been learned or not. For more information, see http://www.wusa.com.

[33]   However, visa restrictions in the United States still restrict the flow of foreign talent into 'organized baseball'.

[34]   This stereotype, until quite recently, was most prevalent in the National Football League, where black athletes were said to not be sufficiently mentally competent for the challenging position of quarterback. The recent emergence of star quarterbacks Donovan McNabb, Daunte Culpepper and Michael Vick have certainly made a mockery of this logic, even if they haven't entirely eradicated the thought process.

[35]   Kelly, 'Exclusionary America', 1045.

[36]   Ibid. Additional quotes from Simon, *Jackie Robinson and the Integration of* Baseball, 34.
[37]   Longman, *The Girls of Summer*, 12.
[38]   Mary Ullmer, 'Half Empty of Half Full? It seems strange to have to justify coverage....'
       Chicago Tribune, 4 July 1999.
[39]   Longman, *The Girls of Summer*, 305.

References

Bordieu, Pierre. *In Other Words: Essays Towards Reflexive Sociology.* Cambridge: Polity, 1990.

Das, Veena. *Critical Events: An Anthropological Perspective on Contemporary India.* New York: Oxford University Press, 1995.

Furet, François. *Interpreting the French Revolution.* Cambridge: Cambridge University Press, 1981.

Hexter, J.H. 'The Rhetoric of History.' In *Doing History,* edited by J.H. Hexter. Bloomington: Indiana University Press, 1971.

Kelly, John. 'Exclusionary America: Jackie Robinson, Decolonization and Baseball not Black and White.' *International Journal of the History of Sport 22,* no.6 (2005): 1036–1059.

Longman, J. *The Girls of Summer: The US Women's Soccer Team and How it Changed the World.* New York: HarperCollins, 2000.

Majumdar, Boria. *Twenty-Two Yards to Freedom: A Social History of Indian Cricket.* New Delhi: Penguin/Viking, 2004.

Markovits, Andrei. S. and Steven. L. Hellerman. *Offside: Soccer and American Exceptionalism.* Princeton: Princeton University Press, 2001.

Sahlins, Marshall. *Apologies to Thucydides.* Chicago: University of Chicago Press, 2004.

Simon, Scott. *Jackie Robinson and the Integration of Baseball.* Hoboken: J. Wiley and Sons, 2002.

Tambiah, Stanley. *Leveling Crowds: Ethnonationalist Conflicts and Collective Violence in South Asia.* Berkeley: University of California Press, 1996.

Tygiel, Jules. *Baseball's Great Experiment: Jackie Robinson and His Legacy.* Oxford: Oxford University Press, 1997.

Epilogue: And the Story Goes On

Kausik Bandyopadhyay and Sabyasachi Mallick

People across the globe like talking, reading and writing about soccer. They love to watch their national soccer team play. They worship their footballing icons. They also invest safely in the 'soccer industry'. However, what is meant by *soccer* here is 'international soccer' where the concerned national team is the crucial adjunct. When it comes to the game on the domestic front, the nature of mass participation depends on a variety of factors, including most importantly the nation's status in the international soccer map. However, even when a country lacks success in international football, the domestic popularity of the game can show both slump as well as jump. It is with this assumption that the present volume has taken into consideration countries such as India, which offer cases of staggering mass popularity of both international and domestic soccer even though the countries are not even a marginal presence in world soccer. On the other hand, soccer still fails to retrieve its sagging fortune in counties such as New Zealand. But if we carefully study the enthusiasm and hype that had followed the qualification of Iran and Australia to the World Cup finals of 2006 we probably come close to a very traditionally powerful answer: 'nothing succeeds like success'.[1]

In trying to document the relationship between soccer and nationalism, contributors have relied heavily on vernacular sources. These sources, largely ignored by earlier analysts, are fundamental to an understanding of the role soccer played in the formation of a nation's identity. Their use, in conjunction with much consulted English language sources, has helped us analyze the relationship between imperialism, nationalism and soccer, between class, community and gender, and between globalization, club culture and national identity. These issues have found a prominent place in the discussions on Africa in general, Senegal, South Africa, Northern Ireland and the USA. *Making It Happen* also tries to bring forth the pertinent question of soccer's new civilizing role in underdeveloped nations like Malawi where soccer has found its way to a new healthy end.[2]

No single volume can cover every inch of ground in its defined field of interest – there is never enough space. However, we have tried to achieve the next best thing. We have tried to pave the way for further and fuller coverage of the significant issues revealed through attitudes to soccer in the polity, society and culture of some relevant 'fringe' nations. Among these are: gender relations (the presence and absence of women within the ambit of the sport); the increasing importance of commerce and its interaction with nationalism; and internecine political and club conflicts within the countries concerned. The two essays on Irish and US women's soccer are efforts to highlight such issues.

Further, the volume has attempted to demonstrate that it is too limited to interpret soccer in terms of the exigencies of the colonial state. Should that have been the case, soccer would not have outlived colonialism to generate the mass following it has done, and one point of this extensive historical, cultural and socio-political inquiry is to understand the currency of the sport in present day national life of various states.

Throughout *Making It Happen* soccer, it is acknowledged, provoked diverse political responses across the globe. Recognition of this fact will help scholars and others better understand the complexities of soccer culture and its future in the nations concerned, while bringing to light the role played by 'soccer' in shaping nineteenth- and twentieth-century societies. While this volume has raised a few issues and addressed a few questions with regard to soccer in the fringe nations, more studies, we expect, will follow to supplement this humble effort.

Notes

[1]   In both countries, soccer is not the national game. For details on this, see chapters by H.E. Chehabi on Iran and Roy Hay on Australia.

[2]   See Sam Mchombo's chapter on Malawi in this volume for details.

INDEX